THE BROOKLYN EXPERIENCE

RIVERGATE REGIONALS

Rivergate Regionals is a collection of books published by Rutgers University Press focusing on New Jersey and the surrounding area. Since its founding in 1936, Rutgers University Press has been devoted to serving the people of New Jersey and this collection solidifies that tradition. The books in the Rivergate Regionals Collection explore history, politics, nature and the environment, recreation, sports, health and medicine, and the arts. By incorporating the collection within the larger Rutgers University Press editorial program, the Rivergate Regionals Collection enhances our commitment to publishing the best books about our great state and the surrounding region.

THE
BROOKLYN
EXPERIENCE

THE ULTIMATE GUIDE
TO NEIGHBORHOODS & NOSHES,
CULTURE & THE CUTTING EDGE

ELLEN FREUDENHEIM

Rutgers University Press

NEW BRUNSWICK, NEW JERSEY, AND LONDON

Library of Congress Cataloging-in-Publication Data
Freudenheim, Ellen.
The Brooklyn experience : the ultimate guide to neighborhoods & noshes, culture & the
cutting edge / Ellen Freudenheim.
pages cm. — (Rivergate regionals)
Includes bibliographical references and index.
ISBN 978-0-8135-7743-2 (paperback : alkaline paper) —
ISBN 978-0-8135-7744-9 (e-book ePub) —
ISBN 978-0-8135-7745-6 (e-book Web PDF)
1. Brooklyn (New York, N.Y.)—Guidebooks. 2. New York (N.Y.)—Guidebooks.   I. Title.
F129.B7F735 2016
917.47'2304—dc23   2015035672

A British Cataloging-in-Publication record for this book is available from the British Library.

Partial proceeds of this book will be donated to two nonprofit organizations, the Brooklyn
Children's Museum and Groundswell.

Visit our website: http://rutgerspress.rutgers.edu

Manufactured in the United States of America

Dedicated to my posse: Daniel, David, Anna, Marina, and Richard

Contents

SECTION 4: WHERE TO GO, WHAT TO DO

SECTION 5: VISITOR INFORMATION

Foreword

This is Ellen Freudenheim's fourth book about Brooklyn in the last twenty-five years. That is a testament to the explosive development of this storied borough—the most famous of New York City's five boroughs—in the last three decades. Brooklyn is booming, in myriad ways, and it is hard to keep up with the story.

And yet, as Ellen makes clear, Brooklyn is still Brooklyn. The hipsters and the entrepreneurs and the writers and the artists are the latest wave of creative talent to find a home in Brooklyn. Compared to its sister Manhattan, it is still affordable. That is the reason I settled here in 1984 after returning from Beirut and Cairo after a six-year stint as a Middle East correspondent for the Associated Press. That is the reason Tom Potter and I started our brewery in an abandoned brewery building in Bushwick, a crime-ridden neighborhood where truck drivers refused to deliver after dark.

Brooklyn has always been a haven for creative and ambitious people. Pfizer pharmaceuticals started in Brooklyn in the nineteenth century. John D. Rockefeller's oil was refined at the Standard Oil refinery on Newton Creek, the waterway between Brooklyn and Queens. National Sugar's refinery on the East River became Domino Sugar and home to the Willie Wonka candies. A man named Carrier invented the air conditioner while working for American Lithograph in Brooklyn. In 1898, when the City of Brooklyn became part of New York City, there were forty-five breweries in Brooklyn. Our Brooklyn Brewery was the first successful brewery to reestablish New York's great brewing tradition. The last two Brooklyn breweries, Schaefer and Rheingold, shut down in 1976. Today, there are six breweries in Brooklyn.

Brooklyn's new companies—Makerbot, Mast Brothers Chocolate, Jacques Torres Chocolate, Etsy, Kickstarter, and hundreds more, including ours—are the latest chapter in the industrial history of Brooklyn. Steiner Studios is home to many of today's successful television productions. HBO's *Boardwalk Empire* was filmed at Broadway Stages in Greenpoint.

Brooklyn is the birthplace of thousands of artists and performers who have shaped American culture. Mae West, Danny Kaye, Aaron Copland, Neil Simon, Neil Diamond, Neil Sedaka, Barbra Streisand all hailed from Brooklyn. Walt Whitman edited the *Brooklyn Daily Eagle* newspaper. Truman Capote had an apartment in Brooklyn Heights. The year after we started selling beer in Brooklyn, Spike Lee began his amazing career with *Do the Right Thing*. I met one of my literary heroes, Norman Mailer, at the Brooklyn Academy of Music in 1988. Today, dozens of successful authors have roots in Brooklyn—Jhumpa Lahiri, Jon Scieszka, Jonathan Lethem, Jennifer Egan, Paul Auster, Adelle Waldman, and others.

The Brooklyn Academy of Music, a beacon of innovative theater, celebrated its 150th anniversary recently. The Brooklyn Cultural District is home to the Mark Morris Dance Company, Theatre for a New Audience, Irondale, and others.

In the early 1980s, people questioned naming our beer after Brooklyn. People equated Brooklyn with crime and urban decay. But they were wrong. Milton Glaser, creator of the "I ♥ NY" logo, encouraged us to "claim Brooklyn," and we did. Brooklyn is still Brooklyn, an incubator for people with big dreams and big ideas. In 2001, the New York Mets located their minor league franchise, the Brooklyn Cyclones, in a great new ballpark in Coney Island. And in 2012, the Brooklyn Nets, an NBA franchise, moved to the Barclays Center, putting Brooklyn back on the map of international sports.

Some have decried the disruption that gentrification has brought to Brooklyn. Brooklyn is constantly changing, but Brooklyn is still Brooklyn. It is still home to big immigrant populations—Russians, Jamaicans, Haitians, Dominicans, Africans, and Chinese, you name it. Many of these strivers hope to move beyond Brooklyn, to New Jersey or Long Island. Once they are gone, they will join the great number of Americans who are proud of their Brooklyn roots.

We now sell Brooklyn beers in more than twenty-five countries around the world. When I visit Stockholm, London, Paris, Rio, or Melbourne, people want to show me their "Brooklyn" neighborhood. Brooklyn is the center of a worldwide movement of artists and entrepreneurs—the population now known as the "creative class." Freudenheim has done a wonderful job capturing the zeitgeist of Brooklyn.

Steve Hindy
Cofounder and chairman of Brooklyn Brewery and
author of *The Craft Beer Revolution*

Preface and Acknowledgments

I never set out to write about Brooklyn. But when I moved here in the 1980s, Brooklyn was like a locked closet. All the things you wanted and needed to know, not just about retail and restaurants but about how the place worked, were, it seemed, oral traditions, shared by word of mouth. Writing a guidebook was a way to discover, to unlock Brooklyn. It was a rougher Brooklyn, then. My mother, who'd briefly lived in Sunset Park after World War II argued, "Brooklyn? Don't you know that's a place everybody leaves?" Brooklyn, in the 1980s, was a sleeper.

But today! Brooklyn's quicksilver and alive as hell. It's a vital place, with a zillion moving parts, ideas, tensions, and trajectories. There's a sense of momentum now, an extraordinary amount of creative capital and energy.

This book is a Brooklyn collage. It features neighborhood profiles, interviews and photos, "best bets" and juicy tidbits, weather-proof family fun, what's free, and over a dozen DIY itineraries. It tries to capture Brooklyn's hydra-headed cultural zeitgeist.

Everyone's talking about hot, hip, happening Brooklyn—but Brooklyn wasn't born yesterday. In a departure from my previous books, all offering bird's-eye views of many neighborhoods, *The Brooklyn Experience* takes the story up a notch, to see what the trends are.

What is the Brooklyn experience? It's hard to define a shape shifter. I talked to experts, soliciting their wisdom. I was surprised by the magnitude of Brooklyn's reach. Contemporary Brooklyn has a global presence. When something's cool, Parisians say it's *très* Brooklyn. Calling it the "power center for the visual arts," Arnold Lehman, the estimable former director of the Brooklyn Museum, said, "Berlin and London are working hard but still running second to Brooklyn." Old-timers laugh out loud, but it's true; Brooklyn's creative global influence is apparent in cuisine, artisanal production, music, and attitude.

Have a Brooklyn experience! Everyone's will be different. Hundreds of scenes are humming along: foodie, literary, political, environmental, artistic, musical, athletic. Brooklyn's like a University of Michigan course catalog on steroids: whatever you want to get into, you'll find it here.

Yes, the borough has real problems. Brooklyn's more ghettoized than many American cities. Class and race issues loom large. The affordable housing crisis is acute. One in five children is food insecure. Once-stable neighborhoods are losing some of the artists, characters, and working-class families that made them robust, varied communities. Priced-out Brooklynites are splitting, for California and Sunnyside, Queens. "Time to find another Brooklyn," they say with a sigh.

Brooklyn's secret weapon is the energy, friendliness, curiosity, and diversity of Brooklynites. It's about the people. Everyone here's got a story, and it's in that telling that you'll find the real Brooklyn experience.

This "Brooklyn book," as we call it, is something of a family project. *Brooklyn: Where to Go, What to Do, and How to Get There* (1991) was a husband-wife effort. I wrote *Brooklyn: A Soup to Nuts Guide* (1998) as Williamsburg was beginning to pop. In 2003, I shared the task with our fifteen-year-old daughter, Anna Wiener, who provided a youthful perspective in the five-hundred-page *Brooklyn: The Ultimate Guide to New York's Most Happening Borough*. Without intending to, my four guidebooks provide time-lag snapshots—in 1991, 1998, 2004, and 2016—of an evolving Brooklyn. Deep apologies in advance for errors herein; we really tried to get it right.

This new book presents almost all new material, a testimony to Brooklyn's true constant: change. One can only hope that the best of old Brooklyn is preserved as the new rolls in.

A huge thank-you to so many who shared their insights with me. I'm especially grateful to Steve Hindy, cofounder and chairman of Brooklyn Brewery, for his wonderful foreword, and to my friend Pam Shelela, for her cover photograph, taken on the Brooklyn Bridge's 125th anniversary.

I'd like to acknowledge the more than sixty people whom I interviewed, either in person, by email, or by phone, between February and July 2015, or who otherwise contributed to the book.

On the literary scene: thanks to Harold Augenbraum, then the National Book Foundation's executive director; Brenda M. Greene, executive director of the Center for Black Literature and chair of the English Department at Medgar Evers College, CUNY; and Johnny Temple, publisher of Akashic Books, cofounder of the Brooklyn Book Festival, and chair of the Brooklyn Literary Council. Thanks to Noreen Tomassi, executive director of the Center for Fiction, and James Peacock, senior lecturer in English and American literature at Keele University, United Kingdom. Rebecca Fitting and Jessica Stockton Bagnulo, coowners of Greenlight Bookstore; Emily Pullen, manager of WORD, and Liz Koch, coproducer and vice president of the Brooklyn Book Festival, were super helpful in recommending reading lists.

My gratitude to Arnold Lehman, former Shelby White and Leon Levy director of the Brooklyn Museum; Elizabeth A. Sackler of the Board of Trustees and founder of the Elizabeth A. Sackler Center for Feminist Art of the Brooklyn Museum; Marco Ursino, founder and executive director of the Brooklyn Film Festival, and artist Deborah Brown.

In the performing arts world, it was inspiring to interview Joseph V. Melillo, executive producer of BAM; Susan Feldman, president and artistic director of St. Ann's Warehouse; Leslie G. Schultz, president of BRIC Arts | Media; Jack Walsh, BRIC vice president and executive producer of BRIC Celebrate Brooklyn!; and Wesley Jackson, founder and executive director of the Brooklyn Hip-Hop Festival. Thanks to Jeff Strabone, chairman of the board of the New Brooklyn Theatre, and Katy Clark, president of BAM. I loved interviewing Elizabeth Streb, director of STREB Extreme Action Company and founder of SLAM, Streb Lab for Action Mechanics; Donny Golden, acclaimed Irish step dancer; and Dick Zigun, founder of Coney Island USA.

Thank you to many civic leaders for your comments: New York City's First Lady, Chirlane McCray; Eric L. Adams and Marty Markowitz, current and former Brooklyn borough presidents; Brooklyn College president Karen L. Gould; Linda E. Johnson, president and CEO of the Brooklyn Public Library; Carlo A. Scissura, president and CEO of the Brooklyn Chamber of Commerce; Carol A. Sigmond, president of the New York County Lawyers Association; and Luis Ubiñas, former president of the Ford Foundation.

The insights offered by leaders in the nonprofit sector were invaluable. Thank you to Colvin W. Grannum, president of the Bedford-Stuyvesant Restoration Corporation; Luis Garden Acosta, founder and president of El Puente; Jason Andrews, cofounder and director of Norte Maar; Kelly Carroll, director of advocacy and community outreach at the Historic Districts Council; Cecilia Clarke, president of the Brooklyn Community Foundation; Jeff Richman, Green-Wood historian; preservationist Christabel Gough; Carolina Salguero, founder and president of PortSide NewYork; Elizabeth C. Yeampierre, executive director of Uprose (United Puerto Rican Organization of Sunset Park); and Andrew Newman of the New York City Parks Forestry Division. A special thanks to Leonard Lopate, host of public radio's *The Leonard Lopate Show* on WNYC, whose unexpected return call one June afternoon left me tongue-tied.

On the food front, what fun it was to schmooze with Junior's owner Alan Rosen and to reconnect with Marc Gold, coowner of Gold's Horseradish. Izabela Wojcik, the James Beard Foundation's director of house programming; Katy Sparks of Katy Sparks Culinary Consulting; Sarah Toland, editor of EatClean .com; and Caroline Mak, cofounder of Brooklyn Soda Works, thank you for your time and insights.

Thanks, too, to Matthew Brimmer, cofounder of General Assembly and Daybreaker; Brooklyn College professor of business Hershey H. Friedman; Monique Greenwood, cofounder and CEO of Akwaaba Mansion; Rabbi Motti Seligson of Chabad-Lubavitch; Lucie Chin, senior docent of the Wyckoff House Museum; artist Charulata Prasada; neighbor Lisa Ann Wilson; Laura McKenna, programming coordinator, Neighborhood Housing Services at Sheepshead Bay; and from abroad, Waterstudio.NL's Koen Olthuis and international relations consultants Bram Donkers and Yazeed Kamaldien.

I appreciated the cooperation of the Rock and Roll Hall of Fame, the Henry Ford Museum, the Brooklyn Historical Society, and the Brooklyn Public Library. Casual conversations with other experts, anonymous people whose pithy comments appear in the book, plus tourists I chatted up on the Brooklyn Bridge informed my work, as did many wonderful publications and blogs, some listed here.

A huge thank you, Marlie Wasserman, for the opportunity once again to write a book about Brooklyn; your Rutgers University Press team, notably Andrew Katz, were wonderful. Artist Florence Neal of FAN Graphics drew our nice map. My gratitude to Carla Craig, Miwa Cogez and her Olympia, Maggie Fenton, Lindy Judge, Peter Justice, Rebecca Nathanson, Barbara Oliver, Fern Square, and Sally Williams for invaluable help, and to Sam Kolich for outstanding photos. Hugs to my amazing big family, and Daniel, my love—how about Amsterdam, soon?

The biggest shout-out is to Brooklyn people—the bodega owners, MTA workers, pickle makers, musicians, teachers, curators, artists, volunteers, kids, parents, entrepreneurs, the whole multiracial, multilingual stew. It's you who make Brooklyn—this complicated, contradictory, and exciting experiment in diverse community—*rock*.

I'm sharing this book's modest proceeds with two terrific nonprofits, the Brooklyn Children's Museum (http://www.brooklynkids.org) and Groundswell (https://www.groundswell.nyc), which both understand the issues facing Brooklyn and are doing their darndest to celebrate diversity, to educate, and to bring everyone together. Please check them out.

How to Use This Book

Brooklyn's insanely dynamic, so by definition one book can't capture it all. *The Brooklyn Experience* has something for everyone: tourists who have already "done" Manhattan; newcomers; parents of college grads who have moved here; Brooklynites trying to keep up; expats; and people who won't ever set foot in Brooklyn but are curious about it, too. *The Brooklyn Experience* gives independent travelers tools to explore Brooklyn's many facets—culinary and cultural, environmental and historical—with minidives into about forty neighborhoods. Throughout, it tries to be honest about the complexities of Brooklyn's rapid gentrification. To hear what local movers and shakers think, read the epigraphs and "Brooklyn Voices" peppered throughout.

Section 1, "Welcome to Brooklyn," explains why you should visit and where Brooklyn is and introduces the Brooklyn Bridge—including how best to walk it and where to go after you do so.

Section 2, "Old Brooklyn and New Brooklyn," connects Brooklyn then and now. Learn about old Brooklyn attitude, brownstones, stoop sitting, ethnic authenticity, mom-and-pops, and the Mafia. Discover the crazy crosscurrents that make contemporary Brooklyn fabulous, the secret sauce in Brooklyn's hot global brand. The new Brooklyn phenomenon is the sum of many factors: the cultural energy here; the tech start-ups; makers and the DIY revolution; artisanal food entrepreneurs and urban farmers; the return of pro sports; adaptive reuse of old industrial buildings; resuscitation of entire neighborhoods; and a community spirit bordering on chauvinism.

Section 3, "The Neighborhoods," introduces the stars of the show. Discover Williamsburg and Coney Island and fathomless Flatbush. For each of dozens of neighborhoods, "Basics" tells you what a local friend might: which subways to take, the best pizzeria (essential information!), shopping drags, hotels, greenmarkets, what's nearby—and where to take a selfie. "Events" lists unique calendar occasions but doesn't list celebrations you'll find nationwide, like July Fourth, Christmas, Hanukkah, Kwanzaa, and Halloween.

Where to start? "Using GPS, orient to . . ." recommends a café, landmark, or other convenient destination for meeting friends and setting out (alternatively, use the recommended pizzeria). "Best Bets" ticks off a half day or more of things to do and see, plus cafés, restaurants, and bars. (The 🏛 symbol indicates "old Brooklyn" restaurants and bars.) For background, read the brief "History Snapshots." In

"Celebs, Films, Fiction," learn about what famous residents lived or live in a given neighborhood and what movies and novels are set in that neighborhood, too. (You can watch these flicks or read these books on your plane, train, or subway ride home!)

Section 4, "Where to Go, What to Do," zeroes in on special interests. "Brooklyn's Cultural Scene" romps through Brooklyn's cultural life in film, literature, art, and more. "Eating and Drinking in Brooklyn" recommends places to eat: old-school classic Brooklyn restaurants, great ethnic and new-Brooklyn farm-to-table eateries, food trucks, and Michelin picks. (We checked all the restaurants and only included those with an "A" rating from the New York City Department of Health.) "Shopping in Brooklyn" offers tips on where to buy cool souvenirs and lists over 260 stores, malls, curated flea markets, pop-up shops, and only-in-Brooklyn shops. "Brooklyn's Waterfront and Parks" will knock your socks off; there's a ton to do outdoors. Please do use your mobile technology: make reservations on Open Table, check crowdsourced reviews, and use smart maps.

Section 5, "Visitor Information," offers a toolbox of insider tips. Find tour guides and fifteen DIY itineraries, street-smart subway dos and don'ts, forty things to do with kids, confusions to avoid, and a monthly calendar. There's a list of local blogs, a bibliography of recommended works by contemporary Brooklyn authors, and a glossary of thirty words you need to know in Brooklyn.

The bookshelf of Brooklyn books is huge these days. Still, it's tougher to ferret out fiction that reflects the neighborhoods than it is to find nonfiction, just because of the way search engines work. That's why this book includes an original list of over seventy novels that in ways large and small shed light on the unique neighborhoods of Brooklyn.

Finally, though it sounds wonky, take a look at the index, too. Kids of all ages will love the "Where to See Things Made" section.

SECTION 1

Welcome to Brooklyn

People doing the tango on Brighton Beach, Brooklyn, 1910. (Courtesy Library of Congress)

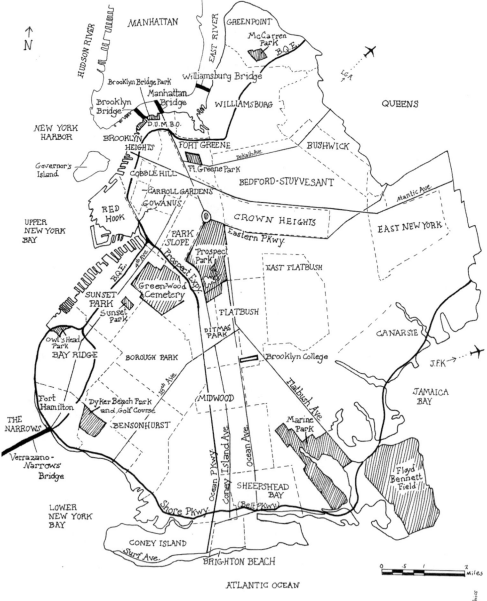

Brooklyn at a Glance: Select Neighborhoods

Brooklyn at a Glance

It'd take a guy a lifetime to know Brooklyn t'roo an' t'roo. An' even den, yuh wouldn't know it all.

—Thomas Wolfe, "Only the Dead Know Brooklyn," 1935

WHAT AND WHERE IS BROOKLYN ANYWAY?

Brooklyn is one of New York City's five boroughs, along with Manhattan, Queens, the Bronx, and Staten Island. With over 2.6 million people, Brooklyn is the largest borough in New York City and the second most densely populated county in the United States. (Yes, Brooklyn is its own county—Kings County.) Brooklyn has seventy-one square miles of land and a twenty-six-mile coastline. Politically, Brooklyn votes solidly Democratic. Geographically, Brooklyn is adjacent to the borough of Queens and is separated from the island of Manhattan and Staten Island by water. Centuries ago, this area was considered part of Long Island.

TWENTY REASONS TO FALL IN LOVE WITH BROOKLYN

1. You can see the sky.
2. You have keys to your neighbor's apartment.
3. The dry cleaner doesn't speak English. His daughter graduated from an Ivy League college.
4. On a spring morning, birds' songs wake you up.
5. There's every kind of skin color on a Brooklyn subway. Nobody seems to notice.
6. People have drive but less competitive edge than in Manhattan.
7. The views of the water, Manhattan, and the bridges never, ever get old.
8. You can see free outdoor movies every night of the week in the summer.
9. The beach is just a subway ride away.
10. You can get seltzer delivered (the kind in squirt bottles).
11. At a Cyclones game, you get baseball, sea breezes, and shtick.
12. You can cross-country ski in Prospect Park. And skate!
13. When you walk to the grocery store, you meet four people you know.
14. It's hopping and creative; something's always going on.
15. You can ad-lib a perfectly wonderful day; people drop by.

16 People in Brooklyn are, for some reason, funny. The water?

17 You can get to Manhattan by subway, but you don't have to stay there.

18 First Saturdays at the Brooklyn Museum, the West Indian American Day Parade, and the Mermaid Parade—all free.

19 You might have a little back garden. With a frog.

20 And everything—food, clothes, rent—seems cooler and more relaxed than in Manhattan.

THIRTY THINGS NOT TO MISS: BROOKLYN BUCKET LIST

What's life without a bucket list? Here's one for Brooklyn:

1 Have a moment—a kiss, an idea, a selfie—atop the Brooklyn Bridge (free).

2 Watch the sunset at Brooklyn Bridge Park (free).

3 Take your honey on a romantic stroll on the Brooklyn Heights Promenade (free).

4 Scream as you ride on the wooden Cyclone roller coaster in Coney Island.

5 Enjoy an outdoor concert in Fort Greene Park (free).

6 Root for the home team at a baseball game at MCU Park, with the Atlantic Ocean in view.

7 Attend the Martin Luther King Day celebration at BAM (free).

8 Watch the July Fourth fireworks over the East River (free).

9 Go to the Atlantic Antic, Brooklyn's biggest street fair (free).

10 Enjoy Bastille Day in Carroll Gardens, because why are they celebrating that there? (free).

11 Tour the historic and revitalized Brooklyn Navy Yard.

12 Join the endless pizza discussion, a hot debate about which is best (free).

13 Take an entertaining trolley tour of historic Green-Wood's "permanent residents."

14 Go to a "Target First Saturday" at the Brooklyn Museum (free).

15 Go vintage shopping in Park Slope or Williamsburg.

16 See a performance at BAM or Bushwick Starr, or a game at Barclays.

17 Sit on a real brownstone stoop or BRIC House's indoor "stoop" (free).

18 Bike down Bedford Avenue through wildly diverse neighborhoods (free).

19 Visit Brooklyn's small oddball museums.

20 Attend Bushwick Open Studios (free).

21 Drink vodka at a Russian nightclub.

22 Graze on farm-to-table food and try to understand every process the waiter describes.

23 Taste amazing small batch . . . pickles.

24 Tour Brooklyn Brewery or other craft brewers and distillers.

25 Take a cooking or DIY brewing class.

26 Take a chocolate tour: watch it made at Raaka in Red Hook.

27 Cheer the New York Marathon runners till you're hoarse (free).

28 Go bowling and hear an indie concert in the same place, at Brooklyn Bowl.

29 Play in the fresh snow in Prospect Park (free).

30 Go to a Brooklyn block party, where nothing and everything happens (free).

The Brooklyn Bridge

> I am with you, you men and women of a generation, or ever so many generations hence. . . . What is it then between us? What is the count of the scores or hundreds of years between us? Whatever it is, it avails not—distance avails not, and place avails not, I too lived, Brooklyn of ample hills was mine.
> —Walt Whitman, *Crossing Brooklyn Ferry* (1856)

The simplest things in life can impart a sense of accomplishment. Walking the Brooklyn Bridge, which spans the East River, connecting two of New York's five boroughs, Brooklyn and Manhattan, is one of those experiences.

An engineering feat in its time, the Brooklyn Bridge, with its soaring gothic arches, immense limestone and granite towers, exhilarating views, and ample pedestrian walkway, won't fail to inspire. The drama and daring of its construction, and the saga of the Roeblings, the family of its chief engineer, are famous. Like an ancient talisman, this 1893 marvel—the world's longest in its era and the first steel-wire suspension bridge—imparts the optimism and energy of New York City's industrial golden age. Stately but sturdy, it's a practical workhorse over which an average of 120,000 vehicles, 4,000 pedestrians, and 3,100 bicyclists cross daily.

The Brooklyn Bridge is the stuff of legend and lore. Lovers propose on it. Reformers hold protest marches on it. The world photographs it: Google pulls up some thirteen million hits on the phrase "Brooklyn Bridge photos." People still use the old saying, pitting a con artist against some gullible rube, "If you believe that, there's a bridge I'd like to sell ya." Of course, the Brooklyn Bridge is not only public, belonging to everyone, but also priceless, Brooklyn's exuberant Eiffel Tower.

But a UNESCO World Heritage site the Brooklyn Bridge is not. And why not? It's a mystery why this national landmark and iconic New York treasure isn't on the world's most prestigious preservation roster.

PRACTICAL TIPS

The Brooklyn Bridge is 1.1 miles (1.8 kilometers) long. Allow an hour to walk it, if you plan to stop for photos or to gaze. It's safe, open all the time, and free. A broad pedestrian walkway above the car lanes accommodates walkers, joggers, cyclists, tightly leashed dogs, and baby carriages. Wear comfy shoes; the bridge's wooden slats are unforgiving to those who are wearing high heels.

For the best views, walk from Brooklyn toward Manhattan and at sunset.

Bring a camera and maybe binoculars, sunscreen or a hat. "Love locks," ten thousand of which were removed by the city in 2015, are discouraged. The bridge has benches but no bathrooms, bike stands, electricity, or food vendors. Pedestrians and cyclists should stay in their respective lanes; collisions do occur. Don't climb the suspension wires. The bridge, a past terrorism target, is under police surveillance.

WHAT TO SEE

The views will melt your heart, starting with a big sky and a bigger skyline. Take in the water views, the powerful East River and New York Harbor, plus all their elements: the Statue of Liberty and Ellis Island; the picturesque Manhattan and Williamsburg Bridges; historic Governors Island; Staten Island and its classic yellow ferry; and brisk river traffic. On the Manhattan side, it's all about height: the Empire State and Chrysler Building skyscrapers, the crazily congested Wall Street skyscape, and the defiant Freedom Tower soaring where the World Trade Center's twin towers stood. Close up, the view of the bridge itself, its soaring arches and thick spun-metal suspension wires, ain't bad either. The views of Brooklyn aren't memorable, though; Brooklyn is more impressive than it appears from its namesake bridge.

HOW TO WALK OR BIKE THE BROOKLYN BRIDGE

In Manhattan, the Brooklyn Bridge pedestrian and bike walkway entrance is located near City Hall. In Brooklyn, there are two points of entry and exit. For a slightly shorter route, enter or exit at the underpass to Washington Street, in Dumbo; note that this involves a flight of steps. Otherwise, enter or exit at the intersection of Boerum Place and Tillary Street, nearer to Downtown Brooklyn and Brooklyn Heights.

Cyclists will find the bridge an easy climb and descent, no matter which end you start from. On summer weekends, the bridge is extremely crowded. Early mornings are perfect in any season for a slow and unencumbered roll—it's also when many photo shoots take place, so you may catch a bride or rock star taking some stills before the crowds arrive. The north side of the crossing is a designated bike lane; if you stop to take photos, or to search out Miss Liberty (best seen from the south side), pull over to the pedestrian path.

WHERE TO GO AFTER CROSSING THE BROOKLYN BRIDGE

Explore on Foot

You've walked the Brooklyn Bridge. You've arrived. Now what?

Nearby Brooklyn Bridge Park is a world unto itself, a long sliver of green built on old shipping piers, each pier offering something different: soccer, grassy spaces, private coves, and free activities including films in the summer.

For shopping, walk to Fulton Mall in Downtown Brooklyn, explore Dumbo's trendy boutiques, or hike over to Atlantic Avenue's boutiques and antique stores.

Mangia, mangia! Snack at the food trucks and stands serving lobster rolls or ice cream, have a drink at Garden Bar, all in Brooklyn Bridge Park. In Dumbo, find excellent pizza, chocolates, and a Sunday bluegrass brunch. Brooklyn Heights and Downtown Brooklyn offer burger joints, wine bars, and old-style Teresa's, a Polish eatery. You'll burn a few calories walking the bridge, so splurge on cheesecake at Junior's, nearby. Smith Street in Carroll Gardens is famous for its cafés, bars, and eateries.

For a cultural outing near the Brooklyn Bridge, explore the New York Transit Museum or Brooklyn Bridge Park's public art and sculpture. In Dumbo, find art galleries, bookstores, the Brooklyn Historical Society's annex, and St. Ann's Warehouse theater. Visit Plymouth Church, an abolitionist center in the Civil War, or take a self-guided literary walking tour (outlined in this book) in Brooklyn Heights.

Children love Brooklyn Bridge Park's many play areas, the Brooklyn Children's Museum in Dumbo, and Jane's Carousel, with its gorgeously restored old horses, dating to 1922.

Explore by Subway, Bike, or Ferry

The Borough Hall subway hub is an easy place to start your Brooklyn adventure. BRIC House, BAM, and the BAM-area Brooklyn Cultural District are close (eight minutes by subway). From here you can also reach Gowanus, Park Slope, Prospect Park, the Brooklyn Botanic Garden, the Brooklyn Museum, Crown Heights (a ten-minute subway ride), Green-Wood, Sunset Park, and Bay Ridge (thirty-five minutes by subway). Coney Island is a forty-minute subway ride away. Take the seasonal East River Ferry to Williamsburg or Greenpoint. On summer weekends, a free ferry runs to Governors Island. You can rent a sturdy green Citi Bike in Dumbo, Brooklyn Bridge Park, and elsewhere.

For a history of the bridge and to learn more about the Roeblings, read the authoritative *The Great Bridge: The Epic Story of the Building of the Brooklyn Bridge* or watch the 1981 Ken Burns documentary *Brooklyn Bridge* or the Douglas McGrath film *Brooklyn Bridge*, under development as of this writing

Old Brooklyn and New Brooklyn

The Brooklyn Bridegrooms baseball team, in a studio portrait, 1889. (Courtesy Library of Congress)

Old and Historical Brooklyn

"The Williamsburg Bridge . . . I pronounce it to be open from this day forward." . . . Such a shout of joyous applause . . . like the breaking of a huge ocean wave. . . . Thousands of steam craft joined to the tumult, . . . the booming of cannon, . . . rejoicing at the joining of the sister borough's by the new bonds of steel.

—"Whole City Cheers Formal Opening of Williamsburg Bridge,"
Brooklyn Daily Eagle, December 19, 1903

One hears the term "old Brooklyn." But what does it mean? And where can you experience it?

"Old Brooklyn," like the French Quarter in New Orleans or the Left Bank in Paris, is a state of mind as much as a physical place. A constellation of images, memories, and ideas, "old Brooklyn" is a hand-me-down recipe that's impossible to replicate—a varied cocktail of nostalgia and ambition, warmth and nerve, bravado and bravery, laced with Irish, Jewish, Italian, Chinese, Polish, African American, Caribbean, and varied Latino flavors. Old Brooklyn straddles chasms of time, from the American Revolution through the 1880s and a century later. Its date line, like Brooklyn's neighborhood boundaries, is negotiable. The one thing everyone agrees on is that old Brooklyn was unequivocally not, ever, Manhattan.

THE BRIEFEST OF BRIEF HISTORIES

Brooklyn is one of America's great metropolises.

Seventeenth-century Breukelen, a Dutch village, gave modern Brooklyn its name, of course. And for years, it was a sleepy rural farming area, comprising six original towns. As Brooklyn developed and eventually consolidated into one city, its micro-urban center was Brooklyn Heights and Downtown Brooklyn, where the modern borough's cultural and educational institutions were founded. In the eighteenth and nineteenth centuries, Brooklyn underwent tremendous growth from farmland to a maritime and industrial powerhouse. East River ferries, bridges, and subways connected Brooklyn to Manhattan, opening frontiers to mostly immigrant families. Starting in the 1830s, millions of immigrants arrived in the United States. Many of them passed through and some settled in Brooklyn. They launched successful entrepreneurial ventures, from German breweries to Scandinavian cooperatives. Some among them and their ambitious children became luminaries in a wide range of fields.

Brooklyn also boasted storied destinations. Coney Island and the Brooklyn Bridge became iconic even before they opened to the public.

By 1900, some of Brooklyn's celebrated residential neighborhoods—Brooklyn Heights, Clinton Hill, Bedford-Stuyvesant, Fort Greene, Park Slope, and Victorian Flatbush, for instance—had already been, literally, set in stone (brownstone and limestone, mostly). Brooklyn was in plain view of Ellis Island, where most immigrants were processed upon arrival in New York after it opened in 1892. Brooklyn experienced immense immigration and population shifts through the mid-twentieth century. It was a vital, roiling, and savvy place—global if not urbane.

Over three decades of decline followed the end of World War II. Mainstay industries—shipping and manufacturing—left New York, as did many middle-class residents. The city struggled economically. Crime, urban decay, and lack of jobs took their toll in the 1950s, 1960s, and 1970s. Immigration continued. The borough began to turn around in the 1980s (mostly in brownstone areas; less so in "deep Brooklyn" neighborhoods like Flatbush and where urban renewal policies and public housing ghettoized the poor). Reviving residential neighborhoods, starting with Brooklyn Heights, Park Slope, Carroll Gardens, and Fort Greene, attracted young professionals who were priced out of Manhattan but rejected suburban life. In fits and starts, with lags during crime waves and national economic downturns, Brooklyn's gentrification has continued. From the 1960s through the 1990s, its hallmarks were the restoration of abandoned parks and derelict public facilities, widespread renovation of old homes, and reconstituting or building new community institutions. Many of those who didn't flee fought for better city services and education.

By the new millennium, 2000, Brooklyn had regained stature. By 2016, it was a media darling, dubbed one of the most desirable places to live and work in the entire United States! Hurtling toward a different future, today Brooklyn is astraddle its old and new identities.

At the end of this chapter, see "Time Line: From Breukelen to BKLYN—How Old and New Brooklyn Are Connected" for a more detailed time line.

You can still see, and feel, much of old Brooklyn today. So we've boiled old Brooklyn down to a dozen facets of the borough as it was until about 1990 when gentrification began to seem transformative, a tidal wave of change. Brooklyn's a huge, morphing, historical entity. As with hands on an elephant, any one experience won't tell the entire story but will help you get a sense of the whole.

BROOKLYN AIN'T MANHATTAN

One of the things that made old Brooklyn Brooklyn was that it was *not* Manhattan.

Much has been made about Brooklyn's rivalry with Manhattan. It certainly exists, though nobody can definitively say why. Brooklyn was an independent city for only about sixty years, from 1833 until 1893, less than the span of a lifetime.

For most of the twentieth century, just about anywhere in Manhattan was considered a glitzier, more sophisticated, and more prestigious address than even the best address in Brooklyn. In 1967, Norman Podhoretz encapsulated the sentiment in his memoir *Making It*, in his quip, "One of the longest journeys in the world is the journey from Brooklyn to Manhattan." Manhattanites didn't want to even set foot in Brooklyn! Brooklyn residents used to poke fun, telling Manhattan friends they'd need a passport to visit. Still, everyone on this side of the bridge knew the best views *of* Manhattan are *from* Brooklyn.

The cost of living in Brooklyn, until recently, was much cheaper than in Manhattan. Affordability was attractive to immigrants, obviously, but also to the middle class: cops and firefighters, nurses and teachers, municipal workers, college grads, young families, and a host of people working in creative, nonprofit, or social service jobs. Artists could afford studio space.

To be sure, mostly hardscrabble Brooklyn had its Gold Coasts and pockets of wealth—in Brooklyn Heights, Victorian Flatbush, Park Slope, and Clinton Hill, along Colonial and Shore Roads in Bay Ridge, and, in its heyday, in parts of Bushwick where the brewery magnates lived. But high culture was more or less the exclusive province of Manhattan, which makes all the more remarkable that a leader in the rarified world of American literature, Harold Augenbraum, told the author, "Brooklyn is what's happening in New York City. And what's happening in New York City is happening in Brooklyn," in 2015.

A PLACE OF IMMIGRANTS AND DIASPORAS

Brooklyn's story is the American story, an optimism-tinged tale of immigrants and working-class Americans in pursuit of a better, or anyway a different, life. Historically, Brooklyn accommodated wave after wave of newcomers, absorbing them geographically, culturally, linguistically, and—most deliciously for tourists and contemporary Brooklynites—culinarily.

Almost everyone in Brooklyn has an immigrant or diasporic connection of one sort or another. It's not uncommon among Brooklynites to be just one or two generations removed from a relative who arrived as an immigrant; the "where did your family come from?" conversation happens all the time among new acquaintances. Brooklyn's influx of out-of-state American-born youth is a largely twenty-first-century phenomenon—but some of these youth proudly trace distant relatives to Brooklyn, too.

ARE *YOU* FROM BROOKLYN?

Many people have roots in Brooklyn.
Start your genealogical research at the
Brooklyn Historical Society or Green-Wood
Cemetery. How can you find photos of
your family's home or business? Ask at the
Brooklyn Public Library, Brooklyn Historical
Society, and Brooklyn Visual Heritage
Project, and search the archives of the
New-York Historical Society. The New York
City Department of Records sells old tax
photos of buildings.

Brooklyn has been the site of many diasporas: members of the African-lineage diaspora,
including African American and Caribbean
American; a Jewish diaspora, with a subset
of Holocaust survivors; and Irish and Italian
diasporas. So many immigrants who were separated by distance from their original home-
lands nonetheless kept the music, language,
foods, and traditions of those places close to
their hearts. Among them are Haitians and
Dominicans, Italians and Irish, Ashkenazi
and Sephardic Jews, Scandinavians, Germans,
Poles, Ukrainians, Mexicans, Puerto Ricans
and other Spanish speakers, Africans, Asians,
Greeks, and Middle Easterners, to name a few.
Some people who settled here were political refugees. "Aristocracy" in the New
England sense of a *Mayflower* legacy traceable to England barely exists; Brooklyn
doesn't have many bluebloods.

One of the most popular services offered by the Brooklyn Historical Society is
its genealogy program, which helps people dig up their Brooklyn roots.

WHERE

Visit the Brooklyn Historical Society, Coney Island Avenue, Bensonhurst, and
Sunset Park.

ETHNIC AUTHENTICITY AND DIVERSITY

"If Manhattan is the thumping heart, Brooklyn is the elusive soul of New York
City. Brooklyn's got personality because it is so ethnically diverse, because it is
human-scaled, and because there are roots here in many neighborhoods . . . that
somehow maintain their ethnic authenticity." That's how this author described
Brooklyn in 1991, in the first independent guidebook to the modern borough. It's
still true.

Where you find immigrant communities, you find ethnic authenticity. It's
reflected in cuisine but also in language, festivals, culture, literature, and outlook.

Immigrant communities, some with deep roots here, define swaths of the bor-
ough. Find them, for example, in Bay Ridge (Muslim immigrants from Egypt,
Morocco, and Levant countries); Bushwick (Latino); Bensonhurst (Asian/Chinese,
Muslim); Brighton Beach (Russian, Mexican); Borough Park (eastern European,
second and third generation); Carroll Gardens (Italian, French); East Flatbush
(Caribbean); Flatbush (Pakistani, Sephardic Jewish, many others); Greenpoint
(Polish); Sheepshead Bay (Asian/Chinese); Sunset Park (Latino, Chinese), and

Annual Tribute to the Ancestors of the Middle Passage, Coney Island Riegelmann Boardwalk. (Photo by E. Freudenheim, 2014)

Williamsburg (Puerto Rican, second and third generation). Obviously, people of a feather don't all cluster together, but the ethnic neighborhoods serve as cultural touch points and heartland shopping centers.

It's no wonder Brooklynites keep winning prestigious National Endowment for the Arts (NEA) "Heritage Fellow" awards: Haitian drummer Frisner Augustin, Irish singer Joe Heaney, Arab American oud player Simon Shaheen, klezmer clarinetist Dave Tarras, and bluegrass clarinet and mandolin virtuoso Andy Statman. Born in 1953, Bay Ridge's Donny Golden is one of the world's most accomplished Irish step dancers and step-dance teachers. Naming him a 1995 National Heritage Fellow, the NEA said, "Golden's choreography is at the cutting edge of innovation within tradition." Jean Butler, the star of the show *Riverdance*, was among his students.

BROOKLYN VOICES

DONNY GOLDEN
World-Class Irish Step Dancer

My parents emigrated from Ireland. They had eight kids and wanted us to grow up with some kind of Irish influence, not on the street. They enrolled us in Irish dance and music classes— which we hated. We wanted to play sports with the kids on the block. But myself and a few of my sisters were good at it. We won many championships.

I studied with Gerry Mulvihill, who had a dancing school down on Thirty-Ninth Street and Fifth Avenue at the back of the Rainbow Bar. Sunday afternoons, the Irish would get together and hold music sessions with people dancing and singing. It was a popular Sunday outing for an Irish Catholic family in Brooklyn.

I won second place in the All-World Championship, and then I danced and taught with Jimmy Erwin for much of my career, in Brooklyn and at the Irish American Center in Nassau. He asked me to take over when he retired. I teach there most of the time now and at the Donny Golden School in Bay Ridge. Some of the kids I'd taught are married; now I'm teaching their kids.

Here, years ago, you had a lot of Irish people. They came for the shipping jobs, as did the Norwegians and Irish. Now fewer Irish are coming over. Still, when I run an Irish dancing competition in Kingsborough College, we get over eight hundred entrants. . . . A lot aren't even Irish!

Although public housing often gets bad press, it was home to many Brooklynites who've climbed the rungs of artistic and economic success, from NBA basketball player Carmelo Anthony to Starbucks founder Howard Schultz. Brooklyn has the largest number of public housing developments in the city, nearly one hundred in all with nearly sixty thousand conventional apartments, according to the New York City Housing Authority (NYCHA) in 2015. Families pay no more than 30 percent of their income for rent. Citywide, working families account for about half of all residents; over a third of households are headed by someone over age sixty-two, and turnover is less than 3 percent. For a rare and positive look at public housing and how it fosters community, see the participatory photography book *Project Lives*, edited by George Carrano, Chelsea Davis, and Jonathan Fisher.

WHERE

Visit any of the aforementioned. (See section 3, "The Neighborhoods.")

BROOKLYN'S NEIGHBORHOODS

Old Brooklyn, if it's been about anything, has been about communities and neighborhoods. Like members of a clan, Brooklyn neighborhoods may have strong similarities but distinct personalities. A visitor might never guess, but it speaks volumes about a Brooklyn resident if he or she grew up in Brownsville or Bay

Ridge or Brooklyn Heights or lived on one side of Prospect Park or the other. There's no Rosetta Stone to crack this code; you live long enough in Brooklyn, gradually you learn.

At its best, the connection to a neighborhood was—and still is!—a way for people to snuggle into a community and preserve a sense of self within a city of more than eight million. Old Brooklyn's strongest neighborhoods were ferociously self-protective, usually somewhat ethnically diverse, and less often racially mixed. People shopped locally. Many residents walked to work. The neighborhood, like a kind of tribe, was the antidote to anonymity, for better and worse. The neighborhood was part of the family, functional or dysfunctional. The family was part of the neighborhood, to a greater or lesser degree. Many people spent months without once going to Manhattan.

WHERE

Everywhere. (See section 3, "The Neighborhoods.")

OLD BROOKLYN AND STOOP SITTING

Stoop sitting is a true Brooklyn tradition and as good a marker as any of the degree to which a neighborhood remains "old Brooklyn." It's absolutely free entertainment. And if this sounds like Larry David's hit TV show *Seinfeld*, which is semiofficially a show about nothing, that's no accident: both Jerry Seinfeld and Larry David grew up in Brooklyn.

For the uninitiated, this is stoop sitting: Someone who lives in a two-, three-, or four-story building plops down on the stoop, for the specific purpose of doing nothing, of having casual conversation with whatever neighbor happens by, or commenting on someone's ability (or lack thereof) to parallel park, while opining on the news of the day. Vital information is exchanged during stoop conversations— gossip about another neighbor's kids or marriage, the weather, and gripes about the mayor. Oh, and jokes! Nothing happens. It's very gratifying.

Sitting on the stoop is an invitation to chat. One successful work-at-home financial writer regularly shared sandwiches on the stoop with his neighbor's three-year-old kid, calling them "businessman's lunches"; it was hard to tell who enjoyed it more. The habit spans generations. Children sell lemonade from their stoop. When the concrete becomes too unforgiving for old-timers, they often place a chair right near the stoop and continue to shoot the breeze and pass the time. At least one enterprise, Bed-Stuy's hip Willoughby General grocery shop, was launched from a stoop conversation. For heart-to-hearts, whether between middle-aged moms or teenagers in love, oddly enough there's nothing quite as intimate as sitting, toe to toe or knee to knee, on a stoop.

Stoop sitting might seem an odd custom to suburbanites who live by automobile or retreat to fenced-in backyards, or to high-rise dwellers who treasure privacy. But in old Brooklyn, the stoop and the street is where that magic word, community, happens.

WHERE

By definition, stoop-sitting culture is an activity one finds in low-rise neighborhoods; find it in such neighborhoods as Bed-Stuy, Fort Greene, Boerum Hill, Carroll Gardens, and Park Slope. (See section 3, "The Neighborhoods.")

BROOKLYN VOICES

LEONARD LOPATE
Host of *The Leonard Lopate Show*, WNYC

My family lived in Williamsburg on Broadway between the Marcy and Hewes Street stations for seven years. It hasn't changed much there—it's just as terrible as it was then. People on the elevated train looked into our window. You didn't want to live there, though there were lots of movie theaters, the Commodore across the street, the Marcy down the block, the Astor. When I went back years later, a Hasidic shopkeeper said, "You look like a foreigner." I said, "What do you mean? I lived most of my childhood here." He looked me up and down and said, "You still look like a foreigner."

In high school, we lived on Washington Avenue between Fulton and Gates. Then it was called Bed-Stuy; now it's Clinton Hill. My parents had four kids and could afford a six-room apartment there. Years later, the Brooklyn Botanic Garden instated me on their Celebrity Path. They gave me a driver, and I said, "I want to show you this awful place I grew up in." We stopped at 475 Washington Avenue—but it was lovely. The lobby was clean, there was no urine in the halls, the elevator was running, and all the bells were working. Clinton Avenue nearby is lovely, too. But when we lived on Washington Avenue, some of those gorgeous buildings were like SROs. And now look at them. They've been reclaimed by wealthy people. It's pretty fancy.

When I was twenty-one, I lived on Strong Place in Cobble Hill. It was an Italian immigrant street. Everyone worked as a longshoreman. I lived on the third of four floors. The owners were in the basement; their son, his wife, and three kids were on the parlor floor; and their newlywed daughter and her husband were on the floor above me. Before a street festival, the neighbors on one side were rehearsing "Paint It Black" and on the other side "I Can't Get No Satisfaction," . . . but if I made noise after ten p.m., my landlord would threaten to call the cops. Today, people of means including actors, and writers like Martin Amis, have bought those same buildings on Strong Place, for millions of dollars.

I wouldn't have predicted that Bushwick or East Williamsburg would become hot. Brownsville, East New York are ghettoized. People are already talking about "good Bushwick" and "bad Bushwick"; we know what that means. Brooklyn will always be segregated. With this economic gap, we'll see more polarization.

I've lived in Prospect Heights, the Slope, and Red Hook. After looking at thirty-five places for my last move, I found a little house for rent in Greenpoint with a big backyard. It's only twelve feet wide but big enough. We grow our own veggies.

BROOKLYN ATTITUDE: HANDS-ON, HUSTLE, SWAGGER

Old-Brooklyn attitude is rooted in swagger, confidence, and a buck-stops-here mind-set. Brooklyn people are feisty.

And for good reason. Brooklyn's immigrants, wherever their origins, had the moxie to leave their homes in pursuit of a better life, adventure, wealth, anonymity, or freedom. The borough still crackles with this energy, of dreamers, seekers, doers, and movers up. At its best, this is a culture that encourages people to cope with adversity, to pick themselves up, dust themselves off, organize collectively, and keep going. At its worst, it produces hustlers and ruthless crooks.

Brooklyn-style hands-on confidence isn't only characteristic of off-the-boat immigrants. It's borough-wide. Take, for instance, an organization called Brownstoners of Bedford-Stuyvesant, formed in 1978. Ignored by the city, Bedford-Stuyvesant lacked basic municipal services. Bed-Stuy's African American residents faced onerous (and now illegal) bank redlining practices. "Young people and families were leaving in alarming numbers, abandoning the large, beautiful brownstone homes, apartment buildings and commercial properties that their parents and grandparents, those first generations of African Americans from the South and the Caribbean, had labored to acquire," Brownstoners' website says. It describes itself as a "hands-on" organization that relies on the resources of its members to improve the neighborhood. And so they did.

Southside Williamsburg was known in the early 1980s as New York's teen gang capital. El Puente, a grassroots organization, was founded and mobilized; they weren't going to give up, either. Across Brooklyn, people fought for their communities and neighborhoods, against the long odds of racism, neglect from city officials, and (at least until scores of New York City journalists themselves decamped to Brooklyn) relentlessly negative media coverage of Brooklyn that focused mostly on crime.

Once you start looking, you'll find this confident Brooklyn attitude expressed, in different ways, across the board. The Brooklyn Children's Museum was the world's first hands-on kids museum; its phone message tells you so. The Brooklyn Navy Yard runs a fabulous "Can-Do WW II" tour, with Turnstile Tours, detailing how women mastered "men's jobs" when the men went into the armed services.

Brooklyn-born, MIT-educated Robert Metcalfe, the inventor of the Ethernet, recalls that his grandmother was "an organized-crime fighter" on Brooklyn's docks, and his grandfather, a chauffeur.

Hands on, can do, give it what you've got. Brooklyn's always had energy and ambition, hustle and swagger.

WHERE

Amazing people lived in Brooklyn: the Brooklyn Botanic Garden Celebrity Path honors Woody Guthrie and Harry Houdini; the three Stooges, Moe, Curly, and

Handmade "sail wagon" in Brooklyn, 1910. (Courtesy George Grantham Bain Collection, Library of Congress)

Shemp Howard; Sandy Koufax; Jacob Lawrence; Mary Tyler Moore; Zero Mostel; Joseph Papp; Floyd Patterson; Maurice Sendak; and over a hundred others. Brooklyn-born talent shows up in all kinds of elite lists: as winners of everything from the Grammys, Oscars, and Emmys, to Pulitzer and Nobel Prizes, MacArthur "genius grants," and Peabody and BET awards, and as inductees into the National Inventors Hall of Fame and the Rock and Roll Hall of Fame.

ICONS AND ARCHITECTURE

Old Brooklyn is visible everywhere. It's in the very architecture of the borough. Visitors can see this in many places.

Start with the bridges. They're of different generations, but many are landmarks: the Brooklyn Bridge, the Manhattan and Williamsburg Bridges, the Verrazano Bridge, and the Third Street, Carroll Street, and Union Street Bridges.

Consider the buildings, too. Old Brooklyn's iconic buildings include the Williamsburgh Savings Bank, the Dime Savings Bank, the Brooklyn Museum, and the Brooklyn Central Library. Coney Island in its entirety is iconic, and its historic rides, landmarks, too—the Cyclone, Deno's Wonder Wheel, and Parachute (the first two still operate). Old Brooklyn—the stuff of memories but also daily life—exists in the brownstone neighborhoods, preserved as if frozen in time, and also in Victorian Flatbush, in the Olmsted and Vaux–designed parks, and in the ivy-covered walls of Brooklyn College. In what was once called the "City of Churches" because of its many spires, old Brooklyn lives on in its churches.

Finally, look at the details. For instance, you could spend a day just touring the Tiffany stained-glass windows all over Brooklyn. They're at the Church of St. Luke and St. Matthew in Clinton Hill, Grace Church and Plymouth Church of the Pilgrims in Brooklyn Heights, the Flatbush Reformed Church on Church Avenue, Grace Reformed Church in Prospect Lefferts Gardens, New Utrecht Reformed Church in Bensonhurst, and Erasmus Hall High School.

WHERE

The NYC Landmarks Preservation Commission has preserved hundreds of buildings in Brooklyn for posterity. (Its reports, freely available online, are fascinating.) Dozens more landmarks are listed on the National Registry of Historic Places. Visit on your own, or take

---

BROOKLYN VOICES

ROBERT METCALFE
Inventor of the Ethernet

Well, I once asked my father what I should do. And he said—and this is a man who never went to college. . . . Brooklyn is a place famous, in those days, for where you could live your whole life and never move three blocks from where you lived. So it was a very closed world. But when I asked what I should do, he says, "Well, it doesn't really matter what you do as long as you're good at it."

(Oral history taken by The Henry Ford Archive of American Innovation in Detroit and reprinted with permission from The Henry Ford's *Collecting Innovation Today, 2008*)

ROCK AND ROLL HALL OF FAME: BROOKLYN INDUCTEES

Beastie Boys
Otis Blackwell
Jimmy Destri and Chris Stein of Blondie
Clive Davis
Neil Diamond
David Geffen
Ellie Greenwich and Jeff Barry
Woody Guthrie
Carole King and Gerry Goffin
Peter Criss of KISS
Little Anthony and the Imperials
Barry Mann
Doc Pomus and Mort Shuman
Marky Ramone
Lou Reed
Jam Master Jay of Run-D.M.C.
Seymour Stein

(List courtesy of Rock and Roll Hall of Fame, March 2015)

an organized tour. (See "How to Visit a Brooklyn Neighborhood," section 3, and "DIY Tours," section 5.)

MOM-AND-POPS OF MAIN STREET, USA

Hand in glove with old Brooklyn's neighborhoods were its legions of small businesses. "Manhattan has corporate headquarters, but we have the corporate headquarters of moms and pops, and there are still thousands and thousands of them today," Bensonhurst native and Brooklyn Chamber of Commerce president and CEO Carlo A. Scissura told the author. "An immigrant can come here and open up a business and do well and send his kids to college and graduate school, and then turn that business over to the member of a different ethnic group. It's great," said Scissura. From the candy shops that Woody Allen recalls to Jewish delis, Italian pizzerias, Latino bodegas, Polish butchers, and German bakers, Brooklyn spawned untold numbers of businesses that stayed small. Many remain in the family. (To get the gist, see the Brooklyn Independent Television video about Circo's Bakery in Williamsburg, online). Some Brooklyn businesses have grown to national prominence: Junior's, Nathan's, Sbarro, and several entertainment empires, like Roc Nation. Brooklyn's produced plenty of left-wing radicals and social idealists, but for generations, capitalism's been good. Main Street USA is alive and well in Brooklyn.

WHERE

Borough-wide. (See "Eating and Drinking in Brooklyn" and "Shopping in Brooklyn," section 4.)

FOLLOW THAT SUBWAY: AS TRANSPORTATION LINES UNFURL, NEIGHBORHOODS GROW

The subway was the main artery of old Brooklyn's growth. Historically, neighborhood development followed its transportation infrastructure—ferries and trollies; the Brooklyn, Williamsburg, and Manhattan Bridges; and most impactfully, the subways. If you build it, they will come, it's said—and so they did. Wherever the subway lines extended, developers, homes, and people followed. This pattern continues even in the twenty-first century. Why are young creatives and hipsters moving to Williamsburg and Bushwick? Partly because they're on the superconvenient L subway line, a straight shot from Fourteenth Street in Manhattan. It's no accident that Brooklyn's Asian population centers—Sunset Park, Sheepshead Bay, and Bensonhurst—are accessible by the N train to Manhattan's Chinatown.

WHERE

Ride the L and N trains.

THE BROOKLYN DODGERS

America's favorite pastime is baseball. And once upon a time, in old Brooklyn, the beloved Dodgers were the pride of the borough. It's hard to think of another baseball team with the mythological aura of the Dodgers. They were full of spunk and humor and won hearts even when they lost games. Some people have said they were the glue that helped bind together a Brooklyn where ethnic and religious groups didn't necessarily mix easily—except in the stands, as Dodgers fans. When the Dodgers left Brooklyn in 1957, fans felt it was an act of personal betrayal.

Ne'er was an apple pie as good as mom's or a team as great as the Brooklyn Dodgers.

WHERE

Alas, there's not much to see of the Dodgers era, unless you happen to catch a special exhibition at a museum. Ebbets Field was torn down, replaced by a housing project that's not particularly recommended for tourists. There's no Brooklyn Dodgers museum. But baseball fans can find memorabilia and stories at the Brooklyn Historical Society and Brooklyn Public Library's Brooklyn Collections and on the shelves of Brooklyn bookstores. You can see vestiges of the ball field used by the Dodgers' precursor team in Gowanus, near Whole Foods. (See "DIY Tours," section 5.)

PATRIOTIC BROOKLYN

To understand old Brooklyn, one needs to understand the sacrifice and patriotism of its people. Brooklyn residents have fought and played a role in every major American war. This patriotic thread of Brooklyn's identity dates to, or even before, the Revolutionary War. George Washington was indeed in Brooklyn—though he probably didn't get much shuteye here. Brooklyn men fought with his ragtag American troops, which were outnumbered, outflanked, and finally overrun by British and Hessian soldiers during the first major battle after the Declaration of Independence in 1776.

WHERE

War memorials are scattered throughout Brooklyn commemorating the Revolutionary War, the Civil War, World Wars I and II, September 11, 2001, and other wars. (To tour Brooklyn's many war-related sites, see "DIY Tours," section 5.)

GANGSTERS, WISE GUYS, AND THE MAFIA

Old Brooklyn was associated with organized crime.

Gangsters made money through hijacking, extortion, loan sharking, bribery, witness tampering, fraud, corruption of labor unions, drugs, and murder. With their made men, paramilitary hierarchies, and decades of illegal dealings, who needs Hollywood?

The infamous twentieth-century Jewish and Italian gangsters, nicknamed "Murder Inc." by the tabloids, had roots in the Brooklyn neighborhoods of Brownsville, East New York, and Ocean Hill. The Mafia was associated with Brooklyn's old Italian neighborhoods: Williamsburg, Carroll Gardens, Red Hook, Bensonhurst, and Dyker Heights. New York's five Cosa Nostra families—the Bonanno, Colombo, Gambino, Genovese, and Lucchese crime organizations—had Brooklyn connections. The Russian mob was linked with Brighton Beach.

It's not entirely ancient history. Dramatic, high-profile mob cases are still occasionally tried in Downtown Brooklyn's federal courthouse. In 2015, octogenarian Vincent Asara stood trial for the nation's biggest cash robbery, a $6 million heist at Kennedy International Airport, a 1978 crime that was the basis for the movie *Goodfellas*. (He was acquitted.)

The intrigue that went on in Brooklyn is dizzying. The following sketches a few major organized-crime cases, by neighborhood, based on the New York County Lawyers Association document *The United States District Court for the Eastern District of New York: A Retrospective (1990–2014)*. It covers thirty-five years of Cosa Nostra litigation.

In Bay Ridge, the Fort Hamilton Army Base was the only place large enough to process the over one hundred mobsters from the Gambino, Genovese, Lucchese, Bonanno, and Colombo families, along with members of the DeCavalcante family of New Jersey, rounded up in a 2011 FBI sting. About a decade prior, on May 26, 1999, according to the U.S. Attorney's Office, an auto dropped off William "Wild Bill" Cutolo, a Colombo family underboss, "at a park near 92nd Street and Shore Road in Bay Ridge," the designated meeting place with Alphonse "Allie Boy" Persico. Cutolo was "never seen or heard from again." (In 2007, Persico was charged with murdering Cutolo.) At the Friendly Bocce Social Club on Eleventh Avenue in Dyker Heights, run by Cutolo, the story unfolded. A case full of twists and turns was made all the more lurid by the discovery during the trial of Cutolo's body, still wearing loafers. In 2009, Persico was sentenced to life imprisonment.

Many mob-related events happened in Bensonhurst.

As for Brighton Beach, in the 1990s, Vyacheslav Ivankov, reputedly head of a Brighton Beach–based Russian mob (who had already spent a decade in a Russian prison), got nearly ten years in a U.S. prison for extorting $3.5 million. He was assassinated in 2009 after deportation to Russia.

In Bushwick, Carmine Galante, head of the Bonanno family, was shot dead while eating at Joe and Mary's Italian-American Restaurant in 1979.

In Carroll Gardens, in 1998, sixty-seven-year-old Gambino associate Joseph Conigliaro, the owner of the One Over Golf Club social club at 497 Court Street (subsequently a dry cleaners), was shot several times. He drove himself to Methodist Hospital in Park Slope, where he died.

There was drama in Downtown Brooklyn. The Lucchese family's Vic Amuso faced a fifty-four-count indictment including nine murders and infiltration of the city's window-replacement union, leading to a case in Brooklyn federal court in 1992. The judge sequestered the jurors in a hotel under armed guard and kept their identities secret. Amuso was sentenced to life imprisonment; John Gotti, the flamboyant leader of the Gambino family, the nation's most powerful criminal syndicate, was convicted of racketeering. During this case, Lucchese insider "Sammy the Bull" Gravano turned government witness. When Gotti, wearing "a black, double-breasted suit with a flame-colored tie and matching pocket square," according to media accounts, received consecutive life sentences on thirteen counts, including racketeering and murder, a crowd of about a thousand rioted in front of the Downtown Brooklyn courthouse in support of the "Teflon Don," who died in prison in 2002.

Also in 2002, after a three-year investigation, seventeen Gambino family associates were prosecuted for infiltrating labor unions, businesses, and pier operators in Brooklyn and Staten Island. In 2003, John's brother, Peter, was convicted of money laundering and attempting to extort $3 million from the movie star Steven Seagal over a meal in Downtown Brooklyn's Gage & Tollner restaurant, as a way to infiltrate the movie industry. In 2004, a nine-week trial found Bonanno boss Joseph Massino guilty of seven murders, arson, loansharking, extortion, and money laundering. Massino defected to the government's side, the first mob boss to do so. In 2011, in the Brooklyn Federal District Court, he revealed tape recordings proving that his successor, Vincent Basciano, had asked for permission to murder Greg Andres, the Assistant U.S. Attorney prosecuting the Bonannos. Basciano was jailed. Massino's sentence was commuted. In 2005, Gambino family members were found guilty of running the nation's largest consumer fraud operation, a half-billion-dollar operation marketing Internet porn and dating services, from 1996 to 2003. In 2009, retired New York Police Department (NYPD) detectives Louis Eppolito and Stephen Caracappa got eighty years to life for working as Mafia assassins and spies, while employed by the NYPD.

Almost straight from the movies, in the 1990s, the Brooklyn Federal District Court heard a murder and extortion case against the Genovese family's Vincent "Chin" Gigante, said to have infiltrated the longshoremen's union, private waste haulers, and construction trades. Starting in the 1960s, Gigante had feigned insanity, wearing old bathrobes on the streets near his Greenwich Village home, acting strangely, and having doctors testify in court that he was mentally unfit— earning him the nickname "Oddfather." He was finally determined to have been faking insanity and the court in Downtown Brooklyn found him guilty in 1997. He went to jail—and was indicted again for conducting mob activities by phone from prison.

You couldn't make this stuff up. Real names include "Sammy" Sammartino, "Scal" Sclafani, "Lefty" Loiacono, "Little Anthony" Pipitone, "Big Frank" Pastore, and "Fat Paulie" Spina (all members of Bonanno family, subject to a thirty-three-count indictment by the Brooklyn U.S. Attorney's office in 2009). The transcripts contain jaw-dropping conversational gems like this 2009 quote: "On one occasion, when a loan shark victim fell behind in payments," the FBI reported, "Bonanno family captain Sclafani allegedly warned, 'You're lucky we don't saw you in half and leave you in the woods.'"

WHERE

The Mafia's power has waned in contemporary Brooklyn. Anyway, it's better for your health not to know too much.

TIME LINE: FROM BREUKELEN TO BKLYN—HOW OLD AND NEW BROOKLYN ARE CONNECTED

Early Days

The land known as Brooklyn originally belonged to the Lenape peoples, the Nayack and the Canarsee, American Indians who farmed corn and tobacco. Giovanni da Verrazano explored New York Harbor in 1524. In 1609, Henry Hudson landed at the rabbit-infested island that the Dutch later named Coinjen Island, or "Rabbit Island." (Coney Island is still hopping, and the bridge bearing Verrazano's name is famously the start of the New York City Marathon.)

1640–1660s

Breukelen was founded (lending Brooklyn its name). It was one of six original towns—along with New Utrecht, Flatlands, Flatbush, Gravesend, and Bushwick—to become Brooklyn. A few early Dutch farmhouses survive. (Visit the tiny 1652 house built by the settler Pieter Claesen Wykhof, now the Wyckoff House Museum in Canarsie.)

1660–1700

Boswijck was chartered by Governor Peter Stuyvesant. (The Dutch name was Anglicized as "Bushwick," a happening neighborhood today.)

1700–1750

Fulton Street (still a major roadway) was laid out in 1704. Ferry services connected Manhattan island and Brooklyn at "Brookland Ferry." (Ferries still run.) The Gowanus Canal was expanded for industrial use in 1774. (Today it's a Superfund site, being remediated of toxic waste created by local industries.)

1776

George Washington lost the Battle of Brooklyn. (With a sleight of hand presaging the borough's subsequent reputation for chutzpah, this rout was reframed as having saved the Revolution.)

1780–1800

Kings County's population was 4,500 people (less than one-third the current Park Slope Food Coop's membership). The first census counted 3,017 white and 1,478 black residents in 1790. Caesar Foster, a slave, was freed in Brooklyn's first act of manumission in 1797.

1800–1850

Things picked up steam in Brooklyn, literally: Robert Fulton's new steam ferry operated from what is now Fulton Ferry Landing, starting in 1814. This fostered commerce and residential growth. Manhattan and Brooklyn vied for control over lucrative shipping (interborough sibling rivalry still exists). In old Brooklyn, industrialists made fortunes. (In new Brooklyn, entrepreneurs are profiting in real estate, hospitality, tourism, and the cyber economy.) Brooklyn's foundational faith and cultural institutions that still enrich life today began to emerge, from Bridge Street African Wesleyan Methodist Episcopal Church in 1818 (still humming in Bed-Stuy) to the Apprentices Library (which became the Brooklyn Museum). Coney Island's first resort opened in 1824. Green-Wood was founded, doing multiple duty as a cemetery, park, and tourist attraction (just as it does today with tours, concerts, and reenactments). Off Red Hook, the Atlantic Basin was completed, enabling Brooklyn to expand its maritime business. New York State abolished slavery in 1827. The City of Brooklyn was incorporated in 1834. In 1838, free black citizens established Weeksville on land owned by the former slave James Weeks, espousing then-radical ideas of economic independence (still resonant today).

1850–1870

The activist writer Walt Whitman, the new editor of the *Brooklyn Daily Eagle*, published his classic *Leaves of Grass* in 1855. (Brooklyn had a long literary history and has enjoyed a recent literary renaissance.) Brooklyn was the nation's third-largest city in 1860 after New York and Philadelphia. (It has ranked third or fourth ever since.) The abolitionist Reverend Henry Ward Beecher put on a mock slave auction at Plymouth Church. Women raised money at the Brooklyn and Long Island Sanitary Fair of 1864 (documented in a colorful 2010 Brooklyn Museum exhibit). During the Civil War (1861–1865), thousands of soldiers from Brooklyn's Fourteenth Regiment and elsewhere were buried in Brooklyn's Green-Wood Cemetery. The U.S. District Court for the Eastern District of New York was signed into existence by President Abraham Lincoln in 1865. Prospect Park was designed by Olmsted and Vaux as an urban pastoral landscape. (It's still great, logging ten million visits annually.) As transportation expanded, farmland was developed into housing, creating the neighborhoods of modern Brooklyn. There was more institution-building: precursors to the Brooklyn Public Library, Brooklyn Academy of Music, and St. Francis Academy (all still alive and well), and taverns (the Brooklyn Inn in Boerum Hill survives).

1870–1890

Brooklyn's growth accelerated as European immigration grew. In 1872, a graft from a tree on the estate of Scotland's Earl of Camperdown was planted near the Prospect Park Boathouse. (It's still there; in 1967, eighty-year-old Pulitzer Prize–winning Brooklyn poet Marianne Moore published "The Camperdown Elm" in the *New Yorker*, helping to save the tree and revive the underfunded park.) In 1877, a subway line opened to Coney Island, transforming it from an elite resort to "the people's playground." U.S. President Chester Arthur attended the 1883 opening of the Brooklyn Bridge; the Carroll Street Bridge in Gowanus also opened—no president. Pratt Institute offered practical education to prepare workers for jobs in Brooklyn's fast-growing manufacturing sector. (It still does, though the jobs have changed.) Brownstone Brooklyn homes were beginning to be built. (They're still in demand.)

1890–1910

Buffalo Bill's Wild West show performed at a Sunset Park waterfront venue in 1894. Brooklyn was consolidated into New York City in 1898 (a loss of independence that some people say caused the borough's chip-on-the-shoulder, tough-guy attitude). The Brooklyn Children's Museum, the world's first, opened in 1899 (kids still love it). More immigrants and newcomers settled in Brooklyn after the Williamsburg and Manhattan Bridges opened in 1903 and 1909, respectively (both still in daily use). Fort Greene Park was designed by Olmsted and Vaux. (It's one of the borough's premier parks.)

1910–1930

Ebbets Field, the Brooklyn Dodgers' home, opened in 1913. Nathan Handwerker started to sell nickel hot dogs at Nathan's in Coney Island, using his wife's recipe. (You can buy Nathan's hot dogs today for four dollars, same location, different recipe.) Margaret Sanger opened the nation's first birth-control clinic in Brownsville in 1916; but she was ahead of her time, and the authorities shut it down after nine days. During Prohibition, Brooklyn's brewery industry took a hit; rumrunners along Sheepshead Bay's shoreline plied their trade, and speakeasies opened. (Brewing and distilling are back; artisanal cocktails and speakeasy-themed places, like Williamsburg's Rye, are fashionable.) The Brooklyn Supreme Court ruled in 1921 that "a reasonable rent was a return of 10 per cent on the present value of a house." (Translated into today's terms, an apartment valued at $600,000 could command $60,000 in annual rent.) Brooklyn soldiers fought and died in World War I. Brooklyn suffered in the crash of 1929 (but Enduro's Sandwich Shop, renamed Junior's, endures). Brooklyn College opened, the city's first public coeducational, four-year liberal arts college, in 1930. (Today seventeen thousand students are enrolled there.) Brilliant inventions came out of Brooklyn: Willis Haviland Carrier invented air conditioning to cool a Brooklyn printing plant, before World War I;

Staubitz Market in Carroll Gardens, one of the city's oldest food shops (est. 1917). (Photo by E. Freudenheim, 2015)

the Brooklyn-born Herman Affel coinvented the coaxial cable at AT&T Bell Telephone Laboratories in 1929, making transcontinental phone and TV transmission possible; both are in the Inventors Hall of Fame. Floyd Bennett Field opened, ushering in the golden age of aviation; Amelia Earhart and others flew from here (read more about Floyd Bennett Field in section 3, "The Neighborhoods.")

1930–1950

Many amenities were built under the federal government's New Deal's Works Progress Administration program, including the Brooklyn Central Library and Olympic-sized pools in the Sunset Park and Red Hook Recreation Centers (still in use today). Some of Brownsville's Jewish and Italian "Murder Inc." gangsters were indicted. And it wasn't just Barbra Streisand; a generation of renowned actors, writers, and professionals burst out of Brooklyn College and onto the world stage. When the United States entered World War II, the Brooklyn Navy Yard doubled in size to over seventy thousand employees, hiring both women, who, surprise, proved capable in formerly male-only jobs as mechanics and technicians, and African Americans, who sought housing in Fort Greene and Clinton Hill.

A Tree Grows in Brooklyn was published in 1943, a novel set in Williamsburg, before Satmar Hasidic Holocaust survivors settled there in 1946 (and well before hipsters and high-rises arrived). Jackie Robinson signed with the Brooklyn Dodgers in 1947, the major league's first African American player.

1950–1970

The suburban dream and GI loans lured Brooklynites to new communities in Long Island. Robert Moses's grandiose urban renewal and highway schemes changed Brooklyn's landscape, especially in Red Hook, Carroll Gardens, what's now called the Columbia Waterfront District, and Sunset Park. (The Gowanus Expressway is still a love-hate affair.) In 1964, the Verrazano-Narrows Bridge, the world's largest suspension bridge, connected Staten Island to Brooklyn. Brooklyn Heights attracted bohemian writers; its civic activists forged New York City's first historic district in 1965. The upheavals of the 1960s took many forms, including riots in Bed-Stuy, leading to the founding of the Bedford-Stuyvesant Restoration Corporation. Newly arrived Caribbean immigrants started the West Indian American Day Parade in 1969 (it still attracts huge crowds). Neighborhoods were recast with fancy names as real estate became more valuable: "Sunset Park" was carved out from "South Brooklyn" and "Boerum Hill" from "Gowanus."

1970–1990

In 1977, a twenty-five-hour citywide power outage triggered looting, arson, and crime. Brooklyn had a bad reputation; Brooklyn stories in major media featured homicides, drugs, and robberies. In 1986, Spike Lee's *She's Gotta Have It*, filmed in African American Brooklyn neighborhoods, helped launch the indie movie industry and depicted inner-city African American life from the inside. Downtown Brooklyn's rejuvenation began with the opening of the MetroTech Center. (Today you'll find residential high-rises, hotels, and shopping there.)

1990–2001

Crown Heights erupted in a three-day riot in 1991, due to tensions between the black and Hasidic communities. (Today it's an up-and-coming destination neighborhood.) The borough's first independent guidebook in fifty years hit the bookstores. Brooklyn Brewery opened in 1996, ushering in a revival of Brooklyn's microbreweries and distilleries. In 1997, NYPD foiled a terrorist bomb plot in the Atlantic Avenue subway station, arresting men with Jordanian passports in Park Slope. A Marriott opened, the borough's first major hotel in decades (now it's one of many). In Carroll Gardens, the bistro Patois opened in 1998, sparking the transformation of low-rent Smith Street into an acclaimed restaurant row. In 1998, New York City allowed the honorific co-naming of streets, resulting in about eight hundred fascinating renamings, each with a backstory (http://nycstreets.info). In 1999, Mayor Giuliani tried to withhold the Brooklyn Museum's city funding because he judged the controversial exhibit *Sensation* offensive; the ensuing brouhaha catapulted the museum, again, to fame. (It has continued to show controversial and inventive blockbusters.) The millennium celebrations passed, with dire Y2K predictions unfulfilled. On September 11, 2001, hundreds of Brooklyn residents plus many first responders who worked in Brooklyn died in the World Trade Center attacks.

2001–2010

The Brooklyn Book Festival, Tech Triangle, and a reinvention of the Brooklyn Navy Yard were launched. Youth of a certain ilk that others called hipsters began moving into Williamsburg, along the L subway line. New York City rezoned almost two hundred blocks in Greenpoint and Williamsburg for development in 2005, promising in exchange the revitalization of Bushwick Inlet Park. Millennials responded to the national enthusiasm for entrepreneurship and the 2008 recession with an explosion of artisanal, craft, DIY, technology, and micro businesses. A public controversy over the development called Atlantic Yards–Barclays Center peaked. (Read the Atlantic Yards/Pacific Park blog online.) Steiner Studios opened a film-production facility at the Brooklyn Navy Yard. A green roof opened in Greenpoint in 2009. During the prodevelopment mayoralty of Michael Bloomberg, Park Slope, Bed-Stuy, Crown Heights, and other neighborhoods rushed to expand their historic districts as rezoning paved the way for increased population density and opened up new areas, including along the North Brooklyn waterfront, for high-rise buildings.

2011–2016

Jay Z opened the Barclays Center with eight sold-out shows. Superstorm Sandy devastated Brooklyn's coastal communities in 2012. Bensonhurst, once Italian, saw the city's greatest growth in Asian population in New York City, according to the 2010 census. Verdant Brooklyn Bridge Park gradually opened in stages, creating a major green amenity, complete with a controversial hotel and apartment complex, built to help finance the park's operation. In 2011, GQ published an article titled "Brooklyn Is the Coolest City on the Planet." The Brooklyn Chamber of Commerce created the "Brooklyn-Made" designation to protect against knockoffs of the Brooklyn brand. Three new roller coasters, the Steeplechase, Soaring Eagle, and Thunderbolt, ushered in a modern generation of amusement-park rides in Coney Island. Williamsburg's hulking nineteenth-century Domino Sugar Factory was mostly demolished to be rebuilt as apartment buildings. Brooklyn progressive Bill de Blasio was elected mayor. Eric A. Adams was elected as Brooklyn's first African American borough president. The Bay Ridge–raised economist Janet Yellen was named head of the Federal Reserve. A decade-long real estate boom rendered swaths of Brooklyn unaffordable to many middle-class or salaried people; Bushwick, once known for gang violence, became the next affordable Brooklyn frontier among some artists and millennials. Dozens of new hotels are slated to open by 2020; the hospitality sector in Brooklyn grew twice as fast as in the rest of the city in 2014.

WHAT HAPPENED TO DUTCH BREUKELEN?

Whatever happened to the original Breukelen, the town in Holland, after which Brooklyn is named? Breukelen, population fourteen thousand, no longer exists, as of 2011. It "was not swept from the planet," said Dutch political consultant Bram Donkers, who'd been involved in a small Brooklyn-Breukelen cultural exchange effort years back. Breukelen was merged into Stichtse Vecht, a larger municipality between Amsterdam and Utrecht, he told the author by email. Suffice it to say, Breukelen didn't fare nearly as well as its namesake.

The New Brooklyn

> I do industrial-strength travel, and everywhere I go, . . . though I am obviously representing BAM, the conversation soon migrates from cultural programming to, "Oh! Tell us about Brooklyn."
>
> —Joseph Melillo, executive producer, BAM

All over the world, people are curious about Brooklyn. But what is the new Brooklyn? This chapter takes a quick trot through some of new Brooklyn's frontiers: its culture, cuisine, craftsmanship, adaptive reuse of buildings, skyscrapers, environmental innovation, technology start-ups, global branding, newly accessible coasts and waterways, and gentrification. All of these ingredients are cooking in the stew pot of old-Brooklyn mores, a multicultural population, and shifting demographics.

CUISINE: NEW BROOKLYN'S AMAZING FOOD SCENE

Eat your heart out. You want Italian? We got Italian. Love babka? Ours is the best. For decades, good, authentic, and cheap ethnic food was what Brooklyn had to offer, along with pizza, dogs, and a few classic holdouts from the last century, like Peter Luger and Junior's. No longer!

Brooklyn has taken its place among the top-ten food capitals of the United States. Its restaurants are winning awards from James Beard, grabbing stars from Michelin, and wooing reader votes in *Zagat*; its chefs are on TV and churning out cookbooks by the dozens. Modern Brooklyn has destination restaurants and a culinary profile. Cocktails are art. Brunch is an event. Dinner is an exploration and adventure. Brooklyn's newly famous eateries are innovative. Menus are religiously seasonal. New York's only Museum of Food and Drink opened in 2015 in Williamsburg, promising "exhibits you can eat."

The Che Guevaras of Brooklyn's farm-to-table revolution are . . . celebrity chefs. Some local stars are Andrew Tarlow (of Reynard, Diner, and others), Andy Ricker (of Pok Pok NY), Elise Kornack (of Take Root), and Dale Talde (of Talde), among others. They're "youthful, adventurous, not tied to traditions, experimental, independent, representing a different generation, and in some ways an embodiment of the diners in Brooklyn," said Izabela Wojcik, a spokesperson for the James Beard Foundation and a self-described "chef wrangler, culinary raconteur, cocktail enthusiast, mom, Brooklynite."

BROOKLYN VOICES

IZABELA WOJCIK

Director of House Programming, James Beard Foundation

The Brooklyn food scene is very dynamic, a complex mash-up of immigrant old-world traditions, established sophisticates, and pioneering youthful artisans, all bound with a do-it-yourself attitude. And epitomized by the construct of a neighborhood.

There's such a delicious proliferation of great things to eat and drink and all the wonderful stories behind them. It's made up of cottage industries, the narrowly focused, single-ingredient-dedicated kind of mom-and-pop shops. There are also pockets of ethnic communities and the intriguing culture and culinary offerings that come with them. And then there are the pioneers that sought out Brooklyn and brought refined techniques and a sense of luxury to define their style to a borough that wasn't at first the obvious choice.

The Brooklyn brand has come to mean . . . a restaurant or business with . . . a strong identity rooted in the idea of a neighborhood gathering place, where the food and drink menus are devoted to local and regional farms and artisans, devoted to the ideals of hand-crafted, and where refined techniques meet urban rustic settings. It also represents revisiting and revitalizing historical recipes, heirlooms, and bringing a sense of purpose to the story behind the foods.

Hungry visitors who want to sample the creative food for which Brooklyn's become famous—or gorge on it in one deliciously efficient scarfing—often graze at Smorgasburg, the foodie flea market. Playfully named to combine *smorgasbord* with *Williamsburg*, where it launched, Smorgasburg is a moveable weekend indie food festival.

New Brooklyn's food culture is pointedly political. Behind the gently crunched kale and sunchoke soup, grass-fed burgers and small-batch everything, the hip food scene delivers a blistering critique of the ecosystem of pesticides, additives, genetically modified animals and produce, industrial husbandry, carbon-guzzling transportation, and corn syrup that corporate agribusiness represents and promotes. Instead, you can eat locally sourced, fresh foods with a smaller carbon footprint, that have been exposed to no or few chemicals, and are seasonal. That healthy food is more expensive, as these foodies see it, is the price of saving the planet.

You can engage with new Brooklyn's food culture in the privacy of your own kitchen. Concoct your own meal: kimchi from Mama O's Premium Kimchi, ribs from Fletcher's BBQ or grass-fed beef from the Meat Hook, McClure's Pickles, Sfoglini Pasta, organic baby arugula, and non-GMO corn, served with Brooklyn-made craft beers and artisanal spirits. Top it off with vegan donuts from Dun-Well.

Some food entrepreneurs work in the former Pfizer pharmaceutical manufacturing building, now called 630 Flushing Avenue; its former labs have been adaptively reused as professional kitchens for over sixty food and beverage businesses.

One example is Madécasse, a social enterprise chocolate maker that imports sustainably farmed Madagascar chocolate.

"Manhattan used to be the progenitor of culinary cool for the rest of the U.S. Brooklyn has stolen that role from her sister borough," Sarah Toland, editor of EatClean.com, told the author by email. "Brooklyn is now the place to be if you want to taste the country's top hot new trends in local, artisanal foods."

WHERE

Farm-to-table restaurants abound. Find many in Williamsburg, Bushwick, Greenpoint, Red Hook, Gowanus, and brownstone neighborhoods. (See "Eating and Drinking in Brooklyn" and, for artisanal, made-in-Brooklyn foods, "Shopping in Brooklyn," both in section 4.)

MILLENNIAL MAKERS AND DIY (DO-IT-YOURSELF)

Add these words to your Brooklyn vocabulary: "maker," "DIY," "indie," and "sustainable." New Brooklyn's "maker movement" and DIY craze is a collection of all kinds of people who make all kinds of things. Some may be software engineers, designers, jewelers, knitters, or chefs. Is this great for shopaholic visitors? Yes! You can

Food truck at Grand Army Plaza. (Photo by E. Freudenheim, 2014)

find tons of Brooklyn-made, unique jewelry, clothing, home accessories, and furniture.

Experimentation and playful creativity are the makers' hallmarks, whether it's chocolate they're burbling or chairs they're building. It's hard not to chuckle at the very idea of Empire Mayonnaise Company's popular "white truffle mayonnaise" (*Saturday Night Live* did). But you name it, they make it: Mast Brothers chocolate bars, Brooklyn Brine artisanal pickles, and Morris Kitchen's ginger syrup.

Irony and insider jokes are part of the fun. A "Gowanus Canal water bottle" is marketed by Brooklyn Rehab; ha-ha, the real canal's polluted. Boundless Brooklyn, which makes and markets DIY model kits of those ubiquitous water towers perched atop so many New York buildings, can't resist a Yiddish pun on its website: "We know the difference between stoop and shtup." For a droll urban gift, how about gold-bullet cufflinks by Snash?

Who are these maker-entrepreneurs, brimming with personality and confidence? They come from surprising walks of life and probably don't have MBAs. For example, Caroline Mak, educated at Stanford and the University of Chicago, cofounded Brooklyn Soda Company in 2010 in the midst of a career as an installation artist. Within five years, the company was annually producing twenty thousand gallons of seasonally varied soda in such flavors as cucumber, lime and sea salt, and red currant and shiso. Mak's art career was on hold. She was working full-time on the business. "We make fun products. We make things we want to drink ourselves," she said.

Millennials—the so-called digital-native generation that grew up with the Internet, aware that Steve Jobs started Apple in his garage and that Jay Z ranks on the 2015 *Forbes* list of world's highest-paid celebrities—are the energy behind new Brooklyn's maker-entrepreneurial-artisanal-DIY thrust. Old Brooklyn was and still is full of small businesses with limited horizons (just spend a few minutes in any corner bodega). In the social media era, now that everybody's a marketer, local entrepreneurship can balloon into a global business. Not a few new-Brooklyn brands have ended up in bigger marketplaces. Williamsburg's Brooklyn Brewery and Brooklyn Bowl have opened in Stockholm and London, respectively. Brooklyn Boulders, a rock-climbing gym, has expanded to Chicago and the greater Boston area.

Old Brooklyn's long been a borough of mom-and-pops. These "small, independent, family-owned businesses, typically with few employees, one location, and a

Man wearing "hipster"-style clothes in Park Slope, better known for stroller gridlock. (Photo by E. Freudenheim, 2015)

local flavor," said Brooklyn College business professor Hershey H. Friedman, are different from entrepreneurs, who are not "afraid of taking a risk and who have a desire to start their own businesses, not necessarily small ones, from the ground up and grow them."

The net result: entrepreneurship, new-Brooklyn style, is a lifestyle, not just a living. Many Brooklyn-made products reflect social or political values or are eco-friendly. It's exhilarating to be your own boss these days; a subculture of twenty- and thirty-something kindred spirits, with one foot in the "sharing economy," are pounding at laptops at cafés or renting cubicles in airy (often postindustrial) shared office hubs. Some are inspired by nineteenth-century craftsmanship, others by twenty-first-century micro capitalism. More than a few have tried corporate jobs and are trading the office cubicle for the freedom to be their own boss, to hold down a day job and yet work on their own ideas (and bike to lunch at a *très* Brooklyn café selling small-batch, vegan walnut-cumin muffins, perhaps). Some hope to do good works while making money. New Brooklyn's DIY and maker scene is joined at the hip with the borough's indie music and zine worlds. Tons of indie bands, small literary magazines and publishing companies, recording studios, and instrument makers have been born here. DIY has social cachet, and so does giving back to the community in which one resides. Entrepreneurship, enabled by social media marketing, is hot.

WHERE

Borough-wide, especially in Williamsburg, Greenpoint, brownstone Brooklyn, Crown Heights. (See "Shopping in Brooklyn," section 4.)

CUTTING-EDGE, POSTINDUSTRIAL PLACES

Raw space. Cavernous, abandoned manufacturing plants. Civil War–era brick warehouses. These are the places where new Brooklyn's creative vibe really begins to hum. Brooklyn's old manufacturing and shipping economy has provided the foundation—often literally—for its new creative economy.

Some of the coolest conversions in Brooklyn are the old warehouses and industrial buildings restored and retrofitted to house high-tech companies, artisanal food start-ups, art studios, restaurants, galleries, and recording and production studios.

Entire areas have been repurposed. Visit the 215-year-old Brooklyn Navy Yard, surely New York's coolest industrial park. It has a four-million-square-foot campus filled with manufacturing cooperatives and small eco-friendly businesses. Brooklyn Grange, a commercial green roof, is there, as is Steiner Studio's movie production facilities, the largest on the East Coast. The Brooklyn Navy Yard, where mighty battleships were built, is today committed to sustainable practices; there too is Kings County Distillery, complete with its own small demonstration cornfield.

In Bushwick, industrial buildings have been repurposed to house artists' studios and galleries. Dumbo—a once seedy waterfront of warehouses, hardly a neighborhood!—today is a chic residential area and tourist destination. Still hanging in the balance between old and new are Gowanus, Red Hook, and Sunset Park's Industry City, all with immense and underutilized industrial spaces.

Century-old decrepit buildings have provided the stage, literally, for Brooklyn's cultural second act. In Flatbush, the 1929 Loew's Kings Theatre, the largest indoor theater in the borough and "inspired by the Palace of Versailles and the Paris Opera House," according to the city's development agency NYEDC, recently reopened as a venue for concerts, plays, and shows. Formerly desolate, Fulton Street's theater district has been revived. BAM's Harvey Theater, repurposed in 1999 by the British director Peter Brook for a production of *The Mahabharata*, was originally the Majestic Theater, dating to 1904. BRIC House renovated the old 1918 Strand Theater. The 1928 Paramount Theater, which has been used for years as the home court for the Blackbirds college basketball team at Long Island University's Brooklyn campus, is being returned to its original purpose, reopening soon.

Many old structures are repurposed into housing. Williamsburg's hulking Domino Sugar Factory (est. 1882), an immense, dreary fixture on the Brooklyn waterfront, has given way to residential development—though not before being turned into a cool installation site for artist Kara Walker's *A Subtlety, or the Marvelous Sugar Baby*, a towering, sugar-coated sphinx-woman.

The roster of repurposed, and retrofitted buildings, missives from the past, that have been transformed in the decades-long rehabbing of Brooklyn's industrial past seems endless.

Stylistically, Brooklyn's "look" marries industrial features with midcentury modern furniture. New Brooklyn has a design vocabulary that riffs on the alphabet of old Brooklyn. Architecturally, the new-Brooklyn décor incorporates recycled beams, stained-glass windows, pressed tin ceilings, and broad wood and steel warehouse-like doorways. Midcentury modern furniture is beyond trendy. When, say, old pharmacies are retrofitted as cafés, ice cream parlors, and restaurants, the old fixtures are kept. Many store signs and names from the 1920s to the 1960s are preserved as treasures: French Garment Cleaners in Fort Greene is a hip clothing store in a former laundry, and Jim and Andy's ancient greengrocer's sign hangs outside a bar in Carroll Gardens. New mimics old here: hilariously, even the bathrooms in some brand-new restaurants evoke the nineteenth century—thankfully, with modern plumbing.

Of course, rehabbing can create controversy.

BROOKLYN VOICES

CHRISTABEL GOUGH
Secretary, Society for the
Architecture of the City

How do you Manhattanize an old town house? First, you pay a seven- or eight-figure price to buy it. Then you destroy it—except, of course, for the street front, if it is in an historic district. You gut it. You toss any Federal or Greek Revival woodwork into the convenient garbage scow outside the front door. You cut in new windows. You tear out the lower back wall. You change the floor levels. You remove some floors altogether to create double-height rooms. That, your architect triumphantly explains, reduces your Floor Area Ratio! You expand the back with a rear yard addition; you expand the top with a rooftop addition; you expand underneath with new underground levels, which may include a swimming pool, a dog grooming room, and other such essentials. If the swimming pool is of Olympic dimensions, you may ask to excavate the entire rear yard as well, turning the existing garden into a roof terrace. Your landscape architect and his arborist will testify that this will have no impact on the neighbors . . . and your engineer will explain that of course there is no danger.

(Reprinted with permission from a speech delivered to the Cobble Hill Association in 2012)

WHERE

Dumbo, Red Hook, Gowanus, parts of Williamsburg, Greenpoint waterfront, Brooklyn Navy Yard, Crown Heights.

A SKYLINE TO CALL ITS OWN

Old Brooklyn never had a skyline. That's sure changing.

The Williamsburgh Savings Bank (now known as One Hanson Place) was, from 1929 until 2010, Brooklyn's tallest building. It stands at a now-quaint forty-five stories high. The fifty-one-story-tall Brooklyner residential tower was the first to surpass it in height. Since 2010, Downtown Brooklyn and Dumbo have been undergoing a high-rise building boom. The result is a new but so far still unremarkable skyline of modern glass-and-steel buildings (although admittedly their rooftops afford amazing views of Manhattan, bridges, and Brooklyn itself). More skyscrapers are on the drawing boards. Further north, Williamsburg's waterfront has been transformed by a row of high-rises. The explosion of Manhattan-like corridors of towering buildings engenders unease in some quarters.

WHERE

Downtown Brooklyn, near Barclays Center and along the Williamsburg and Greenpoint waterfronts.

ECO, GREEN BROOKLYN

New York City's essential urban infrastructure is aging, rapid residential development is straining municipal systems, and Brooklyn's two toxic Superfund sites, the Newtown Creek and the Gowanus Canal, are undergoing remediation.

Greenpoint and Gowanus are the epicenters of Brooklyn's green movement. The Greenpoint Community Environmental Fund has a $19.5 million grant program created by the state of New York and funded by a settlement with ExxonMobil, resulting in a high degree of community engagement with environmental issues. Gowanus activists don't have that kind of money, but they're spirited.

Biking is huge. This is great news for visitors. The number of cyclists has grown more in Brooklyn than elsewhere in the Big Apple, according to the advocacy group Transportation Alternatives. Brooklyn's miles of bike lanes and the introduction of Citi Bikes make cycling an easy way to explore the neighborhoods. You can join fun group rides, including the Brooklyn Public Library's "Bike the Branches" ride, the annual forty-mile Epic Ride (advance registration required), or popular bike tours of the borough.

BROOKLYN VOICES

KELLY CARROLL
Director of Advocacy and Community Outreach at the Historic Districts Council

When you insert out-of-scale developments, it obliterates that sense of place. It alienates people from each other. People moved to low-rise Brooklyn 'hoods because they liked the look and the humanness of it. . . . I don't know whether what's being built in new Brooklyn will be worthy of preservation in a hundred years. Barclays? I don't know if that will be loved, and to be landmarked, a building has to be loved.

Some buildings have LEED status: the Brooklyn Navy Yard's Building 92, Barclays Center, the Brooklyn Botanic Garden's Visitors Center, Whole Foods in Gowanus, Brooklyn Bowl, and Pratt's Myrtle Hall, among others. Downtown Brooklyn's NYU Poly hosts the Urban Future Lab and NYC ACRE, incubators for start-up companies focusing on clean energy and resilient urban technologies adaptable to extreme weather events.

Since Superstorm Sandy ravaged Brooklyn's coastal communities in 2012, millions of dollars have been allocated to flood prevention and protection studies. Meanwhile, horseshoe crabs have returned to funky Plumb Beach, and the Gowanus Dredgers activists hope to reintroduce once-native oysters into the Gowanus Canal.

Food-related green initiatives include green roofs, CSA (community supported agriculture), and Edible Schoolyard programs, and innovations like Brooklyn's Eagle Street Rooftop Farm. Vinegar Hill Community Gardens' raised vegetable beds and rainwater harvesting system are tied in with a citywide antiobesity campaign. The Brooklyn Botanic Garden's Children's Garden is a place for kids and adults to learn about their food sources and connect with nature through gardening. Sprinkled throughout the borough are some three-dozen fiercely protected community gardens.

More than one tree grows in Brooklyn, where centuries-old neighborhood names like Midwood, Greenpoint, and Green-Wood suggest a verdant past. In

Brooklyn Grange farm's rooftop bee boxes against Manhattan skyline. (Photo by E. Freudenheim, 2014)

1946, the borough had some 230,000 trees, increasing to 320,000 by 2015. "Brooklyn is home to some of the city's most historic trees," Andrew Newman of the New York City Parks Department Central Forestry division told the author. Almost all of the native old-growth forest is gone, he said, supplanted by built environments. But groves in Prospect Park, Green-Wood, Marine Park, and other parks, plus greenways such as Ocean and Eastern Parkways, "provide needed respite, a shade canopy in summer, and a natural filter for pollutants."

The tree in *A Tree Grows in Brooklyn*? It's the "tree-of-heaven," or *Ailanthus altissima*. It's known for defying concrete and asphalt and growing in sidewalk cracks and abandoned lots—a tree with Brooklyn attitude. However, it smells bad, U.S. Department of Agriculture experts say—like rancid peanut butter.

WHERE

Borough-wide. See NYC Parks Department Green Thumb, Grow NYC, Green Guerillas (their motto: "It's Your City. Dig It.").

BROOKLYN'S CULTURAL EXPLOSION

The defining feature of new Brooklyn is immense momentum on the cultural front. We've identified six cultural hubs in Brooklyn: the Brooklyn Cultural District; North Brooklyn along the L subway; the Brooklyn Museum and Brooklyn Botanic Garden cluster along Eastern Parkway; Dumbo and Brooklyn Bridge Park; literary events in various locations; and public spaces.

The Brooklyn Cultural District is huge and growing. By 2018, here you will find eight movie screens for art films, over a dozen professional performance spaces, several specialized museums and serious theater venues, a world-class performing arts institution, a state-of-the-art public library, a century-old theatrical archive, an internationally known dance company's headquarters, an eighteen-thousand-seat venue, and a public plaza for events and markets. The Brooklyn Cultural District stretches from Barclays Center to Brooklyn Heights. Its boundaries, like Brooklyn's neighborhood boundaries, aren't set in stone.

In what seems almost like a "race to Brooklyn," new institutions are flocking here. Barclays Center, with seating capacity for world-class concerts and events, opened in 2012, a game changer for Brooklyn. The Center for Fiction and the Shakespeare-centric Theatre for a New Audience are transplants from Manhattan. Local start-ups include Bushwick Starr, Jack arts center, and the New Brooklyn Theatre. Retooled grand-dame venues, like Loew's Kings Theatre in Flatbush and the Paramount Theater downtown, are almost miraculously opening once again.

Existing institutions are expanding. Brooklyn Academy of Music (BAM), a world-class performing arts institution with a 150-year reputation for innovative works across a range of disciplines, is soon opening new venues called BAM Strong and BAM Karen. BRIC, the presenter of Prospect Park's BRIC Celebrate

Brooklyn! series has expanded to year-round programs at its BRIC House cultural center. The century-old Brooklyn Historical Society and Brooklyn Children's Museum have opened new minibranches in Dumbo in 2016.

A vibrant art scene includes everything from galleries to public art and, especially in Gowanus, Bushwick, and Williamsburg, enormous outdoor murals. Brooklyn has many open studio events, too. Community art centers, from the Invisible Dog Art Center in Boerum Hill to the Brooklyn Waterfront Artists Coalition, create cultural momentum.

WHERE

See "Brooklyn's Cultural Scene," section 4.

FESTIVAL FEVER

From Coney Island's famed Mermaid Parade to Williamsburg's eight-day Northside Festival, Brooklyn hosts over three dozen art, music, film, and ethnic festivals annually. That new cultural festivals pop up every year is extraordinary.

"In the past we had to beg bigger-name artists to play here. Their agents would be like, 'What are you talking about? Prospect Park? Are you kidding?'" Jack Walsh, a Park Slope native and executive producer of the free BRIC Celebrate Brooklyn! concert series, told the author over tea in his Windsor Terrace home. "Now we get pitched all the time. Artists come to New York and want to play someplace different. And some understand it's free for the public here; nobody is buying a ticket. Some appreciate the civic value of that."

WHERE

Check listings and blogs for current shows; see the list of blogs in "Tips," section 5.

BARCLAYS CENTER AND PROFESSIONAL BASKETBALL AND HOCKEY

"One thing I can tell you about Brooklyn, the atmosphere as far as sports, it's one of a kind," Nets player and seven-time NBA All-Star Joe Johnson told the website DIME in 2012.

Brooklyn has a new pro sports franchise—actually, two of them: the Brooklyn Nets basketball and New York Islander hockey teams. Plus you can see the single-A baseball team, the Brooklyn Cyclones, play ball in Coney Island's intimate MCU Park, against the backdrop of amusement-park rides and the Atlantic Ocean.

The Brooklyn Nets and New York Islanders play at Barclays Center, New York's first major indoor arena in thirty-five years. The eighteen-thousand-seat Barclays Center rivals Madison Square Garden in size but has modern amenities, such as a green roof, fan-friendly apps, live multicast streaming, and LEED certification. Wi-Fi is free. Over the course of a year, in addition to the Nets and

FESTIVALS IN BROOKLYN

(The abbreviations indicate neighborhoods; see the key in "Shopping in Brooklyn," section 4. For Brooklyn film festivals, see "Brooklyn's Cultural Scene," section 4.)

Afro Latino Festival (FG), http://www.afrolatinofestnyc.com
AfroPunk Fest (FG), http://afropunkfest.com
BAM Next Wave Festival (FG), http://www.bam.org/programs/2015/next-wave-festival
BEAT festival (multiple venues), http://www.beatbrooklyn.com
BRIC Celebrate Brooklyn! (PS), http://bricartsmedia.org/events/performing-arts/celebrate
    -brooklyn
BRIC Jazzfest (multiple venues), http://bricartsmedia.org
Brooklyn Book Festival (multiple venues), http://www.brooklynbookfestival.org
Brooklyn Botanic Garden Cherry Blossom Festival (CH), http://www.bbg.org/collections/cherries
Brooklyn Dance Festival (FG), http://brooklyndancefestival.org/
Brooklyn Flea (multiple venues), http://brooklynflea.com
Brooklyn Folk Festival (BH), http://www.brooklynfolkfest.com
Brooklyn Hip-Hop Festival (various locations), http://www.bkhiphopfestival.com
Brooklyn Hoops Festival (PH), http://www.barclayscenter.com
Brooklyn Renegade Craft Fair (GR), http://www.renegadecraft.com/newyork
Brooklyn Waterfront Artists Coalition Festival (RH), http://bwac.org
Bushwick Open Studios (BU), http://artsinbushwick.org/open-studios/
Central Brooklyn Jazz festival (multiple venues), http://www.centralbrooklynjazzconsortium.org
DanceAfrica Festival (FG), http://www.bam.org
Edible Escape Festival (multiple venues), http://www.ediblemanhattan.com/events
Eighteenth Avenue Santa Rosalia Festival (BE), see Facebook page
Feast of Our Lady of Mount Carmel, Giglio (W), http://www.olmcfeast.com
Festival des Soupes (CG/CH), http://smithstreetbk.com
Festivals at 50 Kent (W), http://www.eventbrite.com
Fort Greene Park Jazz (FG), http://www.fortgreeneparkjazzfestival.com
Go Green Greenpoint Festival (GR), http://www.townsquareinc.com
Gowanus Jazz Fest (GO), http://www.gowanusjazzfest.com
Grand Comics Festival (W), http://www.grandcomicsfest.com
Great Irish Fair (CI), https://www.facebook.com/GreatIrishFairOfNewYork/
Havemeyer Sugar Sweets Festival at City Reliquary (W), http://www.cityreliquary.org
International African Arts Festival (FG), http://www.iaafestival.org
Make Music NY (multiple venues), http://makemusicny.org
Northside Festival (multiple venues), http://www.northsidefestival.com
Our Lady of Guadalupe Festival (BE), http://www.olguadalupe-brooklyn.com
Pow Wow, Red Hawk Native American Arts Council (Floyd Bennett Field), http://redhawkcouncil
    .org/powwows/
Procession of Santa Fortunata (BE), http://www.meetup.com/sicily/events/206181112/
Smorgasburg (multiple venues), http://www.smorgasburg.com
West Indian American Day Parade (CH), http://wiadcacarnival.org
Zlatne Uste Festival (PS), http://goldenfest.org

Islanders games, Barclays Center hosts Top 10 Brooklyn Hoops college basketball and professional boxing. It's a destination, for sure: Britain's Prince William and Duchess Kate attended a Nets game at Barclays Center in 2014.

If the game begins to lag, you can eat and shop yourself silly in the arena, where over fifty food stands sell only-in-Brooklyn specialties like "Mexican-style" cheese-and-chili-covered corn on a stick from the nearby Habana restaurant and Brooklyn's KelSo craft beer. (Outside Barclays Center, explore Prospect Heights' Vanderbilt Avenue or Park Slope's Fifth Avenue to discover small restaurants and bars, some old-Brooklyn, some new-Brooklyn style.)

The Nets look, designed by Jay Z, is by definition very cool. "A lot of international celebrities have been spotted wearing Nets merchandise," said a Barclays spokesperson, citing Beyoncé, Jimmy Fallon, Michael Strahan, and Rihanna.

Nobody knew whether Brooklyn would embrace the Nets. Some locals still poke fun at the Barclays Center's hulking rusty-red building, calling it the "rusty turtle" or "rust bucket." But as Nets player Johnson told DIME, "The way people are so passionate about the Nets coming here to Brooklyn is something new, and it's exciting to everyone."

Barclays Center's elliptical entry, the Oculus. (Photo by E. Freudenheim, 2014)

WHERE

Barclays Center is near the Atlantic Terminal and Brooklyn Cultural District. For tickets, go to ticketmaster.com or brooklynnets.com. To see a Cyclones baseball game in Coney Island, see www.brooklyncyclones.com.

INNOVATION: TECH TRIANGLE, START-UPS, SHARING ECONOMY

Invisible to the naked eye is a very important facet of new Brooklyn: its tech industry. Over twenty thousand people work in Brooklyn's $3 billion tech sector, as of 2015.

Tech Triangle consists of Downtown Brooklyn, Dumbo, and the Brooklyn Navy Yard.

In 2014, the website Technical.ly listed Brooklyn tech companies ranked by number of local employees, citing Amplify, an ed-tech company; ad agency HUGE; 3-D company MakerBot; media giant VICE; e-commerce site Etsy; crowdfunding platform Kickstarter; video-streaming platform Livestream; Department of Defense contractor Cyre Precision; ad agency Big Spaceship; and maker of 3-D printers Solidoo. Not far behind were BioLite, Farmigo, Flocabulary, Genius, Good Eggs, Northside Media, Tinybop, and VHX.

BROOKLYN VOICES

MATTHEW O. BRIMER
Cofounder of General Assembly and
Daybreaker; Tech Entrepreneur

I love living in Brooklyn, and I continue to see more start-ups, creatives, and mischief makers calling BK home base. There's a diversity to Brooklyn that somewhere like Silicon Valley doesn't have. In Brooklyn, you have so many people working on so many interesting things. In a single weekend recently, I got to hang out with Brooklynites building video-sharing apps, designing furniture, making art, bending neon tubes, producing new kinds of music, planning early-morning dance parties, manufacturing technologically advanced underwear, and creating pop-up interior-design experiences. The entrepreneurial energy and diversity of interests is palpable here, which I love.

Other start-ups with significant venture financing include Charged.fm online ticketing site, CartoDB's cloud-based mapping platform, multimedia storytelling platform Atavist, Bandwagon taxi and ride-sharing service, and Maker's Row, which connects designers with U.S.-based manufacturers. TechCrunch's TV show *Built in Brooklyn*, it says, "showcases the intersection of talent, location, and hustle of this iconic NYC borough." Among its first interviews were FlyCleaners, HowAboutWe, Gotham Greens, Wool & Prince, and Atavist. INDMusic, YouTube's largest music network, and Lifebooker are also in Brooklyn.

The sharing economy is a national trend, evident in new Brooklyn, too. For instance, a coliving start-up founded by Common is experimenting with cohousing old town houses; its Crown Heights community was profiled by Bloomberg News in 2015. Silent Barn in Bushwick is a collectively directed cultural event space. Many such initiatives stress their non-hierarchical, alternative organizational structures. On the other hand, while the "sharing economy" is a catchy phrase, the idea's not all new to Brooklyn. Finnish cooperative housing in Sunset Park was founded a hundred years ago, in 1916. (See Sunset Park in section 3, "The Neighborhoods.")

WHERE

Check the website of the Downtown Brooklyn Partnership. Tech Triangle currently comprises Dumbo, Downtown Brooklyn, and the Brooklyn Navy Yard.

SECRET SAUCE OF THE BROOKLYN BRAND: NEW PLUS OLD

New Brooklyn has a brand! Unlike a cereal or detergent brand, Brooklyn's brand more or less evolved organically. The new Brooklyn brand connotes a constellation of pluses—creativity, youth, diversity, urbanity, energy, sustainability, and fun. Above all, it is endowed with the authenticity of the local. As Carlo A. Scissura, president and CEO of the Brooklyn Chamber of Commerce, said, "You can go to China and see Brooklyn stuff, but it's not from Brooklyn."

Brooklyn's brand is different from, say, Portland's, thanks to sheer critical mass of talent and, not to be underestimated, proximity to all that New York City has to offer. One essential ingredient in the secret sauce of the new Brooklyn brand is the synergy between new and old Brooklyn.

WHERE

The new-old-Brooklyn connection is apparent in many ways in the marketing of products, food and beverages, and tourism. Use of the imagery of the iconic Brooklyn Bridge is ubiquitous, as are branding uses of the words *BK*, *BKLYN*, *BKLN*, and *Brooklyn*.

THE SIXTH BOROUGH: WATERFRONT AND WATERWAYS

Like all frontiers, Brooklyn's waterfront spurs the imagination. New Brooklyn is exploring new ways to use its long coastline.

The old-Brooklyn waterfront was defined by three uses: industrial shipping, transportation to Manhattan, and beaches. The latter two have remained constant. But for fifty years after the city's shipping industry sailed off into the sunset of containerization, Brooklyn's decrepit piers and abandoned docks were dangerous and desolate, not the play spaces for picnics or boating one sees in, say, Brooklyn Bridge Park today.

Lots of different ideas are being floated for a reimagined waterfront. The Brooklyn Waterfront Research Center at the New York City College of Technology in Downtown Brooklyn is addressing sustainability. Moneyed interests envision a Gold Coast lined by hotels and high-rise luxury apartments, with entertainment, tourism, and recreation hubs. Environmentalists talk about green technologies, renewable energy, and weather-resilient infrastructures. Community activists advocate maximum public access, use of the waterways for mass transit, and economic development.

Radically remaking Brooklyn's waterfront is not far-fetched. As *Brooklyn* comes from *Breukelen*, it's somehow fitting that lessons be learned today from Holland, where waterways have been incorporated into urban life and even used to ease the shortage of affordable housing, a problem that plagues Brooklyn. "With climate change and urbanisation putting pressure on available living space in New York's post Sandy era," Dutchman Koen Olthuis of the Waterstudio.NL, said by email to the author, "the next step in Brooklyn's evolution could be floating homes on the water, just like you can already find on the water of Yburg: Brigantijnkade, in Amsterdam!" (for pictures, see http://nyti.ms/1NjnCX1).

Elizabeth Yeampierre, executive director of Sunset Park's Uprose, wants waterfront jobs, saying, "In Brooklyn, there has to be a neighborhood where working people can live and thrive. The whole waterfront, once a working waterfront, should not become commercial hotels. It should be used to build environmental sustainability. We need out-of-the-box thinking to create jobs that address the climate needs facing the city and sustain our working waterfront communities." Carolina Salguero, founder and president of the Red Hook nonprofit PortSide NewYork operating from the historic oil tanker *Mary A. Whalen*, docked off Pier 11 near the Brooklyn Cruise Terminal, grew up in Carroll Gardens. She, too, has a broad vision, of a twenty-first-century maritime economy that engages both Brooklyn's waterside and inland communities, creating new opportunities for recreation, education, culture, and business. "The seam between water and land should be a porous membrane with people and things coming and going across it," she told the author.

Gentrification and the devastating wake-up call of Superstorm Sandy in 2012 have focused public attention on how to protect Brooklyn's waterfront from extreme weather and how to better use it for leisure, education, and ecology.

WHERE

Greenpoint, Williamsburg, Wallabout, Dumbo, Brooklyn Bridge Park, Red Hook, Sunset Park, Industry City, Bay Ridge, Coney Island, Brighton Beach, Manhattan Beach.

GENTRIFICATION, MULTICULTURALISM

A challenge for new Brooklyn is how to maintain the diversity—racial, socioeconomic, religious, cultural, and linguistic—that was just a given fact of life in old Brooklyn and, more so, how to lift all boats in the borough's rising economic tide.

"We are a borough of minorities," affirmed Marty Markowitz, former Brooklyn borough president, in a phone interview. "The rest of the country will look like Brooklyn in years to come. Immigrants are moving to America from all over the world; Brooklyn's already been through that. Today in our diversity is the America of tomorrow." You can see this in one subway trip. Especially in immigrant-rich neighborhoods like Bensonhurst, Sunset Park, and Brighton Beach, you can hear different languages. Store signs are often bilingual or just not in English at all. On the subway, John Q. Public could as easily be José, Yankel, Huang, or Haroon.

Gentrification may be buzzy for those who are doing it, but from the point of those who live in places being "gentrified," it hurts.

The ripple effect of changing demographics touches everything, from education to the arts.

"Our greatest concern is losing artists because of rising real estate prices," Arnold Lehman, the former Shelby White and Leon Levy director of the Brooklyn Museum, told the author in the spring of 2015. "City government needs to understand that affordable housing and affordable studio space are critical components in keeping New York the cultural capital of the world." Racing the increasingly powerful wave of Brooklyn's gentrification, artists have hopped from one neighborhood to another for years.

"Gentrification doesn't (always) bring revitalization, not necessarily at all," Kelly Carroll of the Historic Districts Council explained. "A lot of mom-and-pop businesses have been closing, mostly because their landlords sell the buildings. Or owners leave their storefronts empty, waiting to get top dollar. This results in a kind of blight as even the most expensive neighborhoods have fewer amenities, and people who live there don't have choices."

BROOKLYN VOICES

BEDFORD-STUYVESANT RESIDENT

Bed-Stuy used to provide a comfort zone for people of African and Caribbean descent. Today you are subject to feeling like an outsider when you walk into restaurants along streets where you've patronized the businesses for years. In a growing number of establishments, the clientele isn't diverse anymore, and lots of the newcomers give you a questioning second look when you walk in.

BROOKLYN VOICES

JACK WALSH
Executive Producer of BRIC
Celebrate Brooklyn!

Our audiences are less diverse today. In 1982, when I started at BRIC Celebrate Brooklyn!, most of the performers and audiences were black. In fact, Celebrate Brooklyn! was conceived in part to showcase and celebrate Brooklyn's huge number of outstandingly great jazz musicians, choreographers, and dancers. Most lived in Fort Greene. One of our mission statements was to "create a safe, harmonious setting in which to explore each other's cultures." Now when we book a famous black jazz musician, a white audience shows up. We continue to program diverse artists. But that doesn't mean we'll get a diverse audience.

WHERE

In transitional neighborhoods, you can walk down the street and tick off what's old and new Brooklyn: the check-cashing joint and bodega stand in contrast to the organic ice cream parlor or bakery where coffee costs three dollars, with soymilk as an option. Try this in Crown Heights, Bedford-Stuyvesant, and Bushwick.

BROOKLYN VOICES

CECILIA CLARKE
President and CEO of the Brooklyn
Community Foundation

Almost half of the borough lives near
or below the poverty level. That's really
Brooklyn. A lot of it is working class. It's
only a tiny percentage that's this "brand"
and people of growing affluence. We see
neighborhoods that have basically been
forgotten. Brooklyn has experienced a
balkanization of poverty, as people are
being moved into more concentrated areas
of poverty and are isolated and easier to
ignore. On the other hand, there are phe-
nomenal community-based organizations,
with a lot of strength to fight for social and
racial equality.

BROOKLYN VOICES

LUIS GARDEN ACOSTA
Founder and President of El Puente

The changes are absolutely impossible
to grasp. Today Williamsburg has the
highest concentration of poor young
people in Brooklyn, and there's high-end,
upper-income luxury housing next door to
subsidized housing. Across from El Puente
is a building where rents are $4,000 a
month. Next door, the apartments rent for
$400 a month. It's what I saw in Mexico in
the early 1970s, the very poor living next to
the very rich.

Or read articles from blogs and newspapers
from these communities in Voices of New
York (http://voicesofny.org). It is a website
aggregating Chinese, Spanish, and Russian
ethnic media, created by the CUNY Graduate
School of Journalism's Center for Community
and Ethnic Media.

INCOME INEQUALITY AND DEMOGRAPHICS

In 2014, the borough's population was one-
third white, one-third African American,
one-fifth Latino or Hispanic, and just over 10
percent Asian. Over one-third were foreign-
born. Over three in five spoke a language other
than English at home, primarily Spanish, Chinese, Russian, Yiddish, French Creole, Italian,
Polish, and Arabic, according to U.S. Census
Bureau QuickFacts (online, 2014). More than
one in five Brooklyn residents lived below the
federal poverty level. Trends show a decline
in black population and increase in white and
Asian populations.

Despite Brooklyn's newfound shine, it ranks
third in economic inequality among counties
in the United States, according to Cecelia
Clarke, president and CEO of the Brooklyn
Community Foundation.

Many Brooklyn institutions have worked
determinedly on this front for decades. Few
fans are aware that BRIC Celebrate Brooklyn! was created in the hopes that a festival
featuring the music of Brooklyn's different cultures would forge cross-cultural bonds. "For
thirty-five years, BRIC Celebrate Brooklyn!
Performing Arts Festival has been a national
model for civic engagement and community
revitalization through the arts, and is widely considered the best event of its kind
in New York City," said a BRIC document shared with the author.

Challenges exist in new Brooklyn as they did in old Brooklyn, from housing,
jobs, education, and issues of discrimination to communities having a say in their
own futures.

WHERE

CHIPS, at 200 Fourth Avenue, is a soup kitchen in Gowanus, close to pricey Park Slope. Also in Bushwick, Crown Heights, Downtown Brooklyn's Fulton Mall.

Brooklyn Demographics, 2014	
People QuickFacts	**Brooklyn/Kings County**
Population, 2014 estimate	2,621,793
Population, 2010 (April 1) estimates base	2,504,709
Population, percentage change: 4/2010 to 7/2014	4.70%
Persons under 5 years, percentage, 2014	7.60%
Persons under 18 years, percentage, 2014	23.30%
Persons 65 years and over, percentage, 2013	12.10%
Female persons, percentage, 2014	52.60%
White alone, percentage, 2014	49.30%
Black or African American alone, percentage, 2014	32.50%
American Indian and Alaska Native alone, percentage, 2014	1.00%
Asian alone, percentage, 2014	12.10%
Native Hawaiian and other Pacific Islander alone, percentage, 2014	0.10%
Two or more races, percentage, 2014	2.40%
Hispanic or Latino, percentage, 2014	19.50%
White alone, not Hispanic or Latino, percentage, 2014	35.80%
Living in same house 1 year and over, percentage, 2009–2013	90.50%
Foreign-born persons, percentage, 2009–2013	37.50%
Language not English spoken at home, percentage of age 5+, 2009–2013	46.30%
High school grad or higher, percentage of age 25+, 2009–2013	78.50%
Bachelor's degree or higher, percentage of age 25+, 2009–2013	30.60%
Veterans, number, 2009–2013	50,234
Travel time to work (mean minutes), age 16+, 2009–2013	41.1
Housing units, 2014	1,022,498
Homeownership rate, 2009–2013	29.80%
Housing units in multiunit structures, percentage, 2009–2013	85.70%
Median value of owner-occupied housing, 2009–2013	$557,100
Households, 2009–2013	916,025
Persons per household, 2009–2013	2.73
Per capita income past 12 months (2013 dollars), 2009–2013	$25,289
Median household income, 2009–2013	$46,085
Persons below poverty level, percentage, 2009–2013	23.20%

Source: U.S. Census Bureau, State and County QuickFacts, http://quickfacts.census.gov/qfd/states/36/36047.html (accessed September 2015).

The Neighborhoods

A Brooklyn street lined with nineteenth-century brownstone town houses. (Photo by E. Freudenheim, 2014)

How to Visit a Brooklyn Neighborhood

Brooklyn conjures up thoughts of trendsetters in Williamsburg and beat makers of Bed-Stuy, of brownstoners in Park Slope and Coney Island's long-standing sideshow. It's hip, it's chic, it's swagger through and through.
—Eric L. Adams, Brooklyn borough president

It's fun and easy to explore Brooklyn's fast-changing neighborhoods. Visit a few. Don't get stuck in just edgy North Brooklyn or genteel brownstone Brooklyn or the area around Barclays Center. You're in Brooklyn! Mix it up!

To "see" a Brooklyn neighborhood, first of all, get out of the car! You have to hear, smell, and feel it. Go by bike, subway, or car, but explore on foot. Explore diverse areas. Spend some time sleuthing the main shopping drag. Chill in a café or indie bookstore. Eat! We've listed good pizzerias and restaurants in every neighborhood. See what's sold in ethnic grocery stores and food emporiums, in mom-and-pops and boutiques. Pick up a free local newspaper at a supermarket or café. Read a local blog (listed in "Tips," section 5). Visit the library to see what languages the collections are in, a sure barometer of the community's demographic profile. Explore historical sites—the Old Stone House in Park Slope, the Liberty Pole in Bensonhurst, or the Workingmen's Houses in Carroll Gardens—because landmarks may look dull but always have a drama-filled backstory. Absorb the messages in Brooklyn's vibrant street art (find out where to look for street art in "Brooklyn's Cultural Scene," section 4). Attend a concert, festival, or holiday craft fair. If you're thinking of moving to Brooklyn, go online to see what issues a given neighborhood's community board is addressing. In any event, strike up a conversation!

In the following pages, the neighborhoods are listed alphabetically, but we indicate what is nearby geographically.

You can travel cultures and continents in just a few hours in Brooklyn—a trip down Bedford Avenue alone takes you through African American, Hasidic, Latino, and hipster areas. Have fun!

WHAT IS BROWNSTONE BROOKLYN?
WHERE ARE THE HISTORIC NEIGHBORHOODS?

Brooklyn has nearly three dozen landmarked historic districts and over 180 individual land-marked buildings.

"Brownstone Brooklyn" refers to neighborhoods with many brownstone town houses. The word "brownstones" is shorthand for nineteenth-century three-, four- and five-story row houses that are clad in a brown sedimentary building material. "Brownstone Brooklyn" refers generally to neighborhoods where many of these buildings still stand: Bedford-Stuyvesant, Boerum Hill, Brooklyn Heights, Carroll Gardens, Clinton Hill, Cobble Hill, Crown Heights, Fort Greene, Park Slope, Prospect Heights, and Sunset Park. These brownstone neighborhoods encompass large protected historic districts, except Sunset Park, which is seeking that designation.

Other historic districts include the greater Downtown Brooklyn area, the Brooklyn Academy of Music area, the Borough Hall Skyscraper District, Dumbo and Vinegar Hill, Fulton Ferry, and Wallabout. In North Brooklyn, see Greenpoint's Eberhard Faber Pencil Company area and Williamsburg's Fillmore Place. Historic districts in Victorian Flatbush include, among others, Albemarle-Kenmore Terraces, Ditmas Park, Fiske Terrace–Midwood Park, Prospect Park South, Chester Court, and Prospect Lefferts Gardens.

To add to the confusion, there are different kinds of landmarks. New York City's Landmarks Preservation Commission is the official entity that approves city landmarks; strict restrictions apply to landmarked buildings, the façades of which cannot be changed. The National Register of Historic Places identifies national treasures but exerts no constraints on upkeep. New York State also lists historic sites. The National Parks Service has a list of sites under the National Historic Landmarks Program, online. The nonprofit New York Historic Districts Council and many other preservation groups such as the Municipal Arts Society (MAS) advocate for historic preservation and offer excellent tours.

See the New York Historic Districts Council at http://hdc.org for maps and quick profiles of specific historic districts.

Bay Ridge and Fort Hamilton

Hey, you know, Bay Ridge ain't the worst part of Brooklyn.
. . . I mean, you know, it ain't like a hell hole or nothing.
—Tony Manero, in *Saturday Night Fever*

New York City Marathon runners know Bay Ridge as the first Brooklyn neighborhood they enter, encountering wildly cheering crowds, after crossing the Verrazano-Narrows Bridge.

One hour from Wall Street by subway, Bay Ridge has many attractions: a restaurant row, a waterside running and cycling path, Irish pubs, Owl's Head Park, a tiny Revolutionary War cemetery, and the United States Army museum at Fort Hamilton, Brooklyn's only active army base (for which Brooklyn's southernmost area is named). It's suburban-feeling in parts, with some lovely, historic homes, including the quirky "Gingerbread House."

Many homes near the bluff overlooking the water are worthy of historic preservation. Bike or drive Shore Road to see the mansions and Verrazano Bridge views.

You can experience the fabric of a longstanding old-Brooklyn neighborhood in Bay Ridge, where some Irish and Scandinavian families have roots going back generations. Indeed, some idiosyncratic and decades-old institutions still exist: the Norwegian Day Parade, a billiards hall, and stores like Brooklyn Gallery of Coins and Stamps.

Bay Ridge's historically white, middle-class horizons have been stretched in recent decades by the arrival of an immigrant Muslim community sizable enough to support an Arabic-English bilingual pre-K program in the public school. Families from Yemen, Palestine, Lebanon, and Turkey began

BASICS

MAPPING: Using GPS, orient to Robicelli's Bakery. Main drags: 5th and 3rd Avenues. Use R (86th Street) subway. Near Staten Island, the Verrazano-Narrows Bridge, and the neighborhoods of Borough Park, Dyker Heights, Sunset Park. Bounded by 65th and 101st Streets, 7th Avenue, Shore Parkway.

EVENTS: Bay Ridge Storefront Art Walk, New York City Marathon, Norwegian Constitution Day, Ragamuffin Parade, Saint Patrick's Day. Bay Ridge celebrates its 150th anniversary Memorial Day Parade in 2017.

SELFIES AND 'ZA: Selfies on the 69th Street Pier or on the old cannon in John Paul Jones Park. Pizza at Gino's.

GREENMARKET: Saturdays seasonally at 261 95th Street.

ACCOMMODATIONS: Hotel Gregory, Airbnb, Sunset Park and Gowanus hotels.

settling here in the late 1990s, introducing previously unfamiliar languages, dress codes, and faiths—and spicing up the neighborhood's cuisine offerings, with dozens of little eateries. To see the mix, visit the retail stores along Fifth Avenue near Sixty-Ninth Street and the halal and hookah joints near Leif Erickson Park, so named back in the days when Bay Ridge had a sizable Norwegian population.

Bay Ridge is known for discount shopping at Century 21, a charming small botanical garden, a Republican political bent (rare in Brooklyn), and Poly Prep Country Day School with its twenty-five acre campus, complete with duck ponds.

In summer, peep into a "secret garden" (Narrows Botanical Gardens) or rock out at a free "Oldies but Goodies" outdoor concert. If you are traveling with children in the autumn, don't miss the Ragamuffin Parade, by and for kids, and Halloween in Owl's Head Park. Any time of year, it's interesting to tour Revolutionary and Civil War sites (see "DIY Tours," section 5). If you like to play pool, stop in at Hall of Fame Billiards, owned by Jean Balukas, a world-class pool player.

BEST BETS IN BAY RIDGE AND FORT HAMILTON

1 Food! Killer cupcakes, and Irish, Italian, and Middle Eastern fare.
2 Shoreside exercise: On Shore Parkway, walk, jog, or bike, with views of the Verrazano Bridge and Manhattan. (Enter at the Sixty-Ninth Street footbridge.)
3 Historical sites: See the so-called Gingerbread House, Cannonball Park (also called John Paul Jones Park), and Fort Hamilton's Harbor Defense Museum in the historic caponier building.
4 Irish pub crawl: *Sláinte!*
5 Romantic views: At the Sixty-Ninth Street Pier, enjoy sunsets and views of the Statue of Liberty, lower Manhattan, and the Verrazano Bridge, and see a 9/11 memorial.

BAY RIDGE'S RESTAURANT ROW

Hungry? Try Embers for steak or O'Sullivan's for a burger. Dig into family-style Italian at Vesuvio's and Middle Eastern fare at Yemen Café, Haza, Casablanca Restaurant, and Tanoreen. For ethnic takeout, sample Middle Eastern food at the Family Store and Scandinavian sweets at Leske's Bakery. David's Brisket House and Schnitzel Haus win raves. Start your Irish pub crawl at the ever-friendly Wicked Monk, which has stained glass and a wooden bar imported from a chapel in Gallows Green, Cork, Ireland, then head to Kitty Kiernans. For a taste of new Brooklyn, try Brooklyn Beet Company's farm-to-table burgers and Little Cupcake Bakeshop's sweets.

HISTORY SNAPSHOTS

Bay Ridge, a patriotic community that lays claim to the nation's oldest continuously run Memorial Day Parade, held every May, is rich hunting ground for American history sleuths.

Brooklyn's smallest cemetery, just thirty square feet or so, is the Barkaloo family plot, located on Narrows Avenue and Mackay Street in a quiet corner of a residential neighborhood. A plaque there reads, "Revolutionary War Cemetery" (it doesn't reveal which side the deceased were on). A five-minute drive away is Fort Hamilton, a military base that played a role in the disastrous 1776 Battle of Brooklyn. Its Officer's Club is a New York City landmark. On the fort's property is small Denyse Wharf, named after eighteenth-century Dutch farmers. It is one of the spots where, on August 27, 1776, the British invaded Brooklyn. They later overwhelmed George Washington's troops.

History buffs may also find of interest the pre–Civil War–era Bennett-Farrell-Feldmann House, a Greek Revival villa and a city landmark; here lived various colorful characters including Tammany Hall politician James F. Farrell and his son Jack, a promoter with *Buffalo Bill's Wild West* show. Equally surprising is the fact that Confederate generals Stonewall Jackson and Robert E. Lee both worshiped at now-shuttered Saint John's Episcopal Church in the 1840s when they were stationed at Fort Hamilton, before they fought in the Civil War against the North.

OLD/NEW BROOKLYN

For a sense of old Bay Ridge, take a gander at the area's nineteenth-century homes, some whimsical, others elegant, clustered along Shore and Colonial Roads. Manhattan's elite sailed up New York Harbor to these cozy bluff-side summer estates with spectacular New York Bay views. The "Gingerbread House," at Eighty-Second Street near Narrows Avenue, resembles a seventeenth-century British thatched cottage. Contact the Bay Ridge Historical Society for more information.

CELEBS, FILMS, FICTION

As for celebrities, Danny Golden is a world-famous Irish folk dancer. Janet Yellen, head of the Federal Reserve, grew up here. Steve Sasson, an inductee into the Inventors Hall of Fame, created the first digital still camera in 1975 while at Kodak. The railroad magnate "Diamond" Jim Brady built Fontbonne Hall as a "roaring 1890s" party palace for his mistress, the actress Lillian Russell (ironically, it's a Catholic girls' school today). As for film, John Travolta's dancing scenes in the classic *Saturday Night Fever* were set in a Bay Ridge club, long gone, at 802 Sixty-Fourth Street, formerly the 2001 Odyssey Club. Novelist Hubert Selby Jr. grew up here (but set *Last Exit to Brooklyn* in Sunset Park and Red Hook). For fiction set in Bay Ridge between the 1930s and 1950s, read Gilbert Sorrentino's gritty midcentury novel *Steelwork*.

NOSHES, RESTAURANTS, BARS IN BAY RIDGE AND FORT HAMILTON

Areo ☎, 8424 3rd Avenue, (718) 238-0079
Brooklyn Beet Company, 7205 3rd Avenue, (718) 492-0020
Embers ☎, 9519 3rd Avenue, (718) 745-3700
The Family Store, 6905 3rd Avenue, (718) 748-0207
Gino's Restaurant ☎, 7414 5th Avenue, (718) 748-1698
Hazar Turkish Kebab, 7224 5th Avenue, (718) 238-4040
Kitty Kiernans ☎, 9715 3rd Avenue, (718) 921-0217
Leske's Bakery ☎, 7612 5th Avenue, (718) 680-2323
Robicelli's Bakery, 9009 5th Avenue, (917) 509-6048
Schnitzel Haus, 7319 5th Avenue, (718) 836-5600
Tanoreen, 7523 3rd Avenue, (718) 748-5600 (vegan options)
Wicked Monk ☎, 9510 3rd Avenue, (347) 497-5152

SELECT DESTINATIONS

Bennett-Farrell-Feldmann House, 119 95th Street (private home)
Brooklyn Gallery of Coins and Stamps, 8725 4th Avenue, (718) 745-5701
Fontbonne Hall Academy, 9901 Shore Road, (718) 748-2244
Hall of Fame Billiards, 505 Ovington Avenue, (718) 921-2694
Harbor Defense Military Museum at Fort Hamilton, 230 Sheridan Loop,
    (718) 630-4349
Narrows Botanical Gardens, 7200–7398 Shore Road, (718) 748-4810
Owl's Head Park, bounded by Shore Road, 68th Street, and Colonial Road
Revolutionary War sites (see "DIY Tours," section 5)

☞ Like Bay Ridge? Visit Prospect Park South (for elegant homes) and Sunset Park and Windsor Terrace (for bits of Brooklyn Scandinavian and Irish history, respectively).

Bedford-Stuyvesant

Of Bed-Stuy's many attractions, the most stunning for countless visitors of all backgrounds are the beautiful homes and the immense sense of community here. So many people of African American heritage have roots that run deep here.

—Monique Greenwood, owner and CEO of Akwaaba Mansion

Bedford-Stuyvesant (called Bed-Stuy for short) has been an epicenter of black cultural and political life in the United States for decades. And along with Harlem, it's been one of New York's City's two most important African American communities. When Nelson Mandela came to New York on a three-day whirlwind in 1990, Bedford-Stuyvesant's Boys and Girls High School was one of his first stops.

Some of Brooklyn's most beautiful buildings and landmarks grace this neighborhood. It's recently become one of Brooklyn's "hot" and rapidly changing neighborhoods, too.

Bed-Stuy has both creative aristocracy and street cred up the wazoo. The hip-hop artist Mos Def is from Bed-Stuy. Jackie Robinson, the Brooklyn Dodger who integrated baseball, lived in Bed-Stuy for a time. The nation's first black congresswoman and 1972 presidential candidate Shirley Chisholm, comedian Jackie Gleason, singers Lena Horne and Stephanie Mills, and author Frank McCourt grew up here. So did jazz greats Eubie Blake and Max Roach and stars Jay Z, Big Daddy Kane, Biggie Smalls, Chris Rock, and NBA All-Star Lenny Wilkens.

Bed-Stuy is undergoing demographic change, as mostly nonblack young professionals, newcomers in many senses, move into this historically black

BASICS

MAPPING: Using GPS, orient to Macon public library or nearby Peaches. Main drags: Fulton from Troy to Classon, Nostrand from Halsey to Atlantic Avenues. Use A, C, J, Z, S subways to multiple stops. Near the neighborhoods of Bushwick, Clinton Hill, Crown Heights, Williamsburg. Bounded roughly by Flushing, Classon, and Atlantic Avenues, Broadway.

EVENTS: Concerts, SummerStage, movies, events at Herbert Von King and Fulton Parks, "Stoops" community art event.

SELFIES AND 'ZA: Selfies on any brownstone street. For pizza, Saraghina.

GREENMARKET: Saturdays seasonally, Hattie Carthan "After Church Farmers' Market."

ACCOMMODATIONS: Akwaaba Mansion and Sankofa Aban, both bed-and-breakfasts. Airbnb. (Airbnb told the author in 2015 that forty thousand guests stay with its Bed-Stuy hosts annually.)

TIP: "Bed-Stuy" is pronounced "Bed-Sty."

community. The neighborhood's population, according to the 2010 census, was 135,000. The white population grew 150 percent from 2005 to 2010. Housing prices have soared.

Bedford-Stuyvesant's name is hyphenated for a reason: Bedford and Stuyvesant Heights were originally two different areas, with different architectural styles and histories. Bedford, now one-third black, abuts hipster Williamsburg, Crown Heights, and Clinton Hill. Zoning there allows for high-rise residential development, which, as it unfolds, is likely to bring more shops and restaurants to Bedford Avenue. Lower-rise Stuyvesant Heights, with street after street of landmarked, manicured nineteenth-century town houses, affords less opportunity for new housing development.

BEST BETS IN BEDFORD-STUYVESANT

1 Eat! Peaches specializes in southern and soul food. Saraghina is a destination pizzeria. Eliza Coffee Shop makes a Dominican sancocho gumbo. Roew's serves Caribbean. David's Brisket is a Jewish-style deli run by Yemini Muslims (also in Bay Ridge).
2 Tour historic districts: Explore three large historic districts of beautiful, landmarked nineteenth-century homes. In Stuyvesant Heights, for instance, the area bounded by Stuyvesant and Tomkins Avenues and MacDonough Street is full of elegant homes graced with nineteenth-century stained glass and mahogany and marble interiors. Buy a ticket for the Brownstoners of Bedford-Stuyvesant annual house tour. Or just bike these beautiful streets. (For details, see the Historic Districts Council online.)
3 Churches: Many Bedford-Stuyvesant churches are historically important and architecturally notable (see below).
4 Music: Catch some jazz at Sistas' Place coffeehouse, or 966 Fulton, a senior center by day and a weekend jazz club that's hosted the likes of Wynton Marsalis.
5 Arts: Visit the House of Art Gallery. See exhibits at Skylight Gallery at the Center for Arts and Culture, at Restoration Plaza. The Billie Holiday Theatre showcases African American playwrights. A Bed-Stuy museum of traditional African art is rumored to be under consideration.
6 Shop: Find vintage at Shirley and Alice or at Miss Master's Closet. Walk along Nostrand or Fulton Avenues to explore the local retail scene.
7 Books: The landmarked Macon Library on Lewis Avenue is a Carnegie library with a dedicated African American history reading room.
8 Urban gardens: Visit the Hattie Carthan Garden or the Bedford-Stuyvesant Community Garden, a cornucopia of vegetables with unusual vine trellises and decorations. Admire the flower garden and gazebo at Vernon and Throop Community Garden, and see sustainable urban farming at Tranquility Farms (at Throop and Willoughby Avenues).

HISTORY SNAPSHOTS

The Dutch hamlet of Bedford was established in 1663. Even before New York State abolished slavery in 1827, there were free-black communities here, supporting such institutions as the Brooklyn Howard Colored Orphan Asylum (1866) and the Zion Home for the Colored Aged (1869).

Further east, Stuyvesant was built in the roaring 1890s by F. W. Woolworth, of dime-store fame, who lived at 209 Jefferson Avenue. Throughout Stuyvesant Heights and the surrounding area, you can see evidence of its upper-crust beginnings: the Renaissance and Alhambra apartments and Masonic Lodge Boys' High School are good examples. Fulton Park was built to emulate London's elite Bloomsbury Square, complete with elegant homes along Chauncey Street, lining its perimeter.

A Brooklyn resident enjoys a jazz concert by Wynton Marsalis at 966 Fulton; the parasol is reminiscent of a New Orleans "second line" parade. (Photo by E. Freudenheim, 2015)

Rural and southern blacks settled in Bed-Stuy during the 1930s, as did early waves of West Indian immigrants. Some bought homes. During World War II, expansion of the Brooklyn Navy Yard created demand for laborers' housing. As African Americans and Caribbean islanders began to move in, the white population declined, a process accelerated by the end of the war, racism, scaremongering, and discriminatory practices called blockbusting and redlining.

In the politically supercharged 1960s, Bedford-Stuyvesant experienced significant civil unrest. Riots were sparked by the killing of a young boy by a policeman in 1964—an instance of the abuse of power still being protested by the "Black Lives Matter" movement fifty years later. In response, U.S. Attorney General Robert Kennedy helped to establish the Bedford-Stuyvesant Restoration Corporation in 1967, the nation's first community development corporation tasked with advocating for and providing basic services to the community.

Restoration Plaza is the heart of the Bedford-Stuyvesant Restoration Corporation. It may look like just any urban office complex, but because of its origins, it's special. This three-hundred-thousand-square-foot building was constructed from a renovated Sheffield Farms milk-bottling plant with private and public monies. Today it's still a soup-to-nuts revitalization engine. Bed-Stuy's unofficial "downtown," it hosts community meetings and runs the Center for Arts and Culture while advocating for the neighborhood on multiple fronts, from affordable housing to commercial revitalization to entrepreneurship training. The complex incudes a supermarket, a bank, and other community services.

Long gone are The East, a radical culture center from the 1960s and 1970s that helped shape the neighborhood, and the 1910 Regal Theater, renamed the Slave Theater in 1984 to make a political point, at 1215 Fulton Street. Shuttered now, the Slave Theater was a center for activism, where the Reverend Al Sharpton and other leaders held political rallies, protests, and community gatherings from 1986 on. Some parties have expressed interest in renovating and reopening the Slave Theater; a *New York Times* story, "Tug of War over a Civil Rights Legacy," details the convoluted ownership struggle over this historic property.

Bed-Stuy is nothing if not engaged. The Brownstoners of Bedford-Stuyvesant, which still runs the neighborhood's annual house tour, formed in the 1970s as a group of homeowners truly "standing their ground" against erosion of their hard-won homes and neighborhood by crime, drugs, municipal neglect, and middle-class flight. Its house tours were born as a pride-building PR campaign, showcasing the handsome face of Bed-Stuy. The social fabric of Bed-Stuy is woven of such community networks, families, churches of course, and also many social support organizations. The latter aren't visible to tourists. But it's a robust universe, ranging from the venerable United Order of Tents, a direct service agency founded in 1867 by two former women slaves from Virginia, to newer organizations like Bailey's Café, an after-school art and support program for girls.

ARCHITECTURAL AND CHURCH HIGHLIGHTS

The impressive 1890 Twenty-Third Regiment Armory is the most outstanding of all Brooklyn armories. The ornate 1892 Imperial Apartments, by the architect-developer team of Montrose Morris and Louis F. Seitz, promoted the benefits of easy apartment living as an alternative to the burdens of living in a house. Stuyvesant was a wealthy area, and its schools reflected its upper-class status. The 1891 Boys High School at 832 Marcy Avenue, a Romanesque Revival building with a tower, campanile, and architectural flourishes, was built by James Naughton, who also designed Erasmus Hall High School, PS 9 in Prospect Heights, and other landmarked educational buildings.

Some of Bed-Stuy's historic churches were founded as early as the seventeenth and eighteenth centuries. Bridge Street AWME Church is the oldest continuing black congregation in Brooklyn. A pioneer in the civil rights movement, it established an African Free School in the 1820s. Siloam Presbyterian Church was part of the Civil War–era Underground Railroad that helped southern blacks escaping slavery. The pre–Civil War Concord Baptist Church of Christ was founded in 1847. It's one of a handful of extant churches built by the early black residents of Brooklyn. Built in the 1880s: Bethany Baptist Church (the first African American church to move into Bedford-Stuyvesant during the northward migration of rural blacks); Saint Bartholomew's Church (an irregularly shaped small church designed by George Chappel); and two churches designed by architect R. M. Upjohn, Saint George's Episcopal Church and Saint Mary's Church (the former in a high Victorian Gothic style and both with Tiffany windows).

The Berean Missionary Baptist Church was founded in 1635, near Weeksville; it originally included both blacks and whites. It relocated to Bed-Stuy in 1898 and subsequently became an all-black congregation. Our Lady of Victory Roman Catholic Church dates to 1895.

OLD/NEW BROOKLYN

The deepest connection between old and new Bedford-Stuyvesant is of course, the neighborhood's historic urban landscape: the leafy streets, the broad sky, the

BROOKLYN VOICES

COLVIN W. GRANNUM
President and CEO of the Bedford-Stuyvesant Restoration Corporation

Like Harlem, Bed-Stuy is iconic. I wouldn't call them twin neighborhoods. But they are comparable. People don't realize that Harlem and Bed-Stuy are connected by the A train. During the Harlem Renaissance, a lot of exchange happened between people in Harlem and in Bed-Stuy. Bed-Stuy residents took the A train uptown to Harlem to perform or be entertained. They took the A train home to Bed-Stuy.

The cultural richness of Bed-Stuy isn't as well chronicled as Harlem's. But maybe four hundred thousand people of African descent—business owners, artisans, civil servants, teachers, and lots of poor and poorly educated—lived in what was called Bed-Stuy then. It included East Clinton Hill and half of what's now Crown Heights.

Bed-Stuy used to be peppered by lounges, churches, social clubs, and bars where musicians played jazz and the blues, preserving the culture and history of their people who'd migrated from the South. Except for the churches, a lot of these places disappeared after massive disinvestment followed unrest in the 1960s. But Bed-Stuy is still culturally vibrant. At Restoration, we have scores of community meetings and cultural events and performances each month.

Gentrification is scary in the sense that it's all about access to capital. People of African, Caribbean, and Hispanic descent have very limited access to capital. So the opportunity for them to benefit from gentrification in Bed-Stuy, in any way representative of the size of their population or their length of residence in the community, is limited.

A lot of longtime residents feel, and are vulnerable to being, displaced. When newcomers have an attitude that they "discovered" Bed-Stuy, that all that matters is their brownstone and their friends, and that they are going to "improve" the 'hood, people who've lived here for years feel that the newcomers don't respect them. Looking back, after years of complaining about not having nice stores or even adequate municipal services, some long-time residents are saying it wasn't so bad before, at least my presence in the community wasn't being questioned.

human-scaled, low-rise, and ornate buildings. There's historic continuity in the churches and homes. Old and new meet here, as Bed-Stuy once again finds itself at an inflection point.

CELEBS, FILMS, FICTION

See where they lived: Composer and jazz pianist Eubie Blake lived at 284A Stuyvesant Avenue. Drummer Max Roach lived at 475 Nostrand Avenue and attended Boys' High School. The founder and publisher of *Black Enterprise* magazine, Earl Graves, lived at 376 Macon Street. The activist and poet June Jordan lived at 681 Hancock Street. Brooklyn Dodger Jackie Robinson lived at 526 MacDonough Street. Singer Lena Horne lived at 180 Chauncey Street, not far from number 328, where Jackie Gleason grew up. Rev. Al Sharpton lived here. As for film, the Sundance-winning 1999 film *On the Ropes* tells the story of boxers at the New Bed-Stuy Boxing Center, opened in 1980 in part as a community center for youth. See the video online of the celeb-packed twenty-fifth-anniversary street party for Spike Lee's *Do the Right Thing*, held on Stuyvesant Avenue in 2014. For literature, read Paule Marshall's classic 1959 novel *Brown Girl, Brownstones*, and for young-adult fiction, Daniel José Older's 2015 book *Shadowshaper*. Also read Bed-Stuy resident and Pulitzer Prize–winning poet Greg Pardlo's *Totem* and *Digest*.

NOSHES, RESTAURANTS, BARS IN BED-STUY

Alice's Arbor, 549 Classon Avenue, (718) 399-3003
DOCD Southern Desserts Shop, 214 Bainbridge Street, (347) 413-8348
Le Paris Dakar, 518 Nostrand Avenue, (347) 955-4100
Peaches ☎, 393 Lewis Avenue, (718) 942-4162
Saraghina, 435 Halsey Street, (718) 574-0010
Sugar Hill ☎, 609 DeKalb Avenue, (718) 797-1727
Therapy Wine Bar, 364 Lewis Avenue, (718) 513-0686

SELECT DESTINATIONS

Berean Missionary Baptist Church, 1635 Bergen Street, (718) 774-0466
Bethany Baptist Church, 460 Marcus Garvey Boulevard, (718) 455-8400
Concord Baptist Church of Christ, 833 Marcy Avenue, (718) 622-1818
Hattie Carthan "After Church Farmers' Market," 49 Van Buren Street,
     (718) 638-3566
House of Art Gallery, 408 Marcus Garvey Boulevard, (347) 663-8195
Macon Branch, Brooklyn Public Library, 361 Lewis Avenue, (718) 573-5606
Our Lady of Victory Roman Catholic Church, 583 Throop Avenue,
     (718) 574-7772

Restoration Plaza, 1368 Fulton Street, (718) 636-6900
Saint Bartholomew's Church, 1227 Pacific Street, (718) 467-8750
Saint George's Episcopal Church, 800 Marcy Avenue, (718) 789-6036
Sistas' Place, 456 Nostrand Avenue, (718) 398-1766
Washington Temple Church of God in Christ, 1372 Bedford Avenue,
     (718) 789-7545
Willoughby General, 518 Willoughby Avenue, (646) 620-5794

☞ Like Bedford-Stuyvesant? Visit a few other brownstone neighborhoods: Boerum Hill, Clinton Hill, Crown Heights, Fort Greene, and Prospect Heights.

Bensonhurst and Dyker Heights

One of these days . . . POW! Right in the kisser!
—Jackie Gleason in *The Honeymooners*,
set in Bensonhurst

BASICS

MAPPING: Using GPS, orient to Villabate Alba bakery. Main drags: 86th Street, 18th Avenue. Use N subway (Bay Parkway to 86th Street stops). Near the neighborhoods of Bay Ridge, Borough Park, Brighton Beach, Coney Island, Sheepshead Bay. Bounded roughly by 61st Street, 7th Avenue, Avenue U, Shore Parkway.

EVENTS: Columbus Day parade, Dyker Heights Christmas lights extravaganza, Lunar New Year, Italian religious feasts.

SELFIES AND 'ZA: Selfies at the historic Liberty Pole. Pizza at L&B Spumoni Gardens.

GREENMARKET: Sundays seasonally at 18th Avenue at 81st Street.

ACCOMMODATIONS: Airbnb.

TIPS: Greater Bensonhurst is big. Come with wheels—bike or car—to explore.

Spend a few hours in sprawling Bensonhurst (including, here, parts of Dyker Heights and Bath Beach). Though this was once an Italian stronghold and you can find a few Italian bakeries and pizza joints, today as you munch along, you'll more likely be sampling Chinese and Russian foods. Along Bay Parkway, about four out of five shops are now Chinese owned. Get an inexpensive haircut in a salon staffed by Asian immigrants. Buy the cheapest jeans this side of Xinjiang. As a third-generation Bensonhurst woman of Italian descent told the author flatly, "Italian Bensonhurst is done. It's over. They all moved to Staten Island."

Untouched by the gentrification that's transformed Italian Williamsburg and other neighborhoods, Bensonhurst still has the vibe of yesteryear's up-by-the-bootstraps Brooklyn—except now, it's not in Italian but in Chinese, Russian, or Spanish. Bensonhurst saw a nearly 60 percent rise in the Asian population in ten years, according to the 2010 census.

BEST BETS IN BENSONHURST AND DYKER HEIGHTS

1 Christmas lights extravaganza in Dyker Heights: Join thousands who come to see the outrageously elaborate displays of Santas and reindeers on chimneys and entire homes framed in lights. This neighborly, no-holds-barred competition runs from Thanksgiving to New Year's Day, from

Eighty-Second to Eight-Fifth Streets, between Tenth and Thirteenth Avenues, also called Dyker Heights Boulevard.

2 Ethnic cuisine: Shop at Good Fortune Chinese supermarket. Visit Frank and Sal's Italian Market. At Easter, have traditional breads and egg-shaped cakes at Sicilian bakery Villabate Alba.

3 Bargain hunt: Shop for cheap goods and services, including nail salons on Eighty-Sixth Street between Twentieth and Twenty-Fifth Avenues. This street's jammed with outdoor stalls selling food and inexpensive merchandise and chain clothing stores.

4 Italian religious festivals: Time travel to another century, attend the Good Friday procession to Our Lady of Guadalupe Church, the Procession of Santa Fortunata, and the Santa Rosalia Festival. The Columbus Day Parade is an expression of Italian American pride.

5 Landmarks: The 1677 New Utrecht Reformed Church and Cemetery date from the Dutch era. The church is the nation's fourth-oldest Reformed Church congregation; the cemetery contains family plots belonging to early settlers. The New Utrecht Liberty Pole, erected two months after the patriots won independence in 1783, and Magen David synagogue are also landmarks.

HISTORY SNAPSHOTS

In the 1890s, Bensonhurst-by-the-Sea was built as a resort complex with hotels, an amusement park, and racetracks but failed to compete with world-famous Coney Island, nearby. In 1915, mass transit arrived in Bensonhurst, leading to residential development. The area attracted ethnically mixed, and clannish, communities, from Syrian Jewish immigrants who built Magen David synagogue to Italians escaping Manhattan's overcrowded Little Italy.

Fast-forward a century. By the 1970s, majority-white Bensonhurst had a vibrant mix of Italian and Jewish residents. It was famous for its bakeries, elaborate festivals, and Italian men's-only "social clubs"—but infamous for sporadic Mafia-related and racist violence. By about 2000, Russian-run shops and Chinese apothecaries, restaurants, and stores were interspersed among the Italian stores.

OLD/NEW BROOKLYN

Get a street-level eyeful of old Brooklyn just by looking at honorary street names. Robert Merrill Way honors a Brooklyn opera star who belted out some five hundred performances at the Metropolitan Opera (find it at Bay Twenty-Eighth Street, between Benson and Bath Avenues). Tony "The Barber" Nobile Way (on the northwest corner of Sixty-Fourth Street and Eleventh Avenue) honors Sicilian-born Antonio Nobile, whose Dyker Heights barbershop opened in 1973; he's also in the hall of fame at the National Barbers Museum. Louis Liotta Way (corner of Bath and Cropsey Avenues) honors a *New York Post* photo-journalist and lifelong Bensonhurst resident. In 1935, at age fourteen, he worked for the Acme Photo Agency in Manhattan tending the carrier pigeons that flew film from Dodgers games at Ebbets Field direct to the agency. Liberty Pole Boulevard is Eighty-Fourth Street.

CELEBS, FILMS, FICTION

Megastars from the mid-twentieth century who came from Bensonhurst included Phil Silvers, Dom DeLuise, and Abe Burrows. Bensonhurst-raised Maria Bartiromo, a TV journalist, told *Delta Sky Magazine,* "I grew up in Brooklyn. The greatest place on earth. I was very much in a neighborhood." As for movies, in addition to *The Honeymooners*, the car and subway chase scene in *The French Connection* and parts of Spike Lee's *Jungle Fever* were filmed here. *Saturday Night Live* did a devastating episode about race called the "Bensonhurst Dating Game" in 1992. For fiction, read the gritty 1987 *The Boys of Bensonhurst*, by Brooklyn-born Salvatore La Puma.

NOSHES, RESTAURANTS, BARS IN BENSONHURST AND DYKER HEIGHTS

Aunt Butchie's Desserts ☎, 6901 13th Avenue, (718) 256-2933
B&A Pork Store ☎, 7818 13th Avenue, (718) 238-9326
Café Kiev, 1739 West 7th Street, (718) 336-8800
Frank and Sal's Italian Market ☎, 8008 18th Avenue, (718) 331-8100
Hand Pull Noodle and Dumplings House, 7201 18th Avenue, (718) 232-6191
L&B Spumoni Gardens Restaurant ☎, 2725 86th Street, (718) 449-1230
Shabu Shabu, 7204 18th Avenue, (718) 331-1818
Tomasso's Restaurant ☎, 1464 86th Street, (718) 236-9883
Villabate Alba Pasticceria ☎, 7001 18th Avenue, (718) 331-8430

SELECT DESTINATIONS

Dyker Beach Golf Course, 1030 86th Street and 7th Avenue, (718) 836-9722
Good Fortune Chinese Supermarket, 6722 Fort Hamilton Parkway,
    (718) 680-2889
Liberty Pole and Cemetery at New Utrecht Reformed Church, 1827 84th Street,
    (718) 232-9500
Magen David Synagogue, 2130 McDonald Avenue, (347) 762-4363

☞ Like Bensonhurst? Visit what remains of Italian Williamsburg (near the Lorimer L subway stop) or Asian sections of Sunset Park and Sheepshead Bay.

Boerum Hill

I was surprised by the diversity. . . . People of varying
backgrounds and income levels, cuisine, dress, and
businesses [in] the few blocks around our home. Despite
rapid gentrification, they coexist while living in completely
separate worlds.
—Charulata Prasada, former United Nations staffer in
Latin America and Southeast Asia

Speaking of surprises, educated Brooklynites are
shocked to learn that their counterparts in Buenos
Aires have a granular familiarity with Boerum Hill.
After all, it's one of those Brooklyn neighborhoods
that are neither here nor there. Coney it's not. But
what has catapulted Boerum Hill to international
fame, of a sort, is the work of Jonathan Lethem, a
MacArthur "genius" honoree whose popular novels
paint day-to-day life in a Brooklyn on the cusp of gentrification. He's popular in translation, in Argentina.

Boerum Hill, with a population of twenty thousand, harbors a fair share of interesting shops and
bars and, unexpectedly, a small strip of Middle
Eastern stores and a mosque. Its charming nineteenth-century town houses make it worth a look.
Picturesque State Street often wins "best garden"
awards.

BEST BETS IN BOERUM HILL

1 Excellent food and bars! Slurp matzo ball soup
at Mile End Deli. Have brunch or dinner at
Rucola or French Louie. Explore whiskeys at
popular, historic Brooklyn Inn. Down a beer to
live country-western music at Hank's Saloon or
chill at St. Gambrinus Beer Shoppe.

BASICS

MAPPING: Using GPS, orient to Brooklyn
Inn. Main drags: Atlantic Avenue,
Court Street. Use almost any subway
to Atlantic Avenue / Barclays Center
transit hub. Near Barclays Center and
the neighborhoods of Carroll Gardens,
Cobble Hill, Gowanus. Bounded
roughly by Schermerhorn, Warren, and
Court Streets, 4th Avenue.

EVENTS: Atlantic Antic Street Fair, historic
house tour.

SELFIES AND 'ZA: Selfies on a brownstone
stoop. For pizza, Sottocasa or Bedouin
Tent ("pitza").

ACCOMMODATIONS: Nu Hotel, hotels in
Downtown Brooklyn or Gowanus.

2 Culture: Attend an author reading at BookCourt, an experimental music con-
cert at Roulette, or shows at the Invisible Dog Art Center, BAM, or Barclays
Center. All the institutions in the Brooklyn Cultural District are close by.
Don't miss the mother of all street fairs, the Atlantic Antic.

3 Only-in-Brooklyn shops: Check Atlantic Avenue's overstuffed antique shops,
like Horseman Antiques. Rummage through Buffalo Exchange for vintage
finds. Browse the boutiques: Brooklyn Circus, Kimera Design, or Steven Alan.
Get the kids a toy at Acorn.

4 Revolutionary War history: Stand where George Washington stood, at Trader
Joe's! A plaque marks the site where Washington surveyed his troops in the
war's early days, August 27, 1776. (See "DIY Tours," section 5.)

5 Slice of Brooklyn life: Appreciate the random juxtapositions of urban life,
including a muezzin call broadcast from Al-Farooq Mosque, Middle Eastern perfume stores like Madina, the Brooklyn House of Detention, and the
Quakers' austere 1857 Friends Meeting House.

6 Wander: Take a walk along State Street and through the neighborhood's
pretty, preserved old streets. (See the Historic Districts Council online.)

HISTORY SNAPSHOTS

As fans of author Jonathan Lethem know, this tiny neighborhood is packed with
stories. Here's one: 360 Pacific Street (a private home today) from the 1930s through
the 1960s was a residence for Mohawk Indians, imported to work on skyscrapers
as steelworkers. The story was told in a 1949 *New Yorker* article, "The Mohawks
in High Steel," and confirmed by the Smithsonian, which says, "By the 1930s, the
Great Depression and the availability of work in New York had drawn numerous
Mohawk families to New York City. Eventually, more than 800 Mohawk people
were living in the Brooklyn neighborhood of Boerum. . . . By the late 1960s, the
community had virtually disappeared."

OLD/NEW BROOKLYN

Sophisticated yet not showy, historic but not uptight, this diverse neighborhood
was saved from the wrecker's ball in the 1970s by urban homesteaders. They
bought, restored, and basically loved a whole neighborhood of rooming houses,
cheap bars, and decrepit nineteenth-century homes back to its original upper-
middle-class charm.

Along elegant State Street, you can imagine the past and present in split-screen
shots. These renovated, multimillion-dollar, nineteenth-century row houses dating
from the 1840s through the 1870s give you a snapshot of Brooklyn back when it
was an independent city, when cars were a thing of the future, and when travel

fantasies (by balloon) were inspired not by personalized Internet advertising but by Jules Verne's *Around the World in 80 Days.*

CELEBS, FILMS, FICTION

Resident celebs have included actors Ethan Hawke and Keri Russell, Nell Campbell, singer Joan Osborne, former congresswoman Elizabeth Holtzman, and designer Daryl K. For novels set in Boerum Hill, read L. J. Davis's 1971 novel *A Meaningful Life.* And to see what all the buzz is about in Buenos Aires, of course, read former resident Jonathan Lethem's 2004 *The Fortress of Solitude.*

NOSHES, RESTAURANTS, BARS IN BOERUM HILL

Bedouin Tent, 405 Atlantic Avenue, (718) 852-5555
Brooklyn Inn ☎, 148 Hoyt Street, (718) 522-2525
French Louie, 320 Atlantic Avenue, (718) 935-1200
Hank's Saloon ☎, 46 3rd Avenue, http://www.exitfive.com/hankssaloon/
Mile End Delicatessen, 97 Hoyt Street, (718) 852-7510
Rucola, 190 Dean Street, (718) 576-3209
Sottocasa Pizza, 298 Atlantic Avenue, (718) 852-8758
St. Gambrinus Beer Shoppe, 533 Atlantic Avenue, (347) 763-2261

SELECT DESTINATIONS

BookCourt, 163 Court Street, (718) 875-3677
Brooklyn Circus, 150 Nevins Street, (718) 858-0919
Invisible Dog Art Center, 51 Bergen Street, (347) 560-3641
Roulette, 509 Atlantic Avenue, (917) 267-0363

☞ Like Boerum Hill? Visit any brownstone neighborhood: Bedford-Stuyvesant, Brooklyn Heights, Carroll Gardens, Clinton Hill, Cobble Hill, Crown Heights, Fort Greene, Park Slope, Prospect Heights, Sunset Park.

Borough Park

BASICS

MAPPING: Using GPS, orient to Weiss Kosher Bakery; try the babka! Main drags: 13th and 18th Avenues. Use D, B (50th Street), or N (New Utrecht) subways. Near the neighborhoods of Bay Ridge, Bensonhurst, Flatbush, Midwood, Sunset Park. Bounded roughly by 9th, New Utrecht, and 18th Avenues and 38th Street.

SELFIES AND 'ZA: Selfies in front of a wig shop. Try Vincent's Pizzeria (not kosher) or Amnon's Pizza (kosher).

GREENMARKET: Thursdays seasonally at 14th Avenue and 50th Street.

ACCOMMODATIONS: Park House Hotel, Avenue Plaza hotel (both kosher).

TIPS: Dress modestly. Stores are closed on Saturday, during Jewish festivals, and three hours before sundown on Friday.

Venture to a fascinating land, a traditional culture where God looms large, prayer is primary, and the culture is so conservative, it's borderline radical.

And the attire is intense. Men wear long black coats, beards, and *peyot* (sidelock curls). On holidays, you'll see them decked out in big fur hats, *shtreimels*. Women dress modestly, marry young, and, once married, wear wigs or full-coverage hats in public, because hair is deemed sensual and therefore for a husband's eyes only. Even little girls wear long skirts and long sleeves but never shorts or pants. You'll see families of five or six kids trailing a mother down the street, most of them identically dressed. Hewing to tradition, above individuality, is the valued norm.

You will find liquor stores but no bars in Jewish Borough Park. You'll hear klezmer music but not rock. There are jokes galore in Borough Park; most have a Yiddish punch line.

Rigorous religious laws govern life, and if it ain't kosher, they won't eat it. Men and women inhabit separate realms. Matchmakers and parents arrange dates and marriages. Children attend parochial schools. Many among the best and brightest men elect the career of scholar and carry on a millennia-old tradition of Torah study in a yeshiva.

Borough Park (population 130,000) is not exclusively Jewish. Chinese, Polish, and other mostly immigrant residents live in the area. But it's Brooklyn's largest Jewish neighborhood, with the highest concentration of Orthodox Jews outside Israel.

Its Hasidic sects—Satmar, Bobov, Belz, and some dozen more—are generally not Zionists.

Borough Park (like the Hasidic areas of two other Brooklyn neighborhoods, Crown Heights and Williamsburg) makes for a remarkable, eye-opening visit.

BEST BETS IN BOROUGH PARK

1   Sample Jewish food: *Fress* on challah and rye bread, babka and pastries at Korn's, in business since the 1920s, or at Weiss Homemade Kosher Bakery. Eat smoked fish with a schmear at Schwartz Appetizing. Nosh a roll at Sushi Meshuga. It's all kosher here.
2   Train World: Situated under an elevated subway, this hobbyist store sells miniature trains, scenery, figures, and tracks. It's been in business for decades.
3   Shop: Scout the housewares stores, in various price ranges. British Sterling Silver is stocked with well-priced candelabras, Passover Kiddush cups, and cutlery. The Peppermill sells terrific kitchen equipment.
4   Get hats! For women, berets, cloche, beanies, and wide-brimmed styles. For men, black, black, and more black! (Shop at Sherel's for women, at Bencraft Hatters for men.)
5   Explore Jewish culture: Visit a matzo factory where, enacting a centuries-old ritual, workers produce batches of matzo in strict eighteen-minute cycles, sometimes while singing hymns (open only in spring, pre-Passover). To deconstruct the zeitgeist, peruse shelves of Haggadahs, videos, and Jewish-themed coloring books at Eichler's Religious Articles, Gifts and Books store.

HISTORY SNAPSHOTS

In the colonial era, the land that today is Borough Park was part of the Dutch town of New Utrecht. This was farmland until the nineteenth century, when the prominent Litchfield family sold a large parcel of farmland to former New York state senator and developer William H. Reynolds (who also built Prospect Heights and long-gone Dreamland in Coney Island). He built modest, free-standing wood-frame homes with inviting front porches. Initially mixed Irish, Italian, and Jewish, the area has had a growing Jewish population since European Jewish refugees arrived pre– and post–World War II. In the 1970s, more Russian, Hungarian, Polish, Romanian, and Israeli Jews followed. Maimonides Medical Center, today Brooklyn's largest independent teaching hospital, was founded in 1911 and still operates here.

OLD/NEW BROOKLYN

In the past five decades, a growing community of observant Jews, including many Hasidim, has transformed much of Borough Park into a modern-day,

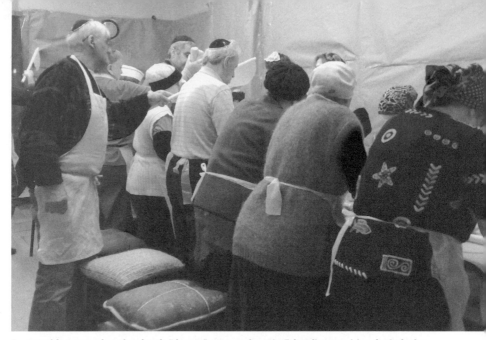

A seasonal factory produces handmade "shmura" matzo under strict Talmudic supervision, for Orthodox Jews. (Photo by E. Freudenheim, 2015)

Internet-wired shtetl, peppered with the signs of an all-encompassing Orthodox religious life: synagogues, yeshivas, and Jewish bookstores. The Hasidim operate kosher hotels, private schools, a volunteer ambulance service, and rabbinical courts. With their faith, family ties, tradition, and a sense of historical mission, everyone seems abuzz, running to study, pray (three times daily), work, tend to kids, and do *mitzvoth* (good deeds).

Brooklyn's Hasidim have amassed significant political clout in New York City politics, and in the world of Brooklyn real estate. Some of the high-rise developments going up in the borough are owned by Hasidic entrepreneurs. But Hasidic Brooklyn, and in particular Borough Park, is not wealthy. Seventy percent of this area's Jewish population earned below $50,000 annually, according to a 2011 UJA Jewish Community report, with the majority (and many have large families) "just managing to make ends meet." The community has had its share of social problems.

CELEBS, FILMS, FICTION

See the PBS film *A Life Apart: Hasidism in America*. Read *A Seat at the Table: A Novel of Forbidden Choices*, by Joshua Halberstam, who grew up in Borough Park, or *Invisible City*, by Julia Dahl.

NOSHES, RESTAURANTS, BARS IN BOROUGH PARK

Amnon's Kosher Pizza, 4814 13th Avenue, (718) 851-1759
Korn's Bakery 🏠, 5004 16th Avenue, (718) 851-0268 (multiple locations)

Vincent's Pizza, 3915 9th Avenue, (718) 851-8838
Vostok, 5507 13th Avenue, (718) 437-2596
Weiss Homemade Kosher Bakery ☎, 5011 13th Avenue, (718) 438-0407

SELECT DESTINATIONS

British Sterling Silver Corporation, 4922 16th Avenue, (718) 436-2800
Eichler's Religious Articles, Gifts and Books, 5004 13th Avenue, (718) 633-1505
The Peppermill, 5015 16th Avenue, (718) 871-4022
Schmura Matza Bakery, 1285 36th Street, (718) 438-2006
Sherel's Hats & Accessories, 4912 13th Avenue, (718) 436-0581
Train World, 751 McDonald Avenue, (718) 436-7072

☞ Like Borough Park? Visit Hasidic sections of Crown Heights and Williamsburg.

Brighton Beach

Ukrainians. These are definitely Ukrainians. I can tell by
their accents.   —young Russian visiting from Moscow

BASICS

MAPPING: Using GPS, orient to Café at Your Mother-in-Law (if only for its name). Main drag: Brighton Beach Avenue. Use B, Q (Brighton Beach Avenue) subways. Near the neighborhoods of Coney Island, Manhattan Beach, Sheepshead Bay. Bounded by the Atlantic Ocean, Corbin Place, Ocean and Shore Parkways.

EVENTS: Brighton Jubilee street fair.

SELFIES AND 'ZA: Selfies at a Russian newsstand or with a "babushka" (elderly Russian woman in a head-scarf), if you turn on the charm. Travel for pizza to Totonno's in Coney Island. Or opt for kasha varnischkes instead.

ACCOMMODATIONS: Airbnb.

"Back in the USSR" indeed. You don't need a visa to get a taste of Russia in Brooklyn's "Little Odessa," a busy neighborhood that seems to be in another time and place, namely, Kiev circa the 1980s and 1990s. Buy pastry and sausages. Look dour and wear fur. Come for blini and to people watch. Join the zaftig ladies and gents in their revealing bikinis on the beach—whenever the thermometer's above fifty degrees. Join a game of chess—but only if you're very good. And for a mind-blowing night out, reserve a table at a Russian nightclub. Carefree Williamsburg feels as far away as the gulag; but you're still in Brooklyn.

"Little Odessa," otherwise known as Brighton Beach, comes as a cultural shock, as bracing as the frigid wintertime ocean braved by local Russian swimmers. Tucked under the elevated train, this neighborhood, with its updated beach bungalows and 1920s apartment buildings, has an old New York feel. But you'll see signs, restaurant menus, and magazines on newsstands written in Cyrillic and, like an afterthought, in English. On the street, you'll hear Russian spoken by young and old alike.

Don't expect California-style smiles or Portlandia "have a nice day" greetings here. You might get a lifted eyebrow from one of the intelligentsia or an ironic shrug of the shoulders from a babushka; the Russians of Little Odessa tend to wear a mask of indifference. If you want to feel at home here, sunbathe in the skimpiest possible bikini and look aloof or perhaps a bit world-weary. Brighton Beach is also one of the few places in Brooklyn where you can wear a full-length sable coat without worrying that an animal-rights activist will snarl at you. And yes, while it's largely unseen, the Russian mob is here (and globally); not to worry, they've got bigger fish to fry than tourists.

BEST BETS IN BRIGHTON BEACH

1   Russian nightclubs: The food and entertainment are beyond legendary. Come with at least half a dozen friends and a designated driver. Never say *nyet* to vodka.

2   Family fun at the beach: Swim, show off your bikini, and learn how to say "sunscreen" in Russian (it's *solntsezashchitnyy krem*).

3   Ethnic food: Tank up on Russian comfort food: borscht, blini, and varnischkes at small cafés. Café Glechik serves Ukrainian dishes. Make an oceanfront picnic of rich cheeses, decadent pastries, black and rye breads, sausages, caviar, canned cherries, imported teas, and walnut spreads, purchased from a Russian emporium like La Brioche Café.

4   People watching: Good everywhere here, especially on the Riegelmann Boardwalk, where you'll find old men on benches and three-generation Russian families out for a European-style stroll.

5   Brunch à la Russe at a boardwalk café: Try Tatiana.

6   Shopping: Try on fur coats, buy a matroyshka (Russian nesting doll), look for a samovar.

7   Russian culture: The Master Theater, formerly the Millennium, is a thirteen-hundred-seat venue where Ray Charles, Jackie Mason, and top performers once appeared. Today it's a center for Russian culture, with many shows from boxing to comedy and also Brighton Beach Ballet performances of *The Nutcracker*. If you read Russian, browse the Black Sea Bookstore.

WORTH SPENDING YOUR RUBLES: A RUSSIAN NIGHTCLUB

Perfect for a birthday, graduation, or anniversary adventure, Russian nightclubs serve gargantuan platters of food, pour vodka flowing faster than the Volga, and entertain with cheesy floor shows. The crowd is mostly Russian (often including large extended families), with a smattering of hipsters and tourists. Your family-style dinner begins with trays of smoked fish, walnut and eggplant spreads, and amazing breads. Then come platters of meats, perhaps shish kebabs on a giant sword, and eventually the music and dancing start. Couples, grandmas with grandchildren, and women dressed to the nines take to the floor to celebrate life, with a taste of irony flavored with a sense of carpe diem. There are fewer Russian nightclubs today than in the past; try the National or Tatiana Grill and Café.

HISTORY SNAPSHOTS

This area was first developed by a German American railroad magnate who built Brighton Beach Bathing Pavilion, a music hall, and a hotel. There were horse races and later automobile races, carousels, and fairgrounds. In the early twentieth century, Brighton Beach became more Jewish, with bungalow colonies and a prominent Yiddish theater. Old-timers will remember the Brighton Beach Bath and Racquet Club and Mrs. Stahl's Knishes (both RIP). The neighborhood became a haven for a large Russian Jewish immigration in the 1950s, the era of dissident "refuseniks" who were aided in their acculturation by local Jewish social service organizations.

Non-Jewish Russians arrived after the 1991 dissolution of the Soviet Union. A growing community of Central Asian immigrants and Mexican, Puerto Ricans, and Dominicans have recently increased Brighton Beach's non-European population. The children of earlier generations of Russian immigrants have grown up American, or Russo-American anyway, with one foot in each culture. Many have moved to Manhattan and New Jersey. Some live in Brighton's upscale, fantasy-pink, Miami-style Oceana apartment complex. Russian-owned stores have popped up in nearby Sheepshead Bay, Manhattan Beach, and other neighborhoods. Still, Brighton Beach remains the commercial and cultural heart of New York's Russian community.

OLD/NEW BROOKLYN

A century ago, Brighton Beach, named for the British resort, was a tony seaside destination. Brighton Beach has lost its sheen, but its essential attractions—ocean, broad sandy beach, and public transportation to all of New York City—remain.

CELEBS, FILMS, FICTION

Feminist Susan B. Anthony and William "Buffalo Bill" Cody, Sophie Tucker, and other stars made an appearance in Brighton Beach in the late nineteenth century. *Brighton Beach Memoirs*, Neil Simon's semiautobiographical play and the subsequent movie starring Jonathan Silverman and Blythe Danner, captures something of the area in the 1940s and 1950s. More contemporary films include *Requiem for a Dream*, directed by Manhattan Beach native Darren Aronofsky (and based on a book by Brooklynite Hubert Selby), *Little Odessa*, *Two Lovers* (starring Joaquin Phoenix and Gwyneth Paltrow), and *We Own the Night* (again with Joaquin Phoenix). *Panic in a Suitcase* by Yelena Akhtiorskaya and Boris Fishman's *A Replacement Life* were both published in 2014.

NOSHES, RESTAURANTS, BARS IN BRIGHTON BEACH

Café at Your Mother-in-Law, 3071 Brighton 4th Street, (718) 942-4088
Café Glechik, 3159 Coney Island Avenue, (718) 616-0766
Café Paris, 3178 Coney Island Avenue, (718) 646-0800
La Brioche Café, 1073 Brighton Beach Avenue, (718) 934-0731
National Restaurant & Nightclub ☎, 273 Brighton Beach Avenue, (718) 646-1225
Skovorodka, 615 Brighton Beach Avenue, (718) 615-3096
Tatiana Grill and Café ☎, 3145 Brighton 4th Street, (718) 646-7630

SELECT DESTINATIONS

Master Theater, 1029 Brighton Beach Avenue, (718) 732-3838
Riegelmann Boardwalk (to Coney Island)

☞ If you like Brighton Beach, visit the remaining Polish shops and restaurants in Greenpoint.

Brooklyn Heights and the Promenade

BASICS

MAPPING: Using GPS, orient to Brooklyn Historical Society. Main drags: Montague, Clark, and Court Streets. Use 2, 3, 4, 5, N, R (Borough Hall, Clark Street) subways. Near the Brooklyn Bridge, Brooklyn Bridge Park, and the neighborhoods of Carroll Gardens, Cobble Hill, Downtown Brooklyn, Dumbo. Bounded by Atlantic Avenue, Cadman Plaza West, and Old Fulton, Furman, Court Streets.

EVENTS: Brooklyn Book Festival, Christmas caroling, Landmark House and Garden Tour.

SELFIES AND 'ZA: Selfies on the Brooklyn Heights Promenade. For pizza, Fascati or Monty Q's.

GREENMARKET: Saturdays, Tuesdays, Thursdays year-round at Borough Hall Plaza.

ACCOMMODATIONS: Esplendor Bossert in the Heights; many hotels in Downtown Brooklyn, 1 Hotel in Brooklyn Bridge Park, Airbnb.

TIP: The elevated Brooklyn Heights Promenade is a third of a mile, about five hundred meters. Enter at Montague Street, overlooking the East River. Walk north to enter Brooklyn Bridge Park.

A stroll on the Brooklyn Heights Promenade is an exhilarating and uniquely New York experience. After the Brooklyn Bridge, it ranks as Brooklyn's second-most-popular destination.

The Promenade is an elevated walkway overlooking the Statue of Liberty, New York Harbor, Manhattan's shimmering skyline, and the iconic spans and arches of the Brooklyn Bridge—and that's just for starters. In the 1960s and 1970s, when Brooklyn was down on its luck and considered déclassé, locals boasted of their losers' trump card: at least nobody *in* Manhattan could ever have views like this *of* Manhattan.

Brooklyn Heights is a wonderful place to imagine genteel old Brooklyn. Much of this neighborhood is a historic district and therefore the façades of buildings are preserved. You can see a full array of nineteenth-century American Victorian life in brick, mortar, and brownstone: churches and banks, private clubs and homes, civic institutions, and public spaces. The Brooklyn Historical Society, itself housed in an elegant landmarked building, is a bottomless resource with exhibits, lectures, and tours. Students of art and literature will be enthralled by the roll call of writers and artists associated with "the Heights:" W. H. Auden, Benjamin Britten, Truman Capote, John Dos Passos, W.E.B. Du Bois, Lena Dunham, Walker Evans, Alfred Kazin, Gypsy Rose Lee, Norman Mailer, Frank McCourt, Carson

McCullers, Arthur Miller, Norman Rosten, Thomas Wolfe, Richard Wright, and Adam Yauch. America's poet, Walt Whitman, published his seminal *Leaves of Grass* at 170 Old Fulton Street (nearby Dumbo claims him at that address, too). And did we mention comic book and Avenger hero Captain America?

Brooklyn Heights is a neighborhood endowed with a patrician backstory and defined by grand old homes. It's considered America's first suburb, according to author Sam Roberts and many others, because it was developed by a wealthy elite who made their money in Manhattan and boated back to Brooklyn to live in splendor. But the Heights is not suburban in a cookie-cutter, homogeneous way. For instance, you can make a pilgrimage to a site associated with high ideals when you pay a visit to the Plymouth Church of the Pilgrims. There, in the 1850s, abolitionist preacher Henry Ward Beecher led his congregation in the struggle to end slavery, even holding a shocking mock slave auction to raise funds to free a young female slave. The Heights was an environment where prominent people, like Beecher, took controversial stands—and, later, where controversial people, mainly authors, became prominent.

A discreetly rich, tiny neighborhood that's easy to explore, Brooklyn Heights is exactly a ten-minute subway ride, and an entire world, away from Manhattan.

BEST BETS IN BROOKLYN HEIGHTS

1 Brooklyn Heights Promenade: Gaze!
2 Eat! To refuel on a budget, have a hearty meal at Teresa's Polish restaurant. Find American fare at Heights Café. Lassen & Henning's Deli is stocked to the gills with salads, sandwiches, and soups. For takeout, Sahadi's excellent Middle Eastern gourmet grocery, a family business started in 1948, is a famous Brooklyn institution. In the oldest section of Brooklyn Heights, near charmingly fruity Cranberry, Pineapple, and Orange Streets, have a pleasant meal at Henry's End, Noodle Pudding, or Brooklyn Heights Wine Bar & Kitchen.
3 Brooklyn Historical Society: Attend excellent programs at this elegant 1881 mansion with its gorgeous, original wood-paneled library; they run tours, too.
4 Historic churches: St. Ann's and the Holy Trinity Church has fifty-five amazing stained-glass windows. The bright blue ceiling of the pre–Civil War Episcopal Grace Church, designed by Minard Lafever, is decorated with a thousand stars. Plymouth Church, self-described as the "Grand Central Depot of the Underground Railroad," hosted Mark Twain, Clara Barton, Booker T. Washington, and, later, Martin Luther King Jr. as speakers. Hear Bach played on the First Unitarian Church's vintage pipe organ.
5 Architecture as history: Stroll down Pierrepont Street, lined with mid-nineteenth-century urban mansions, and back up Remsen Street. Imagine Grace Court Alley, a mews off Hicks Street, in its original incarnation as a

stable alley for the fine homes on Remsen Street. Explore Hunts Lane mews off Henry Street, and quiet Garden and Sidney Places, too. The Federal-style homes at 155–157 Willow Street date from about 1829. The Manhattan-facing homes on Columbia Heights have amazing harbor views.

6   Shop: Tucked among mostly chain stores are three gems—the nonprofit Brooklyn Women's Exchange for handmade gifts, Tango for women's wear, and Housing Works Thrift Shop.

7   Literary celebs: Brooklyn Heights was the crucible for extraordinary literary talent; read on.

FOR BREATHTAKING VIEWS, THE PROMENADE

Indulge in one of New York's kaleidoscopic pleasures: a stroll on the Brooklyn Heights Promenade. It affords expansive views of New York's sensational skyline, the Statue of Liberty, the harbor, East River bridges, and the Empire State Building. Here, above the fray, you can embrace New York with all its vibrant beauty and leave behind the daily hassle, sweaty subways, and crowded streets. The grandeur of the Promenade views is Grand Canyon–esque. And as in the Grand Canyon, you can hang on a railing or sit on a bench and spend a good half hour just absorbing the panorama.

The Promenade is manmade. Prior to its construction in the 1950s, there was just a steep natural bluff, atop which were the homes you now see bordering the esplanade.

People standing on the Promenade on September 11, 2001, unfortunately had a front-row seat to the World Trade Center's twin towers during and after the Al Qaeda–sponsored aerial terrorist attack that killed three thousand people and crumpled the twin skyscrapers. For weeks after, the Promenade was littered with papers and ash—and tears. Today one can see where Manhattan's Freedom Tower, nearby the National September 11 Memorial Museum, rises in defiance.

HISTORY SNAPSHOTS

Until 1898, Brooklyn Heights was the urbane heart of the independent city of Brooklyn. Its residents were wealthy Protestant bankers, industrialists, and shipping magnates, some with New England roots. Among these proper folk were civic leaders, philanthropists, and even a mayor of New York, Seth Low. They left as their legacy many of Brooklyn's foundational institutions or their precursors: the Brooklyn Historical Society, the Brooklyn Philharmonic, the Brooklyn Academy of Music, Packer Collegiate Institute, Brooklyn Borough Hall, and many churches.

And what a life the burghers and bankers of nineteenth-century Brooklyn Heights enjoyed! Old Brooklyn's theater district, along Fulton and Flatbush in what today is Fort Greene, was within walking or carriage distance. Spiffy Abraham

& Strauss, a megashopping department store founded in 1865 by a Bavarian immigrant, had amazing attractions including a mineral spa, lounges, and, by the 1920s, a brass-and-glass elevator (still operating in Fulton Mall's Macy's today). The St. George Hotel was famous, too, for its rooftop pool and elegant dining. There were the federal courts, the roiling energy of the working waterfront (the original docks where bucolic Brooklyn Bridge Park now sits), and ferries to Manhattan. It was the best of all worlds, with fresh air and space, a small-enough social pond in which to be a big fish, schools and churches and social clubs intimate enough to feel a sense of community—yet close to Manhattan's throbbing economic engine. Brooklyn Heights was a civilized place when the rest of Brooklyn was rough around the edges or rural.

Brooklyn's history is inextricably tied up with transportation. The long-awaited opening of Brooklyn Bridge in 1883 enabled the masses to cross the river not by paid ferry but for free. And just as the extension of the subways into faraway Coney Island and Bay Ridge transformed elite resorts into escapes for Everyman, Brooklyn Heights became less exclusive. Fifteen years later, in 1898, when Brooklyn was absorbed into New York City, the area lost its power base and, with it, cachet. Some of Brooklyn Heights' elite drifted away, to such newer neighborhoods as Clinton Hill (where Charles Pratt built elegant homes) and Park Slope's "Gold Coast," along Prospect Park West.

Still, with easy access to Manhattan and Brooklyn's municipal life percolating nearby, elements of Brooklyn Heights' high society remained. In 1991, the *New York Times* profiled generations-old Victorian private clubs, some single gender, still operating in the Heights: the Rembrandt Club, Mrs. Field's Literary Society, Ihpetonga Club, Wednesday Music Club, and one whose name says it all, the New England Society in the City of Brooklyn.

After World War II, much of Brooklyn Heights became seedy, pulled down by the borough's overall decline. It was a time of tectonic shifts, caused by the rising appeal of Long Island's expanding suburbs and the slow death of Brooklyn's mainstay shipping and manufacturing industries. Energy leached from Brooklyn. People left. Dereliction was a real danger. Some dropouts, musicians, and artists moved in; Brooklyn Heights was cheap and off the beaten path. Bob Dylan's "Tangled Up in Blue" lyrics evoke a bohemian Montague Street of the 1970s: smoke-filled cafés and roiled talk of Black Panthers and revolution. Some out-of-work former dockworkers and artists and writers had points of connection. For instance, *Angela's Ashes* author and Pulitzer Prize winner Frank McCourt (1930–2009) lived upstairs from Montero Bar & Grill, a dive where bohemian writers mixed it up with longshoremen.

Meanwhile, civic-minded stalwarts were hard at work; a vigorous preservation movement lobbied for about eight years to obtain landmark status, and in 1965, Brooklyn Heights became New York City's first historic district. As the neighborhood began a slow recovery, things began to happen: restaurants opened, as did an erudite used bookstore and the much-missed Cousin Arthur's, Brooklyn's first children's bookstore, owned by a poet-publisher couple who hosted author readings. The neighborhood's renaissance was spurred as an influx of wealthy lawyers, bankers, and professionals arrived through the 1970s and 1980s. Today homes are affordable only to the proverbial "one-percenters."

BOHEMIAN LITERARY BROOKLYN HEIGHTS

Iconoclasm was in the air in the early to mid-twentieth century, and the Heights' fraying elegance and comfortable neglect appealed to a certain kind of artist, one who might taunt Manhattan's social codes and hierarchies but on the other hand didn't want to be too far from "the city." Starting in the 1920s, bonhomie-seeking creative types coalesced "over in Brooklyn." Like the fomenting art scene in Bushwick today, there was a scene here, too, and a fascination with the tangible raw energy of the nearby shipping docks. Rents were cheap. Acquaintances from Manhattan couldn't be bothered to drop by. There was opportunity to pursue one's muses, romances, and, for those who were homosexuals, which was outlawed, sexual proclivities in relative privacy.

Old Brooklyn was seen as inferior, in class and culture, to Manhattan; as Truman Capote wrote in his 1959 *Holiday* magazine essay, "Brooklyn: A Personal Memoir," "I live in Brooklyn. By choice." (This essay and David Attie's previously unseen photos of Capote from the 1950s were republished in 2015 in *Brooklyn: A Personal Memoir*—worth a look.)

So while Manhattan commanded the upper hand as the nation's kingdom of culture, Brooklyn Heights, especially in its decades of decline, was roiling with strong undercurrents of creative energy. An astonishing number of writers who became American literary luminaries lived here in the twentieth century. The Nobel Prize winner Thomas Wolfe (1900–1938) rented at 5 Montague Terrace in 1934, the year before the *New Yorker* published his "Only the Dead Know Brooklyn" about Red Hook. Arthur Miller, who wrote memorably gut-wrenching scenes of struggling, upwardly mobile, postwar Brooklynites in *Death of a Salesman* and *View from the Bridge*, spent a decade at 155 Willow Street. He finished *Salesman* when living at 31 Grace Court, a home he later sold to an elderly W.E.B. Du Bois. During this period, actress Marilyn Monroe visited Miller in Brooklyn, and in a 1955 NBC radio interview, Monroe called Brooklyn her "favorite place in the world" because of the people, the Manhattan views, and the atmosphere and said she'd like to retire to Brooklyn (http://www.nbcnews.com/video/nbc-news/48494970). Truman Capote, author of *Breakfast at Tiffany's* and *In Cold Blood*, rented at 70 Willow Street and in his *A House on the Heights* gave the world a peek into a Brooklyn Heights that was less conventional than today's. (In a sign of the times, Capote's house sold in 2012 for over $12 million to an executive at Rockstar Games, of Grand Theft Auto fame.) Joseph Brodsky, a refugee, Nobel Prize–winning

Russian poet, and U.S. poet laureate, resided at 22 Pierrepont Street until he died. (His house was bought by the MacArthur "genius" award winner and filmmaker Errol Morris.) Norman Mailer, a neighborhood fixture, outlasted them all, holding court in a floor-to-ceiling book-lined apartment with spectacular views, at 142 Columbia Heights, until his death in 2007.

Number 7 Middagh Street was a bohemian writers' group house. Its revolving door of artists included W. H. Auden, stripper and writer Gypsy Rose Lee, Jane and Paul Bowles, and composer Benjamin Britten, among others. Some of the residents patronized the sailors' bars and red-light district, called Barbary Coast, along Sands Street in what is now Dumbo. The house at 7 Middagh might have been a literary museum today. Brooklyn's loss, it was razed in an urban development deal when the Brooklyn-Queens Expressway was built under the aegis of Robert Moses (the complex antihero of Robert Caro's *Power Broker* biographical opus).

There's enough literary history here to fill a book. Indeed, Evan Hughes's *Literary Brooklyn* and Sherry Tippet's *February House* do just that. Meanwhile, take a tour. (See "DIY Tours," section 5.)

OLD/NEW BROOKLYN

Plus ça change, plus c'est la même chose—the more things change, the more they stay the same.

Many century-old Brooklyn Heights institutions still occupy their original sites: churches, banks, schools, and municipal buildings. The private Heights Casino was renovated and reopened in the 1990s. The Bossert Hotel reopens soon. St. Francis College, founded in the 1880s by Franciscan Brothers to aid immigrants' children, is still serving immigrant students. Brooklyn's oldest independent school, Packer Collegiate Institute, founded in 1845 as an institute for young ladies, is one of the city's best-known private schools. Today girls and boys trot into class with laptops through a building adorned with pinnacles, Gothic arches, Tiffany windows, and a tower. Plymouth Church, where abolitionist preacher Henry Ward Beecher (brother of Harriet Beecher Stowe) joined Brooklyn's Civil War–era Underground Railroad, remains a progressive institution.

New Brooklyn is mostly represented today by an influx of wealth and, recently, celebrity. But it's worth noting, given the neighborhood's history of civic leadership, that Brooklyn Heights residents were instrumental in the twenty-year push to create extraordinary Brooklyn Bridge Park nearby.

CELEBS, FILMS, FICTION

Brooklyn Heights has its share of celebrities, in addition to the aforementioned writers. Björk bought a town house in 2009. Lena Dunham attended one of the neighborhood's private schools, Saint Ann's (unrelated to the historic St. Ann's church), and bought an apartment on Henry Street in 2014. A park was named as a memorial to musician Adam Yauch of the Beastie Boys of "No Sleep till Brooklyn" fame, who grew up near Atlantic Avenue. As of 2015, rumor had it that Dan Stevens of *Downton Abbey*, Broadway and film actor Paul Giamatti, and *Broad City's* Abbi Jacobson live in Brooklyn Heights. Presidential aspirant Hillary Clinton opened a campaign office here, at One Pierrepont Plaza in 2015.

Francis Ford Coppola filmed *The Godfather's* Luca Brasi murder scene in the St. George Hotel (now Brooklyn Law School dorms and apartments), against an interior window of carved glass fish. *Annie Hall, Saturday Night Fever,* and *Moonstruck* all feature scenes shot on the Promenade. A scene in Robert Redford's film *Three Days of the Condor* was shot at 9 Cranberry Street. *Captain America*, of comic book and Avenger film fame, was set near the St. George Hotel in the 1930s and 1940s.

Here's a variety of fiction set in Brooklyn Heights in different eras: *The Heights* by Peter Hedges, *Milk* by Darcey Steinke, *A House on the Heights* by Truman Capote, *Desperate Characters* by Paula Fox, and *May Wine on Brooklyn Heights* by Robert Leary. Also a fun read: the Brooklyn Heights Crime Series by former Brooklyn historian John Manbeck.

NOSHES, RESTAURANTS, BARS IN BROOKLYN HEIGHTS

Brooklyn Heights Wine Bar & Kitchen, 50 Henry Street, (718) 855-5595
Fascati Pizza, 80 Henry Street, (718) 237-1278
Heights Café Restaurant, 84 Montague Street, (718) 625-5555
Henry's End ☎, 44 Henry Street, (718) 834-1776
Lassen & Henning's Deli ☎, 114 Montague Street, (718) 875-6272
Montero Bar & Grill ☎, 73 Atlantic Avenue, (646) 729-4129
Monty Q's, 158 Montague Street, (718) 246-2000
Noodle Pudding ☎, 38 Henry Street, (718) 625-3737
Oriental Pastry & Grocery ☎, 170 Atlantic Avenue, (718) 875-7687
Roebling Inn, 97 Atlantic Avenue, (718) 488-0040
Sahadi's ☎, 187–189 Atlantic Avenue, (718) 624-4550
Yemen Café, 176 Atlantic Avenue, (718) 834-9533

SELECT DESTINATIONS

Adam Yauch Park, 27 State Street, (212) 639-9675
Brooklyn Book Festival, http://www.brooklynbookfestival.org
Brooklyn Historical Society, 128 Pierrepont Street, (718) 222-4111
Brooklyn Women's Exchange, 55 Pierrepont Street, (718) 624-3435
Grace Episcopal Church, 254 Hicks Street, (718) 624-1850
Heights Casino, 101 Clark Street, (718) 624-5388
Landmark House and Garden Tour, http://brooklynheightsassociation.org

St. Ann's and the Holy Trinity Church, 157 Montague Street, (718) 875-6960

St. George Hotel, 100 Henry Street (currently Brooklyn Law School dorms)

☞ Like Brooklyn Heights? Visit other brownstone neighborhoods: Bedford-Stuyvesant, Boerum Hill, Carroll Gardens, Clinton Hill, Cobble Hill, Crown Heights, Fort Greene, Park Slope, Prospect Heights, Sunset Park.

Bushwick

Brooklyn, with its million and a half people, produces nearly 2,500,000 barrels of lager beer, ale and porter. This would seem to indicate that in the houses, the clubs and the cafes of this borough . . . every man, woman and child in Brooklyn drinks a little less than two barrels of malted product every year. . . . [A] seemingly enormous consumption of the product of local breweries disappears down Brooklyn throats every year.

—Brooklyn Daily Eagle, October 5, 1907

BASICS

MAPPING: Using GPS, orient to Roberta's pizzeria. Main drags: Flushing Avenue, Broadway. Use L, J, M, Z subways (multiple stations). Near the neighborhoods of Bed-Stuy, Brownsville, East New York, Williamsburg, and in the borough of Queens, Ridgewood. Boundaries are rough—they keep shifting: Flushing Avenue, Broadway, Queens, the Cemetery of the Evergreens.

EVENTS: Afro-Latino Festival, Beat Night Art Crawl, BushwigNYC drag festival, Bushwick Film Festival, Bushwick Open Studios, Cinco de Mayo.

SELFIES AND 'ZA: Selfies outdoors at Bushwick Collective murals. Pizza at Roberta's.

GREENMARKETS: Saturdays seasonally at Maria Hernandez Park. Saturdays, Thursdays at Bushwick Farmers' Market (locations online).

ACCOMMODATIONS: Airbnb and hotel (under construction as of this writing) at 232 Siegel Street.

TIPS: Weekday parking is scarce. Bushwick is big, so be prepared to walk or come with wheels (even a unicycle).

Bushwick is, as the French might breezily say, *très* Brooklyn. Or to be long-winded, diverse with a mostly blue-collar population and a bustling industrial zone, Bushwick is also a bohemian art, music, and exuberant party scene, with a significant amount of social activism.

Since about 2005, unpretty, crime- and poverty-plagued Bushwick has gained unimaginable momentum in Brooklyn's fast-moving creative culture. It's on the contemporary frontiers of art and music—with arresting street murals, bars, indie bands, clubs, cooperatives, inventive food, edgy style, and a whole lot of fun places to visit. There's gritty industry here, but even the Tortilleria Chinantla taco factory is decorated with a huge mural. Artists' workspaces are wrought out of rough industrial buildings. Bridges across socioeconomic ravines are built, through art. Bushwick's story will read as a major chapter in the book of new Brooklyn's reinvention.

Serious creative work goes on in dozens of studios. Many galleries are nonprofits. Young artists patronize each other's art shows, bands, bars, boutiques, and barbershops. You may encounter a refreshing collectivist mentality—as in "we are all in this together"—self-consciously contrasted with the competitive commercial art scene in Manhattan. The life of an artist is never easy, and money can be tight. The cool vibe, edgy style, and youthful energy of the entire Bushwick endeavor generates a certain conviviality. The art community, common wisdom has it, is largely well educated, white, young, and not native New Yorkers. Artists make up a fraction of Bushwick's population of 112,000.

Bushwick is the longstanding home to a Latino community, too. It's Brooklyn's largest, according to 2010 data—a *sancocho*, or stew, of Mexicans, Ecuadorians, Dominicans, and Puerto Ricans. Spanish-speaking Bushwick is largely poor, aided by a handful of robust community groups, including Make the Road NY, Sista-II-Sista, and Williamsburg-based El Puente.

As real estate developments rise, with microneighborhoods such as Morgantown and Jefftown being carved out and renamed by real estate interests, concerned locals from all walks of life are confronting the ethical and human issues of displacement of older, poorer residents as moneyed newcomers roll in.

Weekdays, the place is abuzz with industry, literally: there are active machine shops, warehouses, loading docks, metal shops, and businesses with Spanish, Chinese, and English signage. This mixed-use neighborhood has forty-six acres of industrial and manufacturing land. It's tough to find street parking on a weekday.

Hipsters and artists are transforming Bushwick into a place where innovation happens. For example, EcoStation:NY, a social and environmental justice organization, is seeking to expand its urban agriculture project to a ten-thousand-square-foot space atop a building called Mayday, a community center that houses social-change nonprofit organizations. Local Woodhull Hospital initiated a barter system in 2010, the Artist Access Program, allowing artists to work—say, by teaching yoga or decorating a clinic waiting room—for health care credits to be applied toward prescriptions and doctors' fees.

Urban memory runs short, and it is hard to overstate how rough Bushwick was. The story of Maria Hernandez, after whom the local park is named, tells the tale. A resident of Bushwick, she had a degree in accounting from NYU and a bookkeeping job in New Jersey.

VOICES ABOUT BROOKLYN

LUIS UBIÑAS
Former President of the Ford Foundation

A vibrant creative community is a constant feature of places that have rebounded from decline. I saw it in Soho in the 1970s and 1980s and later in Chelsea and Williamsburg, Brooklyn, in the South End of Boston in the 1980s and 1990s and in SOMA in San Francisco. Rio de Janeiro, Berlin, and London prove the same point. Each of these places took distressed neighborhoods that housed burgeoning arts scenes and through a combination of rezoning, infrastructure investment, and private development turned them into powerful engines of local economic growth. Art is not a luxury; art is a precondition to success in a world increasingly driven by creativity and innovation.

(Excerpted with permission from "A Commitment to the Arts That Will Transform Communities," by Luis Ubiñas, published by National Endowment for the Arts, 2011)

She was also a visible community leader who actively fought the drug trade in her neighborhood. Five bullets tore through her home and killed her as she was getting dressed for work, in August 1989. This was Bushwick.

Bushwick might serve as a case study in the relationship between art and revitalization in distressed urban areas.

BEST BETS IN BUSHWICK

1   Edgy street art: Wander around Bushwick Collective's extraordinary mural zone. It's like an informal outdoor gallery. Start where Troutman Street, Scott Avenue, and Saint Nicholas Avenue intersect.

2   Eclectic food: Have comfort food at the Michelin-rated Northeast Kingdom. Roberta's is an institution, touted for amazing pizza, community activism, a rooftop garden, and its Heritage Radio Network, broadcast out of two shipping containers. Blanca is a Michelin-rated restaurant; Vietnamese Falansai made the Michelin Bib Gourmand, as did Faro. Try Momo Sushi Shack, Café Ghia, and the British-country-squire-themed Dear Bushwick or La Tortilleria Mexicana Los Tres Hermanos. Calories be damned, have a cannoli at Sicilian Circo's Pastry Shop (est. 1945) or a bar of Bushwick-made chocolate created by Fine & Raw (est. 2013).

3   Indie bands: Explore tons of venues like the Wick, a music venue in a former brewery; Pine Box Rock Shop, in a former coffin shop; Pearl's Social & Billy Club; The Shop; and anything-goes Bizarre.

4   Galleries galore: Refer to the site Bushwickgalleries.com for current shows. The Bushwick Open Studios event is an indoor/outdoor summer extravaganza showcasing artwork, performances, and bands.

5   Shop vintage: Fish around at Mary Meyer + Friends Vintage. Green Village is a packrat's heaven. For years, Domsey Express (also in Williamsburg) has been selling fashions so dowdy that they're in again.

6   Theater: Bushwick Starr Theater is hot; the *New York Times* called it "boldly experimental, . . . fun, . . . a bright spot on the Off Off Broadway map."

7   Booze tours: See old Bushwick's fabled "Brewer's Row," a twelve-square-block area, not yet landmarked, once the heart of the German brewery industry (Linden Street and Gates and Bushwick Avenues). Tour a new distillery, the Noble Experiment.

8   Park: Maria Hernandez Park is to Bushwick what Washington Square Park was to 1950s beatniks: a community green space, meeting spot, and performance center. It's jammed with kids.

ART HERE, THERE, EVERYWHERE

In sections, Bushwick resembles a free outdoor museum. You can barely go a block without noticing wall murals, a fantastically painted rooftop water tank, or a door decorated by an artist's hand. An unpainted warehouse wall feels like a blank canvas.

One reason for this is the Bushwick Collective, founded in 2012. As many as fifty murals, painted by individual or teams of artists, might be visible at any given time, all bearing the signature "Bushwick Collective." Some of the pieces are huge—and so is the endeavor. There's not one location; the sites and artists (only some local) rotate. There's a festival day when you can watch as some murals are being painted and enjoy food trucks and a DJ. It coincides with the Bushwick Open Studios weekend. The Bushwick Collective is a volunteer, collaborative local arrangement; one hopes these walls aren't turned into billboards for paid advertising.

Bushwick's galleries run the gamut. At BogArt, see Robert Henry Contemporary, Theodore: Art, Fresh Window, Momenta Art (formerly of Williamsburg), and NurtureArt. Nearby on Knickerbocker Avenue is Interstate Projects. Microscope Gallery specializes in the moving image, sound, digital, and performance artists. Signal stages exhibitions by emerging artists. Storefront Ten Eyck shows new and emerging artists. Luhring Augustine Bushwick, a prestigious Manhattan gallery, has an exhibition space for large-scale installations. Some galleries operate out of private apartments, by appointment.

BROOKLYN VOICES

DEBORAH BROWN
Bushwick Artist

There's not a "Bushwick school" of art. There are artists of all ages and career levels working here, including well-established artists like sculptor Ursula von Rydingsvard, Jules de Balincourt, and Rashid Johnson. Until recently, studio space was plentiful and reasonable. Most of the Bushwick galleries are run by artists. There are sixty-five galleries today, compared to about five a few years ago. In the last few years, the area has exploded with bars and restaurants. It's now a social and nightclub scene as well as an art community. Being an artist out here is a wonderful thing. Bushwick's got a great vibe.

Working together has always been a hallmark of the cultural scene in Bushwick. We got together and created a website listing all the galleries [BushwickGalleries.com], because they're spread out and can be hard to find. We organize joint gallery walks and art fairs in conjunction with Armory Week in March and Frieze NY Art Week in May. Our big event is Bushwick Open Studios the first weekend in June. But you can see art any time of the year.

HISTORY SNAPSHOTS

Settled by the Dutch, Bushwick was a separate town, merging in 1855 with five other towns to create the original, independent city of Brooklyn. The land was used to grow food and tobacco. Working-class immigrant Italians and later Puerto Ricans and Dominicans settled here.

Bushwick was in ferment, literally, in the late nineteenth century, when brownstone Brooklyn was just on the drawing board. By the 1870s, German immigrants had established a major beer-brewing industry, founding some of the nation's most prominent brewers, including Rheingold and Schlitz. The brewery entrepreneurs were rich, as you can see at 670 Bushwick Avenue, the Catherina Lipsius House, home of the Claus Lipsius Brewing Company's owners, also a landmark.

Numerous brewing establishments dotted Williamsburg, Greenpoint, and especially Bushwick. By the 1880s, eleven breweries operated in a fourteen-square-block area, according to the NYC Landmarks Preservation Commission; most of these were shuttered by Prohibition, which lasted over a decade, from 1920 to 1933. Go see 31 Belvidere Street, the landmarked main building of the William Ulmer Brewery. It was founded by a Bavarian immigrant and mentioned by the *Brooklyn Daily Eagle* newspaper in 1875 as the largest of Brooklyn's dozens of breweries, complete with a private stable. Funnily, over a century later, a November 2015 *Brooklyn Daily Eagle* article titled "Bushwick Nostalgia," describes development plans for some of Bushwick's old brewery buildings.

Other landmarks: Brooklyn Fire Engine Co. 252 was built in 1896–1897 and is still in use. According to the NYC Landmarks Preservation Commission, "the design of the firehouse, a Flemish Revival–style structure with a prominent scrolled front gable and stepped end gables, may allude to the seventeenth-century history of Bushwick as a Dutch settlement." The neighborhood's 1904 DeKalb library is one of Brooklyn's first branch libraries, built with funds from Andrew Carnegie's philanthropic library program.

At the risk of oversimplification, the general arc of Bushwick's post–World War II fate went like this: Bushwick experienced white flight and a decline in municipal services, exacerbated by a lethal cocktail of the 1970s riots, systemic racism, New York City's economic crisis, and a rise in drug-related violence. Bushwick succumbed to a downward spiral. By the 1980s, to outsiders Bushwick was synonymous with violence, intractable poverty, and gang activity. New and poor Spanish-speaking immigrants from Mexico and Latin America settled here in the 1990s.

Early in the twenty-first century, artists and hipsters who were being displaced by Williamsburg's rising rents (or disaffected by its having become tamer) began to move along the L subway line to Bushwick in search of cheap spaces and new frontiers. The L train afforded ready access back to Williamsburg's restaurants, bars, shops, and social life and to Manhattan.

Morgan Avenue L subway station in Bushwick. (Photo by E. Freudenheim, 2015)

Politically progressive members of Bushwick's art community work in various ways with local organizations to address the community's challenges, including access to fresh food and educational opportunities for its underserved youth. Bushwick in the first decades of the twenty-first century is ground zero in New York's well-worn playbook of gentrification, in which real estate developers follow artist "pioneers" into a low-income, industrial, or neglected area. Bushwick is the new Williamsburg; Williamsburg was the new Soho; both make Dumbo, whose successful evolution was nurtured like a hothouse flower by a family-owned development company and patron of the arts, seem as suburban as Park Slope. As of 2015, rising rents in Bushwick threaten to price out some artists. The next frontiers appear to be East New York, Brownsville, Ridgewood (Queens), Philadelphia, upstate New York, and maybe Detroit.

OLD/NEW BROOKLYN

If old and new Bushwick seem schizophrenic, it's not entirely so. The fluid strains of change and continuity are apparent in a few ways.

First, Bushwick is a place where physical things are made. It's home and worksite for many laborers, artisans, and artists who work with their hands. "Many employees of businesses within the industrial and manufacturing sectors reside in Bushwick," a 2015 Pratt Institute report said. Manufacturing still employs some four thousand residents, or 15 percent of Bushwick's working population. Some synergy has grown among the artist community and Bushwick's manual laborers. When the Boar's Head factory closed off its one-block lane, Rock Street, allowing the Bushwick Open Studios organizers to create a temporary urban sculpture park, that's old meets new Brooklyn.

Second, many popular restaurants, bars, and cafés retain in their design vestiges of old Brooklyn: tin ceilings, heavy wood beams salvaged from industrial buildings, and vintage styles with tropes from the Great Depression through the 1960s.

Third is a green theme. Bushwick was originally named Boswijk, or "town in the woods," by Governor Peter Stuyvesant. The Reformed Church of South Bushwick, landmarked as "an exceptionally handsome example of late Greek Revival Church architecture, with a soaring steeple silhouetted against the sky," has a small yard that "still reminds the passerby of the original rural character of the area." And though it's a stretch, the rooftop garden at Roberta's and Bushwick's other urban agriculture initiatives in some way hark back to Bushwick's original connection to the land.

CELEBS, FILMS, FICTION

Mos Def attended Philippa Schuyler Middle School 383 in Bushwick. See the *Saturday Night Live* "Bushwick Brooklyn 2015" skit online. Henry Miller's *Tropic of Capricorn* mentions Bushwick. For microviews of the neighborhood, read the short-story collection *Bushwick Nightz*, edited by Dallas Athent, Daniel Ryan Adler, and Nathaniel Kressen, and Ariel Schrag's novel *Adam*.

NOSHES, RESTAURANTS, BARS IN BUSHWICK

Café Ghia, 24 Irving Avenue, (718) 821-8806
Circo's Pastry Shop ☎, 312 Knickerbocker Avenue, (718) 381-2292
Dear Bushwick, 41 Wilson Avenue, (929) 234-2344
La Tortilleria Mexicana Los Tres Hermanos ☎, 271 Starr Street, (718) 456-3422
Momo Sushi Shack, 43 Bogart Street, (718) 418-6666
Northeast Kingdom, 18 Wyckoff Avenue, (718) 386-3864
Roberta's, 261 Moore Street, (718) 417-1118
Tina's Restaurant ☎, 1002 Flushing Avenue, (718) 821-9595
Wyckoff Starr, 30 Wyckoff Avenue, (718) 484-9766

SELECT DESTINATIONS

Arts in Bushwick (artists, galleries), http://bushwickgalleries.com
The BogArt Galleries, 56 Bogart Street, (718) 599-0800
Brooklyn Fire Engine Company 252, 617 Central Avenue
Brooklyn Public Library's DeKalb Branch, 790 Bushwick Avenue, (718) 455-3898
Bushwick Starr Theater, 207 Starr Street, (917) 623-9669
Catherina Lipsius House, 670 Bushwick Avenue
The Noble Experiment, 23 Meadow Street, (718) 381-3693
Shea Stadium BK, 20 Meadow Street
Silent Barn, 603 Bushwick Avenue, (800) 628-7666
The Wick, 260 Meserole Street, (347) 338-3612

☞ If you like Bushwick, visit adjacent Ridgewood (technically in the borough of Queens).

Canarsie and East New York

The area around Broadway Junction, where three subway lines and regional rail converge, has the potential to support substantial development and become a major outer borough destination with places to work, shop, socialize, and enjoy.

—*Sustainable Communities: Overview, East New York*,
NYC Department of City Planning, 2015

BASICS

MAPPING: Using GPS, orient to Brooklyn Terminal Market. Main drags: Rockaway Parkway, Remsen and Flatlands Avenues. Use 2, 3, 4, 5, L subways, Long Island Railroad. Canarsie is near Mill Basin, East Flatbush, Brownsville, East New York. Bounded by Paerdegat Basin, Fresh Creek, Jamaica Bay, Avenue D, East 108th Street. East New York is near Bedford-Stuyvesant, Brownsville, Bushwick, Canarsie. Use L train. Bounded roughly by Atlantic and Van Sinderen Avenues, 108th Street, Linden and Conduit Boulevards, Jamaica Bay.

SELFIES AND 'ZA: Take a selfie at the "Canarsie Pier" sign. Try Original Pizza (est. 1970).

GREENMARKET: Saturdays seasonally at Schenck Avenue between New Lots and Livonia Avenues.

Canarsie and East New York aren't typical "tourist" areas, but two things make it worth the trip: the Wyckoff House Museum and the Gateway National Recreation area. For shopping, Gateway Center mall is off the Belt Parkway.

Nature enthusiasts often come to Canarsie, without knowing (or caring) that it's Canarsie, to visit a marshy nature preserve, go kayaking at the extraordinary Sebago Canoe Club, or pick up low-cost food and garden supplies at the Brooklyn Terminal Market, a retro-looking retail/wholesale market dating to 1942. "Way out in Brooklyn," East New York and Canarsie share easy access to Jamaica Bay, relatively inexpensive housing, the thrum of jets from Kennedy International Airport and, in sections, higher crime rates than other neighborhoods.

BEST BETS IN CANARSIE AND EAST NEW YORK

1 Mother nature: Go canoeing! Paddle out with the Sebago Canoe Club. Bird-watch and walk the pathways at Fresh Creek Nature Preserve, forty-two acres of salt marsh that's hospitable to wildlife, birds, butterflies, and fish. You won't believe you are in New York City.

2 Old Dutch New York: Tour New York City's oldest Dutch farmhouse, the Wyckoff House Museum.

3 Really? Cricket? Watch cricket games in Canarsie Park's regulation-size cricket field and high school rugby. Visit Canarsie Skateboard Park for urban skateboarding.

4 Canarsie Pier: On the six-hundred-foot pier, which today is part of the Gateway National Recreation Area, watch the seagulls and, in the summer, take kayak or paddle-boat trips. People fish for bluefish and fluke here, as they have for about three hundred years. The pier has had a facelift; the old food stand is gone, but locals still play checkers and backgammon on stone tables.

5 Baseball and racial equality: Run-down 5224 Tilden Avenue was the home of Dodger Jackie Robinson in the late 1940s. A plaque honors "The 1st African-American Major-League Player."

6 Shop: Visit the suburban-style Gateway Center mall. The 1940s-era Terminal Market, a food and flower market, still in operation, is picturesque in its way.

7 See how people live: Drive through residential areas, say from East Ninety-Eighth Street to Fresh Creek Park around Seaview Avenue and Avenues L, M, and N.

WILL AFFORDABLE HOUSING—OR ART— TRANSFORM EAST NEW YORK?

There are twin pressures for change on the subneighborhoods within East New York: New Lots, Spring Creek, Cypress Hills, and City Line. New York City planners have identified East New York as a frontier for affordable housing development, a new industrial area, and new mixed-use buildings with housing along Atlantic Avenue, Fulton Street, and Pitkin Avenue. Why? In a word: transportation. A Long Island Railroad station provides easy access to JFK Airport, and numerous subway lines serve the area. Plus, there's a sociological pattern at work: artists (and then gentrification) have in recent years settled in one neighborhood after another along the L subway line. For example, Norte Maar for Collaborative Projects in the Arts is a nonprofit, one of the first to have made a stake in once-blighted Bushwick. It relocated to Cypress Hills in East New York in 2015.

BROOKLYN VOICES

JASON ANDREW
Cofounder and Director of Norte Maar

East New York is Brooklyn in the raw and Cypress Hills has the same sense of potential as we once saw in Bushwick ten years ago ... Here we will once again have room to experiment and create. . . . We see in East New York the same underserved and neglected community that Bushwick was ten years ago. Bushwick hasn't always been known for its arts scene. When we first began programming in Bushwick the crime rate was much higher than the number of coffee shops, bars, and galleries!

(Excerpted with permission from Norte Maar's website, where in 2015 Andrew announced the organization's move from Bushwick to East New York.)

HISTORY SNAPSHOTS

You see remnants of New York City's Dutch colonial era in this area. In the colonial era, Canarsie belonged to the Flatlands, one of five founding Dutch towns that were granted local rule by Peter Stuyvesant and later joined to become Brooklyn. The Dutch stayed until the late nineteenth century.

Visit the Wyckoff House Museum, a historic Dutch farmhouse first built in 1652. You can feel what it was like to live in colonial days as guides bring to life how eleven children and their parents crammed into one room and "cooked on this very hearth." Popular among European tourists, it's surprising to learn that this out-of-the-way site's biggest audience is some fifty thousand descendants of the former indentured servant Pieter Classen Wyckoff and his wife, Gertie, who built this home. "Most of our visitors are Wyckoffs," said Lucie Chin, the head docent. "And they are all cousins."

Nearby are the Old Dutch Reformed Church, Kings Highway Flatlands Dutch Reformed Church, and the Joost Van Nuyse House. The 1719 Lott House is under restoration through late 2016. See a reconstructed seventeenth-century Dutch farmhouse, the 1775 Jan Martense Schenck House, at the Brooklyn Museum.

OLD/NEW BROOKLYN

In the first half of the twentieth century, Canarsie and East New York were thriving immigrant neighborhoods, with little shops along Pitkin Avenue, stores with

The Wyckoff House, one of the city's oldest Dutch colonial homes. (Courtesy Wyckoff House Museum)

BROOKLYN VOICES

LUCIE CHIN
Head Docent, Wyckoff House Museum

As Brooklyn grew, this property [the Wyckoff family farm] became too valuable to farm. Almost every farmer between 1890 and 1910 profitably sold their farmland to developers and moved, mainly to Long Island—where they bought more farmland. The area remained a mix of Irish and Italian. In the 1970s, with New York City in bad straits, these communities also decamped. The next wave to settle in their place was newly arrived Caribbean immigrants.

And that's interesting for us, because in the seventeenth century, the Dutch owned this part of North America, plus 90 percent of the Caribbean. Which is why we have people attending our Saint Nicholas Day celebrations who remember that holiday from their childhood in the islands, sing along in French, and know the recipes used in Dutch ovens.

---

names like Kishke King, and horse-pulled laundry trucks. Some Brooklynites may remember their parents or grandparents talking about Grabstein's Delicatessen, the 1920s carousels, the Seaview Club, Ruby the Knish Man, and the Thomas Jefferson Club. But things changed. For the complex story of how the ascendant suburbs, civil rights school busing, and other pressures impacted Canarsie, see Jonathan Rieder's 1985 *Canarsie: The Jews and Italians of Brooklyn against Liberalism*.

During the 1920s and 1930s, East New York and neighboring Brownsville were home turf for "Murder Inc.," the Jewish and Italian gangs who carried out contract killings. Some operated out of Midnight Rose's candy store at Livonia and Saratoga Avenues. Contemporary East New York faces challenges. In 2012, forty-nine members of the rival Very Crispy Gangsters and Rockstarz gangs were charged by then Brooklyn district attorney Charles Hynes with having "terrorized parts of the East New York community as they recklessly shot at one another in crowded parks and busy streets with no regard for innocent bystanders." And the Louis Pink Houses public housing complex is where in 2014 a controversial police shooting death of an innocent and unarmed black man took place. Still, if the city's plans proceed, East New York is in for changes in the coming years. It's happened before: think Crown Heights, Williamsburg, and of course, Bushwick.

CELEBS, FILMS, FICTION

East New York gave us George Gershwin, Danny Kaye, Shelley Winters, Jimmy Smits, and Tony Danza. Starbucks founder Howard Schultz lived in Canarsie's Bay View Housing Projects. The *Canarsie Courier* lists stars from that neighborhood: NBC's TV weatherman Al Roker and his CBS counterpart, Allen Craig; the Guardian Angels' Curtis Sliwa; and rockers Peter Criss of KISS and Warren

Cuccurullo of Duran Duran. Local high school grads include many actors: Danielle Brisbois, Michael Goldfinger, Annabella Sciorra, Tony Award winner Randy Graff, William Forsythe, and Steven Keats. Athletes include basketball pros Lloyd Free, John Salley, and Geoff Huston and pro baseballers Dan Morogiello and Wayne Rosenthal. East New York's quaint past is captured in a nostalgic YouTube video: "East New York: The Classic Brooklyn Neighborhood 1920–1960." For fiction set here, read Michael Stephens's 1994 novel, *Brooklyn Book of the Dead*.

NOSHES, RESTAURANTS, BARS IN CANARSIE AND EAST NEW YORK

Bamboo Gardens Restaurant, East 95th Street, (718) 272-3175
Gateway Center, 501 Gateway Drive: Applebee's, Panera Bread, Buffalo Wild
    Wings, and Smashburger
Original Pizza ☎, 9514 Avenue L, (718) 531-3559

SELECT DESTINATIONS

Brooklyn Terminal Market, 21 Brooklyn Terminal Market, (718) 444-5700
Canarsie Pier (at the foot of Rockaway Parkway)
Cypress Hills Cemetery, 833 Jamaica Avenue, (718) 277-2900
Fresh Creek Nature Preserve, East 108th Street and the water, (718) 965-8900
Sebago Canoe Club, 1400 Paerdegat Avenue N, (718) 241-3683
Wyckoff House Museum, 5816 Clarendon Road, (718) 629-5400

☞ Like this facet of Brooklyn? Visit Crown Heights (for Caribbean culture), Bushwick (for art), and Floyd Bennett Field (for nature lovers).

Carroll Gardens and Cobble Hill

There's too much traffic now. All the old Italian people you used to see on the street, almost nobody's around. And not that many of the old stores either. But you want a pizza pie? The best in the neighborhood is still Sal's. The place is just the way it was in the 1950s.

—third-generation Carroll Gardens shopkeeper on Court Street

Come to the contiguous neighborhoods of Carroll Gardens and Cobble Hill for cool cafés and bars, authentic French croissants or pommes frites, the freshest mozzarella, and an assortment of artisanal foods.

Carroll Gardens and Cobble Hill are side-by-side residential areas of nineteenth-century town houses with classic stoops and wrought-iron railings, punctuated by a handful of new apartment buildings. If there's a faintly European air in Carroll Gardens, it's a layer of French je ne sais quoi that fits snugly atop the neighborhood's century-old Italian American legacy. Lovely if not diverse, accessible, and boasting one-of-a-kind shops, both neighborhoods are human scaled and family friendly. The young professionals who flock here may be wealthy, but they don't flaunt it, or as old-timers say, they don't wear their money on their backs.

Stylish scruffiness is the mode du jour. Smith Street, once an unsavory strip, is a mile-long ribbon of humble four-story, painted brick buildings with front-facing iron fire escapes, their façades often graffiti tagged. As on the Left Bank in Paris, these old buildings house expensive apartments above cool ground-level shops, bars, and restaurants.

Relax in Cobble Hill Park and Carroll Park. Both often have children's activities, concerts, and festivals.

BASICS

MAPPING: Using GPS, orient to Carroll Park. Main drags: Court and Smith Streets. Use F, G (Bergen Street, 9th Street), 2, 3, 4, 5 (Borough Hall). Near the Brooklyn Cultural District, Atlantic Avenue, and the neighborhoods of Boerum Hill, Brooklyn Heights, Columbia Waterfront, Gowanus, Red Hook. Cobble Hill is bounded roughly by Court and Degraw Streets, Atlantic Avenue, Gowanus Expressway; Carroll Gardens by Degraw and Hoyt Streets, Gowanus Expressway.

EVENTS: Bastille Day, Court Street Festival, "Festivale des Soupes," PS 29's holiday Eat Pie and Shop, Smith Street Funday Sunday, Smith Street Stage.

SELFIES AND 'ZA: Selfies at G. Esposito & Sons Pork Store, with the funny apron-wearing pig. For pizza, Lucali.

GREENMARKET: Sundays year-round at Carroll between Smith and Court Streets.

ACCOMMODATIONS: Airbnb; hotels in Gowanus and Downtown Brooklyn.

TIPS: Weekdays are quiet, weekends busy; some places close on Mondays.

Cobble Hill Park, with its faux-antique benches, is near the onetime home of writer Thomas Wolfe. Carroll Park has a bocce court and summer theater.

BEST BETS IN CARROLL GARDENS AND COBBLE HILL

1   Foodies alert: You will find sophisticated gourmet food shops and restaurants here. The trend started when chefs who'd trained in excellent Manhattan restaurants opened little eateries closer to home. Head to Frankies 457 Spuntino, Prime Meats, or Jolie Cantina. Take Root and La Vara are both Michelin rated. Go to a wine tasting at Smith & Vine. Have a cannoli from Court Pastry Shop. Take home cheesy delectables from Stinky Bklyn. Enjoy the like-your-bubbie's lox and bagels from Shelsky's of Brooklyn. Relax at Bar Tabac; practice your French.

2   Only-in-Brooklyn boutiques: Walk down Smith and Court Streets, stopping in trendy boutiques such as Refinery; By Brooklyn specializes in Brooklyn-made items.

3   Ideas: Give a shout-out to social reformer Alfred Tredway for his nineteenth-century Workingmen's Cottages, designed as socially enlightened housing for low-wage workers.

4   Picturesque history: Explore quaint side streets like hobbit-sized Dennett Place, formerly called Cats Alley, a quirky row of small antique houses with gnome-sized doors. It's tucked behind St. Mary Star of the Sea Church, where in 1918 Brooklyn native Alphonse (Al) Capone (1899–1947), who was a petty thief here and later became the Chicago Mafia's notoriously violent leader, was married.

LITTLE FRANCE TODAY, LITTLE ITALY YESTERDAY

French expats have introduced French food, fashion, and language classes to once-Italian Carroll Gardens, opening restaurants, boutiques, and cultural venues. For French fare, try Bar Tabac, Provence en Boite, and the acclaimed bakery Bien Cuit. The foreign-language bookstore Idlewild offers language classes. And *oui, oui*, don't miss Smith Street's annual July fourteenth Bastille Day festival, complete with *pétanque* tournament.

Why has this neighborhood lured the French? It's surely not the oysters—though the nearby polluted Gowanus Canal was once full of them. More likely, the French bilingual educational programs in two local schools attract French residents, of whom there were some three thousand, a French embassy official told the *Wall Street Journal* in 2009.

And love it they do: "Like many of us, I'd really prefer to just not cross the East River," sniffed one French entrepreneur from Brittany, from his little shop on Smith Street.

HISTORY SNAPSHOTS

Cobble, Carroll . . . what's the difference? The adjacent neighborhoods of Carroll Gardens and Cobble Hill share shopping streets, subway services, and an enviable swath of brownstone town houses. Both neighborhoods boast pre–Civil War churches and landmarks.

Cobble Hill is about forty blocks in size, smaller than Carroll Gardens. Its nineteenth-century residences were built for the upper-middle class and are characterized by elaborate ironwork and architectural detail. "Cobble Hill" dates to the 1950s and 1960s, when brownstone revivalists were seeking to differentiate their neighborhood from workaday "South Brooklyn." They resuscitated the Revolutionary War–era name for a nearby strategic hillock, "Cobbleshill." The area's seventeenth-century Dutch farmers had their own colorful name for Cobble Hill: Punkiesberg.

Carroll Gardens was settled by first Irish and Italian immigrants. Along with Bensonhurst and part of Williamsburg, this was a major Italian population center in Brooklyn in the twentieth century. Many locals worked on the docks, a rough world powerfully dramatized in Arthur Miller's *A View from the Bridge* and Elia Kazan's film *On the Waterfront*. In the 1960s, New York City's shipping industry declined, killing off a lifeline of employment. A core of the Italian community remained in Carroll Gardens through the turbulent, sometimes violence-plagued 1970s and 1980s, when non-Italians and "outsiders" who weren't part of a local extended family began to trickle in as renters and home buyers. A handful of small, pioneering restaurants and stores geared to young professionals opened on Smith Street in the mid-1990s, garnering media accolades for Smith Street as Brooklyn's new "restaurant row."

Stroll the two historic districts. Carroll Gardens Historic District (you can get the gist along President and Carroll Streets between Hoyt and Smith Streets) features classic Brooklyn homes with deep front yards. The area's original surveyor, Richard Butts, laid out these ample front plots that lend the word "Gardens" to the neighborhood's name. In Cobble Hill, the Workingmen's Cottages, Cobble Hill Towers, once known as "Model Tenements: Home and Tower Buildings," on Warren Place between Hicks and Henry Streets, were the nation's first high-quality, low-income housing development, built by philanthropist Alfred Tredway White in 1879. Inspired by London's new Victorian apartment buildings and model worker housing, White introduced ventilation, indoor plumbing, and natural lighting. (Find details at the Historic Districts Council website.)

Brooklyn was known as the "city of churches." Sacred Hearts and Saint Stephen Church (108 Carroll Street), Brooklyn's oldest Italian parish, has a Good Friday procession guaranteed to transport you to medieval Italy. Also, see the landmarked Romanesque Revival South Congregational Church (corner of Court and President Streets). It took over forty years to erect and has a ladies' parlor and rectory;

sections have now been repurposed into apartments. Kane Street Synagogue (236 Kane Street), which is home to Brooklyn's oldest Jewish congregation and still serves the neighborhood in which it was founded, was erected in 1855 as the United Brethren Society.

Here's a story for the kids: around 1915, the carriage house at 173 Pacific Street housed the zebras from Ringling Brothers and Barnum & Bailey Circus, and the building next door housed the elephants. They arrived by train into the Flatbush Terminal, according to a 1983 *New York Times* report.

Every neighborhood deserves a mystery. Here it's the pre–Civil War, half-mile Atlantic Avenue Tunnel. This underground subway tunnel is a historic site brought to public attention by Bob Diamond of the Brooklyn Historic Railway Association. Years ago, Diamond gave tours; today the tunnel, deemed unsafe, is off-limits to visitors. Urban lore speculates that pirate booty and/or John Wilkes Booth's diary might be buried here.

OLD/NEW BROOKLYN

New and old go together here as well as eggplant and Parmesan—better, croquet and monsieur. If there's a recipe for hip Brooklyn, it's in this mixture of then and now, nineteenth to twenty-first centuries.

Old Brooklyn is still palpable in Carroll Gardens. Caputo's Fine Foods and F. Monteleone's bakeries, D'Amico's Coffee, Sam's Restaurant, Sal's Pizzeria, and Staubitz Market, a butcher shop, have been in business for decades. Their storefronts haven't changed much. Everybody who was anybody was laid to rest at Scotto's Funeral Home or at F. G. Guido Funeral Home, the latter still housed in a 1840s landmarked building. The 1905 Carroll Gardens Library, the site of many a first library card, and the 1925 Cobble Hill Cinema, the site of many a first kiss, recall earlier eras. Both still draw patrons. For authentic midcentury retro, Marietta's across from Carroll Park still sells granny flannel nightgowns and chintzy housecoats, though to whom it's unclear. In disarray, the old Smith Union Market resembles a Broadway stage set from yesteryear. Jim and Andy's greengrocers used to be run by cranky brothers who had a Midas touch for picking ripe melons. The meticulous little market has been replaced by an attractive bar that's retained the original "Jim and Andy" shop sign. For a sign of the real-estate-obsessed times, see churches-turned-condos at South Congregational Church (360 Court Street) and Old Westminster Church (450 Clinton Street). Forever gone are the legions of Italian ladies wearing black and peering out of lace window curtains, "watching the street," or sitting in plastic chairs on the sidewalk of an evening. Carroll Gardens' Italian population dropped from half to just over one-fifth of all residents between 1980 and 2012.

New Brooklyn is everywhere, too, in the gourmand-pleasing farm-to-table cuisine, craft beers, unusual cocktail recipes, and independent boutiques along Atlantic

G. Esposito & Sons Pork Store, a third-generation Carroll Gardens family store (est. 1922). (Photo by E. Freudenheim, 2015)

Avenue and Smith and Court Streets. To experience real estate sticker shock like a native, see 177 Pacific Street, which the media excitedly reported as having sold in 2015 for $15.5 million to former Manhattanite, octogenarian, and award-winning photographer Jay Maisel. Locals hope rising prices don't undermine the idiosyncratic charms of Smith and Carroll Streets. But unless the neighborhood's retailers own the buildings from which their businesses operate, displacement from escalating rents is a real risk.

Invisibly, old-Brooklyn history runs beneath the surface. For instance, the big residential development called Sackett Union (est. 2013) was erected on the site of the "Anthony Anastasio Memorial Wing of the Brooklyn Longshoremen's Medical Center" at 339 Court Street (est. 1963). The popular clinic served former dockworkers; its flagpole was rescued from the demolition and honorarily placed at 102 First Place. But the factoids that go unstated are that "Tough Tony" Anastasio headed Local 1814, which was associated with the Gambino family, and his brother was Albert Anastasia of "Murder Inc." and a Gambino crime boss. The best part of the story is that you'll never know.

CELEBS, FILMS, FICTION

In 1931, Thomas Wolfe lived at 40 Verandah Place. Celebrities who lived or still live in these neighborhoods include Grammy winner Norah Jones, Sarah Jessica Parker, Beastie Boy Mike D, and *Cobble Hillbillies* / *Real Housewives of New York City* cast members Alex McCord and Simon van Kempen. A celeb of sorts for busy home cooks, Clarence Birdseye, founder of Birds Eye Foods, was born in 1886 at

368 Clinton Street; he's in the Inventors Hall of Fame for having figured out how to preserve foods through freezing.

Moonstruck (starring Cher and Nicholas Cage) was filmed at 502 Henry Street, the formerly characterful Cammareri Bakery. The TV show *Seinfeld*'s "Money Episode" was shot at D'Amico's Coffee, when Elaine buys George a bag of Arabian mocha java. The 2015 movie *Brooklyn* has some echoes of the neighborhood but was not shot here. For novels, read *Friendship* by Emily Gould, *Motherless Brooklyn* by Jonathan Lethem, *Brooklyn, a Novel* by Colm Toibin—and, of course, Thomas Wolfe's 1935 classic *Only the Dead Know Brooklyn*.

NOSHES, RESTAURANTS, BARS IN CARROLL GARDENS AND COBBLE HILL

Bar Tabac Café, 128 Smith Street, (718) 923-0918
Bien Cuit, 120 Smith Street, (718) 852-0200
Brooklyn Farmacy & Soda Fountain, 513 Henry Street, (718) 522-6260
Buttermilk Channel, 524 Court Street, (718) 852-8490
Caputo's Fine Foods 🏛, 460 Court Street, (718) 855-8852
F. Monteleone Bakery and Cafe 🏛, 355 Court Street, (718) 852-5600
Frankies 457 Spuntino, 457 Court Street, (718) 403-0033
G. Esposito & Sons Pork Store 🏛, 357 Court Street, (718) 875-6863
Jolie Cantina, 241 Smith Street, (718) 488-0777
Lucali, 575 Henry Street, (718) 858-4086
Prime Meats, 465 Court Street, (718) 254-0327
Provence en Boite, 263 Smith Street, (718) 797-0707
Sal's Pizzeria 🏛, 305 Court Street, (718) 852-6890
Take Root, 187 Sackett Street, (347) 227-7116

SELECT DESTINATIONS

By Brooklyn, 261 Smith Street, (718) 643-0606
Dennett Place (aka Cats Alley), between Nelson and Luquer Streets
Smith & Vine, 268 Smith Street, (718) 243-2864
Workingmen's Cottages and Cobble Hill Towers, Hicks Street

☞ Like Carroll Gardens and Cobble Hill? Visit Red Hook and the Columbia Waterfront District or any brownstone neighborhood.

Clinton Hill

I love Brooklyn. New York City needs to thank Brooklyn every day just for existing. That's how I feel about it.
—Mos Def, now known as Yasiin Bey
(quoted with permission from Yazeed Kamaldien, "Yasiin Bey: Cape Town Is Crazy," *Mail and Guardian Online*, March 7, 2014)

BASICS

MAPPING: Using GPS, orient to Red Lantern Bicycles. Main drags: DeKalb and Myrtle Avenues, Fulton Street. Use C (Clinton and Washington), G (Classon Avenue, Myrtle and Willoughby) subways. Near the Brooklyn Navy Yard and the neighborhoods of Bedford-Stuyvesant, Crown Heights, Prospect Heights, Williamsburg. Bounded roughly by Flushing, Atlantic, Vanderbilt, and Classon Avenues.

EVENTS: Biannual house tour. Events in nearby Fort Greene Park.

SELFIES AND 'ZA: Selfies at the Pratt Institute Sculpture Park. For pizza, Speedy Romeo.

GREENMARKET: Saturdays year-round, at 205 Washington Park between DeKalb and Willoughby Avenues.

ACCOMMODATIONS: Airbnb, hotels in Downtown Brooklyn.

A study in contrasts, Clinton Hill is multiracial, diverse, and eclectic. It's elegant and genteel, rough and tumble. Within its borders are mansions and public housing. It's a place where Walt Whitman and Biggie Smalls have roots. It's fancier and whiter than it was twenty years ago.

Count among Clinton Hill's attractions its excellent restaurants, bars, and cafés with a very chill vibe. It's the site of New York's largest sculpture garden. The lifestyle of Brooklyn's nineteenth-century ultrarich industrialists is evident in the handsome houses, with their ample stoops and swooping stairways, built by the profiteers of mass production during the city's Gilded Age. Enjoy the broad, leafy streets (great for biking) and the arty influence of Pratt Institute, a major art and design school, located here.

"A rarity," Clinton Hill is "one of the few areas where the residential architecture built for affluent families lasted almost a century," according to the NYC Landmarks Preservation Commission. Inside, these nineteenth-century homes are spectacular, graced with stained glass and mahogany trimming, beautiful bannisters, carved marble mantelpieces, high ceilings with ornate plaster details, and parquet floors.

BEST BETS IN CLINTON HILL

1 Culture and entertainment: Clinton Hill is a stone's throw from BAM and the Brooklyn Cultural District. Attend a play, concert, or dance performance at Jack. Hear jazz at Five Spot Soul Food and Supper Club. Drop in at Kinz + Tillou Fine Art gallery. See new and emerging artists at Corridor gallery, run by artist and poet Danny Simmons, of the influential entertainment industry family. Visit Sisters for entertainment; it used to be Sisters Community Hardware Store.

2 Great food: Oooh! Such a plethora of little bars and restaurants to choose from here. Locanda Vini e Olii is located in a charmingly renovated old pharmacy. Try American fare at the Finch; the Michelin guide liked it! Sample "Southern-fused cuisine" melding Cajun and soul flavors at SoCo. Nosh café food at Annex, wonderful prepared treats at Greene Grape, and life-changing doughnuts at Dough. Red Lantern Bicycles is a café and bike shop. Speedy Romeo is co-owned by a casting director for *The Sopranos* and an associate of celeb chef Jean-Georges Vongerichten and is located in a former auto-parts store.

3 Churches: Among several important churches in Clinton Hill, don't miss the popular Emmanuel Baptist Church and its imposing 1887 Gothic Revival Romanesque building. Historic Church of Saint Luke and Saint Matthew has Tiffany stained-glass windows.

4 Pratt Institute: Pratt Institute has its own historic district on the National Register of Historic Places. Stroll in the free, publicly accessible sculpture garden, a revolving exhibit of about fifty contemporary works.

5 "Millionaires' Row": Tour society hill by bike; ride along mansion-lined Clinton Avenue, home to oil magnate Charles Pratt and his peers. (See "DIY Tours," section 5.)

6 New York City's largest concentration of pre–Civil War wood frame houses: Built for Brooklyn Navy Yard workers, they're tucked in the twenty-two blocks between Classon, Carlton, Flushing, and Myrtle Avenues in the historic section called Wallabout.

HISTORY SNAPSHOTS

A stage coach in Brooklyn? Yup. The Knickerbocker Stage Coach Line ran along Myrtle Avenue in the mid-nineteenth century. But the story here is really all about Charles Pratt, the granddaddy of Standard Oil, once the wealthiest man in Brooklyn and clearly a force of nature. Pratt built such elaborate homes for himself and his sons that his friends, multimillionaires even by today's standards, followed suit, transforming Clinton Avenue into a veritable Gold Coast—as a trip down Clinton between Myrtle and Gates Avenues will reveal.

Today we think of Google and Apple as pioneering companies, working on the frontiers of technology. But in the nineteenth century, megawatt entrepreneurial success was achieved by men (99 percent men) who dealt in the physical world. They made fortunes on such products as coffee (John Arbuckle), typewriters (the Underwoods), machine-made lace (A. G. Jennings), and food items we don't think twice about today but then for the first time were mass marketed, for example, baking soda (the Hoagland family). Arbuckle, the Underwoods, Jennings, and C. N. Hoagland, peers of Charles Pratt, all lived here. Many of these magnates lived within walking distance of their offices and factories.

There's wonderful architecture in Clinton Hill. See photos on the Society for Clinton Hill and Historic Districts Council websites.

OLD/NEW BROOKLYN

Today, Clinton Hill (population thirty-five thousand in 2010) is a place where residents often stop to chat with their neighbors and volunteer on a park-cleanup day. That's partly cultural, because this classy, expensive neighborhood pulled itself back up by its bootstraps, in that old-Brooklyn can-do, hands-on spirit. Some people call it the Clinton Hill Revival.

Today things are looking good. But crime was a problem here, for decades. Locals wryly called Myrtle Avenue "Murder Avenue" in the 1980s. Some mansions went to seed, evident in collapsed floors, broken windows, rampant graffiti, and decrepit stoops. Late twentieth-century Clinton Hill suffered from the citywide crack-cocaine epidemic, resulting in drug dealing on corners and in playgrounds and a disquieting incidence of shootings, robberies, and car break-ins. Residents banded together in block associations. They cleaned up block after block. They gradually reclaimed the parks. They won historic-district status. They demanded better police protection and improved living conditions in public housing projects. A revival along Clinton and DeKalb Avenues began in the 1990s, with essential help from local organizations such as the Myrtle Avenue Brooklyn Partnership and Pratt Institute.

The gorgeous homes built by social climbers and successful businessmen 150 years ago are gorgeous once again. And an attendant new-construction housing boom has transformed the area. Where there was once a warehouse, an abandoned church, an empty lot, the movie theater, the supermarket, a White Castle, and an old gas station, apartments now stand.

From 2000 to 2010, Clinton Hill's white population more than doubled to over 35 percent, and the black population declined by about 30 percent, according to the U.S. census. The microneighborhood Wallabout, near the revitalized Brooklyn Navy Yard, hasn't popped yet; it's just a matter of time.

CELEBS, FILMS, FICTION

There's a fair sprinkling of celebrity fairy dust here: residents have included actors Susan Sarandon, Rosie Perez, Jeffrey Wright, *Entourage* star Adrian Grenier, rapper Himanshu Suri (known as Heems), and Yasiin Bey (formerly Mos Def). Biggie Smalls grew up on Saint James Place. Theater genius Robert Wilson is one of many influential Pratt graduates. In 1967, Patti Smith and Robert Mapplethorpe rented at 160 Hall Street, not far from 99 Ryerson Street, Walt Whitman's home when he published *Leaves of Grass* in the 1850s.

Check out Dave Chappelle's 2005 documentary *Block Party*, featuring musicians Kanye West, Mos Def, Jill Scott, and Erykah Badu.

NOSHES, RESTAURANTS, BARS IN CLINTON HILL

Clementine Bakery, 299 Greene Avenue, (718) 483-8788
The Finch, 212 Greene Avenue, (718) 218-4444
Five Spot Soul Food and Supper Club ☎, 459 Myrtle Avenue, (718) 852-0202
Green Grape Annex, 753 Fulton Street, (718) 233-2700
Locanda Vini e Olii ☎, 129 Gates Avenue, (718) 622-9202
Red Lantern Bicycles Café and Shop, 345 Myrtle Avenue, (718) 889-5338
SoCo, 509 Myrtle Avenue, (718) 783-1936
Speedy Romeo, 376 Classon Avenue, (718) 230-0061

SELECT DESTINATIONS

Jack, 505 1/2 Waverly Avenue, http://www.jackny.org
Mural of Biggie Smalls, aka Notorious B.I.G., 991 Fulton Street
Pratt Institute, 200 Willoughby Avenue, (718) 636-3886
Wallabout Historic District, http://www.myrtleave.org

☞ If you like Clinton Hill, visit other brownstone neighborhoods: Boerum Hill, Brooklyn Heights, Carroll Gardens, Cobble Hill, Crown Heights, Fort Greene, Park Slope, Prospect Heights, Sunset Park.

Columbia
Waterfront District

Until about 2011, there was a live-poultry plant here. Every so often, a chicken would escape.

—anonymous local resident

Once part of Red Hook, the Columbia Waterfront District is a sliver of a neighborhood that feels like a teensy town. It's vaguely off the beaten track and a low-key place to explore that's very close to Brooklyn Bridge Park.

As an amuse-bouche is to a full meal, so the Columbia Waterfront District is to the full Brooklyn experience: an appetizing teaser. Seinfeldian to the max—that is, nothing at all, yet everything happens here—the Columbia Waterfront District looks gritty and is understated. You'll find a few delightful surprises: a small theater and a few outstanding restaurants.

Residents have reclaimed empty lots, turning them into a half dozen community gardens named Human Compass, Amazing, Summit Street, Pirate's Cove, the Backyard, and the Urban Meadow gardens. Columbia Waterfront Park, still rough, is a two-acre segment of the evolving coastal Brooklyn Greenway.

Visit the hobbyist shop Brooklyn General Store. Brooklyn Collective describes itself as an artisan gallery showing "designers whose work ranges from the elegant to the obscure." Freebird, a bookstore, runs events and doubles as a community center. Freebird has collaborated with Brooklyn Bridge Park on its *Books beneath the Bridge* literature series and a game of Scrabble on a giant board. Fine and funky, the Jalopy Theatre and School of Music has shows, concerts, and music classes like ukulele workshops.

BASICS

MAPPING: Using GPS, orient to Alma Mexican restaurant. Main drags: Union and Columbia Streets. Poorly served by subways. Near Brooklyn Bridge Park and the neighborhoods of Brooklyn Heights, Carroll Gardens, Cobble Hill. Bounded roughly by Atlantic Avenue, Gowanus Expressway, East River, Brooklyn Battery Tunnel.

EVENTS: Columbia Waterfront Fall Festival.

SELFIES AND 'ZA: Selfie at Freebird Books or Alma's rooftop bar. Try Luzzo's Pizza or House of Pizza and Calzones.

ACCOMMODATIONS: Airbnb, Comfort Inns on Butler and Seabring. Nearby, Nu Hotel; hotels in Gowanus, Downtown Brooklyn, and Brooklyn Bridge Park.

BEST BETS IN THE COLUMBIA WATERFRONT DISTRICT

1 Great food: Have Thai at Michelin-starred restaurant Pok Pok NY, fish at Petit Crevette, and pastries at Margaret Palca Bakes. Enjoy margaritas and rooftop Manhattan views at Alma Mexican restaurant.
2 Brooklyn Bridge Park: Pier 6 beckons with views, open space, volleyball courts, playgrounds, seasonally free Governors Island ferry, and Smorgasburg.
3 Enjoy Jalopy Theater shows and events.

HISTORY SNAPSHOTS

This area was once part of the Red Hook–Carroll Gardens continuum. Just walk uphill away from the water, on any street, to see the Gowanus Expressway, which leads into the Brooklyn-Queens Expressway (BQE). It was built in the 1940s by Robert Moses, and you can see how it separates the neighborhood (and nearby Red Hook) from Carroll Gardens. For decades, the area around Columbia Street— renamed as the fancier-sounding Columbia Waterfront District—was isolated, a backwater with close-knit families but plagued by low-grade crime. Words fail; go look.

OLD/NEW BROOKLYN

An 1860s paper manufacturing plant (1 Tiffany Place) and a 1920s industrial building (42–60 Tiffany Place) were among the neighborhood's first buildings to be repurposed as apartments. Ferdinando's Focacceria, operating since 1904, is one of Brooklyn's oldest restaurants; its recipe for Sicilian rice balls, *arancina*, is still good!

CELEBS, FILMS, FICTION

Was Robert Moses a local celebrity? Both famous and infamous, the midcentury urban planner didn't live here. But the Gowanus Expressway, which truncated this area from Carroll Gardens and Red Hook, was his initiative, so his presence rumbles hourly through the neighborhood. Read Jim Mason's *Positively No Dancing*, published by local Freebird.

NOSHES, RESTAURANTS, BARS IN THE COLUMBIA WATERFRONT DISTRICT

Alma Restaurant, 187 Columbia Street, (643) 643-5400
Ferdinando's Focacceria Restaurant ☏, 151 Union Street, (718) 855-1545
Margaret Palca Bakes ☏, 191 Columbia Street, (718) 802-9771
Petit Crevette ☏, 144 Union Street, (718) 855-2632
Pok Pok NY, 117 Columbia Street, (718) 923-9322

SELECT DESTINATIONS

Freebird Books, 123 Columbia Street, (718) 643-8484
Jalopy Theatre and School of Music, 316 Columbia Street, (718) 395-3214

☞ Like the Columbia Waterfront District? Visit Red Hook and Industry City in Sunset Park.

Coney Island

Coney is Times Square at the beach. It's where popular culture flowered out of New York and spread to the world. It's where the Victorian era broke into unstructured play, where men met women they hadn't been introduced to if they struck up a conversation on the beach. You could get a ticket and go on a roller coaster and . . . buy a few minutes of closeness, and if you were lucky, you could go in the tunnel of love and steal a kiss.

—Dick Zigun, founder of Coney Island USA

BASICS

MAPPING: Using GPS, orient to Coney Island USA's Freak Bar. Main drags: Stillwell and Surf Avenues. Use Q, F (West 8th Street), D, Q, N, F (Stillwell Avenue) subways. Near the Atlantic Ocean and the neighborhoods of Brighton Beach, Sheepshead Bay. Bounded by Belt and Ocean Parkways, Atlantic Ocean, Norton's Point.

EVENTS: Brooklyn Cyclones games, Coney Island Film Festival, Coney Island Sand Sculpting Contest, Irish Fair, July Fourth fireworks, Mermaid Parade, Nathan's Hot Dog Eating Contest, New Year's Day Polar Bear Club swim, New Year's Eve ball drop, Seaside Park concerts.

SELFIES AND 'ZA: Pix on the beach, on the B&B Carousel, on a roller coaster. Pizza? Totonno's (est. 1924).

ACCOMMODATIONS: Sleep Inn.

TIPS: The Visitors Center in the Stillwell Avenue subway station has brochures, maps, and discount coupons. Also, see the Coney Island Fun Guide online.

If ya ain't been to Coney Island, ya ain't been to Brooklyn.

Brave the historic wooden Cyclone roller coaster and new "Scream Zone" rides. Walk on the boardwalk. Frolic at the beach. Eat a hot dog. Sip a lime rickey. See summer fireworks, outdoor movies, and the most wonderful New York Aquarium. Bring the kids! Over fifteen million people a year, from ten thousand miles and ten minutes away, flock to this populist play land.

Coney has its own special occasions. At Nathan's Famous International Hot Dog Eating Contest, an extreme eater downs sixty-nine dogs in ten minutes. At the annual sand-sculpting contest, artists carve porpoises and sea gods, castles and cars. And during the annual Mermaid Parade, New York's own Mardi Gras, "mermen" and "mermaids" in scant, sea-themed costumes dance down the street and prance atop floats.

Once and always a place of spectacle and pressing of the flesh, Coney's safe but not sanitized. It's still authentic—which is why New Yorkers love it.

The subway from Manhattan to Coney Island takes nearly an hour. But it's worth it. Rounding the bend, you spy the fabulous amusement-park landscape, the ocean and boardwalk, and the crowds. And at night, the rides are lit up.

BEST BETS IN CONEY ISLAND

1 The Atlantic Ocean! Go to the beach, fish from the pier, walk the boardwalk.
2 Beach snacks: Eat clams on the half shell, fries, knishes, and corn on a stick. People swear by the hot dogs at the original Nathan's Famous restaurant.
3 Amusement park and trapeze: There's something for everyone at Luna Park and Deno's Wonder Wheel Amusement Park. Enjoy over fifty rides including new roller coasters like the Thunderbolt, with a ninety-foot drop, and the thrilling 1927 wooden Cyclone. Deno's has tot-friendly rides, and the historic B&B Carousel is old-school. Learn to fly at the New York Trapeze School— or just take the terrifying Slingshot ride high in the air.
4 Mermaid Parade: Exuberant and bare, it opens the beach season.
5 Free fun: Monday Flicks at the Beach, Friday fireworks. Weekends, Coney Island History Project's exhibits.
6 Coney traditions: Enjoy the Coney Island Circus Side Show's old-fashioned sword swallowers and fire eaters in a no-holds-barred joint. See the Coney Island History Project, too.
7 New York Aquarium: See sea lions, sea otters, harbor seals, and exotic fish, with marine and freshwater habitats from around the world.
8 Baseball and MCU Park: MCU's a small-town ballpark in the Big Apple. Attend a Brooklyn Cyclones baseball game. Visit the Jackie Robinson and Pee Wee Reese statue, and the Brooklyn Wall of Remembrance, a 9/11 memorial.
9 Ice-skate: Abe Stark Rink is an indoor ice-skating rink dating from the 1970s. Limited weekend hours.
10 Souvenirs and T-shirts: Shop at Coney Island USA, Lola Star, Nathan's, and a seasonal Brooklyn Flea market.

CONEY BEACH FOOD AND BREWS

Feast on all-day breakfast, traditional Brooklyn egg creams, and lime rickeys at Tom's Coney Island on the boardwalk. For Mexican, eat at Doña Zita. Have beer, sausages, and clams at Paul's Daughter, a fifty-year-old Coney institution. There's Wahlburgers, IHOP, and other restaurant chains and, rare for New York City, a drive-through Starbucks on Cropsey Avenue off the Belt Parkway. Find indie food vendors at Smorgasburg. Sit down for an old-school Italian red-sauce meal of baked clams and pasta at Gargiulo's. Have the best pizza of your life—but hope the dough doesn't run out—at Totonno's. The Coney Island Nathan's Famous is the granddaddy of them all, so have a hot dog!

Tour the Coney Island Brewing Company and sample brews with funny names: Coney Island Hard Root Beer, Mermaid Pilsner, and wittiest of all, Seas the Day IPL.

HISTORY SNAPSHOTS

Coney's had its own ups and downs. It started as a world-class seaside resort, patronized by Herman Melville, Walt Whitman, and actress Lillian Russell, along with plenty of other rich and famous people. The opening of mass transit transformed Coney Island into the people's playground. Visualize the scene: the energy of workers escaping crowded, hot tenements; kids running in the sand; barkers hawking their wares; steaming sexuality; a babel of languages and the cacophony of a hard-driving city at play. Relief from overcrowded Manhattan, steaming in the summer, was just a subway ride away at the beach, complete with entertainment, food, and fun.

Images of early twentieth-century Coney Island are the stuff of American populist romance: Steeplechase and Luna Park, the racetracks, beach pavilions, flashy hotels, and championship prizefights. Charles Feltman, a German immigrant, invented the hot dog by sticking a sausage in a long roll, a hit at his Coney Island concession.

Coney Island took a dive after World War II. Steeplechase Park closed in 1965, public housing displaced bungalows, and hotels and entertainment venues (but not the entire amusement park) closed. Coney became dirty, dangerous, and down on its luck. Public controversy and litigation ensued as old Coney families, like the owners of Astroland, were bought out by investors. In 2012, Superstorm Sandy flooded many rides and buildings. But today, Coney Island is back!

Recommended reading for history and stories: Charles Denson's *Coney Island: Lost and Found* (2004) and *Coney Island: Visions of an American Dreamland, 1861–2008*, edited by Robin Frank (2015).

OLD/NEW BROOKLYN

Take a ride on, and in, history! The vintage 1927 Cyclone and 1920 Deno's Wonder Wheel are protected landmarks but still operate as rides.

Deno's Wonder Wheel, with its mile-high ocean views, was constructed from 1918 to 1920 by the Eccentric Ferris Wheel Company, using Bethlehem Steel forged on-site. Test your mettle by hanging upside down on the historic wood-framed Cyclone roller coaster, dating to 1927. You can look at (but not ride) the Parachute Jump, built for the New York World's Fair of 1939–1940 and transported to Steeplechase Park. Around Twelfth Street on the Riegelmann Boardwalk, drop a quarter into an arcade machine, and a toy woman will dance, a holdover from the 1930s. Spookarama has been in the same place (under Deno's Wonder Wheel)

The 150-foot Deno's Wonder Wheel in Coney Island is a New York City landmark (opened 1920). (Photo by E. Freudenheim, 2015)

since the 1950s. Eldorado Bumper Cars, with a 1970s disco sound system, has been in business since, well, the age of disco.

On the far west of Coney Island is Brooklyn's only gated community, Sea Gate, not open to tourists. Built in the 1890s, its ninety-acre, eight-hundred-odd home community remains under the aegis of the Sea Gate Association. Surrounded on three sides by water, it still has some rambling Victorian homes. The population is a polyglot mix of Russian and eastern European immigrants, Orthodox Jews, and others.

New Brooklyn is coming, fast. Smorgasburg and Brooklyn Flea have arrived. In 2015, the Trapeze School of New York opened year-round. Art dealer Jeffrey Deitch mounted a sponsored street-mural exhibit. The amusement parks have new rides like the Thunderbolt. The once alternative Mermaid Parade now attracts up to eight hundred thousand visitors and is the city's largest art parade. Brooklyn Cyclones games draw family-friendly crowds of over seven thousand fans. The 1923 Child's Restaurant building, with its fanciful façade—a New York City landmark, bedecked with terracotta seashells, wriggling fish, gargoyles, sailing ships, and a seaweed-draped Neptune—will reopen as a five-thousand-seat, indoor-outdoor concert amphitheater in 2016.

Follow the money, the wisdom goes: Thor Equities now owns a big chunk of Coney Island. The supermarket billionaire John Catsimatidis is developing expensive waterfront condo towers, the first in this mostly low-rent community, population fifty thousand (about the size of Galveston, Texas). A 2015 New York City plan identifies Coney Island for "targeted infrastructure investments to help spur affordable housing development." Everyone's got their eye on Coney Island's Atlantic Ocean waterfront property.

CELEBS, FILMS, FICTION

It's fun to watch old movies that depict Coney Island (though not all were shot here): D. W. Griffith's *Monday Morning* is set in a Coney Island Police Court (1908). Harold Lloyd and Ann Christy's *Speedy* (1928) and *The Shopworn Angel* (1938), with James Stewart, depict Coney Island in the earlier twentieth century. Red Skelton's *The Clown* (1953) captures its heyday. Sylvester Stallone's *The Lords of Flatbush* (1974) depicts a darker world, as does the cult film *The Warriors* and Lee Strasberg and Ruth Gordon's *Boardwalk* (both 1979). Woody Allen waxes nostalgic in *Annie Hall* (1977). The 2015 *Brooklyn* with Saoirse Ronan depicts romance on the beach in the 1950s. You can see the old amusement rides in *Enemies* (1989), starring Angelica Huston, and *Angel Heart* (1987), starring Mickey Rourke and Robert DeNiro. Amy Nicholson's 2013 indie film *Zipper: Coney Island's Last Wild Ride* investigates Coney Island's gentrification. *Last Summer at Coney Island* by J. L. Aronson describes the transformation undertaken by private developers. Read Kevin Baker's 1999 novel *Dreamland*, *Coney* by Amram Ducovny (2000), and former Brooklyn poet laureate Norman Rosten's *Under the Boardwalk* (1968).

NOSHES, RESTAURANTS, BARS IN CONEY ISLAND

Coney Island Brewing Company, 1904 Surf Avenue, (718) 996-0019
Gargiulo's Restaurant ☎, 2911 West 15th Street, (718) 266-4891
Nathan's Famous Hot Dogs ☎, 1310 Surf Avenue, (718) 333-2202
Tom's Coney Island, 1229 Boardwalk, (718) 942-4200
Totonno's Pizzeria Napolitano ☎, 1524 Neptune Avenue, (718) 372-8606

SELECT DESTINATIONS

Abe Stark Rink, Coney Island Boardwalk and West 19th Street, (718) 946-6536
B&B Carousel, Boardwalk West, (718) 373-5862
Coney Island History Project, at Deno's Wonder Wheel, West 12th Street (free)
Coney Island USA / Coney Island Circus Side Show / Coney Island Museum, 1208 Surf Avenue, (718) 372-5159
Deno's Wonder Wheel Amusement Park, 3059 Denos Vourderis Place, (718) 372-2592
Luna Park, 1000 Surf Avenue, (718) 373-5862
MCU Park, 1904 Surf Avenue, (718) 449-8497
New York Aquarium, 602 Surf Avenue, (718) 265-3474

Seaside Park and Community Arts Center, 3052 West 21st Street (under
   construction)

☞ Like Coney Island? Sorry, there's nothing else like it! (But for beaches, try
Brighton or Manhattan beaches, nearby.)

Crown Heights

Nearly thirty thousand Hasidim live in Crown Heights, home to the world headquarters of the Chabad-Lubavitch movement.   **—Rabbi Motti Seligson**

BASICS

MAPPING: Using GPS, orient to Chavela's restaurant. Main drags: Franklin, Utica, and Nostrand Avenues. Use 3, 4, A, C (Franklin, Nostrand, Kingston, or Utica Avenues) subways. Near Brooklyn Botanic Garden, Brooklyn Museum, Prospect Park, and the neighborhoods of Bedford-Stuyvesant, Brownsville, Clinton Hill, East Flatbush, Prospect Heights. Bounded roughly by Empire Boulevard and Ralph, Washington, Atlantic Avenues.

EVENTS: Black History Month events at Medgar Evers College, Martin Luther King Jr. concerts, West Indian American Day Parade.

SELFIES AND 'ZA: For selfies, Berg'n. For pizza, Barboncino or Basil Pizza.

ACCOMMODATIONS: Airbnb; homestay for Orthodox Jews; La Quinta opening soon.

TIP: The express subways sometimes run on the local track.

If heterogeneity makes the world go round, then Crown Heights is spinning. Racially, ethnically, and socioeconomically diverse, and also in the midst of a real estate boom, Crown Heights is one of the borough's hottest new-old neighborhoods.

Come for jazz, for a beer hall with new Brooklyn-style food stands, for intimate cafés, and to see renovated brownstone town houses and beautiful nineteenth-century freestanding homes. Savor the contrasts here: wealth and poverty, faith and secularism, beautiful architecture and beat-up buildings. Visit not one but two children's museums.

There's a quiet but radical undercurrent in Crown Heights, past and present. You can see it in Weeksville, a historic and largely self-sufficient community developed by free black men and former slaves, prior to the Civil War. The Brooklyn Children's Museum (fun for all ages) revolutionized "hands-on" experiential education for generations of museum-going children. At Medgar Evers College during Black History Month, you can attend excellent, incisive public lectures and discussions about race in America today.

Crown Heights is a random marriage of the oddest of demographic bedfellows: Hasidic Jews, Caribbean Americans, hipsters, and young professionals (and, lately, investors in absentia).

BEST BETS IN CROWN HEIGHTS

1 Food and drink: At Berg'n, the mommy crowd comes during the day with strollers, and the work crowd arrive later for fresh craft brews. It's a hip venue with artisanal food stands familiar from Smorgasburg. For restaurants, eat Senegalese at Café Rue Dix, Indian food at Pearl, Mexican fare at Chavela's. Drink beer to live music at Franklin Park, a bar in a former garage. Sample island drinks at Glady's and Creole and Cajun brunch at Catfish. Enjoy dinner and jazz at the Classon Social Club. Try the soul food at Arboceno. Or chill at cafés like The Pulp and the Bean, Breukelen Coffee House, and retro Little Zelda.

2 Diversity: Drive along Franklin Avenue on both sides of Eastern Parkway to see a very mixed population. Shop for Caribbean and Jewish ethnic fare. Shop Nostrand and Utica Avenues for inexpensive clothes and Caribbean food markets. If you're traveling by bike, take a ride to nearby Park Slope, Prospect Park, or Bed-Stuy.

3 Destination checklist: See Weeksville Heritage Center (by appointment), the Hasidic community, historic homes, landmarked districts, the nearby Brooklyn Museum and Brooklyn Botanic Garden.

4 Family friendly: Visit the Brooklyn Children's Museum and the Jewish Children's Museum.

5 Culture: Check out the Franklin Park Reading Series. The FiveMyles Arts Center, founded in 1999, focuses on experimental work of underrepresented artists, featuring non-Western themes.

6 African diasporic diversity: Visit Medgar Evers College. The Jackie Robinson School was built on the site where America's first black major league baseball player lived. Tour Weeksville. See P-Tech, the school President Obama visited in 2013, calling it "the first school in the nation to seamlessly connect high school, college, and job training, aided by private-sector partnerships." The Ronald K. Brown / Evidence dance company combines traditional African dance with contemporary choreography and spoken word; the Haiti Cultural Exchange and organizers of the West Indian American Day Parade, WIADCA, are based in Crown Heights. There's also a Chassidic Art Institute gallery.

HISTORY SNAPSHOTS

The Brooklyn Church of God in Christ (renamed the Washington Temple in 1951 in honor of its founder) had a longstanding traditional gospel choir. The *Encyclopedia of the City of New York* says that in the 1940s, the church was "the best known" gospel concert venue in the city at a time when gospel debuted at Harlem's Cotton Club. Its choir was led by the "Songbird of the East," the pastor's Little Rock–born

One of hundreds of West Indian American Day Parade marchers wearing custom-made feather costumes. (Photo by E. Freudenheim, 2014)

wife, Ernestine B. Washington, who sang in the style of Mahalia Jackson. (She's fascinating; see the online *Encyclopedia of American Gospel Music*.)

The calm, multiethnic conviviality of Crown Heights today is a hard-won accomplishment. It's a far cry from 1991, when violence was triggered by the traffic death of a seven-year-old black child, Gavin Cato, accidentally run over by a Hasidic driver. Shortly thereafter, a young student, Yankel Rosenbaum, was murdered by a group of young black men. Since the Crown Heights riots, strenuous efforts by such groups as the Crown Heights Youth Collective to build bridges and improve relations have resulted in cross-cultural basketball teams, cross-community outreach, and ongoing dialogues.

WEEKSVILLE HERITAGE CENTER

Weeksville Heritage Center is an important site. It marks a nineteenth-century independent, free black community. Founded in the 1830s (before the Civil War), within decades it had grown into a thriving community with its own newspaper and other institutions. Today it's a living museum. Hear about the times and lives of residents of four small wood-frame houses, dating to the 1860s, 1900s, and 1930s, a story of generations of African Americans who survived the Civil War, world wars, and the Great Depression while living here.

Prominent residents included Moses R. Cobb, a black policeman from North Carolina, the son of slaves, said to have walked from North Carolina to New York to live as a free man; and Major Martin Delaney, the grandson of an enslaved West African prince who was an Underground Railroad activist and writer for Weeksville's newspaper, *Freedman's Torchlight*. Dr. Susan Smith McKinney-Steward, the nation's third black female doctor, was born in Weeksville in 1847 and lived here.

Named after James Weeks, the man who purchased this property in 1838, eleven years after New York State abolished slavery, the site was forgotten after World War II. It was rediscovered in the late 1960s when historians James Hurley and James Hughes flew a helicopter over the area, searching for the remains of what historical documents indicated had been a thriving black community. Decades of archaeological work, fundraising, and reconstruction, often driven by the late Joan Maynard, ensued. Four houses (circa 1840 to 1883), known as the Historic Hunterfly Road Houses, are listed in the National Register of Historic Places and are New York City landmarks. The nonprofit StoryCorps, based locally in Fort Greene, has collected over 120 Weeksville oral histories. Visits by appointment.

HASIDIC COMMUNITY HQ

The Hasidic community, concentrated in Crown Heights, Borough Park, and Williamsburg, is part of the fabric of Brooklyn life. It's made up of various sects, differentiated by subtleties in rituals, spiritual leadership, and even dress codes such

---

BROOKLYN VOICES

RABBI MOTTI SELIGSON
Spokesman for Chabad-Lubavitch

[Crown Heights] is an international destination, annually drawing hundreds of thousands of Jewish visitors from nearly every part of the world. They come for holidays and programs, and to stroll streets where Judaism is alive in shops, restaurants, and cultural institutions, including the largest Jewish children's museum in the United States.

Individuals can arrange in advance to visit some of the Chabad-Lubavitch movement's offices, culminating with the world-renowned 770 Eastern Parkway, where the Lubavitcher Rebbe—Rabbi Menachem M. Schneerson, of righteous memory—set into motion the post-Holocaust revolution of Judaism, as well as the movement's priceless Judaica library.

---

as the style of hat and height of socks. Number 770 Eastern Parkway is the head-quarters of the global Chabad-Lubavitcher Hasidic movement.

OLD/NEW BROOKLYN

You'll find new bars and music venues in Crown Heights. Perched on once-derelict Franklin Avenue, 341 EPW is an apartment building the name of which evokes a pricey Manhattan address, CPW, shorthand for Central Park West. In 2014, studio apartments here rented for $2,200 a month. 1000 Dean Street, a former 1920s Studebaker auto building, was "reimagined as the 21st century home for Brooklyn's creative community," its website says. On the ground floor is the food hall and bar Berg'n.

In the 2010 census, about three in four of Crown Heights' 150,000 residents identified as black, a mix of African Americans, Caribbean Americans, and Caribbean immigrants. The Hasidic community numbers 25,000, or one in six residents. Some 7,000 whites arrived from 2000 to 2010, with a 25 percent increase in the population of twenty-four- to thirty-year-old whites.

CELEBS, FILMS, FICTION

The roster of celebrities associated with Crown Heights is wildly diverse. It includes rapper Skoob of the Das EFX and Lubavitcher Rebbe Menachem Mendel Schneerson, who although he died in 1994 is still spoken of in the present tense by his followers. Presidential candidate Shirley Chisholm, the U.S. Congress's first black female member, first elected in 1966, and former Brooklyn borough president Marty Markowitz lived here. For literature, read Chaim Potok's 1967 *The Chosen*.

NOSHES, RESTAURANTS, BARS IN CROWN HEIGHTS

Barboncino Pizza, 781 Franklin Avenue, (718) 483-8834
Basil Pizza, 270 Kingston Avenue, (718) 285-8777
Berg'n, 899 Bergen Street, (718) 857-2337
Chavela's, 736 Franklin Avenue, (718) 622-3100
Classon Social Club, 807 Classon Avenue, (718) 484-4475
Franklin Park Bar and Beer Garden, 618 St. Johns Place, (718) 975-0196
Glady's, 788 Franklin Avenue, (718) 622-0249
Pearl Indian Restaurant, 738 Franklin Avenue, (718) 622-9500

SELECT DESTINATIONS

Brooklyn Children's Museum, 145 Brooklyn Avenue, (718) 735-4400
Brooklyn Flea, 1000 Dean Street, http://brooklynflea.com
Chassidic Art Institute, 375 Kingston Avenue, (718) 774-9149
FiveMyles Arts Center, 558 St. Johns Place, (718) 783-4438
Hullabaloo Book Shop, 711A Franklin Avenue, (917) 499-3244
Jewish Children's Museum, 792 Eastern Parkway, (718) 467-0600
Jewish Hassidic Walking Tours of Brooklyn, 305 Kingston Avenue,
    (718) 953-5244
P-Tech, 150 Albany Avenue, (718) 221-1593
Weeksville Heritage Center, 158 Buffalo Avenue, (718) 756-5250

☞ Like Crown Heights? Visit hipster Bushwick, Williamsburg, and Gowanus; Hasidic Borough Park and Williamsburg; and Caribbean East Flatbush.

Downtown Brooklyn and Fulton Mall

> You cannot re-create the place where you put an engagement ring on a piece of cheesecake!
>
> —Alan Rosen, third-generation owner of Junior's

BASICS

MAPPING: Using GPS, orient to the steps of Brooklyn Borough Hall. Main drags: Boerum Place, Flatbush Avenue, Fulton Street, Schermerhorn Street. Use 2, 3, 4, 5 (Borough Hall), A, F, R, N (Jay Street), D, Q, R, N (DeKalb Avenue) subways. Near the Brooklyn and Manhattan Bridges, Brooklyn Cultural District, and the neighborhoods of Brooklyn Heights, Cobble Hill. Bounded roughly by the BQE, Schermerhorn and Court Streets, Flatbush Avenue.

EVENTS: Brooklyn Book Festival, official Christmas-tree and thirty-foot-tall menorah lightings at Brooklyn Borough Hall, free midday jazz at MetroTech Commons.

SELFIES AND 'ZA: Selfies on the marble steps of historic Brooklyn Borough Hall. Pizza at Forno Rosso or Luciano's.

GREENMARKET: Saturdays, Tuesdays, Thursdays year-round at Borough Hall Plaza.

ACCOMMODATIONS: New York Marriott at Brooklyn Bridge, Hampton Inn, Sheraton Brooklyn, Holiday Inn, other major chains.

You've arrived!

Downtown Brooklyn is the name of the place you arrive in the borough of Brooklyn after you cross the Brooklyn Bridge (if you don't go to Dumbo or Brooklyn Bridge Park first). With amazing subway connections and a gaggle of name-brand hotels and upscale fast-food restaurants, it's a great place to start exploring. It's also a fast-growing hub for businesses, restaurants, hotels, entertainment, office workers, lawyers, students, tourists, and shoppers—and spiffy high-rise apartment buildings. Eventually a greenbelt called the Brooklyn Strand may link the area's small parks with Brooklyn Bridge Park nearby.

Downtown Brooklyn has long been the borough's civic bellybutton, the center for courts and municipal administration, first for the independent city of Brooklyn and today for the overlapping entities of the borough of Brooklyn and Kings County.

Don't expect to find a traditional "neighborhood" in Downtown Brooklyn. (For that, visit adjacent Brooklyn Heights, a gorgeous brownstone community with a centuries-long patina of history.) Downtown Brooklyn is a business district in transition as new hotels and apartments are built. The projected population is thirty or forty thousand as residential skyscrapers with Manhattan-style amenities like swimming pools, rooftop grills, and aerial views rise. Downtown Brooklyn's new, vertical "instant neighborhood" has a major benefit: convenience to both Manhattan and Brooklyn destinations.

Downtown Brooklyn (which some parties want to rebrand as "DoBro," like Soho and Dumbo) is also a multicollege campus, of sorts, with a total student population of sixty thousand mostly commuter students, part- and full-time, graduate and undergraduate. They study at Brooklyn Law School, Long Island University on Flatbush Avenue, NYU-Poly (formally known as Polytechnic Institute of New York University), City Tech (New York City College of Technology, CUNY), the nation's second-oldest private engineering school, and Saint Francis College in Brooklyn Heights.

Downtown Brooklyn has a number of technology companies and at least one small-business incubator dedicated to urban environmental sustainability. It's one leg of Brooklyn's Tech Triangle. (See "Innovation: Tech Triangle, Start-Ups, Sharing Economy" in "The New Brooklyn," section 2.)

BEST BETS IN DOWNTOWN BROOKLYN AND FULTON MALL

1 Shop Fulton Mall: This long-profitable pedestrian mall has a reputation for hip-hop street style, and you can find sneakers, jeans, hats, T-shirts here, plus bling jewelry. Popular for decades with Caribbean and African American shoppers, of late corporate retailers are displacing independently owned shops. As of this writing, retailers include Brooklyn Industries (great for souvenir T-shirts), Aeropostale, Gap, Macy's, Century 21, Cookies, H&M, T. J. Maxx, Nordstrom Rack, and Armani Exchange. Nearby chains include Neiman Marcus Last Call and Sephora. (See "Shopping in Brooklyn," section 4.) For a political history, read *Street Value: Shopping, Planning, and Politics at the Fulton Mall*, by Rosten Woo.

2 Family-friendly New York Transit Museum: A cool place that's worth the time to visit. You can board old New York City subway cars, steer a mock city bus, and learn about New York's century-old system in the *Steel, Stone, and Backbone* exhibit. (See "Brooklyn's Cultural Scene," section 4.)

3 Food: Nosh at such popular eateries as Hill Country Barbecue and Shake Shack. Enjoy a sit-down dinner at the traditional Italian restaurant Queen. Snack on cheese, bread, and fruit at the greenmarket. In the Fulton Mall, City Point's DeKalb Market will include Katz's Delicatessen, Fletcher's Brooklyn Barbecue, Arepa Lady, and Sunday Gravy—all Big Apple specialties.

4 Brooklyn Borough Hall: The seat of government for the independent city of Brooklyn, this 1851 Greek Revival–style building, topped by a stunning statue of Justice, houses ornate rooms and the Brooklyn borough president's office. The useful Visitors Center is open weekdays.

5 Culture and entertainment: Hear the award-winning Brooklyn Tabernacle gospel choir, buy discount tickets to Broadway shows at the TKTS booth, catch a movie at Alamo Drafthouse Cinema, see avant-garde performances at Issue Project Room.

6 Chill! Sit on the inviting broad marble steps of Brooklyn Borough Hall and
   watch multiethnic Brooklyn—lawyers, students, vendors, businesspeople, of
   all races and backgrounds—bustle by. Wander through Cadman Plaza Park.

7 "Skyscraper Historic District": Take a brief walking tour of the Borough Hall
   Skyscraper Historic District and of Fulton Mall. (See "DIY Tours," section 5.)

8 Junior's: Junior's is a tourist attraction and iconic meeting place—for cheesecake! It's been around so long that Brooklynites don't think twice about
   it—until, that is, the media reported in 2014 that the owner turned down a
   $45 million bid on Junior's building. That kind of money is a lot of cheesecake.

HISTORY SNAPSHOTS

Downtown Brooklyn has historical importance, as the civic center of the once
independent city of Brooklyn. This gravitas is evident in elegant Brooklyn Borough Hall, the Duffield Street Houses (where abolitionists lived), and Abraham &
Straus (now Macy's), one of the nation's first department stores.

It is also a place where judicial history was made. The Theodore Roosevelt
United States Courthouse at 225 Cadman Plaza East opened in 2006. It houses
the Brooklyn Federal Courthouse, seat of the storied Eastern District court of
New York, which was created in 1865 when a fast-growing shipping industry
spawned disputes and hence spurred litigation. It hears cases in Brooklyn and in
Islip, Long Island.

Recent cases have included high-profile terrorism conspiracies to blow up JFK
Airport, the subway, and the Federal Reserve Bank and to help the Islamic State,
ISIS. The serial killer nurse Michael Swango was tried here, as were prominent

---

BROOKLYN VOICES

ALAN ROSEN
Owner of Junior's Restaurant

Junior's is where people got married and had graduations and first dates. People came at three
a.m. after rock-and-roll concerts at the Paramount or after the clubs to get a cheeseburger
deluxe. We've had CEOs and lawyers and city workers. Mead Esposito was wiretapped here. It's
part of the people's history, a time line.

Our clientele is a melting pot. It's always been a kaleidoscope. You could have the president
of Pfizer and the garbage man sitting next door. Guys used to come here from the Navy Yard
factories. At 12:04 p.m., there was a line out the door. Back in the 1950s, we were not segregated.
My grandfather and his brothers came from Russia and Poland, and they wouldn't have it.

Today we sell La Colombe espresso and craft beers. We added jerk chicken, salmon escovitch,
and barbecue ribs. We don't serve stuffed derma or chicken pot anymore. Cheesecake? We ship
millions, as far away as South Korea.

Duffield Street Houses, formerly Johnson Street Houses, homes of abolitionists, 1835–1845. (Photo by E. Freudenheim, 2015)

drug traffickers and human smugglers trafficking in Chinese immigrants. The court heard influential class-action suits, for instance, against Frito-Lay for labeling products as "natural," against firearm makers' marketing practices, and against Swiss banks on behalf of Holocaust survivors. The 1977 Abner Louima police-brutality case was heard here, presaging national attention to an explosive issue.

Older court dramas include an influential ruling against President Franklin D. Roosevelt's New Deal initiatives; the World War II trial of some thirty German spies who had infiltrated American industry, called the Duquesne Spy Ring (the case was the basis for the film *The House on 92nd Street*); and controversial school busing and integration cases. In the 1970s and 1980s, the court heard cases related to Vietnam, abortion, environmental issues, labor law, employment discrimination (including a Title VII case against the New York Fire Department), and organized crime. (Read details about the Mafia in "Old and Historical Brooklyn," section 2.)

In Downtown Brooklyn, the truism holds: what stories they could tell, if only these walls could talk.

OLD/NEW BROOKLYN

Old Brooklyn is well represented here, architecturally. Highlights include the ornate Romanesque-style post office building on Cadman Plaza West, Brooklyn Borough Hall, homes of nineteenth-century antislavery activists, and the serene Quaker meeting house. Landmarked Gage & Tollner restaurant has not yet been revived. The New York Transit Museum (in a decommissioned subway station) tells many stories about old New York.

New Brooklyn is all around, too, visible in the furious pace of high-rise construction and as Fulton Mall morphs upscale. Of course, as this is Brooklyn, the shop selling pricey jeans will be right next to the discount wig shop, while outside a street vendor is hawking incense. As ever, the civic center of Brooklyn remains full of hustle.

CELEBS, FILMS, FICTION

The Kings County Supreme Court building at 320 Jay Street is the set for a *Sex and the City* wedding scene and the trial of Denzel Washington's character in *American Gangster*. Junior's is where *Sex and the City*'s Carrie and Big have a wedding party. Kelly Anderson's 2012 social documentary *My Brooklyn* explores the Fulton Mall's gentrification.

NOSHES, RESTAURANTS, BARS IN DOWNTOWN BROOKLYN AND FULTON MALL

Forno Rosso, 327 Gold Street, (718) 451-3800
Junior's 🏠, 386 Flatbush Avenue Extension, (718) 852-5257
Luciano's, 15 MetroTech Roadway, (718) 855-6668
Queen 🏠, 84 Court Street, (718) 596-5955

SELECT DESTINATIONS

Brooklyn Borough Hall, 209 Joralemon Street, (718) 802-3700
Brooklyn Friends Meeting House, 110 Schermerhorn Street, (212) 777-8866
Brooklyn Tabernacle, 17 Smith Street, (718) 290-2000
Brooklyn Tourism and Visitor Center, Borough Hall, 209 Joralemon Street, (718) 802-3846
Fulton Mall, Fulton Street, (718) 403-1608
Issue Project Room, 22 Boerum Place, (718) 330-0313
New York Transit Museum, 130 Livingston Street, (718) 694-1600
TKTS booth, 1 MetroTech Center (limited hours)

☞ Like Downtown Brooklyn? Visit nearby Dumbo and Williamsburg near the Bedford Avenue L train stop.

Dumbo, Fulton Ferry Waterfront, and Vinegar Hill

Everything here is "high end" now. How about just regular? Just give me regular. —Dumbo resident

Picturesque, unique Dumbo is the first spit of Brooklyn land you can touch after a stroll across the Brooklyn Bridge.

With light bouncing off the water, the long, meandering riverside park, and romantic sunset views of Manhattan, the neighborhood is a photographers' and lovers' delight. You'll often see wedding limos parked while the blissful couple poses against the backdrop of the Manhattan skyline and Brooklyn Bridge.

Dumbo is a bite-sized neighborhood, easy to visit, filled with charming contradictions. Its cobblestoned streets lead to chic high-rises. Its nineteenth-century warehouses are inhabited by many twenty-first-century tech companies. After walking across the Brooklyn Bridge from Manhattan, you get the sense that, finally, you've arrived! In Brooklyn! Truth is, Dumbo is a one-off, unlike any other Brooklyn neighborhood. Dumbo is a tourist, technology, and commercial center, as well as a residential area. It's a wonderful first foray into Brooklyn. But if you only get as far as Dumbo, you haven't totally experienced Brooklyn.

The adjacent microneighborhood of Vinegar Hill is a ten-block hike from the heart of Dumbo. Known as Irishtown in the late 1700s, its name was changed by land magnate John Jackson to commemorate the 1798 Irish Rebellion's Battle of Vinegar Hill. Vinegar Hill's early days were as a simple, waterfront, working-class, residential area that followed the boom-bust cycles of the nearby Brooklyn Navy Yard.

BASICS

MAPPING: Using GPS, orient to Brooklyn Roasting Company. Main drags: Water and Main Streets. Use East River Ferry or A, C (High Street), 2, 3 (Clark Street), or for Vinegar Hill, F (York Street) subways. Near Brooklyn Bridge Park, Brooklyn Navy Yard, and the neighborhood of Brooklyn Heights. Dumbo is bounded by the East River, Old Fulton, Sands, and Bridge Streets. Vinegar Hill is bounded by the East River, the Brooklyn Navy Yard, and Sands and Bridge Streets.

EVENTS: First Thursday gallery walks, July Fourth fireworks (when over the East River), July marathon reading of Walt Whitman's "Song of Myself," open studios.

SELFIES AND 'ZA: Selfies at Fulton Landing, with a backdrop of Manhattan's skyline. Pizza at Juliana's or Grimaldi's.

Vinegar Hill is a mixed bag. Farragut Houses, a public housing complex, is located here. So is the "Commander's Quarters," a stately, gated 1805 mansion that is listed on the National Register of Historic Places. A private home today, it was built by Charles Bulfinch, the architect of the U.S. Capitol building, for Captain Matthew C. Perry of the Brooklyn Navy Yard. Romantic Vinegar Hill House restaurant is located on a cobblestone street lined with quaint historic row houses.

BEST BETS IN DUMBO, FULTON FERRY WATERFRONT, AND VINEGAR HILL

1 The views! Soak in the panoramic views of Manhattan's East Side, New York Harbor traffic, and the Statue of Liberty. Photo ops are everywhere, notably at Fulton Landing and Brooklyn Bridge Park.

2 Ferry rides: Hop the East River Ferry to Williamsburg or the summertime-weekend, free Governors Island Ferry.

3 Brooklyn Bridge Park: This modern park has it all, including food, culture, views, nature, and wonderful free activities.

4 Eat! Relax at the Brooklyn Roasting Company's cool café and workspace with a cup of Fair Trade or Rainforest Alliance coffee. Relish Superfine's bluegrass brunch or an intimate dinner at Vinegar Hill House. Splurge at fancy River Café. Nibble a croissant at Almondine. Indulge in small-batch, artisanal ice cream in handmade waffle cones at Brooklyn Ice Cream Factory, housed in a landmark lighthouse. Have yummy chocolate at Jacques Torres.

5 Culture: St. Ann's Warehouse, a cultural heavyweight, is a performing arts center known for collaborations with the likes of the National Theater of Scotland and for experimental works by emerging artists. Hear live classical music at Bargemusic, a renovated 1899 Erie Lackawanna coffee barge anchored in the East River since 1978; concertgoers have bird's-eye views of Manhattan's skyline. Attend an author reading or event at powerHouse Arena. Learn about independent film and technology at the prestigious Made in NY Center by IFP. Appreciate the historic buildings, like Empire Warehouse. In the Manhattan Bridge Archway, literally under the Manhattan Bridge, rock to free concerts or maybe join fun events like a huge World Cup viewing party.

6 Art: Attend popular First Thursday Gallery Walks. Visit the nonprofit gallery Smack Mellon or the galleries at 16 Main Street, including Minus Space, United Photo Industries, Klompching Gallery, Masters Projects, and the feminist A.I.R.

7 Family fun: Enjoy the Brooklyn Children's Museum annex, the beautifully restored antique horses on Jane's Carousel, housed in a modern glass building, and many inventive play areas in Brooklyn Bridge Park.

8 Shop! Visit Journey and Stewart/Stand for housewares and furniture and one of three bookstores in the area: powerHouse Arena, Beryl's Poetry Shop, and P.S. Bookshop.

9 Scream! Well, don't alarm anyone. But the ruckus of the subways rumbling
   over the Manhattan Bridge affords the perfect moment to let it all hang out.
   Otherwise, just feel your smallness as you stand under the vast structures
   supporting the Brooklyn and Manhattan Bridges; they're awesomely huge.

HISTORY SNAPSHOTS

This is a very old part of Brooklyn. Starting in the 1600s, boats carried people,
livestock, and produce, connecting rural villages to the City of New York, then
just Manhattan. General George Washington fled his first major battle, the Battle
of Brooklyn, departing from the "Brookland Ferry" landing, here, under cover of
night on August 29, 1776. Tom Paine lived near today's Cadman Plaza West and
Sands Street. On unassuming Doughty Street, Charles Doughty took the radical
act of freeing his own slave in 1797 and then worked for the abolition of slavery in
New York State.

For sixty years, starting in the 1830s, Fulton Ferry thrived as a river town, with
taverns for overnight travelers, and farmers carting produce by horse to an open
market. Today's street layout and names echo that era: Front, Water, and Fulton
Streets remain central arteries in Dumbo. Banks, insurance companies, and law
firms clustered on Front Street. The neat red-brick building at 5 Front Street (now
Gran Eléctrica restaurant) was the 1835 Long Island Insurance Company, where
Henry Cruse Murphy, a mayor of Brooklyn, helped lay the legal foundation for
the building of the Brooklyn Bridge. Blacksmiths, ship carpenters, and a chandlery,
as well as coopers, painters, and warehouse businesses, lined Water Street. The
1860s Empire Stores warehouse, revitalized today into a retail and cultural center
housing St. Ann's Warehouse theater, was a storage facility for sugar, molasses, and
coffee. The four-story brick buildings on Fulton Street, now housing restaurants
and pizzerias, once had oyster saloons, shops, and modest hotels.

The opening of the Brooklyn Bridge in 1883 rendered ferry transportation
obsolete. By the mid-twentieth century, when the shipbuilding business from the
Brooklyn Navy Yard dried up, the area became desolate, with few residents and
little commerce. In the 1970s, New York's urban planners began to think of ways
to repurpose the city's many abandoned manufacturing buildings. In Manhattan's
Soho, the city was allowing qualified artists to move into abandoned industrial
lofts. Brooklyn's brownstone revival movement had already begun. Preservationists
and officials took a second look at Dumbo's enduring assets: historic architecture
and waterfront access.

David Walentas, founder of Two Trees Management, began to buy buildings in
the area in 1974. Later, its new name, "Dumbo," an acronym for the somewhat tortured "Down Under the Manhattan Bridge Overpass," was adopted both for fun
and for marketing purposes. Two Trees Management acted as a patron of the arts,
subsidizing artists' studio space and rent. In the 1980s, artists began to work and

live in some of the industrial buildings underneath the bridges, sometimes reno-vating the spaces themselves. The buildings offered light, huge spaces, and views. Dumbo was "desolate, decrepit, even creepy" in the late 1990s, this author's 2004 guidebook said, but it offered artists "splendid isolation."

By the twenty-first century, the area had become, once again, an important and visible part of New York City life. The opening of fabulous Brooklyn Bridge Park has given Dumbo a burst of energy.

OLD/NEW BROOKLYN

The entire twenty-five-block neighborhood of Dumbo is a historic district. Barge-music is a floating concert hall on an old barge. Brooklyn Bridge Park is con-structed, in part, from bits of the old pier. Many industrial buildings have been adaptively reused into work and living spaces. For instance, the Eagle Warehouse at 28 Old Fulton Street, built in 1893, is one of Brooklyn's few remaining build-ings by Frank Freeman, dubbed "Brooklyn's greatest architect" by the *AIA Guide to New York*. Atop the building is a huge clock, visible from the Brooklyn Bridge. Today it's apartments.

As for new Brooklyn, Dumbo's economic engine is thrumming with real estate, culture creation, tourism, and technology businesses. Among its many tech com-panies are Etsy (which went public as a socially responsible B Corporation in 2015 for $1.8 billion) and Kickstarter (a global crowdfunding platform that's raised over a billion dollars). Many cultural institutions flourish here, too: small publishers, the Brooklyn Arts Council, the Brooklyn Historical Society annex, the New York Foundation for the Arts, the Asian American Arts Alliance, New York Studio School's sculpture studio, and several competitive artist residency programs. The transformation of this riverfront backwater into an economic dynamo is a remark-able Cinderella story.

CELEBS, FILMS, FICTION

Washington and Whitman (George and Walt, that is) walked these streets. Actress Anne Hathaway bought (and sold) a multimillion-dollar condo in Dumbo. An enormous number of fashion shoots and advertisements are set in Dumbo. As for fiction, one could imagine Emily Barton's fictional *Brookland* set here.

NOSHES, RESTAURANTS, BARS IN DUMBO, FULTON FERRY WATERFRONT, AND VINEGAR HILL

Brooklyn Ice Cream Factory, 1 Water Street, (718) 246-3963
Brooklyn Roasting Company, 25 Jay Street, (718) 855-1000
Gran Eléctrica, 5 Front Street, (718) 852-2700

Grimaldi's Pizza 🏮, 1 Front Street, (718) 858-4300
Juliana's Pizza, 19 Old Fulton Street, (718) 596-6700
River Café 🏮, 1 Water Street, (718) 522-5200
Smorgasburg, http://www.smorgasburg.com
Superfine 🏮, 126 Front Street, (718) 243-9005
Vinegar Hill House, 72 Hudson Avenue, (718) 522-1018

SELECT DESTINATIONS

Bargemusic, 2 Old Fulton Street, (718) 624-4924
Brooklyn Children's Museum, 1 John Street, (718) 735-4400
Eagle Warehouse, 28 Old Fulton Street (condos)
Empire Warehouse, formerly 53–83 Water Street (enter through St. Ann's
    Warehouse)
First Thursday Gallery Walks, (718) 222-2500, http://www.dumbo.is
Galleries at 16 Main Street
Jane's Carousel, Dock Street, (718) 222-2502
Made in NY Media Center by IFP, 30 John Street, (718) 729-6677
Smack Mellon Art Studios, 92 Plymouth Street, (718) 834-8761
St. Ann's Warehouse, 45 Water Street, (718) 254-8779

☞ Like Dumbo? Visit Red Hook . . . or Manhattan.

Flatbush

On any given day, a visitor to Brooklyn College might hear more than one hundred languages spoken or meet students born in 150 countries.

—Brooklyn College president Karen L. Gould

BASICS

MAPPING: Using GPS, orient to Brooklyn College. Main drags: Avenues J and M; Church, Coney Island, Ocean, and Nostrand Avenues; Cortelyou Road; Kings Highway; Ocean Parkway. Use Q, F, 2, 5 subways (multiple stations). Flatbush touches Prospect Park and the neighborhoods of Borough Park, Flatlands, Marine Park, Sheepshead Bay. Bounded roughly by Rogers, Ralph, and Remsen Avenues, Prospect Park, with zigzags from Coney Island Avenue to Ocean Parkway.

EVENTS: Mardi Gras along Avenue M, Pakistani Independence Day, Victorian house tours.

SELFIES AND 'ZA: Selfies at Brooklyn College. For pizza, Di Fara's.

GREENMARKETS: Sundays year-round at Cortelyou and Rugby Roads. Saturdays seasonally at Flatbush and Nostrand Avenues.

ACCOMMODATIONS: Bed-and-breakfasts, Airbnb.

TIP: For Yelp, specify subneighborhood names like Ditmas or Midwood.

Flatbush, a large swath of "deep Brooklyn," is vaguely mysterious to the uninitiated—and for good reason, because it's a vast and variegated area. It encompasses Brooklyn College, immigrant-rich neighborhoods where a babel of languages are spoken, and beautiful Victorian homes. Flatbush doesn't have many Starbucks coffee shops, a barometer of disposable income. It is immensely culturally diverse. Depending on where you are, Flatbush is located half an hour by subway to the Atlantic Ocean in one direction and forty-five minutes to Manhattan in the other.

Flatbush is fantastic, in a Brooklyn kind of way.

English is the lingua franca of New York; it's not, however, the mother tongue of about half of Flatbush's one hundred thousand or so residents. You'll rub elbows here with people who are, in various combos, Haitian, Trinidadian, Caribbean, African American, Syrian, Turkish, Pakistani, Russian, Chinese, Jewish, Muslim, Christian, Buddhist, Rastafarian, multigenerational American, and more. A cacophony of languages, cultures, and religions greets you in Flatbush. In the human geography of Flatbush, unlike that of the real world, you can travel from Haiti to Pakistan in minutes.

For the causal day-tripper, we've sliced the Flatbush foray into three digestible bites: Jewish Midwood and Brooklyn College; Victorian Flatbush, an architectural feast; and East Flatbush, a center of

Caribbean life. You can do the whole thing in a day, sustained by bourekas, kebabs, roti, callaloo, jerk chicken, pierogi and dumplings, and halva.

BEST BETS IN FLATBUSH

1 Ethnic eats: In Caribbean East Flatbush, have bammy (cassava-flour flat-bread), spinachesque callaloo, or okra-based coo-coo. Your Jewish food tour might stop at Essen Deli, Mansoura's Mediterranean pastries (a sixth-generation family business), and Chiffon's bakery. Have farm-to-table at Farm on Adderley, Mimi's Hummus, and Lea, a Michelin pick.

2 Bike: The path along Ocean Parkway Mall from Prospect Park to the Atlantic Ocean, Coney Island, and Brighton Beach is an easy, fun ride.

3 Woody Allen: See Woody's childhood homes and haunts, some evoked in his films. (See "DIY Tours," section 5.)

4 Diversity: Religious schools—madrassas, yeshivas, a Buddhist temple—dot Flatbush. See the first two along Coney Island Avenue, around Avenue J. The Cambodian Buddhist temple Watt Samakki Dhammikaram sits a block away from historic homes in Victorian Flatbush. Visit busy Kings Highway public library, where multilingual programs serve fifty thousand people annually. Brooklyn's Little Pakistan is one of the nation's largest Pakistani enclaves. In August, the *mela* (Sanskrit for "gathering") street fair celebrates Pakistan's 1947 independence from Great Britain.

5 Shop: Kings Highway, a shopping drag since the 1930s, has various clothing stores, including the original Chuckie's shoe store. Near Brooklyn College is Flatbush Junction, a micromall with Target and a few national brands. (See "Shopping in Brooklyn," section 4.)

6 Live shows: Loew's Kings Theatre is a renovated ornate 1920s movie house that reopened in 2015, with shows by Stephanie Mills, Stephanie Scott, Moscow Ballet's *Nutcracker*, and the National Beard and Moustache Championships. Kids' shows are always fabulous at the Brooklyn Center for the Performing Arts' new $55 million facility at Brooklyn College.

7 Victoriana: See a swath of eye-candy Victorian homes with playful turrets, big porches, and stained glass galore. In a rush? A walk along East Seventeenth Street between Dorchester and Ditmas Avenues affords a glimpse of some lovely homes. See grassy Knickerbocker Field Club, a Victorian-era tennis club. The annual Flatbush house tour is terrific (organized by the Flatbush Development Corporation).

8 Colonial Flatbush: The 1800s Johannes Van Nuyse House and the late eighteenth-century Joost and Elizabeth Van Nuyse House (Coe House) date to Brooklyn's Dutch era. Also not to be missed is the Flatbush Reformed Church, built by order of Governor Peter Stuyvesant in 1654, with Tiffany stained-glass windows.

9 Famous schools: Brooklyn College is a must-see. Midwood, Murrow, and James Madison High Schools are huge (each has more than three thousand students). The spacious campus and fraying façades of the once-renowned Erasmus Hall High School will impress. All have long rosters of stellar alumni.

GETTING ORIENTED: MAIN ROADS IN FLATBUSH

Three parallel arteries define the touristic geography of Flatbush: Ocean Avenue, Coney Island Avenue, and Ocean Parkway. All run through Brooklyn from Prospect Park to the Atlantic Ocean; there are bike lanes on Ocean Parkway. Retail corridors worth exploring are Church Avenue, Cortelyou Road, Kings Highway, and Avenues J and M.

Gritty Coney Island Avenue and Ocean Avenue are lined with a jumble of light industry and humdrum businesses: tire and car-repair shops, mom-and-pop grocery stores, insurance companies, plumbers, funeral homes, appliance stores, and discount shoe outlets, mostly in two- to four-story buildings. Many are mixed use, with apartments above street-level businesses.

Get a whiff of South Asia around Avenue H and Parkville on Coney Island Avenue, where you can find a Pakistani enclave, with small shops selling strong spices in bulk containers, condiments, enormous sacks of rice, and other necessities for the home chef who is ten thousand miles from home. When you see shops and eateries with the same name, like Punjab Grocery, Punjab Sweets, and Punjab Restaurant, chances are they are all owned by one extended family.

Between Coney Island Avenue and Ocean Parkway are beautiful suburban-style homes, with manicured lawns.

Ocean Parkway: Park architects Olmsted and Vaux designed the broad green malls along this urban highway. You can enjoy benches and plantings, a nice bike path to the ocean, and outstanding people-watching. On Friday nights and Saturdays, you may see Orthodox Jewish families shuttling back and forth between home and synagogue around Avenue J, in the subneighborhood of Midwood.

Kings Highway is a busy shopping street. It's also a name you can say to former Brooklynites—even if they've been living in a Tibetan monastery—and get a reaction. In fact, you could use this as a Rorschach test to ascertain if someone who claims to be from Brooklyn really is. Some buildings, like the decorative building at 815 Kings Highway, date to the 1930s. On Saturdays and Jewish holidays, most stores are closed for Jewish religious observances.

BROOKLYN COLLEGE AND MIDWOOD

Part of the public City University of New York (CUNY) system, Brooklyn College is a four-year liberal arts college offering graduate programs. As it always has done, Brooklyn College serves all kinds of students including a large contingent of immigrants and first-generation Americans, many the first in their families to attend college.

Brooklyn College has a pretty campus with a green quadrangle and stately neo-Georgian brick buildings. It has an observatory, a greenhouse, and, now dated but still something to brag about, a particle accelerator. Since the college's founding in 1930, it has turned out Nobel and Pulitzer Prize winners, poets, actors, scientists, and equally importantly, legions of aspiring men and women who might otherwise have been unable to obtain higher education. The current student body numbers seventeen thousand. Tuition runs about $6,000 a year for in-state residents. Scholarships average $3,400. Of those reporting ethnicity, about 30 percent of students are white, 18 percent are African American, 17 percent are Hispanic, and 15 percent are Asian, according to 2014 City University of New York data. Half of the students graduate within six years; many hold down jobs. Midwood High School is associated with Brooklyn College. "Due to their diverse background and the strong education we provide," Brooklyn College president Karen L. Gould said by email, "our students are especially well prepared to succeed in their chosen field with a global view."

For cultural entertainment, the on-campus Brooklyn College Center for Performing Arts hits the high notes of Brooklyn's xylophone of diverse cultures, featuring touring acts like the Vienna Boys Choir, Step Afrika, Darlene Love, and Chinese dancers. It's a fun outing for kids, with plenty of space for them to run around outside après show.

Midwood has a strong Jewish influence, and one can see many Jewish bakeries, synagogues, and shops along Avenue J. Notable among the distinctive Jewish communities in Midwood is the world's largest group of Sephardic Jews outside Israel. Syrian Jews from Aleppo and Damascus have built a close-knit community, which preserves a three-thousand-year tradition in its own schools, synagogues, and a summer getaway in Deal, New Jersey. Brooklyn's first Sephardic Jews arrived in the early twentieth century, founding the Magen David synagogue in Bensonhurst in 1921. Immigration picked up after 1948, when Israel was created and hostilities broke out in the region. Jordache jeans and Duane Reade were founded by members of this community.

VICTORIAN FLATBUSH

Visitors who assume that Brooklyn is all high-rises, projects, and row houses are in for a surprise. South of Prospect Park are miles of freestanding homes with knock-your-socks-off details like wrap-around porches, ample bay windows, stained glass, and other exuberant nineteenth-century embellishments. With Neoclassical-, Queen Anne–, and Colonial-style homes, Victorian Flatbush seems (because it is, in fact) transported from a slower era. After you explore the area,

A 1900 Colonial-style home in Prospect Park South, designed by J. J. Petit. (Photo by E. Freudenheim, 2014)

wash down your astonishment with some excellent, locally sourced food at Farm on Adderley.

Within biking distance of Prospect Park are eleven distinct and landmarked Victorian neighborhoods: Albemarle-Kenmore Terraces, Beverley Square East and West, Caton Park, Ditmas Park, Ditmas Park West, Fiske Terrace–Midwood Park, Prospect Park South, South Midwood, and West Midwood. Each little enclave has a unique history and a fiercely proud and protective community of homeowners. Victorian Flatbush is within a thirty- or forty-minute subway ride to lower Manhattan. If "Garden in the City" sounds like a headline straight out of *Architectural Digest*, these neighborhoods were designed to be just that.

Prospect Park South is Brooklyn's most elegant in-city suburban community, a neighborhood of villas and homes with distinctive architectural flourishes. A veritable who's who of high fliers built and lived in these homes, among them the founders of Ex-Lax, Gillette, Fruit of the Loom, and Sperry Gyroscope. The interiors are even more detailed than their exteriors. The Prospect Park South Neighborhood Association (est. 1905), they say, is one of the nation's oldest continuously operating neighborhood associations. It's fun to join the annual house tour, but otherwise, just stroll or bike along Albemarle Road between Marlborough and Stratford Roads to get the flavor of Victorian Brooklyn. Or take a brief self-guided walking tour of Prospect Park South. (See "DIY Tours," section 5.)

EAST FLATBUSH

Should you be in the mood for Haitian, Jamaican, Trinidadian, or other Caribbean food, a bead-covered calabash, or Rastafarian gear, East Flatbush is your 'hood. There's reggae, calypso, and soca music blaring from the cars in summer and in some stores year-round. Brooklyn has the largest Caribbean diaspora in the Northeast, which explains such honorary street names as Bob Marley Boulevard and Toussaint Louverture Boulevard, both Caribbean cultural heroes. New York Republican politician Rudy Giuliani grew up here when it was a white, Italian

WHEN AN OLD HOUSE IS PART OF THE FAMILY

Owning an old and landmarked home—and thousands of Brooklynites do, given the housing stock in the borough—involves a dance with history. The house becomes like family: one loves and cherishes it but may also find it exasperating at times. Eventually the houses outlast their owners.

Victorian Flatbush is landmarked, meaning that building façades must conform to historical standards, so repairs are expensive and permitting arduous. Prospect Park South was the first of the Victorian neighborhoods in Flatbush to be revived, in the 1980s. Its urban pioneers would despair about their homes being "money pits" and "sinkholes," all the while pointing lovingly to "the details": sweeping oak bannisters, elaborate stained glass, high plaster ceilings, servants' back staircases, mahogany decorative grillwork, marble sinks, dumbwaiters, and signs of old craftsmanship even where it couldn't be seen. Crime was a worry, and one had to drive to Park Slope for a cappuccino; renovation was a labor of love.

Years of Dumpsters on the streets and punch lists on many a fridge paid off. Victorian Flatbush has more or less been returned to its original splendor, plus Wi-Fi. Along Cortelyou Road, a shopping drag with a Caribbean beat, a microneighborhood of cool cafés and restaurants is emerging. The fabric of community life here is woven, in part, from shared interest in the architecture and history of the historic homes and by the care and tending of the neighborhood itself.

This picturesque area attracts so many film and TV crews that the community board has appealed to the city to "ensure against oversaturation" and to incentivize the crews to patronize the local shops, complaining that the frequency of shoots "begins to wear on the community's patience."

A spin around Victorian Flatbush spirits you to a different time zone. Its leafy spaciousness evokes Savannah, Georgia. Its street names suggest London. The area's riotous variety of architectural styles is a radical break from severe uniformity of brownstone Brooklyn's rows of attached houses. Victorian Flatbush, then and now, is about having it all: country living in the big city.

For details, see the Historic Districts Council or NYC Landmarks Preservation Commission online.

neighborhood—but no streets have been named in honor of the law-and-order former mayor.

For the flavors of the Caribbean, try Trinidadian oxtail, beef roti, and dough in tamarind at Bake and Things, or coconut-fried chicken, jerk wings, and plantains at fusion Mango Seed.

The city's densest Caribbean population lives in East Flatbush. "Caribbean" doesn't even begin to describe its cultural diversity. East Flatbush residents (or their families) spoke English in Trinidad, Grenada, and Barbados; English Creole in Jamaica; Dutch, English, and Creole-like Papiamento in Aruba and Curaçao; Spanish in Puerto Rico and the Dominican Republic; and French and Creole dialects in Martinique, Guadeloupe, and Haiti.

Brooklyn's Caribbean immigration began in the early twentieth century, with newcomers settling here and in Bedford-Stuyvesant and Crown Heights. Immigration accelerated midcentury. Since the 1980s, more than eight hundred thousand Caribbean immigrants settled in New York, and by 2000, the city's West Indian population made up a quarter of the city's black population. Twenty-two thousand foreign-born Flatbush residents hail from Jamaica, Trinidad, Guyana, and Mexico. Flatbush's largest immigrant group is Haitians, numbering about thirteen thousand. East Flatbush is among the poorer areas in Flatbush.

And should you notice a disproportionate number of people dressed in medical whites or scrubs, that's because SUNY Downstate Medical Center is nearby.

If time allows, explore off-the-beaten-track, over-150-year-old Holy Cross Cemetery. (See "Brooklyn's Cultural Scene," section 4.)

HISTORY SNAPSHOTS

Settled in 1634 by Dutch farmers, Flatbush was a sleepy backwater until 1878, when mass transit arrived, in the form of the Brooklyn, Flatbush and Coney Island Railroad. In the 1920s, after the subway was extended to Coney Island, large apartment buildings on Ocean Parkway were erected. Fast-forward a century: in the 1970s, a new wave of immigrants, including Hispanic, Caribbean, African, Pakistani, and others, settled here. In 2011, about half the population of Flatbush was foreign-born, with the prevalent languages Spanish and Haitian Creole, followed by Russian, Indic languages, Urdu, and French, according to CAMBA, a community group. In a boggling vignette that says it all, 130 languages were spoken at a single elementary school in Flatbush, according to Brooklyn Community Board 14 in 2014.

OLD/NEW BROOKLYN

Flatbush isn't frivolous. It doesn't have a roller coaster or amazing Manhattan views, and you'll walk a long mile to find an artisanal cocktail with locally grown lime—but don't let that fool you. Flatbush is essential Brooklyn, girded by the fundamental optimism of immigrants. It has always been a place where people from diverse backgrounds bounce off one another and are more or less forced to get along. They may share little, perhaps, but the desire for a new life, a commitment to family, and the exacting transition of living in a different culture than that of one's homeland. This diversity makes Flatbush's extraordinary enclaves well worth a visit, whether on your own, with a local, or with a private tour.

Flatbush stands as testimony to the nation's ability to successfully accommodate and engage with generation after generation of immigrants. The grease in the wheels of this extraordinary American experiment is public education: schools, colleges, and libraries. Walk into any public library in Flatbush, and you will find books, resources, and community programming in three, four, six languages. They offer a roster of services, too. In school, bi- or multilingual children learn to navigate a global world—starting in kindergarten. Hidden in plain sight, ungainly, almost-too-big-to-swallow Flatbush is a living lesson in the ongoing saga of the United States as a nation of immigrants.

While this book celebrates the yin and the yang of old and new Brooklyn—its historic architecture, culinary revolution, and revival of "maker industries" like brewing—an unsettling reality of Brooklyn's past persists: poverty. In 2010, more than one in five families in Flatbush lived in poverty, according to the Citizens Committee for Children.

To get the full Brooklyn experience, Flatbush is something to see, to celebrate—and to grasp.

CELEBS, FILMS, FICTION

More success stories and Hollywood stars than you can count lived in, survived, and left Flatbush. Woody Allen, Marisa Tomei, and Gil Hodges (Brooklyn Dodgers first baseman) lived here. Barbra Streisand was born at 457 Schenectady Avenue in East Flatbush and watched movies at the now-renovated Loew's Kings Theatre. Senator Charles Schumer, 2015 presidential aspirant Senator Bernie Sanders, Cousin Brucie, Wendy Wasserstein, and Judge Judy all lived and went to school here. So did Supreme Court Justice Ruth Bader Ginsburg, who in 2015 became an Internet sensation through the Tumblr site and book *Notorious R.B.G.*, a pun on fellow Brooklynite and rapper Notorious B.I.G. Rappers who came from, or lived in, East Flatbush include Busta Rhymes, Bobby Shmurda, Rowdy Rebel, Shyne, Joey Bada and Flatbush Zombies, and the Underachievers. Actress Michelle Williams bought a Ditmas Park home on Albemarle Road, in 2015.

As for literature, playwright Arthur Miller lived in the modest home at 1350 East Third Street, said to be an inspiration for *Death of a Salesman*. *Sophie's Choice*, the 1979 novel by William Styron, is set in Victorian Flatbush; the movie was filmed at 101 Rugby Road. The 2001 Pulitzer Prize–winning novel *The Amazing Adventures of Kavalier and Clay* by Michael Chabon and the mid-twentieth-century *Strictly from Brooklyn*, by William Heuman, are set in Flatbush.

NOSHES, RESTAURANTS, BARS IN FLATBUSH

Am Thai Bistro, 1003 Church Avenue, (718) 287-8888
Café Madeline, 1603 Cortelyou Road, (718) 941-4020
Café Tibet, 1510 Cortelyou Road, (718) 941-2725
Farm on Adderley, 1108 Cortelyou Road, (718) 287-3101
Fisherman's Cove, 2017 Church Avenue, (718) 859-1580 (five locations)
Mango Seed, 757 Flatbush Avenue, (347) 529-1080
Mimi's Hummus, 1209 Cortelyou Road, (718) 284-4444
Oxcart Tavern, 1301 Newkirk Avenue, (718) 284-0005
Purple Yam Restaurant, 1314 Cortelyou Road, (718) 940-8188
Shayna's Restaurant, 907 Church Avenue, (718) 282-8190
Wheated Pizza, 905 Church Avenue, (347) 240-2813

SELECT DESTINATIONS

Brooklyn College, 2900 Bedford Avenue, (718) 951-5000 (also home to Brooklyn
    Center for the Performing Arts)
Flatbush Dutch Reformed Church, 890 Flatbush Avenue, (718) 284-5140
Holy Cross Cemetery, 3620 Tilden Avenue, (718) 284-4520

☞ Like Flatbush? Visit the rest of Brooklyn.

Fort Greene

There are tons of writers here, Pulitzer Prize winning, best-selling, and diverse. In Fort Greene alone, Jhumpa Lahiri, Jennifer Egan, Colson Whitehead, and Nelson George at one point all lived within five blocks of each other.
— Johnny Temple, Fort Greene resident,
Brooklyn Book Festival cofounder,
Brooklyn Literary Council chairman,
and publisher of Akashic Books

Fort Greene is the buzzy heart of the Brooklyn Cultural District. With a dozen theaters and cultural institutions, it's a juggernaut of creative energy, acclaimed performance, and live music. In a feat of adaptive reuse, in Fort Greene performance spaces have been carved out of just about everything: churches, Salvation Army buildings, and decrepit old theater palaces. (See "Brooklyn's Cultural Scene," section 4.)

Residential Fort Greene has allure, too. Once an arty, primarily African American neighborhood—where filmmaker Spike Lee and jazzman Wynton Marsalis lived—today it's wealthier, though still diverse. The neighborhood is a Brooklyn classic, with many fine three- and four-story brownstone town houses. Explore Fort Greene Park, enjoy sitting in a café, dining at a cool restaurant, and catching a performance.

BEST BETS IN FORT GREENE

1 Food: Walter's serves southern cuisine. French bistro Chez Oskar has been serving up both great flair and fare since 1998. Have brunch at Black Iris, tasty short ribs at the Smoke Joint,

BASICS

MAPPING: Using GPS, orient to BRIC House. Main drags: DeKalb and Myrtle Avenues, Fulton Street. Use 2, 3, 4, 5 (Barclays), B, Q, D, N, R (DeKalb), A, C (Lafayette), and G (Fulton) subways. Near Barclays Center and the neighborhoods of Clinton Hill, Downtown Brooklyn, Prospect Heights. Bounded roughly by the Brooklyn Navy Yard and Atlantic, Vanderbilt, and Flatbush Avenues.

EVENTS: Fort Greene Park Jazz Festival and concerts, movies, events in Fort Greene and Commodore Barry Parks and Brooklyn Cultural District.

SELFIES AND 'ZA: Selfies in Fort Greene Park. Pizza at Graziella's or Lean Crust (gluten-free).

GREENMARKET: Saturdays year-round at Fort Greene Park, off DeKalb Avenue.

ACCOMMODATIONS: Hotels in Downtown Brooklyn, Airbnb. A Marriott is opening near BAM.

TIP: What officialdom calls the "Brooklyn Cultural District," Brooklynites know as the names of neighborhoods: Fort Greene, Barclays Center area, and Brooklyn Heights.

and farm-to-table fare at Roman's. Frank's Cocktail Lounge has a long history and occasionally colorful clientele. At Madiba Restaurant, named for Nelson Mandela, sample South African fare. Try adorable Lulu & Po.

2   Culture: Drench yourself in the Brooklyn Cultural District. Chill at BRIC House; something is always going on. Attend an author reading at Greenlight Bookstore.

3   Historic neighborhood: Bike or walk along Carlton Avenue between Willoughby and DeKalb Avenues along streets that seem architecturally frozen in the nineteenth century. Peek into the old Williamsburgh Savings Bank; its sparkly lobby ceiling evokes a planetarium. See Brooklyn Technical High School, a New York City institution. Don't miss the Revolutionary War Prison Ship Martyrs' Monument in Fort Greene Park.

4   See celeb sites: It won't last forever, so take a photo of *Commandante Biggie*, the wall mural of Biggie Smalls, aka Notorious B.I.G. painted by street artist Lee Quiñones at Fulton Street and South Portland Avenue. Spike Lee grew up at 165 Washington Park. His production company, 40 Acres and a Mule, was founded in 1985 in the renovated firehouse Engine Company 256, moving to nearby 75 South Elliot Place in 2008. Jazz vocalist Betty Carter resided at 117 Saint Felix Street from 1972 until she died in 1998. Trombonist "Slide" Hampton lived at 245 Carlton Avenue, renting rooms to his friends Eric Dolphy, Wes Montgomery, and Wayne Shorter, all Downbeat Hall of Fame jazz musicians.

5   Shop: Browse independent boutiques along Fulton Street and DeKalb Avenue and the summertime Brooklyn Flea.

6   Parks: Historic Fort Greene Park is the soul of residential Fort Greene. It's a place where you can jog, picnic, play tennis (permit needed), enjoy seasonal festivals, and munch your way through a popular greenmarket. Commodore Barry Park, which dates to 1836, is the site of the International African Arts Festival and other festivals and concerts, playing fields, and a pool.

HISTORY SNAPSHOTS

A community of free black shipbuilders and their families lived here in the first half of the nineteenth century. The Hanson Place Baptist Church (now the Hanson Place Seventh-day Adventist Church) harbored runaway slaves, part of the Underground Railroad. By the 1870s, the decade after the Civil War, more than half of Brooklyn's black population lived in Fort Greene. Irish, Italian, German, and English immigrants built much of what's now a historic district. Fort Greene's economy was tied to the nearby Brooklyn Navy Yard, which remained segregated, as the U.S. Navy did, through the mid-twentieth century.

Fort Greene Park was Brooklyn's first official park, designed by Frederick Law Olmsted and Calvert Vaux, architects of Central and Prospect Parks. Major

General Nathanael Greene first developed this steeply graded land as a fort in 1776 during the Revolutionary War. The towering Prison Ship Martyrs' Monument (1907), designed by Stanford White, honors 11,500 Revolutionary War patriots who died aboard British prison ships anchored nearby. Another fort was built here during the War of 1812. Walt Whitman advocated for this area to be designated a public park.

Fort Greene's residential and commercial vitality went downhill after World War II and was pulled back up by Brooklyn's, and especially BAM's, gradual ascendancy. From 1967 until 1999, BAM's executive director Harvey Lichtenstein helped catalyze remarkable transitions in BAM, greatly impacting its immediate surroundings. There's an active music and cultural scene here, the Greene Hill Food Coop, author readings, and discussion groups.

With a population of under thirty thousand that in 2010 remained predominantly nonwhite, Fort Greene on paper looks more racially and economically diverse than many neighborhoods. That's due in part to the coexistence of NYCHA public housing projects and expensive homes. "Apartments down the street you couldn't give away," an African American flautist and retired sound engineer who has lived here since the 1980s told the author, "are selling for a million bucks."

Spike Lee went on an amazing rant about newcomers to his old Brooklyn neighborhood "bogarting," slang for appropriating, it. (Read the transcript in the *Guardian*, February 2014.)

OLD/NEW BROOKLYN

Walt Whitman opined in his *Brooklyn Daily Eagle* that Fort Greene Park would be "a place of recreation where, on hot summer evenings, and Sundays, [people] can spend a few grateful hours in the enjoyment of wholesome rest and fresh air." He was prescient; that's certainly the case today.

Brooklyn's original "skyscraper," formerly the Williamsburgh Savings Bank (now condos called One Hanson and eclipsed by taller towers), was Brooklyn's tallest building—"bigger than London's Big Ben!" boosters would brag. It was visible from twenty-five miles away. Its four-faced clock retains most of its original mechanisms and equipment. Also see Brooklyn Technical High School, one of New York's best public high schools, founded in 1922 and still housed in a hulking, almost-century-old building.

Other points of continuity are the neighborhood's ongoing literary preeminence and the rebirth of cultural life and theaters along Fulton Street.

CELEBS, FILMS, FICTION

The honor roll of famous artists, musicians, poets, and writers who have lived in Fort Greene runs long. The writers Walt Whitman, Richard Wright, and Marianne

Moore, singer Betty Carter, and musicians Steve Coleman, Lester Bowie, Wayne Shorter, Slide Hampton, and Branford Marsalis lived in Fort Greene. More recent residents include Nelson George, Chris Rock, Cecil Taylor, and Rosie Perez.

Movies that shed light on aspects of Fort Greene include Spike Lee's films *She's Gotta Have It, Do the Right Thing,* and *Crooklyn. Brooklyn Boheme* depicts the Black Arts Movement in Fort Greene of the 1970s and 1980s, as told by writer/historian and resident Nelson George, featuring Chris Rock, Spike Lee, Branford Marsalis, Rosie Perez, Saul Williams, Lorna Simpson, and Talib Kweli. For fiction set here, read *Outerborough Blues*, by Andrew Cotto.

NOSHES, RESTAURANTS, BARS IN FORT GREENE

Black Iris 🏛, 228 DeKalb Avenue, (718) 852-9800
Chez Oskar 🏛, 211 DeKalb Avenue, (718) 852-6250
Frank's Cocktail Lounge 🏛, 660 Fulton Street, (718) 625-9339
The General Greene, 229 DeKalb Avenue, (718) 222-1510
Graziella's, 232 Vanderbilt Avenue, (718) 789-5663
ICI Restaurant: French Country Kitchen, 246 DeKalb Avenue, (718) 789-2778
Lean Crust, 737 Fulton Street, (718) 852-7567
LuLu & Po, 154 Carlton Avenue, (917) 435-3745
Madiba Restaurant 🏛, 195 DeKalb Avenue, (718) 855-9190
Roman's, 243 DeKalb Avenue, (718) 622-5300
The Smoke Joint, 87 South Elliott Place, (718) 797-1011
Walter's Fort Greene, 166 DeKalb Avenue, (718) 488-7800

SELECT DESTINATIONS

Note: Because destinations in Fort Greene overlap with the Brooklyn Cultural District, for BAM, BRIC House, MoCADA, the Mark Morris Dance Center, Irondale Ensemble Project, Theatre for a New Audience, and other cultural institutions, see "Brooklyn's Cultural Scene," section 4.

"Commandante Biggie": Biggie Smalls mural, corner of Fulton Street and South Portland Avenue

☞ Like Fort Greene? Visit other still-diverse brownstone neighborhoods: Bedford-Stuyvesant, Boerum Hill, Crown Heights, Prospect Heights, or Sunset Park.

Gowanus

Fact: A one-year-old harp seal was spotted swimming in the algae and garbage-littered Gowanus Canal in April 2003. It was rescued and named Gowanda before being returned to open waters.

Tiny Gowanus, named for the Gowanus Canal, is smack dab in the thick of things, proximate to desirable brownstone neighborhoods and not far from Prospect Park, BAM, and Barclays Center. New developments along the canal waterfront are changing the neighborhood, which some people predict will become Brooklyn's "Little Venice."

Oozing local color—the colors of red brick, industrial gray, and toxic sludge, to be precise—Gowanus is both decrepit and divine. A small spit of land and water separating Carroll Gardens and Park Slope, this unique ecological and industrial landscape bears almost no resemblance to the bourgeois brownstone neighborhoods it abuts. Painters, photographers, and romantics love its picturesque drabness. Gowanus is the spiritual sibling of that other Brooklyn post-industrial waterfront neighborhood, Red Hook.

Once-desolate Gowanus has sprouted nightlife, small bars, hip cafés, and popular restaurants. You can stand on a nineteenth-century bridge and watch the sunset light play on the water, help turn a compost heap, take a boat ride on the little canal, and drink cocktails. Cool. Or. What.

BEST BETS IN GOWANUS

1 Entertainment and culture: Check out the Morbid Anatomy Museum. The Bell House, a converted 1920s warehouse, is a popular concert and

BASICS

MAPPING: Using GPS, orient to Third Street Bridge or The Roof café at Whole Foods. Main drags: Union Street, 3rd and 4th Avenues. Use F, G (Smith and 9th Streets), R (4th Avenue and Union Street) subways. Near the neighborhoods of Carroll Gardens, Greenwood Heights, Park Slope, Sunset Park. Bounded roughly by the Gowanus Expressway, Butler and Hoyt Streets, 4th Avenue.

EVENTS: Earth Day, Gowanus Jazz Festival, Gowanus Open Studios, Oktoberfest, Rooftop Films.

SELFIES AND 'ZA: Selfies on the historic 1889 Carroll Street Bridge. For pizza, Bar Tano.

ACCOMMODATIONS: Gowanus hotels, Airbnb.

TIPS: Parking is tough. Although bikeable and walkable, at night Gowanus can feel lonely.

event venue. Littlefield's hosts parties and events. Royal Palms Shuffleboard is not your granny's shuffleboard; with expensive drinks and a food truck, it's a hip, young scene.

2   Eat! The new Brooklyn food aesthetic is well represented in Gowanus. Enjoy Runner & Stone's bakery-café; artisanal Pickle Shack with its humorous, pickle-centric snacks and craft brews; and the Pines' seasonal menu. At Littleneck, obviously, eat clams. For BBQ, try Dinosaur BBQ (a chain) or Fletcher's Brooklyn Barbecue. For sweets, Ample Hills Creamery's ice cream—including, on occasion, a special-to-Gowanus "toxic sludge" flavor—and Four and Twenty Blackbirds café's delicious pies satisfy.

3   Drink! Join a creative and professional crowd that gathers at such watering holes as Lavender Lake, Lowlands Bar, Halyards with its pool table, and pet-friendly Canal Bar. For an Aussie vibe, have a cold one at Sheep Station.

4   Hidden gems: Aficionados of vintage guitars, banjos, and other string instruments will be blown away by Retrofret's gorgeous curated selection and musical miscellany at its sister store, Musurgia. Build It Green sells cool salvaged stuff and surplus building materials.

5   Green eco-fun: Take a canal boat tour with the Gowanus Dredgers. The Gowanus Canal Conservancy, central to the waterway's revitalization, hosts volunteer weekends; help hoist ten thousand pounds of food scraps onto its compost piles. If you're interested in climate change and coastal sustainability, learn about award-winning 2nd Street Sponge Park, which sounds cuter than it looks.

6   Historic bridges: Walk the three oldest and most colorful of the canal's five historic bridges, at Carroll Street (1889), Third Street (1905), and Union Street (1905).

7   Climb! Brooklyn Boulders' indoor rock-climbing gym is a hit with families, energetic daters, and both the upwardly and downwardly mobile.

HISTORY SNAPSHOTS

This area was named by the Dutch after the indigenous Gowanus tribe, so if "Gowanus" sounds more Native American than Dutch, that's because it is.

Few people give the Gowanus Canal credit, but it was one of the factors that helped catapult Brooklyn from farmland to an industrial giant in the late nineteenth and early twentieth centuries. Gowanus also happened to have played a central role in the Revolutionary War's Battle of Brooklyn (see "DIY Tours," section 5).

In 1866, just after the Civil War, New York State approved the enlargement and straightening of the natural canal to allow barges to float goods via the Gowanus and New York Bays. The result was today's hundred-foot-wide, two-and-a-half-mile-long Gowanus Canal stretching from Gowanus Bay in New York Harbor to Douglass Street.

Brooklyn's subsequent industrial maritime history was, pun intended, water under the bridge. By 1880, dozens of lumber, coal, hay, grain, oil, and building materials companies were located near the canal. Later, gas and electric utilities, which required coal and coke, were built nearby.

The Gowanus was the nation's busiest—and most polluted—canal after World War I. Its use peaked in the 1920s, when some twenty-five thousand vessels carried goods from over fifty different manufacturers through it. Use dropped after World War II. Construction of the Gowanus Expressway in 1964, a Robert Moses plan, diminished reliance on waterways for industrial transportation. The canal became a stinking dumping ground for toxic material, garbage, and waste, with tires, garbage, and ooze floating on it. The 1905 pumping station at 209 Douglass Street and still in use almost a century later was not quite up to the task of flushing the canal. In 1998, a $450 million sewage-treatment plant was installed. Voilà! Soon after, fish, oysters, waterfowl, and even the seal named Gowanda were sighted. Still, at the bottom of the canal, a toxic mix lurks. And in heavy rains, sewage has overrun into the canal. Over the city's dead body—it wanted to handle the problem itself, still, after all these years—the federal Environmental Protection Agency designated the Gowanus Canal a Superfund site in 2010, to be remediated by 2020 (fingers crossed, but nobody is holding their breath).

Gowanus was a mixed-use, largely industrial neighborhood. Today a few surviving "authentic Gowanus homes" have sold for millions as antiques or been torn down to make way for the multistory apartment buildings now rising.

CEMENT SHOES AND THE GOWANUS CANAL: FACT OR LEGEND?

Gowanus was once associated with oysters, manufacturing plants, the Mafia, and a rough crowd. A review of over a century's worth of newspaper stories suggests that some pretty dirty business has been associated with Gowanus. In 1888, the *New York Times* reported that Mrs. Wall said that her murdered husband was dumped in the canal after a man "came knocking" at her door. In 1931, a Gowanus racketeer's body was pulled from the canal, and his murderer was indicted. In 1936, in an era when the mob was muscling itself into the dockyards, the paper reports that the president of the local Grain Handlers Union "was discovered, bound and garroted in Gowanus waters," and his killers were also found guilty of shooting to death another shipyard owner. How many bodies ended up in the Gowanus Canal? Nobody's saying, and nobody knows for sure.

Teddy Roosevelt, campaigning in Brooklyn in 1898 to become governor, found here a "brickbat district" and the "home of the stiletto" knife. Gowanus was subsequently infamous for toxic brownfields and stench. Now it's chock-a-block with hotels, restaurants, bars and cafés, and condos.

OLD/NEW BROOKLYN

The very word *Gowanus* resonates with the grit of its namesakes: the Gowanus Expressway, Gowanus Houses (a fourteen-building public housing project with over twenty-five hundred residents), Gowanus Parole Center (a New York State facility serving hundreds of parolees), and of course, the Gowanus Canal.

New Brooklyn is bursting out all over old Gowanus. Just blocks from Two Toms Restaurant, a well-liked, old-school-Brooklyn meat-and-potatoes eatery, is a rather special Whole Foods store, designed with a green roof and a café and powered by wind turbines. Saint Lydia's bills itself as a "dinner church and co-working space" and a GLBTQ-affirming congregation. The nonprofit Textile Arts Center engages people in textile arts; you can see them through the big windows, weaving on big floor looms. Groundswell, a nonprofit that engages high-risk teens by creating outdoor building murals (visible all over Brooklyn), and the nonprofit GallopNYC, dedicated to helping disabled people through therapeutic horsemanship, are based here. Spanking-new town houses have been built with exteriors that mimic those of old-Brooklyn brick homes (442 Union Street, for instance). Eight residential towers are in the pipeline; in this industrial area of brown sludge and red brick, the development, named Gowanus Green, is betting on a new color scheme. Green, of all things, is the one color that old Gowanus never was.

The nonprofit Build It Green in Gowanus sells salvaged, surplus building materials. (Photo by E. Freudenheim, 2015)

Stirring up old and new as though in a petri dish, Gowanus is in a huge transition. The link between past, present, and future is the Gowanus Canal itself.

CELEBS, FILMS, FICTION

Monte's Restaurant, an old Brooklyn and Gowanus fixture since 1906 (renovated beyond recognition in 2011) was used as a film set for both John Huston's 1985 *Prizzi's Honor* and John Turturro's 1990 *Men of Respect*. For a memorable quote about the stench of the old Gowanus Canal, read Thomas Wolfe's otherwise not very Brooklyn *Of Time and the River*.

NOSHES, RESTAURANTS, BARS IN GOWANUS

Ample Hills Creamery Ice Cream, 305 Nevins Street, (347) 725-4061
Fletcher's Brooklyn Barbecue, 433 3rd Avenue, (347) 763-2680
Monte's Restaurant ☎, 451 Carroll Street, (718) 852-7800
Pickle Shack, 256 4th Avenue, (347) 763-2127
The Pines, 284 3rd Avenue, (718) 596-6560
Runner & Stone, 285 3rd Avenue, (718) 576-3360
Two Toms Restaurant ☎, 255 3rd Avenue, (718) 875-8689
Whole Foods Café, 214 3rd Street, (718) 907-3622

SELECT DESTINATIONS

Bar Tano, 457 3rd Avenue, (718) 499-3400
The Bell House, 149 7th Street, (718) 643-6510
Brooklyn Boulders, 75 Degraw Street, (347) 834-9066
Gowanus Canal Conservancy, Smith Street at 8th Street, (718) 541-4378
Gowanus Canal Dredgers Launch, 2nd Street and Canal, (718) 243-0849
Groundswell, https://www.groundswell.nyc/, (718) 254-9782
Royal Palms Shuffleboard Club, 514 Union Street, (347) 223-4410
Saint Lydia's, 304 Bond Street, (646) 580-1247
Textile Arts Center, 505 Carroll Street, (718) 369-0222

☞ Like Gowanus? Visit Red Hook, Dumbo, and Bushwick.

Greenpoint

The *Monitor* has been called the most famous ship in American history. . . . Swedish-American engineer John Ericsson presented a conceptual design of a steam-powered, ironclad ship with a rotating gun turret to the U.S. Navy and promised to build it in 100 days. On January 30, 1862 . . . the USS *Monitor* launched from Greenpoint.

— USS *Monitor* brochure, NOAA.gov

BASICS

MAPPING: Using GPS, orient to McGolrick Park near the Monitor Memorial statue. Main drags: Greenpoint and Manhattan Avenues. Use East River Ferry or G (Greenpoint Avenue) or L (Bedford Avenue) subways. Near the neighborhoods of Williamsburg and Long Island City in the borough of Queens. Bounded roughly by North 14th Street, Newtown Creek, the BQE, the East River.

EVENTS: Concerts in McCarren Park, Go Green! Greenpoint Festival, other events by nonprofit Town Square.

SELFIES AND 'ZA: Selfies at landmark cast-iron street clock, 753 Manhattan Avenue. Pizza at Paulie Gee's.

GREENMARKET: Saturdays year-round at Union and Driggs Avenues.

ACCOMMODATIONS: Box House, Hotel Norman, Airbnb, hotels in Williamsburg, Greenpoint YMCA.

How can you not love a place where Lena Dunham's series *Girls* was filmed, where a laundromat has vintage pinball machines, and where the battleship the *Monitor* was launched?

Welcome to Greenpoint, one of North Brooklyn's smallest neighborhoods. It's adorable with numerous cafés, bars, and interesting small venues mixed in with mom-and-pop stores run by the long-established Polish community. Brooklyn's most European-feeling area, Greenpoint has a nice mix of newish hip cafés, bars, and restaurants, alongside old-timers' places like Peter Pan Donut & Pastry Shop and Kiszka and Sikorski, both butchers with kielbasa hanging in the windows. There's human-scaled and genteel McGolrick Park and a still-gentle pace. It's located about half a mile as the crow flies across the East River from Manhattan's Stuyvesant Town, at about East Twentieth Street. Mid-Manhattan's skyscrapers, visible from many places, look like a distant Oz.

Visitors can "do" Greenpoint in a few hours. Don't miss Transmitter Park with its classic New York City views. Take your pick of appealing small shops—clothing boutiques, awesome vintage stores, even a specialty shop with old vinyl records.

As the joke goes, Greenpoint is "suburban Williamsburg." Indeed, it's a respite from crowded, condo-dense Williamsburg, just a ten-minute walk away. Expansive McCarren Park sits between the two neighborhoods, a green buffer and point of connection.

If Greenpoint were a cocktail, it'd be a Williamsburg with a twist of Krakow. Once a seemingly timeless, quiet community with a large Polish (combined with Irish and Italian) population, it's been enlivened by the arrival of young professionals and college grads. According to Pandora's "What's Playing in New York City" 2014 music map, Greenpoint's listening to hair bands, hipster BBQ, and hipster cocktail-party music.

It used to be tough to find a place to rent or buy in Greenpoint. As in many ethnic neighborhoods, Greenpoint's landlords preferred to rent and sell apartments within their community network to friends and family. The rise of Williamsburg changed the game.

Local issues involve the environment and gentrification. Greenpoint activists are demanding public waterfront access, in the form of the proposed twenty-eight-acre Bushwick Inlet Park (so called despite not being located in Bushwick). Bushwick Inlet Park was promised to the community by the city as part of a 2005 development deal. As developers erect apartment towers in Greenpoint, and given the construction of five thousand apartments in ten waterfront towers called Greenpoint Landing, slated for completion by 2025, rents will likely only go up. Some artists and old-timers are being displaced, and the ethnic character of the area is slowly being diluted.

BEST BETS IN GREENPOINT

1   Eat and drink: Have cocktails at Ramona, brunch or dinner at Habitat, Enid's, Five Leaves, or Anella. Sample the raw bar at Greenpoint Fish & Lobster Company. Bring the kids to LaFond for brunch. Chill over a craft beer and tacos at Greenpoint Heights. Have Scandinavian tidbits at Michelin-rated Luksus. Stuff your face on hardy workingman's meals at Polish restaurants like Karczma. Dive into a cream-filled doughnut at Peter Pan Donut & Pastry Shop.

2   Waterfront: Paddle with the North Brooklyn Boat Club. Near the waterfront, splurge on Glasserie's Mediterranean fare, savor a sandwich at Eagle Trading, or just ogle the Manhattan views at Transmitter Park.

3   Shop: Try on vintage gear at Beacon's Closet, People of 2morrow, Seven Wonders Vintage, and Fox & Fawn. Get vinyl records at Co-op 87. Browse the shelves at WORD independent bookstore and in curated clothing and lifestyle boutiques such as Wolves Within.

4   Architecture/history: The huge old factory at 1155 Manhattan Avenue is Greenpoint Manufacturing and Design Center, repurposed to house small

entrepreneurs; it's full of artists' studios and light manufacturing companies. Walk by the Queen Anne–style historic Astral Apartments, dating to the 1880s. The building was commissioned by industry baron Charles Pratt for workers at his Astral Oil Works refinery. The historic *Monitor* warship was built near Quay Street over 150 years ago; look for the sign describing the *Monitor*'s history. Join a tour offered by Preservation Greenpoint or other history organizations.

5   Ferry and bike: You can board a seasonal East River Ferry and head to Dumbo. Hop a Citi Bike and take a short ride to PS 1 MOMA art museum in Long Island City.

6   Green: Visit Eagle Street Rooftop Farm, a commercial green roof, open to visitors during the growing season on Sundays. Get the scoop on Bushwick Inlet Park.

7   Bargain fish: The city's biggest wholesaler of smoked fish, Acme, opens its smokehouse to the public every Friday.

8   Kitchen sink: Vast and modern, Brooklyn Expo Center is an event space that hosts all kind of events: animal-adoptions, chef showcases, craft and food markets, and record fairs. Check their calendar.

9   Environmental education: Visit the new Greenpoint library branch, one of the system's busiest. It has a large Polish collection. And with funds from the Exxon settlement, it's building the Greenpoint Environmental Education Center.

HISTORY SNAPSHOTS

The Dutch bought this land in 1638 from the Keshaechqueren Indians. By the mid-1800s, Greenpoint was an industrial center for the "five black arts": glass making, pottery making, printing, refining, and the manufacture of cast iron. Shipbuilding thrived. The Civil War iron gunship the *Monitor* was launched in 1862 from a dock near Oak and West Streets. A Monitor Trail sign marks the original site of the Continental Iron Works; it's part of a historic trail being created by the National Oceanographic and Atmospheric Administration.

In the historic district, streets perpendicular to the East River were named alphabetically: Ash, Box, Clay, Dupont, Eagle, Freeman, Green, Huron, India, Java, Kent, Greenpoint (formerly Lincoln), Milton, Noble, and Oak Streets. Meander around what's probably the only landmarked area named after a tool from your elementary school backpack: the "Eberhard Faber Pencil Factory District."

Polish, Russian, and Italian immigration to Greenpoint began in the late 1880s and continued after World War II. For decades, Greenpoint was a blue-collar ethnic neighborhood. Since 2005 zoning changes to the waterfront and the growth of nearby Williamsburg, Greenpoint's rate of gentrification has accelerated.

THE POLISH CONNECTION

Greenpoint is the heart of New York's Polish community, and St. Stanislaus Kostka Church is the heart of Polish Greenpoint. Pope John Paul II visited Saint Stanislaus Kostka twice—as pope in 1979 and as Karol Cardinal Wojtyla in 1969. In 2010, the church held a special service in honor of the thirtieth anniversary of the independent trade union Solidarity, which helped win Polish independence from the Soviet Union. The Polish & Slavic Center, founded in 1972, provides social services.

OLD/NEW BROOKLYN

You can find many points of continuity in Greenpoint between past and present. The legacy of Brooklyn's industrial past weighs heavily in four-mile-long Newtown Creek, separating Brooklyn from Queens and designated a polluted Superfund site in 2010. Exxon agreed to a $25 million settlement, of which $19.5 million was earmarked for environmental improvement, payback for years of oil-storage-tank spills in the soil underneath Greenpoint. The neighborhood is embroiled today in a tug-of-war with municipal officials and commercial interests over the very thing that made it an attractive area for industrial manufacturing barons over a hundred years ago. It's still all about waterfront resources: who has access, and what kind of access, to valuable land, property, and waterways.

The brilliantly conceived Greenpoint Manufacturing and Design Center (GMDC) was formed in 1992 as a nonprofit dedicated to rehabbing abandoned industrial buildings into affordable workspaces for artists, artisans, and light industry. Its first successful project was the behemoth 1155 Manhattan Avenue, which once housed such businesses as a rope factory and die works. Today its tenant list includes woodworkers, architects, metal fabricators, and other "makers." GMDC is New York's premier nonprofit industrial developer. It seeks to create a replicable model for other postindustrial cities seeking manufacturing-job-creation strategies.

Greenpoint illustrates Brooklyn's pivot from its past muscular industrial economy of belching smokestacks, polluted waters, and brut physical labor. This author's 2004 guide *Brooklyn! The Ultimate Guide to New York's Most Happening Borough* said, "Suddenly, there's a buzz going on about—of all places—Greenpoint. For years 'Greenpernt' as it was pronounced by true Brooklynites, was dispatched with an airy wave of the hand. Greenpoint, a destination? No way." Yes way. Thanks to real estate, hospitality, retail, tourism, and artisanal businesses, "Greenpernt" is a thing of the past.

CELEBS, FILMS, FICTION

WNYC's popular radio host Leonard Lopate lives here (read his "Brooklyn Voices"). Lena Dunham's HBO television series *Girls* is set in Greenpoint. For fiction, read *The Astral* by Kate Christensen and *The Lullaby of Polish Girls* by Dagmara Dominczyk.

NOSHES, RESTAURANTS, BARS IN GREENPOINT

Bar Matchless, 557 Manhattan Avenue, (718) 383-5333
Black Rabbit, 91 Greenpoint Avenue, (718) 349-1595
Café Grumpy, 193 Meserole Avenue, (718) 349-7623
Eastern District, 1053 Manhattan Avenue, (718) 349-1432
Luksus at Torst, 615 Manhattan Avenue, (718) 389-6034
Paulie Gee's, 60 Greenpoint Avenue, (347) 987-3737
Peter Pan Donut & Pastry Shop ☎, 727 Manhattan Avenue, (718) 389-3676
Ramona, 113 Franklin Street, (347) 227-8164
Rosemary's Greenpoint Tavern ☎, 188 Bedford Avenue, (718) 384-9539

SELECT DESTINATIONS

Astral Apartments, 184 Franklin Street between Java and India Streets
Beacon's Closet, 74 Guernsey Street, (718) 486-0816
Brooklyn Expo Center, 72 Noble Street, (718) 775-3315
Eagle Street Rooftop Farms, 44 Eagle Street, http://rooftopfarms.org
Greenpoint Clock, 753 Manhattan Avenue, between Norman and Meserole
    Streets
NOAA Monitor Warship Marker, 56 Quay Street, Bushwick Inlet and
    East River
North Brooklyn Boat Club, 437 McGuinness Boulevard, http://northbrooklyn
    boatclub.org, (347) 915-6222
Saint Stanislaus Kostka Church, 607 Humboldt Street, (718) 388-0170
Sunshine Laundry, 860 Manhattan Avenue, (718) 475-2055
WORD Brooklyn, 126 Franklin Street, (718) 383-0096

☞ Like Greenpoint? Visit Williamsburg, Bushwick, Red Hook, or Clinton Hill.

Greenwood Heights

Whether you are interested in history, sculpture, architecture, trees, birds, spring bloom, fall foliage, or just a quiet stroll, Green-Wood is the place for you. Our motto: "Come visit while you still can leave!"
  —Jeffrey I. Richman, Green-Wood Cemetery historian

Greenwood Heights is a residential neighborhood on a hill; in places, you can enjoy a clear sightline to the Statue of Liberty. Nestled between South Park Slope and Sunset Park, teeny Greenwood Heights takes its name from verdant, park-like Green-Wood, an arboretum, historic cemetery, and event venue. It's a low-key place to eat, drink, and chill.

Formerly lumped in with Sunset Park or just "South Brooklyn," the area had a working-class and ethnically diverse population of Latino, Polish American, and Italian American residents. It was rechristened "Greenwood Heights" and gussied up in the late 1990s by realtors and developers seeking to attract buyers priced out of Park Slope, half a mile away. Since then, housing prices and apartment buildings in Greenwood Heights have both risen. More than one characterful, unrenovated, century-old home owned by the same family for fifty or seventy years has sold for nearly a million dollars—just to be bulldozed and replaced with nondescript condos.

BEST BETS IN GREENWOOD HEIGHTS

1 Bar fun: Greenwood Park is a big, friendly, indoor/outdoor beer garden. Enjoy comedy, live music, and bar food at retro Freddy's Bar. It was driven out of its longstanding Fort Greene location when Barclays Center was built.

2 Really good food: Find good pizza here, or gobble down Korzo Haus's fried
   burgers and Hungarian langos bread. For new American cuisine, go to Lot 2.
   Baked in Brooklyn sells fresh-baked goods also sold in Baked café in Red Hook.
3 Green-Wood: Green-Wood is a beautiful setting for a stroll, entrance-free.
   Book online to take a trolley tour to learn about its exciting "permanent
   residents." Green-Wood's Visitors Center opens in 2016 in the renovated,
   all-glass, 1895 Wier Greenhouse, a landmark. (See "Brooklyn's Cultural Scene,"
   section 4.)
4 Sunset views of New York Harbor: Feast your eyes from atop Twenty-First
   and Twenty-Third Streets. (Or, if you stay at Freddy's till closing, see the view
   at sunrise.)
5 Stories: Find an old-timer to schmooze with, for a memorable experience.

HISTORY SNAPSHOTS

When this area was first developed, in the late 1800s and early 1900s, many of
its residents labored in Green-Wood Cemetery or in shipping or heavy industry
in Sunset Park and Gowanus. The houses were practical; many still have vinyl
siding. Today it's a cozy little neighborhood, though in the middle of it is a block-
wide utility plant. Still, you can time-travel back a century or so by strolling down
Webster and Jackson Places, lined by attractive old row houses that are typical of
old Brooklyn.

NOSHES, RESTAURANTS, BARS IN GREENWOOD HEIGHTS

Baked in Brooklyn Bakery Store, 755 5th Avenue, (718) 788-3164
Beer Garden at Greenwood Park, 555 7th Avenue, (718) 768-0131
Breuckelen Distilling, 77 19th Street, (347) 725-4985
Freddy's Bar ♟, 627 5th Avenue, (718) 768-0131
Guiseppina's, 691 6th Avenue, (718) 499-5052
Korzo Haus, 667 5th Avenue, (718) 499-1199
Toby's Public House, 686 6th Avenue, (718) 788-1186

SELECT DESTINATIONS

Green-Wood Cemetery and Arboretum, Visitors Center, 500 25th Street,
   (718) 768-7300

☞ Like Greenwood Heights? Visit Brooklyn Botanic Garden and other historic
cemeteries. (Learn more about both in "Brooklyn's Cultural Scene," section 4.)

Marine Park

> Join [the] Urban Park Rangers as your guides to the solar system, discussing the science, history, and folklore of the universe.
>
> —Marine Park Geminids Meteor Shower skyviewing, NYC Parks Department, 2015

If the Big Apple, city of nine million, has small-town enclaves, count Marine Park as one of them.

Come to visit the park for which this neighborhood is named, an eight-hundred-acre marshy area, with a public golf course and playing fields. The educational Salt Marsh Center makes for a cool outing for kids, because what kid doesn't love squishy hands-on encounters with small sea creatures? Find tasty and affordable Italian food and roast beef. Marine Park, Mill Basin, and the neighborhoods of Bergen Beach and Georgetown (not covered in this book) have a total population of about forty-five thousand, almost 75 percent white—a medley of Irish, Italian, and Jewish residents.

BEST BETS IN MARINE PARK

1 Old-Brooklyn cuisine: Do as generations have done: stuff your face with roast beef at Brennan & Carr, one of Brooklyn's oldest eateries (est. 1938). Enjoy traditional Italian Sunday lunch at Michael's of Brooklyn.
2 Year-round golf: Play eighteen holes of golf on a waterfront public course.
3 Marine Park and outdoor sports: Play tennis or baseball, run on a track, stretch your legs—all within vast Marine Park. Or watch a cricket

BASICS

MAPPING: Using GPS, orient to Brennan & Carr's. Main drags: Quentin Road, Avenue S. No convenient subway. Drive, bike, or take a bus. Near Gateway National Recreation Area and Kings Plaza Mall and the neighborhoods of Flatlands, Midwood, Mill Basin, Sheepshead Bay. Bounded roughly by the park, Kings Highway, Avenue P, Gerritsen and Flatbush Avenues.

EVENTS: Kite-flying, bird-watching, biking, bocce, summertime concerts.

SELFIES AND 'ZA: Selfies at the Salt Marsh Center or a cricket match. One reviewer called Frank's Pizza the "Sophia Loren" of pizza.

ACCOMMODATIONS: Airbnb.

match or the annual bocce contest. Rent pedal boats or kayaks from Wheel Fun Rentals to explore Gerritsen Creek.

4   Environmental education: Visit the Salt Marsh Nature Center (seasonal).

5   Model-plane hobbyists: Watch radio-controlled planes flown at John V. Lindsay Model Airport.

6   How people live: Drive or bike through the tiny, half-mile-wide residential waterfront neighborhood of Gerritsen Beach next to Marine Park, with its modest beach-bungalow ambiance. Many homes have small docks.

7   Visit the historic Hendrik I. Lott House, an 1800s Dutch farmhouse (reopening 2016–2017).

OLD/NEW BROOKLYN

Remarkable because it's so unremarkable, Marine Park is old school—a close-knit community of working- and middle-class families, some with roots going back to when much of the area's housing was built, in the 1930s. It's the kind of place where the Little League chapter is named for homegrown hero Joe Torre, former Yankees manager. It's not notably progressive; a brouhaha over the bocce club's exclusion of women didn't erupt until . . . 2013.

CELEBS, FILMS, FICTION

When James Gandolfini's last movie, *The Drop* (formerly titled *Animal Rescue*), was filmed here, it's said he bonded with the "regular" working-class people. *St. Vincent*, starring Bill Murray, was shot here; you can find the title character's house on Batchelder Street and Avenue T. Read the novel *Marine Park* by native Mark Chiusano.

NOSHES, RESTAURANTS, BARS IN MARINE PARK

Brennan & Carr ☎, 3432 Nostrand Avenue, (718) 646-9559
Frank's Pizza ☎, 2134 Flatbush Avenue, (718) 377-8100
Jay & Lloyd's Kosher Deli ☎, 2718 Avenue U, (718) 891-5298
Michael's of Brooklyn ☎, 2929 Avenue R, (718) 998-7851

SELECT DESTINATIONS

Boat and bike rental: Wheel Fun Rentals, Avenue U and East 33rd Street, (917) 533-6196
Hendrik I. Lott House, 1940 East 36th Street, http://www.lotthouse.org
John V. Lindsay Model Airport, Gerritsen Avenue between Seba and Lois Avenues behind the Seba Playground

Marine Park Golf Course, 2880 Flatbush Avenue, (718) 252-4625
Salt Marsh Center, Avenue U and East 33rd Street, (718) 421-2021

☞ Looking for "Deep Brooklyn"? You've found it.

Mill Basin and Floyd Bennett Field

A crowd of more than 50,000 watched as "23 leading avia-trices" competed in this 40-mile race for $850 first prize." Amelia Earhart was the race Starter . . . (June 4, 1933).
—National Park Service, "Floyd Bennett Field Historic Flights"

BASICS

MAPPING: Using GPS, orient to Kings Plaza Mall or Aviator Sports. Main drags: Flatbush Avenue, Avenue U, Aviator Road. Best to drive or bike. Near Belt Parkway, Kings Plaza Mall, Jamaica Bay, Marine Park. Bounded by Jamaica Bay, Avenue U, Mill Basin / Mill Island Inlet.

EVENTS: Antique Automobile Association of Brooklyn rally, Native American Pow Wow, North Forty Nature Trail walk.

SELFIES AND 'ZA: Selfies at Floyd Bennett Field. Try Lenny and John's Pizzeria, flipping pies since 1969.

ACCOMMODATIONS: Airbnb at nearby Neponsit, a beachfront community in Queens. No passport required.

An unpredictable pairing: the marvelously untamed Floyd Bennett Field and the neighborhood of Mill Basin are at the southeast tip of Brooklyn, at the end of Flatbush Avenue. They're also near to two places in another New York City borough, Queens, worth knowing about: Riis Park beach and the Rockaways' arty bungalow community and surfboarding beach.

This is New York? Floyd Bennett Field, a historic airfield within the Jamaica Bay Unit of the National Park Service's Gateway National Recreation Area, is full of opportunities for unlikely urban adventures. Eloise of Plaza fame would have loved it all: the real live powwows, the tromping through the bushes to go bird-watching, the crazily fast bicycle races, and hanging around Hangar B watching expert volunteers restore vintage aircraft, which, if you are lucky, you might be able to clamber inside. You can sign up for overnight summertime outdoor camping (bare bones), go horseback riding nearby (not bareback), and watch the zucchinis grow in hundreds of garden plots reminiscent of Britain's victory gardens. You can see the Empire State Building's spire in the distance.

Aviator Sports and Events Center, located on-site in Floyd Bennett Field in a converted airplane hangar, offers such indoor activities as rock climbing, gymnastics, and ice-skating even in sweltering summer.

In contrast, adjacent Mill Basin is small, residential, and conservative, a waterfront neighborhood of about thirty-five thousand residents. Some homes have private docks. If you see boats bobbing in the water when driving past Kings Plaza, en route to Floyd Bennett or Riis Park beach, that's Mill Basin. On the map, it's a tiny area surrounded by water on three sides.

BEST BETS IN MILL BASIN AND FLOYD BENNETT FIELD

If you're interested in shopping, go to Kings Plaza Mall (for the roster of stores there, see "Shopping in Brooklyn," section 4). Otherwise:

1 Eat! Have ices at the classic Dolly's Ices. For Italian food, head to Avenues N and T for favorites like Massimo's Ristorante and "to-go" meals at La Torre Pork Store. La Villa, which has a twin in Park Slope, serves up tasty pizza and enormous Italian entrees. Moretti Bakery is a fave for its fresh-baked breads.
2 Historic aircraft at Floyd Bennett Field: Visit the 1930s Ryan Visitor Center for exhibits on the age of aviation in New York City. Also see vintage aircraft at the Historic Aircraft Restoration Project (HARP); limited hours.
3 Golf: Enjoy an urban driving range and miniature golf at the Brooklyn Golf Center.
4 Family fun at Aviator Sports and Events Center: A million visitors a year come to rock climb, play basketball, skate, watch competitions and shows, do water-balloon battle, run 5K "Color Run" races while covered in paint, and compete in obstacle-course events.
5 Outdoors-in-the-city adventures: Enjoy hiking trails, fishing, kayak trips, ecology expeditions, gardening events, urban camping, and group stargazing at Floyd Bennett Field. Walk, jog, or bike the waterside Jamaica Bay Greenway.
6 Riding, both horses and bikes: At Jamaica Bay Riding Academy, ride horses along wooded trails. At Kissena Cycling Club's weekly bicycle-racing series, you can watch cyclists zoom around the track at Floyd Bennett Field.
7 Explore the coast by bike: Cycle across the Marine Parkway Bridge to Queens to explore Fort Tilden, Riis Park, and the Rockaways.
8 Kid friendly: Don't miss the Kings County Fair and the Redhawk Native American Arts Council powwow, called Gateway to the Nations.

HISTORY SNAPSHOTS

Floyd Bennett Field was New York City's first municipal airport. It was named after a Congressional Medal of Honor–winning pilot who was the first person to fly over the North Pole; at the 1931 dedication ceremony when it opened, 672 Army planes did a flyby. Howard Hughes, Douglas "Wrong Way" Corrigan, Wiley Post, Laura H. Ingalls, and other famous pilots flew from this airport, as did future astronaut John Glenn.

Amelia Earhart was here, too. She was the race starter for an all-women's race in 1933, watched by a crowd of fifty thousand spectators. She participated in an all-women's Bendix Trophy Race from Floyd Bennett Field to Burbank, California, in 1936. An air parade was held here months after she disappeared over the Pacific Ocean in 1937; at the parade, according to the National Parks Service, "civilian planes joined those from the Navy, Coast Guard and Army in the fly by."

Floyd Bennett Field was converted into a Naval Air Station in 1941 and during World War II was the nation's most active airport. (Learn more in "Brooklyn's Waterfront and Parks," section 4; for Bennett's biography, see the National Park Service website.)

OLD/NEW BROOKLYN

Floyd Bennett Field is a trip, in many ways, including to the past. And Mill Basin is, too; the farm-to-table-type restaurants and the hipster aesthetic of the new-Brooklyn renaissance are decidedly absent.

CELEBS, FILMS, FICTION

Comedian Jimmy Kimmel was born and stayed in Mill Basin until the ripe age of nine. The 1933 film *King Kong* includes a scene shot at Floyd Bennett Field. A fake North-South Korean border was built in Floyd Bennett Field as a set for the 2010 film *Salt*, with Angelina Jolie and Liev Schreiber.

NOSHES, RESTAURANTS, BARS IN MILL BASIN

Dolly's Italian Ices ☎, 5805 Avenue T, (347) 582-1072
La Villa Restaurant ☎, 6610 Avenue U, (718) 251-8030
Lenny and John's Pizzeria ☎, 2036 Flatbush Avenue, (718) 252-9710
Mill Basin Kosher Deli ☎, 5823 Avenue T, (718) 241-4910
Moretti Bakery ☎, 4524 Avenue N, (718) 377-5364

SELECT DESTINATIONS

Aviator Sports and Events Center, 3159 Flatbush Avenue, (718) 758-7500
Brooklyn Golf Center, 3200 Flatbush Avenue, (718) 253-6816
Floyd Bennett Field, North Forty Nature Trail, Historic Aircraft Restoration
    Project, 50 Aviator Road, (718) 338-3799
Jamaica Bay Riding Academy, 7000 Shore Parkway, (718) 531-8949

☞ Like Mill Basin? For off the beaten track, visit Red Hook.

Park Slope

Whether Bill and I are dining at our favorite eatery, enjoying an art experience at the Brooklyn Museum, or taking a stroll through Prospect Park, we can't help but feel the energy that makes Brooklyn so special. From Williamsburg to Park Slope to Red Hook, Brooklyn is truly a beautiful mosaic of neighborhoods and communities and a place we're so proud to call home.

—Chirlane McCray, First Lady of New York City, Park Slope resident

Park Slope, named for its proximity to Prospect Park, is arguably Brooklyn's most famous brownstone neighborhood. "The Slope" includes a vast historic district of nineteenth-century town houses; outstanding historical architecture; genteel, tree-lined streets; and an engaged community.

Jog, bike, or walk in the park. Admire the rows of decorative row houses and the "Gold Coast" urban mansions along Prospect Park West. Oscar the Grouch doesn't live in a Brooklyn trash bin, but some brownstone streets, with their stoops, resemble a stage set from *Sesame Street*. Peruse the one-off boutiques. Chill at the Gate bar, the Chocolate Room, or Guerilla Coffee. Attend a reading or musical performance at intimate Barbès. Play indoor bocce and have drinks while snuggled up near a working fireplace at Union Hall.

Somewhat to the neighborhood's own surprise, Park Slope has been lauded as one of New York's most desirable residential areas, by *New York* magazine, the American Planning Association, and others. It's got a winning mix: access to transportation, controlled population density, parks, stores, restaurants, good schools, and civic engagement. It's a casual

BASICS

MAPPING: Using GPS, orient to the Old Stone House. Main drags: 5th and 7th Avenues. Use 2, 3 (Grand Army Plaza), F, G (9th Street), Q, B (7th Avenue), R (Union Street, 4th Avenue) subways. Near BAM, Barclays Center, Brooklyn Cultural District, Prospect Park, and the neighborhoods of Gowanus, Prospect Heights, Windsor Terrace. Bounded roughly by 4th and Flatbush Avenues, Prospect Park West, 16th Street

EVENTS: BRIC Celebrate Brooklyn! summer festival, Christmas-tree and huge menorah lightings, PRIDE, Prospect Park's New Year's Eve fireworks, St. Patrick's Day parade.

SELFIES AND 'ZA: Selfies on a brownstone stoop. For pizza, Franny's.

GREENMARKETS: Saturdays year-round at Grand Army Plaza. Sunday and Wednesday afternoons year-round in Washington Park. Wednesdays year-round at Bartel-Prichard Square.

ACCOMMODATIONS: Hotels in Gowanus, Airbnb, local bed-and-breakfasts.

place—but, now, expensive! Brownstone homes that cost $250,000 in the 1980s now sell for $3 million. Today that original quarter of a million dollars could buy you just a "car condo garage" at the Park Slope Garage Condominium, literally a condominium for parking spots.

BEST BETS IN PARK SLOPE

1 Munch, brunch, and drink! For restaurants, try al di la Trattoria, Applewood, Talde, and Fonda. Weekend brunch at Miriam and Bogota are popular. Try Alchemy and Pacific Standard bars, near Barclays Center, or the Owl Farm, offering an esoteric beer menu.

2 Brooklyn literary culture: Hear an author read at the Old Stone House or the Park Slope Community Bookstore, about which a customer once said, "They sell books with a tenderness you'd expect from people selling puppies."

3 Prospect Park: Bring the kids to the Prospect Park Zoo, the old-fashioned Carousel, and free events at the Historic Lefferts House or Audubon Center. Rent a novelty bike, kayak, or pedal boat, go ice- and roller-skating. (For details, see "Brooklyn's Waterfront and Parks," section 4.)

4 Cool boutiques and shops: So many stores, so little time—and such names! Lulu's is a kids' hair salon and toy store. Kiwi, Bird, and Otto are all women's boutiques. Clay Pot is known for gifts, unusual jewelry (some by local designers), and engagement and wedding rings. Babeland is the coolest sex-toy shop in Brooklyn. Park Slope has a dozen vintage stores including Beacon's Closet. Food stores range from Fleisher's Craft Butchery to artisanal, farm-to-table food at BKLYN Larder. Purchase a can of "immortality" at Brooklyn Superhero Supply, a tutoring center ingeniously fronted by a fantasy store. Cyclists might want to visit the bricks-and-mortar shop of R&A, known to online shoppers. (See "Shopping in Brooklyn," section 4.)

5 Landmarked nineteenth-century homes and buildings: Wander to your heart's content. The best blocks are between Prospect Park and Seventh Avenue, from Union to Third Streets. See the Montauk Club and the lavish 1892 Grand Prospect Hall (now renovated into a catering hall and beer garden), where Enrico Caruso, Sophie Tucker, Mae West, Sonja Henie, and Fred Astaire once performed. (For more information, see the Historic Districts Council online.)

"NORTH," "SOUTH," AND "PC" PARK SLOPE

People refer to the "North" and "South" Slope. It's all one neighborhood. The invisible line of demarcation is Ninth Street. The North Slope boasts bigger, fancier homes. The South Slope's once-more-modest homes have been gussied up, and nearby are a slew of casual bars, cafés, and interesting restaurants. On Fifth Avenue, from Ninth to Sixteenth Streets, rows of stores selling hardware and cheap

BROOKLYN VOICES

PARK SLOPE FOOD COOP MEMBER #9008D

A lot of Park Slopers wouldn't be caught dead here. But I love it. The Park Slope Food Coop is the largest member owned and run food cooperative in the United States. People poke fun at it (thanks, Jon Stewart). But what other $50 million supermarket do you know that uses largely volunteer labor? And runs like a democracy? I've been a member since the 1980s.

Here's what I love about it. The corn and beets and broccoli sprouts. And apples! And gluten-free vegan chips! All this sustainably grown organic produce is priced below 25 percent of cost. On my squad, I stacked bread, then eggs, and repackaged spices. I worked with a Sudanese lawyer, a sculptor, a mom, a writer, a yoga teacher, and a professor. I met a retired MTA worker who schleps here from Bay Ridge. "After all those years working on the subway underground I want to eat healthy," he said. I know a hedge-fund guy who shops here—you'd never guess he's a one-percenter. There's a sense of community and mission. You couldn't invent this place if you tried.

kids' clothing and shoes are reminiscent of Park Slope circa the 1980s. Almost all of North and South Park Slope are now historic districts and safe from wreckers' balls and McMansions, except along Fourth Avenue, rezoned for high-rise development.

Park Slope's hallmarks are progressive politics and a block-by-block sense of community. New Yorkers joke about its stroller gridlock and PC attitude. It has its share of idiosyncratic institutions: the Lesbian Herstory Archives, the Park Slope Child Care Collective (est. 1971), the activist Park Slope Community Bookstore, and Park Slope Parents, an information-filled website that's a favorite among helicopter parents. Aside from local schools, it's the Park Slope Food Coop that takes the cake (gluten-free, perhaps), as the neighborhood's best-known institution.

HISTORY SNAPSHOTS

Park Slope's turnaround, over decades, is remarkable. Fifth Avenue, filled with restaurants and shops today, was so crime-ridden in the 1980s that residents went to lengths—for example, a husband and wife leaving home surreptitiously and separately for vacation—in order to foil would-be burglars.

Park Slope's renaissance, rooted in real estate, can be traced in part to the late Everett and Evelyn Ortner. This remarkable couple began a renovation of their 1886 four-story home at 272 Berkeley Place in 1963 and ended up, five years later, cofounding the Brownstone Revival Coalition. Advocates for preserving and landmarking brownstones, they renovated seventeen dilapidated town houses on nearby St. Johns Place. They were helped in this endeavor by Senator Robert F. Kennedy, local parishes, a foundation, and Hugh Carey, who lived, with his wife and fourteen children, nearby at 61 Prospect Park West, prior to becoming the governor of New York in 1975. The Park Slope Civic Council on its website recalls how

Grand Army Plaza Soldiers' and Sailors' Memorial Arch. (Photo by E. Freudenheim, 2014)

it "fought bank redlining, planted thousands of trees, and launched [an] annual House Tour to present Park Slope as an alternative to would-be suburbanites."

Take a guided tour if you can. Park Slope's glorious swaths of row houses speak for themselves. But there are lots of good tidbits and stories here. The gargoyle-decorated Montauk Club, at the corner of Eighth Avenue and Lincoln Place, was a nineteenth-century men's club. To feel the smack of that era's chauvinism, just compare the men's majestic main entrance with the simple, functional women's door. A few blocks away, the corner of Sterling Place and Seventh Avenue was the site of a terrible midair collision in 1960. Pretty 153 Lincoln Place, next to the lovely Brooklyn Conservatory of Music (est. 1881), was until about 2004 a discreet "hot sheet" hotel, politely ignored by the neighbors but frequented by people who arrived and departed in private cars with frosted windows. It's now condos.

OLD/NEW BROOKLYN

If possible, try to visit inside a brownstone home. In five minutes, you'll see the intimate, quotidian melding of old and new Brooklyn. If you're accustomed to modern houses with windows on four sides, you'll be surprised by these old attached town houses. Most are three or four stories high, about twenty feet wide and sixty deep, with steep external stoops, internal stairs, beautiful wooden floors, stained glass, and working fireplaces. They have pocket doors, natural light on only two sides, and postage-stamp-sized backyards. Some have dumbwaiters, internal airshafts, and other Victorian features.

As for the neighborhood, the Park Slope Civic Council's website features this poignant glance backward: "The Park Slope we know and love did not just happen. It was preserved, protected, and nurtured by dedicated volunteers."

CELEBS, FILMS, FICTION

John Turturro, a top character actor, and Steve Buscemi, who stars in the award-winning TV series *Boardwalk Empire* (shot partly in Brooklyn) live in Park Slope. So does actor Sir Patrick Stewart, a septuagenarian whose enthusiastic bite-by-bite report of his first slice of pizza in a local pizzeria was widely retweeted. U.S. Senator Charles Schumer is a longtime resident. New York City Mayor Bill De Blasio raised his family and owns a home at 442 Eleventh Street. President Barack Obama spent time as a student at his girlfriend's apartment at 640 Second Street, according to *Barack Obama: The Story*, by David Maraniss. Film crews are often seen on location. At Le Pain Quotidian on Fifth Avenue (formerly a funeral home), Meryl Streep played Julia Child lunching in Paris for *Julie and Julia*. *Prizzi's Honor* and *The Royal Tenenbaums* were shot at the Grand Prospect Hall. Noah Baumbach's indie *The Squid and the Whale* was shot at 167 Sixth Avenue.

Novelists Jonathan Safran Foer and Nicole Krauss (once called the "too-successful-to-stomach physical embodiment of literary Brooklyn" by *New York* magazine) lived in the Slope, as do many writers for major media. For local flavor, read Paul Auster's *Winter Journal* and *The Brooklyn Follies*, Amy Shearn's *The Mermaid of Brooklyn*, Amy Sohn's *Prospect Park West*, and—though memoir, not fiction—Pete Hamill's 1994 classic, *A Drinking Life*.

NOSHES, RESTAURANTS, BARS IN PARK SLOPE

al di la Trattoria, 248 5th Avenue, (718) 783-4565
Barbès, 376 9th Street, (347) 422-0248
Franny's, 348 Flatbush Avenue, (718) 230-0221
Los Pollitos ☎, 148 5th Avenue, (718) 623-9152
Miriam, 79 5th Avenue, (718) 622-2250
The Owl Farm, 297 9th Street, (718) 499-4988
Pacific Standard, 82 4th Avenue, (718) 858-1951
Pork Slope, 247 5th Avenue, (718) 768-7675
Rose Water, 787 Union Street, (718) 783-3800
Santa Fe Grill ☎, 62 7th Avenue, (718) 636-0279

SELECT DESTINATIONS

BKLYN Larder, 228 Flatbush Avenue, (718) 783-1250

Brooklyn Superhero Supply Store, 372 5th Avenue, (718) 499-9884

Clay Pot, 162 7th Avenue, (718) 788-6564

Grand Prospect Hall, 263 Prospect Avenue, (718) 788-0777

Lesbian Herstory Educational Foundation, 484 14th Street, (718) 768-3953

Montauk Club, 25 8th Avenue, (718) 638-0800

Old Stone House Museum, 336 3rd Street, (718) 768-3195

Park Slope Community Bookstore, 143 7th Avenue, (718) 783-3075

Park Slope Food Coop, 782 Union Street, between 6th and 7th Avenues,
(718) 622-0560

Prospect Park and Washington Park (see "Brooklyn's Waterfront and Parks,"
section 4)

Puppetworks, 338 6th Avenue, (718) 965-3391

Union Hall, 702 Union Street, (718) 638-4400

☞ Like Park Slope? Visit any brownstone neighborhood: Bedford-Stuyvesant, Boerum Hill, Brooklyn Heights, Carroll Gardens, Clinton Hill, Cobble Hill, Crown Heights, Fort Greene, Prospect Heights, or Sunset Park.

Prospect Heights and Pacific Park

Tom [of Tom's Restaurant] and Gus and his family were the only people when we got to New York who knew and cared whether we lived or died.... And they were like that with everybody.

—Lisa Ann Wilson, former tenant of
Tom and Gus Vlahavas of Tom's Restaurant

Location, location, location!

Prospect Heights packs a punch. It's home to the Brooklyn Museum, the Brooklyn Botanic Garden, Barclays Center, and Pacific Park. It is within walking distance of some very happening places: the Brooklyn Cultural District and BAM. It's cheek-by-jowl to the Brooklyn Central Library and Park Slope.

Prospect Heights boasts a huge swath of historic, landmarked, nineteenth-century brownstone homes with a growing stable of good, small restaurants, cafés, and bars. Stoop sitting and neighborliness remain well-honed arts in this handsome, diverse neighborhood. Come for a meal or drinks, and go exploring.

Tom's Restaurant, a beloved institution, serves up all-day breakfast. (Tom's has a branch on the Coney Island boardwalk.) James specializes in seasonal American fare. If you love the Kimchi Taco food-truck fare, you can pick up the same snacks in its Prospect Heights restaurant. Eat in or take out at Stocked. Or bar hop from one block to another: start at Weather Up on Vanderbilt, progress to Bar Sepia at Underhill Avenue, and end up back at Soda Bar.

Barclays Center is theoretically located in Prospect Heights. But it's so big that the neighborhood can't quite swallow it whole. It is home to the Brooklyn Nets basketball team and the New York Islanders

BASICS

MAPPING: Using GPS, orient to the Vanderbilt, Tom's Restaurant, or Brooklyn Museum. Main drags: Vanderbilt, Washington, and Underhill Avenues, Eastern Parkway. Use any subway to Barclays Center / Atlantic Avenue, B, Q (7th Avenue), 2, 3 (Grand Army Plaza). Near Atlantic Malls, Barclays Center, Brooklyn Cultural District, Brooklyn Central Library, Prospect Park, and the neighborhoods of Crown Heights, Park Slope. Bounded by Atlantic, Flatbush, and Washington Avenues, Grand Army Plaza, Eastern Parkway.

EVENTS: Events at Barclays Center, Brooklyn Museum, Brooklyn Botanic Garden.

SELFIES AND 'ZA: Selfies at Barclays Center Oculus or Tom's Restaurant. Pizza at Cataldo's.

ACCOMMODATIONS: Airbnb.

hockey team and is a venue for concerts, circuses, and special events. The development of the Barclays Center and Atlantic Yards (now called Pacific Park) was controversial for a decade starting at its inception, for a host of reasons including the use by developer Forest City Ratner of eminent domain. But many residents now enjoy having sporting events and major concerts right on their doorstep, rather than having to travel to Manhattan's Madison Square Garden.

BEST BETS IN PROSPECT HEIGHTS AND PACIFIC PARK

1 Cafés, bars, restaurants: Grab a burger at Rose's Bar & Grill on Flatbush Avenue, stop in bakeries and cafés along Vanderbilt, eat French fare at Gamin, or try Cheryl's Global Soul. People love Mitchell's for soul food. Have a drink at Sharlene's.

2 Bike routes: Vanderbilt Avenue has a broad bike lane running from Prospect Park to Fort Greene.

3 Shop: Browse Vanderbilt and Washington Avenues stores, from the small bodegas that represent the neighborhood's yesteryear to new-Brooklyn-style trendy spots, such as O.N.A. clothing boutique.

4 Barclays Center: Check its calendar of basketball, hockey, boxing, and other sporting events, as well as concerts and such spectaculars as *Disney on Ice*.

5 Nineteenth-century brownstone town houses: Walk along Vanderbilt and Carlton Avenues, Bergen Street, and Park Place. See historic Public School 9 Annex. (For more information, see the Historic Districts Council online.)

PACIFIC PARK: LOW-RISE NEIGHBORHOOD GETS A HIGH-RISE NEIGHBOR

Prospect Heights is a low-rise neighborhood that had about twenty thousand residents in 2010. A development of fourteen residential skyscrapers known as Pacific Park (formerly Atlantic Yards) is rising on its periphery, bounded roughly by Atlantic, Flatbush, and Vanderbilt Avenues and Dean Street. With some buildings slated to open in 2017, the new Pacific Park development may add as many as fifteen thousand new residents to Prospect Heights. How this 75 percent increase in population will play out remains to be seen.

Pacific Park, according to its designers, SHoP Architects, is "a project of eight million square feet of mixed use development across a 22-acre site and into the surrounding neighborhoods. . . . It will include an eight acre public park, 247,000 square feet of retail, 336,000 square feet of commercial space and 6,430 units of housing, 2,250 of which will be affordable for low, moderate, and middle income families."

BROOKLYN VOICES

LISA ANN WILSON
Tenant above Tom's Restaurant

Tom's Restaurant is a Brooklyn institution. It was founded by Greek immigrant Tom Vlahavas and run by his son Gus, who died in 2014. I moved upstairs from Tom's Restaurant in 1995 out of college. I'm from Louisiana. My roommate was from Oregon. We were as far as could be from home. Ours was the first generation, a postcollege wave that moved to Brooklyn instead of Manhattan.

Often we'd come down on busy Saturday mornings to pass out oranges to customers waiting on the line or pour coffee. We'd go through the kitchen, scoot behind the line cooks, pour our own coffee behind the counter. We learned about Greek Easter when we went to Gus's for Greek Easter dinner. During the blackout, we took all the meat from restaurant and grilled it in their backyard.

Cops were at the restaurant all the time; they had their special tables. We used to go to Mooney's Bar on Flatbush. Kevin Mooney was straight from Ireland, so he'd opened a bar, like Tom was Greek, so he'd opened a diner. When it was late, Kevin would . . . turn to some off-duty cop hanging at the bar, and they'd have a patrol car trail us the few blocks home, back to Tom's. [It was] because they liked Tom and [because] we were his tenants.

Tom's became our connection to the street, and it became like a small neighborhood in New Orleans. My Brooklyn story: a little neighborhood in the big city.

OLD/NEW BROOKLYN

Old meets new here, as across Brooklyn, in the adaptive reuse of old schools, factories, and once-dilapidated structures. In the place of a one-story garage at 280 Saint Mark's Avenue, there's now a four-story condo. News Walk Condos, at 535 Dean Street, was one of the first conversions in the area. It began life in 1927 as the *New York Daily News* printing plant. Apartments have also been carved out of the renovated, abandoned commercial Spalding Ball factory (manufacturers of those pink rubber balls that bounced through Americans' childhoods and that New Yorkers called "Spaldeens") and a school, PS 9 on Sterling Place and Vanderbilt, a handsome Renaissance Revival building. Although much of Prospect Heights is a protected historic district, changes in use are permissible, as long as original façades remain intact.

For new Brooklyn, see the handsome glass apartment building by Richard Meier at Grand Army Plaza and the cute cafés and restaurants along the neighborhood's main streets.

This author's 2004 guidebook said, "A decade ago, some Manhattanites wouldn't be caught dead here. Today, these same people are spending big bucks to buy a floor of a brownstone in Carroll Gardens or Prospect Heights." Until the 1990s, Prospect Heights was a mixed Caribbean, African American, and white community with beautiful homes in varying states of repair. There's been a gold rush. In 2013, the home at 206 Park Place sold for a then-record high of $4.3 million.

CELEBS, FILMS, FICTION

The award-winning TV workplace sitcom *Brooklyn Nine-Nine*, starring Andy Samberg, is modeled on the real-life 78th New York City Police Department Precinct. You could make a movie (someone did) of the tortured history of the Barclays Center–Atlantic Yards–Pacific Park project, with its community protests, backroom deals, eminent domain evictions, and most unlikely, a Russian oligarch who swooped in and acquired partial ownership of an American basketball team. This truth-is-stranger-than-fiction drama is captured in the 2011 advocacy film *Battle for Brooklyn*. For fiction set here, read *The Love Affairs of Nathaniel P.* by Adelle Waldman.

NOSHES, RESTAURANTS, BARS IN PROSPECT HEIGHTS AND PACIFIC PARK

Bar Sepia, 234 Underhill Avenue, (718) 399-6680
Cataldo's Restaurant, 554 Vanderbilt Avenue, (718) 857-6700
Cheryl's Global Soul, 236 Underhill Avenue, (347) 529-2855
James, 605 Carlton Avenue, (718) 942-4255
Kimchi Grill, 766 Washington Avenue, (718) 360-1839
Little Cupcake Bakeshop, 598 Vanderbilt Avenue, (718) 783-0770
Mitchell's, 617A Vanderbilt Avenue, (718) 789-3212
Sharlene's Bar, 353 Flatbush Avenue, (718) 638-1272
Tom's Restaurant ☎, 782 Washington Avenue, (718) 636-9738
Weather Up, 589 Vanderbilt Avenue, (212) 766-3202

SELECT DESTINATIONS

Barclays Center, 620 Atlantic Avenue, (917) 618-6100
Brooklyn Botanic Garden, 1000 Washington Avenue, (718) 623-7200
Brooklyn Museum, 200 Eastern Parkway, (718) 638-5000
NYPD 78th Precinct, corner of Bergen Street and Sixth Avenue near
    Flatbush Avenue
PS 9 School, 689 Vanderbilt Avenue

☞ Like Prospect Heights? Visit other brownstone neighborhoods: Boerum Hill, Brooklyn Heights, Carroll Gardens, Clinton Hill, Cobble Hill, Crown Heights, Fort Greene Park Slope, or Sunset Park.

Prospect Lefferts Gardens

Even kale, which used to be a weed, costs too damn much. Everything made a 180-degree turn here.
—local resident since 1986

Prospect Lefferts Gardens is residential, a tad off the radar screen, and close to subways, the Brooklyn Botanic Garden, and Prospect Park. Call this Flatbush or PLG, a melting-pot neighborhood where you can have interesting food and feel like you've seen where "real New Yorkers" live.

Prospect Lefferts Gardens' socioeconomically diverse population of almost 170,000 includes Caribbean-born Americans and immigrants, Asians, African Americans, and young people from across the world. A charming historic district includes a range of housing styles and one of the city's early twentieth-century experimental "planned communities."

Real estate is a perennial conversational hot button in New York, and Prospect Lefferts Gardens is suddenly topical. This once-sleepy neighborhood has gotten a lot of attention as young professionals, frustrated by astronomical house prices in the borough—"You can't find anything even with a million dollars in cash in Park Slope," complained one stymied house hunter—have ventured further into Brooklyn. Real estate prices are hitting the stratosphere; homes along Rutland Road (for instance, numbers 33, 55, and 118) sold for close to $2 million in 2014.

BASICS

MAPPING: Using GPS, orient to Gratitude Cafe. Main drags: Nostrand and Flatbush Avenues. Use B, Q (Prospect Park, Parkside), 2, 5 (Sterling, Winthrop Streets) subways. Near Prospect Park and the neighborhoods of Crown Heights, Flatbush. Bounded roughly by Empire Boulevard and Clarkson, Ocean, and New York Avenues.

EVENTS: House tour organized by Lefferts Manor Association.

SELFIES AND 'ZA: Selfies on pretty Rutland Road. For pizza, Gino's Trattoria.

ACCOMMODATIONS: Airbnb and Gowanus hotels.

BEST BETS IN PROSPECT LEFFERTS GARDENS

1 Cycle along neighborhood streets: Bike down pretty Rutland Road. Explore Lefferts Manor,

designed as a planned community. Continue down to Coney Island or into Prospect Park.

2   Caribbean chill pill: Take a vegan ice cream break at Scoops, a local institution thanks to the charms of its owner, Tony, who sports Rastafarian dreadlocks. Sample Jamaican patties and "the world's best" currant rolls at Allan's Bakery, which has been doing business since 1961. Have waffles for brunch at Delroy's Cafe. Try flying fish cutters or oxtail and cou-cou with sorrel at Culpepper's, a Barbadian eatery. Shop at Tafari Tribe for ethnic fashion, jewelry, and home accessories.

3   Tour the landmarked areas: There are Tiffany windows at the Grace Reformed Church at 108 Lincoln Road. (A precursor of the church was a Sunday school built by the 1860s-era Society for the Amelioration of the Colored Population of Flatbush. It was subsequently under the aegis of the Flatbush Dutch Reformed Church, one of the city's oldest Protestant denominations.) Read more in the NYC Landmarks Preservation Commission Designation report online.

OLD/NEW BROOKLYN

Over eight hundred homes make up the Prospect Lefferts Gardens historic district. It includes the microneighborhoods of Midwood, Maple, and Rutland off Flatbush and Rogers Avenues, sections of Lincoln Road and Fenimore Street. In Lefferts Manor, a planned community, the population is limited by a rare one-family covenant in the land deed, a mandate from the past that maintains low population density.

See the 1898 Romanesque Revival–style homes at 50 to 60 Rutland Road and further down the street, between Flatbush and Bedford Avenues, a row of 1915 neo-Tudor houses. Find neo-Georgian- and neo-Renaissance-style homes at 13–49 and 74–88 Midwood Avenue.

For decades, New York City's oldest black-owned art gallery, Dorsey's Frame Shop, which showed African diasporic artists James Denmark, Jacob Lawrence, Tom Feelings, and Ernie Crichlow, was tucked away here. It closed in 2003.

CELEBS, FILMS, FICTION

Pulitzer Prize winner Alice Walker, author of *The Color Purple*, and politicians Christine Todd Whitman and Hugh Carey lived in Prospect Lefferts Gardens. So did Mae West's mother, herself a burlesque actress.

NOSHES, RESTAURANTS, BARS IN PROSPECT LEFFERTS GARDENS

Allan's Bakery 🏛, 1109 Nostrand Avenue, (718) 774-7892
Culpepper's 🏛, 1082 Nostrand Avenue, (718) 940-4122

Delroy's Cafe ☎, 14 Duryea Place, (347) 770-9300
Gino's Trattoria ☎, 548 Flatbush Avenue, (718) 287-1277
Gratitude Cafe, 499 Rogers Avenue, (347) 413-7944
Scoops Ice Cream ☎, 624 Flatbush Avenue, (718) 282-5904

SELECT DESTINATIONS

Grace Reformed Church, 163 Lincoln Road, (718) 287-4343
Tafari Tribe, 593 Flatbush Avenue, (347) 365-6197

☞ Like Prospect Lefferts Gardens? Visit Windsor Terrace and Victorian Flatbush.

Red Hook

BASICS

MAPPING: Using GPS, orient to Hope & Anchor. Main drags: Van Brunt and Van Dyke Streets. Poorly served by subways; use G, F (Smith Street); both are three-quarters of a mile away. New York Water Taxi runs from Wall Street's Pier 11 to Red Hook's Ikea; Ikea shuttle bus runs from Brooklyn Borough Hall. Near Brooklyn Battery Tunnel, Gowanus Expressway, and the neighborhood of Carroll Gardens. Bounded by Buttermilk Channel, Gowanus Bay, Gowanus Canal, Gowanus Expressway.

EVENTS: Red Hook Film Festival, Red Hook Fest, BWAC free art shows, Red Hook artists annual open-studio tours, 9/11 memorial Stephen Siller Tunnel to Towers 5K Run & Walk.

SELFIES AND 'ZA: Selfies at Beard Street Piers. For pizza, Pizza Moto.

ACCOMMODATIONS: Airbnb or hotels in Gowanus.

TIPS: On weekdays, Red Hook feels like the industrial zone it is, filled with truck traffic and lifting and hauling activity. Tourists flock here in the summer and for special events.

The views are stunning; the public transportation, exasperating. From Valentino Pier, the Statue of Liberty seems close enough to wave at.

Gritty, artsy, and slightly disaffected, semi-industrial Red Hook remains part of Brooklyn's working waterfront. Culturally, it's part of the constellation of Brooklyn's hipper neighborhoods, along with Gowanus, Williamsburg, Greenpoint, and Bushwick.

Red Hook's saving grace is also its nemesis: it lacks good public transportation. Come by Ikea's ferry, car, or bike. Proposals have been floated for years about the revival of trolley transit connecting Red Hook to Downtown Brooklyn. If and when affordable ferry or streetcar transit service is instated, the Red Hook scene will explode.

Red Hook is beloved by photographers and iconoclasts for its evocative landscape and historic architecture, salty attitude, good dive bars, sense of space, and water-diffused light. The two anchor stores are Ikea and a Fairway supermarket. But what really anchors the neighborhood are its roots in Brooklyn's rich maritime past. Coastal Red Hook still evokes the powerhouse port that Brooklyn once was. (See "Brooklyn's Waterfront and Parks," section 4.)

Come for open studios, kayaking, outdoor movies, and art shows. Have a party at the renovated, 150-year-old Liberty Warehouse. It's all about ambiance in Red Hook. Just stare for a few minutes at the 1850s warehouse overlooking New York Harbor that's above Fairway market, itself housed in an old coffee warehouse; it's gorgeous. So are the 1870 Beard Street Piers, housing artists' studios today; both have been adaptively reused.

BEST BETS IN RED HOOK

1   Eats: Brunch at New England–style Brooklyn Crab or Home/Made; have coffee at Court Street Grocers; dine at the Good Fork or Hope & Anchor. Baked is a destination bakery; Steve's Authentic Key Lime Pies is a Brooklyn religion. Treat yourself to a lobster roll at the Red Hook Lobster Pound. At Defonte's, dig into a delicious, overstuffed sandwich, sized for the muscled dockworkers the shop originally served. Huge Fairway supermarket sells picnic-ready foods, fresh breads, and coffee.

2   Statue of Liberty: Valentino Pier and Fairway's outdoor café overlook Lady Liberty.

3   Biking: Cycle Van Brunt Street, explore Beard Street Pier and the area's nineteenth-century streets, Pier 44 Garden, and Ikea's waterfront Esplanade.

4   Ferry: Ikea's ferry from lower Manhattan to Red Hook is twenty minutes of sheer pleasure.

5   Summer fun: Kayaking with Red Hook Boaters, and Red Hook Flicks, outdoor movies on Valentino Pier.

6   Drinks and dive bars: Have drinks at Sunny's Bar or Rocky Sullivan's roof deck. Visit Widow Jane Distillery, Six Point Brewery, and Red Hook Winery.

7   Ball-field food: Visit Red Hook Recreation Area, a fifty-eight-acre park, for soccer and Red Hook ball fields' legendary food stands. They sell hot chicken tamales, pupusas, and fresh lemonade. Vendors are from El Salvador, Guatemala, Colombia, Mexico, and the Dominican Republic. (Summer Sundays.)

8   Art shows: See exhibitions at Red Hook open studios, Brooklyn Waterfront Artists Coalition (BWAC) shows, and Kentler International Drawing Space. Visit Pioneer Works, an arts center. Look North, an Inuit art gallery, is located here.

9   Historic boats: The Waterfront Museum on the 1914 *Lehigh Valley No. 79* barge has periodic exhibitions and performances. The 1938 *Mary A. Whalen*, billed as "the only oil tanker cultural center in the world" by its owner, the nonprofit PortSide New York, hosts smart, curated programs, educational displays, and open-air opera. Both boats are listed on the National Register of Historic Places.

10 Watch the *Queen Mary 2* enter or depart from the new Brooklyn Cruise Terminal.

HISTORY SNAPSHOTS

The Dutch occupied Red Hook, one of Brooklyn's earliest settlements, in 1636. It was a landing site for General George Washington (1732–1799). He ordered the construction of Fort Defiance, the westernmost flank in a series of fortifications along the coast of Brooklyn that included Cobble Hill Fort, Fort Box, Fort Stirling, Fort Greene, and Fort Putnam (where Fort Greene Park now exists). A marshy area unsuitable for farming, Red Hook was transformed by the development of New York Harbor, becoming one of the nation's premier shipping centers by the 1840s.

Typical industrial harbor life grew up here: working docks, boisterous bars, affordable eateries, ship-repair shops, and flophouses. The colorful, rough, sometimes violent waterfront was dominated by Italian, Irish, Scandinavian, and German dockworkers and the International Longshoremen's Association.

In 1938, the public housing project Red Hook Houses opened, providing homes for dockworkers. Construction of the Gowanus Expressway and the Brooklyn Battery Tunnel after World War II geographically isolated Red Hook from nearby Carroll Gardens and led to economic decline and a spike in crime. In the late twentieth century, the O'Connell Organization and artists began to rehab and settle in Red Hook.

SUPERSTORM SANDY AND CLIMATE CHANGE

In October 2012, Superstorm Sandy exposed New York's vulnerability to rising sea levels and extreme weather. Red Hook suffered significant damage and disruption. Floodwaters from a tidal surge that overcame the Brooklyn Battery Tunnel, plus some from the toxic runover from Gowanus Canal, ran six feet high. Sewage permeated streets and basements. Residents and businesses were displaced; power outages lasted a month in parts. Residents of Red Hook Houses, the city's second-largest public housing project and Brooklyn's largest, were hit hard. In 2014, New York City and State funded a $100 million integrated flood-protection plan in Red Hook. (See a dramatic video of waters rising: https://www.youtube.com/watch?v=OHJqazqui9M.)

RED HOOK'S FUTURE

Brooklyn's love affair with its old and still-functioning industrial areas is in full heat in Red Hook. It is one of only sixteen industrial business zones in New York City. Community organizations have fought to retain the historical industrial character of the neighborhood. Meanwhile, new restaurants and retail stores have vastly improved the neighborhood's tourist appeal. Red Hook Initiative and other groups are fighting for community involvement in development decisions about possible future residential towers, hotels, and big box stores.

Red Hook's population in the 2012 census was fifteen thousand and included black, Hispanic, Italian, and Irish families. About five thousand people reside inland in the Red Hook Houses public housing complex. The smaller, arty-hipster community lives in renovated old homes and buildings near Fairway Market and the Beard Street warehouse, near the waterfront. This demographic profile could change radically if improved transportation were to be introduced into this still-roughhewn waterfront area.

OLD/NEW BROOKLYN

As for old Brooklyn, Red Hook slyly exudes its past in many small ways, if you know where to look. For instance, on Dwight and Walcott Streets, Heritage Trail signs mark Red Hook Lane, an Indian trail used by Washington and his Continental Army in August 1776, during the Battle of Brooklyn.

Note the many nineteenth-century shipping-era buildings that have been adaptively reused. Inside the handsome, pre–Civil War–era Beard Street Warehouse, bedecked with 250 arched iron shutters, massive original beams define modern workspaces. Inside, makers and creatives do everything from glassblowing (once a Brooklyn specialty, revived by Brooklyn artists) to composing music. The landmarked Brooklyn Clay Retort and Fire Brick Works building at 76 Van Dyke Street, another relic of New York's late industrial history, today houses a glass-making company. The immense, long-abandoned 1910 New York Dock Building, rechristened as 160 Imlay, was retrofitted into apartments with spectacular harbor views. You can see the old streetcar tracks behind Fairway; the Brooklyn Historic Railway Association is promoting revival of streetcar service to address Red Hook's public transit needs. Kentler International Drawing Space, a gallery, has created the Red Hook Archives.

The Ikea Esplanade weaves giant-sized, colorfully painted winches, ropes, and seaport artifacts with explanatory signage into a free, airy, outdoor micromuseum.

George Washington built Fort Defiance; today you can dine at Fort Defiance restaurant. As evocative names go, there's Hope & Anchor and Erie Basin jewelry store, the latter named for Red Hook's harbor. Kentler International Drawing Space, one of Red Hook's first art organizations, took its name from its 1877 building, where "Kentler" is chiseled atop what had been a men's haberdashery for the seaport workers.

Generations of Italian and Irish Catholic dockworkers attended the hulking mid-nineteenth-century Visitation of the Blessed Virgin Mary Church. When you pass this church and walk on uneven Belgian blocks in Red Hook's streets, you're likely walking on the same road those workers did.

Corruption thrived on Brooklyn's waterfront. It hasn't totally disappeared. In a 2015 case, the police stumbled on a large marijuana operation in a Red Hook maraschino cherry factory, with dramatic consequences.

New Brooklyn's entrepreneurial, epicurean trends are apparent in the cuisine, shops, and bars here. Visitors should head to Van Brunt Street, the main drag for the small, trendy section of Red Hook, which has a few restaurants and picturesque shops displaying interesting jewelry, textiles, foods, and wine.

CELEBS, FILMS, FICTION

Locals included Colombo mobster Carmine "The Snake" Persico and Al Capone. Type O Negative bassist Peter Steele was born as Peter Ratajczyk here (his family moved to Bensonhurst). Rapper Shabazz the Disciple and NBA basketball player Carmelo Anthony grew up in the Red Hook Houses. Brooklyn's only comic book crime-busting hero, Captain America, aka Steve Rogers, led the Avengers from a Red Hook pier in comic books and films from 2002 to 2007 (see https://www .youtube.com/watch?v=KP7FIhaqaJA).

As for literature, Arthur Miller's plays *A View from the Bridge* and *The Hook* depict dockworkers' lives. The latter inspired Elia Kazan's classic movie *On the Waterfront*, starring Marlon Brando and depicting human drama and union thuggery among Brooklyn's longshoremen. Hubert Selby Jr. wrote *Last Exit to Brooklyn* about Red Hook; it also became a movie in 1989. For more scenes of Red Hook, watch *Extremely Loud and Incredibly Close* (see Sunny's Bar) and the 2010 Academy Award–winning short *God of Love*, by Brooklynite Luke Matheny.

For fiction set in Red Hook, read Ernest Poole's 1915 book *The Harbor* or H. P. Lovecraft's xenophobic 1927 story *The Horror of Red Hook*. Of more recent vintage, read Ivy Pochoda's 2013 *Visitation Street* and two mysteries, Reggie Nadelson's *Red Hook: An Artie Cohen Mystery* and Gabriel Cohen's *Red Hook*.

NOSHES, RESTAURANTS, BARS IN RED HOOK

Baked, 359 Van Brunt Street, (718) 222-0345
Botanica, 220 Conover Street, (347) 225-0148
Brooklyn Crab, 24 Reed Street, (718) 643-2722
Defonte's 🏛, 379 Columbia Street, (718) 625-8052
Hope & Anchor, 347 Van Brunt Street, (718) 237-0276
Rocky Sullivan's 🏛, 34 Van Dyke Street, (718) 246-8050
Sonny's Bar, 253 Conover Street, (718) 237-8888
Steve's Authentic Key Lime Pies, 185 Van Dyke Street, (718) 858-5333
Widow Jane Distillery / Cacao Prieto, 214 Conover Street, (347) 225-0130

SELECT DESTINATIONS

Brooklyn Cruise Terminal, 72 Bowne Street, (718) 855-5590
BWAC (Brooklyn Waterfront Artists Coalition), 499 Van Brunt Street,
   (718) 596-2507

Coffey Park, bounded by Verona, Dwight, King, and Richards Streets

Fairway Market, 480 Van Brunt Street, (718) 254-0923

Flickinger Glassworks, 204 Van Dyke Street, (718) 875-1531

Ikea, 1 Beard Street, (888) 888-4532

Kentler International Drawing Space, 353 Van Brunt Street, (718) 875-2098

Look North, Inuit Art Gallery, by appointment, 275 Conover Street,
    (347) 721-3995

Mary A. Whalen, Pier 11, next to Brooklyn Cruise Terminal at 72 Bowne Street,
    (917) 414-0565

Pioneer Works, 59 Pioneer Street, (718) 596-3001

Red Hook Boaters, http://www.redhookboaters.org

Red Hook Pool, Park, Recreational Area, Bay and Clinton Streets

Red Hook Winery, 204 Van Dyke Street, (347) 689-2432

Waterfront Museum, 290 Conover Street at Pier 44, (718) 624-4719

☞ If you like Red Hook, visit Gowanus and Sheepshead Bay, both waterfront communities, or landlocked Bushwick, for edgy art and Brooklyn attitude.

Sheepshead Bay and Manhattan Beach

Well, I love the eggplant parmigiana at Il Fornetto, the Saint Peter's fish at Liman, and the kunefe at OPera—oh, and the apple cake at Apani (when I can get it!).
—Laura McKenna, programming coordinator, Neighborhood Housing Services at Sheepshead Bay

BASICS

MAPPING: Using GPS, orient to Randazzo's; enjoy some fried clams. Main drags: Emmons Avenue, Sheepshead Bay Road, Avenue U. Use B, Q (Sheepshead Bay / East 16th) subways. Near the Belt Parkway and the neighborhoods of Brighton Beach, Marine Park, Midwood, Mill Basin. Bounded roughly by Avenue T, Kings Highway, Gerritsen Avenue, Knapp Street, Plumb Beach Channel, Ocean Parkway.

EVENTS: Bayfest street fair, Kingsborough Community College summer concerts.

SELFIES AND 'ZA: Selfies near the fishing boats or at Jordan's Lobster Dock. Pizza at Delmar.

ACCOMMODATIONS: A few motels.

What do Joan Rivers, Woody Allen, and Rodney Dangerfield have in common? Sheepshead Bay.

Sheepshead Bay is situated along a small inlet near the Atlantic Ocean. This neighborhood is known for four things: fishing party boats, its beach, its weird name (it was named for a local fish that people thought resembled a sheep's head, now extinct), and its contribution to the American comedy scene through a little, long-gone club called Pips on the Bay.

As for the nearby community of Manhattan Beach, there's absolutely nothing "Manhattan" about it. It's an oceanfront residential community of about a thousand homes, including a few McMansions, a beach, Kingsborough Community College, a CUNY campus which runs a nice summer concert series, and a substantial Russian-speaking community.

Calmer than Coney, a thousand times grittier than the Hamptons, Sheepshead Bay is best experienced as a cheapo summer getaway. You can go out with a half-day fishing boat from the Emmons Avenue piers in the morning, or come in the afternoon to purchase the day's catch. Eat lobster at Jordan's Lobster Dock, pretend to be vacationing in Rhode Island, and later sleep in your own bed at home in Brooklyn, all for the price of a subway ride (and the lobster!). If you crave anonymity, off-the-tourist-track Sheepshead Bay is a good place to find it—unless you grew up here, in which case you'll probably bump into someone who never left but remembers you from high school.

BEST BETS IN SHEEPSHEAD BAY AND MANHATTAN BEACH

1 Old-Brooklyn-style affordable food on the Emmons Avenue waterfront: Chow down at Randazzo's Clam House, Clemente's Maryland Crab House, and, for roast beef, Roll-n-Roaster. (You could probably spark a genial argument among expat Brooklynites in Florida about which of these places is "da best.") Feast on Turkish meals at OPera and Liman and takeout Georgian food at Apani.
2 Canal-side stroll: Take a stroll along Emmons Avenue and on the charming Sheepshead Bay Foot Bridge.
3 Manhattan Beach's beach: This public beach is nice, but it's inconvenient to reach by subway, and parking is expensive.
4 Go fishing! Fishing party boats depart from the Emmons Avenue piers. Book ahead for *Sea Queen VII*, *Ranger VI*, *Flamingo III*, and others. For an adventure, book with New York Kayak Fishing Guide Services.
5 Brooklyn's second "Chinatown": Visit Avenue U, one of Brooklyn's burgeoning Chinatowns.
6 Cycle: The Shore Parkway Greenway Trail goes from Emmons Avenue to Brooklyn Marine Park (beware the highway stretch).
7 The Holocaust Memorial Mall Park: A small memorial on Emmons Avenue at Shore Boulevard was erected in honor of the thousands of survivors who moved to this part of Brooklyn.

HISTORY SNAPSHOTS

Back in the nineteenth century, much of Brooklyn was forest or farmland, muck or sawdust, but Manhattan Beach had fancy hotels and resort homes; in the late 1800s, a horse-racing track ran along what is today Ocean Avenue between Jerome Avenue and Neck Road. After horse racing was outlawed, the racetrack tried unsuccessfully to shift from horses to cars, reinventing itself as the Sheepshead Speedway. That too gave way in the 1920s to residential development. In the 1930s, the piers along Emmons Avenue were built as part of a WPA project. In the 1950s, the Robert Moses initiative, the new Belt Parkway, facilitated access to Sheepshead Bay, which stimulated the growth of a middle-class Jewish and Italian community.

OLD/NEW BROOKLYN

Along with Pips on the Bay, Lundy's is long gone. Lundy's was Brooklyn's renowned seafood restaurant from its opening in 1934 through the 1960s. Lundy's, in its distinctive Spanish Colonial Revival building, served twenty-eight hundred customers at a time. The landmark building today houses Cherry Hill Market, a Euro-Russian food emporium and café.

Sheepshead Bay (population sixty-four thousand) reflects old-Brooklyn values in certain ways. Here's a vignette: The neighborhood's annual Bayfest street fair features live local bands, speeches, kids' games, and dancing. But there's nothing to buy—an astonishing accomplishment given that the city's commercialized street festivals generally feature hundreds of vendors. "Not everyone has money to spare. We don't want anyone to feel left out," one of the organizers told the author.

Speaking of old Brooklyn, former residents often remark that, at least on the Sheepshead Bay waterfront, nothing much has changed since they left years ago. Emmons Avenue is still lined with fishing boats and restaurants. There's parking, and the subway station, pharmacies, doughnut shops, and inexpensive stores on Sheepshead Bay Road. However, further inland, reflecting an increase in Asian immigration to Brooklyn, Avenue U has developed into a thriving Asian retail strip.

CELEBS, FILMS, FICTION

Pips Comedy Club in Sheepshead Bay opened in 1962 and closed in the early 2000s. It was one of the nation's first comedy clubs. The young stars-to-be who cut their teeth here included Woody Allen, Richard Belzer, David Brenner, George Carlin, Andrew Dice Clay, Rodney Dangerfield, Andy Kaufman, Lisa Lampanelli, Adam Richman, Joan Rivers, and Jerry Seinfeld. They faced a tough, heckling Brooklyn audience. Seth Schultz, son of Pips' founder, once described the club as "the Gleason's Gym of comedy." Watch a video about Pips online: bit.ly/1Hd9MVr. For fiction, read the Moe Praeger series by Reed Farrel Coleman, set here and in other Brooklyn neighborhoods.

NOSHES, RESTAURANTS, BARS IN SHEEPSHEAD BAY AND MANHATTAN BEACH

Apani, 1520 Sheepshead Bay Road, (347) 462-4733
Clemente's Maryland Crab House 🏛, 3939 Emmons Avenue, (718) 646-7373
Delmar Pizzeria, 1668 Sheepshead Bay Road 🏛, (718) 469-7766
Il Fornetto, 2902 Emmons Avenue 🏛, (718) 332-8494
Liman Restaurant, 2710 Emmons Avenue, (718) 769-3322
OPera Cafe & Lounge, 2255 Emmons Avenue, (718) 676-2992
Randazzo's Clam Bar, 2017 Emmons Avenue, (718) 615-0010
Roll-n-Roaster 🏛, 2901 Emmons Avenue, (718) 769-6000

SELECT DESTINATIONS

Fishing trips: *Sea Queen VII*, *Ranger VI*, *Flamingo III*, and others; New York
   Kayak Fishing Guide Services
Kingsborough Community College, Leonard Goldstein Performing Arts Center,
   2001 Oriental Boulevard, (718) 368-5596
Lundy's landmark, now Cherry Hill Market, 1901 Emmons Avenue,
   (718) 616-1900
Manhattan Beach, Oriental Boulevard between Ocean Avenue and
   Mackenzie Street
Shore Parkway Greenway Trail / Shore Parks Conservancy, 9728 3rd Avenue,
   #402, (646) 355-3709

☞ Like Sheepshead Bay? Visit Coney Island, Brighton Beach, and maybe Red
Hook. For Asian food and shops, visit Sunset Park or Bensonhurst.

Sunset Park

It's the definition of coolness to have a diverse community. Brooklyn has always been a place that has a little of everything. People have to work and play and study and experience each other. Engaging in diversity expands people's resiliency and that of the whole community.

—Elizabeth C. Yeampierre, Executive Director, Uprose (United Puerto Rican Organization of Sunset Park)

BASICS

MAPPING: Using GPS, orient to Tacos El Bronco. Main drags: 5th and 8th Avenues. Use D, N, R (4th Avenue at 36th and 59th Streets) subways. Near Green-Wood, Industry City, Brooklyn Army Terminal, Gowanus Expressway, and the neighborhoods of Bay Ridge, Borough Park, Greenwood Heights, Park Slope. Bounded roughly by 39th to 65th Streets, 9th Avenue, Upper New York Bay.

EVENTS: Lunar New Year celebrations.

SELFIES AND 'ZA: Selfies atop Sunset Park at sunset. Pizza at Johnny's Pizzeria.

GREENMARKET: Saturdays seasonally at 4th Avenue and 59th Street.

ACCOMMODATIONS: Airbnb, Comfort Inn and Days Inn (near 39th Street).

Sunset Park is a Latino-Chinese neighborhood, where the two communities live together but apart. You'll want to wander pretty nineteenth-century streets, camera in hand. Sunset Park is interesting and fun to explore—and not far from such top tourist destinations as Green-Wood and the Brooklyn Museum and goings-on at Industry City.

Sunset Park bears the name of its eponymous twenty-four-acre park. The park is perched high enough to afford nice views of New York Harbor and Lady Liberty. The sunsets are, as you would expect, gorgeous. There are many brownstone and limestone houses here. Sunset Park is on the National Register of Historic Places, but it's not a New York City historic district, yet.

During a visit here, you might catch Chinese women practicing tai chi in the park, see where Norwegians implemented the European idea of a cooperative, and learn about Brooklyn's World War II history. You can order a taco in Spanish, have dim sum, or if it's summer, swim laps in a landmark, Olympic-sized, admission-free outdoor pool built by the Works Progress Administration in 1936.

Like a clamshell with two distinct halves, Sunset Park has parallel main drags, Eighth and Fifth

Avenues. They are almost mirror images of each other. Latino shops are arrayed along Fifth Avenue. Asian-owned stores line Eighth Avenue (which, by no accident, is on an express subway route to Manhattan's Chinatown). You'll find ethnic food stores, housewares, and inexpensive kids' clothing stores on each avenue. Here, Spanish is spoken; there, Chinese. Latino-run *botánica* stores have windows filled with saints and figurines. Chinese apothecaries sell herbal cures. Come for authentic ethnic food, romantic sunsets, and a weekend bike ride around the industrial waterfront.

The demographics in the neighborhood continue to shift, of course. Today the Latino community is a mash-up of Caribbean, Latino, Mexican, Central American, Ecuadorian, Dominican, Puerto Rican; the Chinese are mainly immigrants from Fujian province. It's an organized community thanks to such groups as the local Brooklyn Chinese American Association. Meanwhile, attracted by the housing stock, many young American professionals are moving in.

Sunset Park boasts of being the Big Apple's largest "walk to work" community. Activists, advocating for good jobs at a living wage on the waterfront, are fighting forces of gentrification. "See what a thriving walk-to-work community looks like," said Elizabeth Yeampierre, a champion of blue-collar workers and executive director of Uprose, a grassroots environmental justice group that's one of Brooklyn's oldest Latino community organizations. "It's the small businesses, bodegas and taquerias, and the variety of entrepreneurial business that make . . . Sunset Park so interesting. People working on the waterfront work in everything from mom-and-pop shops to auto-salvaging shops. These are the kinds of businesses that people without a formal education set up if they are entrepreneurial."

BEST BETS IN SUNSET PARK

1   Authentic ethnic food: Bánh mì and tacos, authentic Mexican, Malaysian, and Chinese cuisine. Have Malaysian at Nyonya. Try the steamed prawn dumplings at East Harbor Seafood Palace, which was selected for the Michelin Bib Gourmand list. For tacos, it's Tacos El Bronco.

2   Sunset romance: Pink and orange sunsets over New York Harbor are visible from Sunset Park's park. In summer, picnic at a free outdoor movie screening of a blockbuster classic.

3   Cheap shopping: Shop for inexpensive food, toys, basic clothes, and shoes. Walk downhill toward the water to Frankel's (est. 1890s) for discounted name-brand work boots and work clothes.

4   Industry City: Bike around Industry City (formerly Bush Terminal) and the Brooklyn Army Terminal. Snack at Industry City Food Hall, which features Colson Patisserie, Blue Marble ice cream, Ninja Bubble Tea, Liddabit Sweets, and Steve & Andy's Organics. In 2015, Smorgasburg and Brooklyn Flea were held at Industry City (they move around).

5 Environmental justice: Book in advance for a minitour of the neighborhood
with Uprose; you won't forget it. Visit the new waterside Bush Terminal Park,
for which the community lobbied for some fifteen years.

6 Arts and vibe: Visit Industry City's annual Open Studios or Tabla Rasa, an
admission-free art gallery with a social conscience. Shop the supermarkets for
hard-to-find vegetables, spices, breads, and other specialty ethnic ingredients.
Mingle with the Chinese, Latino, and hipster locals over darts at Soccer Tavern.

HISTORY SNAPSHOTS

As in much of Brooklyn, the subway played a major role in Sunset Park's evolution.
The area uphill of Fourth Avenue "remained largely undeveloped until the 1890s
when the Brooklyn Union Elevated Railway Company built a Third Avenue" subway, according to the NYC Landmarks Preservation Commission report on the
neighborhood. Sunset Park was settled by Irish Catholics fleeing the potato fam-
ine, followed by Polish and Scandinavian immigrants. "Little Norway" ran from
Forty-Fifth to Sixtieth Streets. Between World Wars I and II, a one-hundred-
thousand-person strong Finnish population supported many cooperatives—for
groceries and housing. You can still see the city's first not-for-profit cooperative
apartments, built by Finnish immigrants, at the Sunset Home Association at 549
Forty-First Street. Sixteen families who formed the Finnish Home Building Association in 1916, started the Alku and Alku Toinen Finnish Co-ops, a few blocks
away. Italian immigrants settled here in the early twentieth century, too, many
finding work in waterfront-related jobs.

South Brooklyn went into decline in the Depression and in ensuing decades
took a double hit with the demise of New York's shipping industry and the construction of Gowanus Expressway (Interstate 278), which carved the waterfront
away from the residential and retail heart of the neighborhood. This part of South
Brooklyn was recast as "Sunset Park" in the 1960s. In the 1980s, Latin American
and Asian immigration continued. By the 1980s and 1990s, when New York's crime
rate was high, Sunset Park was riddled by crack-cocaine use and violence. Greg
Allman's song "Don't Stand in My Way" describes a gunfight in Sunset Park.

Safety gradually improved, spurred by community activists, interventions by
Lutheran Medical Center, and a citywide drop in crime.

OLD/NEW BROOKLYN

You can see traces of old Brooklyn in Sunset Park's buildings: the rows of brownstone homes on the long, steep streets and the medieval-fortress-like former
Seventy-Eighth Police Precinct on Fourth Avenue, a New York City landmark
that is also listed on the National Register of Historic Places. Visit Saint Rocco's

Chapel, formerly a center of Italian life, and Fatih Camii Mosque, built in the 1980s on the site of an Irish and Norwegian dance club. And if you like really old bowling lanes reminiscent of the 1960s, bowl a few at Melody Lanes.

New York City has long been trying to breathe life back into Sunset Park's mile-long, once-vibrant industrial maritime properties. Finally, things are happening. Gargantuan, obsolete facilities (remnants of New York's glory days as a premier port) have been rehabbed into twenty-first-century work sites for artisanal manufacturing, food production, light industry, and storage. A fascinating mélange of small enterprises and arts organizations have moved into Industry City (formerly Bush Terminal), including the American Museum of Natural History, which stashes a collection of Native American canoes there. Visitors can attend special events at Industry City, eat at the new indoor food court, and walk along the waterfront in Bush Terminal Park. In 2015, a $1 billion makeover plan was announced for the Sunset Park industrial waterfront.

Should ferry or trolley service ever connect the Sunset Park waterfront to, say, Red Hook or Williamsburg, a new chapter in the neighborhood's economy would quickly open. (See "The Sixth Borough: Waterfront and Waterways," in "The New Brooklyn," section 2.)

CELEBS, FILMS, FICTION

In the 2006 film *The Departed*, Leonardo DiCaprio orders a cranberry juice at Irish Haven (5721 Fourth Avenue). For fiction, read Brooklynite Paul Auster's 2010 novel *Sunset Park*. Hubert Selby's 1964 novel *Last Exit to Brooklyn* roams through various neighborhoods, including Sunset Park.

NOSHES, RESTAURANTS, BARS IN SUNSET PARK

Industry City Food Hall, 220 36th Street
Johnny's Pizzeria ☎, 5806 5th Avenue, (718) 492-9735
Pacificana Chinese Restaurant ☎, 813 55th Street, (718) 871-2880
Soccer Tavern, 6004 8th Avenue, (718) 439-9336
Tacos El Bronco ☎, 4324 4th Avenue, (718) 788-2229

SELECT DESTINATIONS

Alku and Alku Toinen Finnish Co-op, at 826 and 816 43rd Street
Bush Terminal Park, Marginal Street between 44th and 50th Streets; enter at
    43rd Street
Fatih Camii Mosque, 5911 8th Avenue, (718) 438-6919
Industry City events, http://industrycity.com

Sunset Park and Sunset Park Recreation Center (see "Brooklyn's Waterfront and
   Parks," section 4)
Tabla Rasa Gallery, 224 48th Street, (718) 833-9100

☞ Like Sunset Park? Visit Gowanus, Bay Ridge, Avenue U (Chinese), and Bushwick (Latino).

Williamsburg

An Homage to the Unpaid and Overworked Artisans Who
Have Refined Our Sweet Tastes from the Cane Fields to the
Kitchens of the New World on the Occasion of the Demoli-
tion of the Domino Sugar Refining Plant
> —subtitle of Kara Walker's *A Subtlety or a*
> *Marvelous Sugar Baby* **art installation**
> **at the Domino Sugar Factory, 2014**

Williamsburg's hip and edgy, fun and famous—but
not necessarily spiffy. Emerge from the L subway at,
oh, the Graham Street station, one of several serving
Williamsburg. You'll likely see a ninety-nine-cent
store, nail salons, and a pizzeria. A hardware store
advertises "back and foot rub for men and women,"
near rolls of linoleum displayed on the sidewalk. If
you've come a long way, say, from Tokyo or California, you might think you got off at the wrong stop.
Absent is any visible fabulousness, no Times Square
lights ablaze.

Relax! Grit is half of Williamsburg's charm. Make
the pilgrimage to the palaces of new North Brooklyn: Brooklyn Brewery, Brooklyn Bowl, the Wythe
Hotel, and Mast Brothers Chocolate Makers. Experience the waterfront views (and ride the seasonal
East River Ferry). Williamsburg boasts all kinds of
interesting creative action: indie bands, zines, creative cuisine, and eclectic entertainment.

Williamsburg's easy to reach by ferry, foot, bike,
and subway. It's diverse: home to hipsters and Latino
and Hasidic communities. You can drink in fashionable retro bars where mixologists delicately balance
flavors. Williamsburg is a playground of nightlife
options. Local chefs are rewriting the book, cooking
up outstanding, thoughtfully creative farm-to-table

BASICS

MAPPING: Using GPS, orient to Brooklyn
Brewery. Main drags: Bedford, Driggs,
Union, and Graham Avenues, Lorimer
and Grand Streets. Use L, G, J, M,
Z subways, at multiple stops, and
ferries. Near the Williamsburg Bridge
and the neighborhoods of Bushwick,
Clinton Hill, Greenpoint, Wallabout.
Bounded roughly by the East River and
Kent, Flushing, Nassau, and Bushwick
Avenues.

EVENTS: Brooklyn Flea and Smorgasburg
(weekly in summer), Giglio Feast at Our
Lady of Mount Carmel Church, many
concerts and film events in McCarren
Park and 50 Kent.

SELFIES AND 'ZA: Selfies on the Williamsburg Bridge. Pizza at Motorino or
Best Pizza.

GREENMARKET: Saturdays year-round at
McCarren Park at 12th Street.

ACCOMMODATIONS: Wythe Hotel, the
Hoxton, the Pod, William Vale, McCarren Hotel, Williamsburg Hotel, Airbnb.

cuisine. You can linger in bookstores, buy organic small-batch cheeses, and contemplate a delightful array of vintage clothes, books, records, and furniture. It's a social scene for the postcollegiate set (many of whom can't afford to live here except in group apartments). This approximately 150-year-old neighborhood has turned a nifty trick: it seems to be getting both younger and richer, simultaneously.

Williamsburg is huge. Its distinct sections include Northside, Southside, and South Williamsburg. (The contentious boundaries of "East Williamsburg" are as variable as Mark Twain's New England weather. In 2014, the *Brooklyn Paper* said they don't acknowledge the existence of "East Williamsburg." Nor do we! It's just Williamsburg.) That said, Northside was once very Italian and still has an Italian flavor, diluted by many new young arrivals and hipsters. Across Grand Street, Southside was historically Puerto Rican and Latino. South Williamsburg today is largely Satmar Hasidic. Fleeing Europe in the 1940s, many Hasidic sects settled in the area defined by Division Avenue, Broadway, and Heyward Street to the Brooklyn Navy Yard, with shops along Lee Avenue. (The media have a field day punning about the bearded ones: the hipsters and the Hasidim. So do some hipsters. Williamsburg's pork specialty restaurant Traif was opened by a reform Jew. *Traif* means "unkosher" in Yiddish, an insider's joke.)

Largely, these groups live side by side, not intersecting except over real estate and on the subways. "Bahia is the one restaurant that is integrated in Williamsburg," a man in a local park told the author. "You see black, Latino, white Americans there. In the new restaurants, you are only going to find middle-class white kids." The gentrified Williamsburg waterfront—with high-rises, a ferry, weekend Smorgasburg, the foodie flea market, and a Trader Joe's—is as much a Manhattan outpost as Hasidic Lee Avenue is a throwback to nineteenth-century Hungary.

If your feet ache, you can explore Williamsburg just by hopping on and off the L subway line at various stops, from Bedford to Lorimer, Graham, and Grand Avenues.

BEST BETS IN WILLIAMSBURG

1 Iconic Brooklyn: Visit the Brooklyn Brewery. Bowl a game and catch a concert at Brooklyn Bowl. Sip your cocktail and contemplate the skyline at the Ides Bar atop the Wythe Hotel. For something quite different, visit the historic onion-domed Russian Orthodox Cathedral of the Transfiguration of Our Lord (est. 1922), which straddles Greenpoint.
2 Wowza food! Have breakfast at Egg and dinner at Maison Premiere, Zenkichi, Antica Pesa, or Reynard. Try Michelin-ranked Semilla. For old Brooklyn, it's Bamonte's for Italian or Peter Luger for steak (reservations required). For kosher eats, have the stuffed cabbage, chicken paprikash, and kugel at Gottlieb's Restaurant; mix it up with the Hasidic clientele. Visit Café El Puente

Restaurant for authentic Dominican fare. For more Latino ethnic eats, in South Williamsburg, Moore Street Market, one of New York's few extant indoor markets, has stalls selling authentic Caribbean, Puerto Rican, and Dominican foods. Williamsburg is the birthplace of Smorgasburg; in season on Saturdays, you can graze all day.

3 Bars! So many cool and varied places—dozens! The bar and cocktail scene is big and active and changes frequently. Start at Night of Joy or Skinny Dennis, Dram, the Camlin, Spuyten Duyvil, or Mugs Ale House, and proceed, carefully.

4 Walk a bridge, ride a ferry: Walk or bike across the beautiful Williamsburg Bridge. Hop the seasonal East River Ferry down to Dumbo—a great ride.

5 Waterfront, Manhattan skyline views! Williamsburg's views of mid-Manhattan's skyline are wonderful, so take a walk on the waterfront.

6 Entertainment and indie culture: See what's on at the Knitting Factory, Music Hall of Williamsburg, Pete's Candy Store, Output, or Brick Theater. (See "Brooklyn's Cultural Scene," section 4.)

7 Shops: Williamsburg's an excellent place to find both curated and just plain cheap vintage gear. Or, gents, go in the other direction and have a bespoke suit made at Brooklyn Tailors, on Grand Street. Don't miss GGrippo, a cashmere recycler, or Life:Curated gift store.

8 Flicks! Enjoy outdoor summer movies, Brooklyn Film Festival, and many film events. Go to a midnight show at Nitehawk Cinema and have dinner served by seemingly invisible waiters. UnionDocs Center for Documentary Art presents over a hundred films and events annually.

9 Chill, flirt, or exercise in McCarren Park: Enjoy this busy urban park—play soccer or baseball, or swim in the Olympic-sized outdoor McCarren Park Pool.

10 Diversity and activism: Go to El Puente's Three Kings Day Christmastime celebration, a Broadway-like musical with a social justice theme. Visit Northside Town Hall community center.

ART, FOOD, ACTIVISM

Art

Williamsburg is home to scores of artists, musicians, writers, and talented folks who work in New York City's vast creative economy. You'll find a lot of small art initiatives and cultural institutions here. The newest is the Museum of Food and Drink. One of the oldest, Pete's Candy Store (a bar in a former candy shop), presents regular readings. The Brooklyn Art Library hosts the innovative Sketchbook Project, a crowdsourced archive of over thirty thousand sketchbooks contributed by people from dozens of nations. City Reliquary is an Everyman's museum. Take some time exploring; each of Williamsburg's quirky cultural institutions has an interesting backstory.

For instance, take the open-to-the-public space called SLAM (an acronym for Streb Lab for Action Mechanics), where you can watch art being made, in a sense. SLAM was created by choreographer Elizabeth Streb, a 1997 MacArthur "genius grant" recipient who moved to Williamsburg when it was still raw. At her organization's space, you can wander in and watch Streb's troupe—"extreme action specialists," she calls them—rehearse. Streb describes her work as "a mixture of slam dancing, exquisite and amazing human flight, and a wild action sport which captures kids, older people, and the general public's hearts and minds and bodies." It's an open space where a lot of different things happen simultaneously: kids fly on the trapeze, while the Streb team explores moves on huge hardware gizmos. (Inventing these contraptions, Streb said, is like "designing instruments for a new kind of orchestra.") SLAM's openness, said Streb, who grew up working class, "demythologizes the idea of privacy in the dance and the arts." Streb's work plays with conceptual assumptions about space, gravity, time, fear, and human capacity.

Brooklyn's Locavore Food Scene

Restaurants and food shops featuring creative, organic, and locally sourced foods abound here. Tourists who don't have time for a sit-down meal can get the idea by

---

BROOKLYN VOICES

ELIZABETH STREB
Director of the SLAM Extreme Action Company at SLAM, the Streb Lab for Action Mechanics

My notion was that humans could fly. Real flight is a grisly sport, and the drama is in that moment of impact, when flight fails. The traditional dance world's mimicking of lightness, so technically, in ballet, in my view wasn't flight at all. It was a pretending technique. Peter Pan never really lands. I'm redefining human flight. . . . It's abrupt and not durational. You could say I disagree with the classical calibration of movement that's been theatricalized.

I came to Brooklyn in 1995 in search of an empty garage. In my Manhattan studio, when we landed all eight dancers, the whole building shook. I needed a place where first and foremost I didn't have to be careful of the real estate and I could do whatever I needed to do, whatever the action required. You need that freedom if the action is going to be extreme and vivid.

At SLAM, I wanted to have cotemporal activity, with no walls. I'm honoring the source of our funding. I thought, "We are a nonprofit company, so this is going to be a public space." I think most art nonprofits operate privately. I just let it rip.

I'm completely clear that Brooklyn is the future. I know for sure my work over the past thirteen years wouldn't have evolved like this if I hadn't been working in a garage in Brooklyn, with the doors wide open.

visiting the Brooklyn Kitchen and the Meat Hook. They are two adjoining shops, the former a kitchenware and organic-food store and the latter a butcher, operating in a single storefront near the BQE (look for the painted cow outside). And don't be surprised if the young apron-wearing staff have degrees in philosophy from fine liberal arts colleges.

The Brooklyn Kitchen is a destination cook shop where you might find just the perfect gift—fish-bone tweezers, anyone?—or stock up on a curated selection of jams, breads, specialty cheeses, and organic vegetables. Their popular two-hour classes sometimes feature pizza making with a chef from famous Roberta's restaurant in Bushwick.

The Meat Hook is the one place where you may actually want to see how the proverbial sausage is made. (You can, every weekday.) Specializing in locally sourced meats, the Meat Hook goes whole hog: it purchases entire animals—grass-fed cows, lambs, pigs, turkeys, and chickens—from small family farms and prepares them on-site. The store has a policy of minimal waste, so it uses every part of the animal. It makes more than fifty kinds of sausages with about a dozen available at any given time, and it may be the only butcher you'll meet that displays beautiful cows and pigs on its website and talks about paying small farmers a living wage.

The Meat Hook and Brooklyn Kitchen are much beloved, are highly regarded, and double as a social environment too. If reading this makes you hungry, make a beeline to the Meat Hook Sandwich Shop.

See "The New Brooklyn," section 2.

Activism

Williamsburg isn't all art, commerce, food, drink, and play. Community activists are working to help Williamsburg's low-income residents. In North Williamsburg, Firehouse 212, built in 1869, was occupied in the 1970s by Williamsburg residents protesting a pattern of municipal neglect; in 2016, it finally reopened as Northside Town Hall Community and Cultural Center. Southside community activism has been led by the nonprofit organization El Puente.

HISTORY SNAPSHOTS

The village of Williamsburgh was chartered in 1827. German immigrants settled here in the mid-nineteenth century. In 1855, Williamsburgh joined Brooklyn (and dropped the *h* in its name).

Williamsburg was a getaway for the one-percenters: the Vanderbilts, Commodore Perry, and William W. Whitney came to dine at fancy hotels and restaurants in the city across the way, Brooklyn. Peter Luger, the steak restaurant, founded in 1887, is a survivor of that era. In 1903, the Williamsburg Bridge opened. A stream

BROOKLYN VOICES

LUIS GARDEN ACOSTA
Founder and President of El Puente

When I founded El Puente in 1982, everyone in the Southside of Williamsburg was Latino. Seventy percent were on some form of government assistance. In 1980, the Southside was the city's teenage gang capital, according to the media. Today maybe half of the Southside of Williamsburg is Latino. Even the Latino professionals from the Southside who got priced out [of Williamsburg] and used to move to Bushwick can't afford that now. Instead they are moving to the Bronx, Astoria—as far away as they have to go to afford housing.

That's the challenge for all of us. We have people coming into a neighborhood—a place that was one class and color, one Latino community—of a different class, color, and language. We are both living in our own silos. Our challenge is to create community.

I'd tell visitors that the Southside of Williamsburg is filled with brilliant, wonderful people who have been here a long time and led a movement to reclaim what was once a very difficult place. Would you stay in a place where in a square mile, virtually one adolescent died every week? In 1979, it was a horror. But people stayed, and organizations like El Puente dealt with the gangs. Soon there were no more gangs, that's an incredible piece of history. It took us fifteen years to get a park near the Domino Sugar Factory. We fought development of a fifty-five-foot incinerator in coalition with the Hasidim. We developed affordable housing and created El Puente Academy of Peace and Justice. This is a vibrant and resilient Latino community. We know how to work hard and get things done.

of immigrants fled into the relative openness of Williamsburg, leaving Manhattan's overcrowded, sickly slums. The *New York Tribune* of the era referred to the Williamsburg Bridge as "Jews Highway."

Heavy industry was sited along the waterfront. Precursors to Standard Oil and Corning Glassware (Astral Oil and Brooklyn Flint Glass, respectively) and to Pfizer Pharmaceutical Company were located here. They've left as a legacy a picturesque postindustrial landscape but a very polluted Newtown Canal in nearby Greenpoint.

OLD/NEW BROOKLYN

Williamsburg was a place where things were made, which explains why apartments have been carved out of an old mustard-manufacturing plant on Metropolitan Avenue and why the Mini Mall building on Bedford Avenue was, in its first incarnation, the Real Form Girdle building. The former Domino Sugar Factory, now a rising apartment complex, had for over a century produced sugar, generating steady work for residents. Penicillin was first mass-produced in a Williamsburg-area Pfizer plant that's now incubating small food companies. Williamsburg textile mills supplied the garment industry; Newcastle Fabrics on Wythe Avenue still does.

The intersections between old and new Brooklyn are poignant in Williamsburg's only landmarked district, one-block-long Fillmore Place between Roebling Street and Driggs Avenue north of the Williamsburg Bridge. Built before the Civil War, in the 1850s, it imparts a distinct sense of historic, old Brooklyn in the midst of Williamsburg's fast-changing contemporary scene.

Hipster Williamsburg's dynamic art, foodie, indie music, and energetic DIY culture have helped propel Brooklyn into global visibility. But as apartment towers and rents have both risen, some of the vital art scene has already relocated to Bushwick and beyond. Felicitously for some, ominously for others, chains are arriving; a Ralph Lauren store opened its first Brooklyn shop, in Williamsburg, in 2015. The urban pioneers who moved to Williamsburg in its freewheeling days of the 1990s may one day reminisce, "I lived there when . . ."

Taka Sasaki, a stylist, at Williamsburg's Krasi hair salon. (Photo by E. Freudenheim, courtesy of Sasaki and Krasi, 2015)

CELEBS, FILMS, FICTION

Actor Mel Brooks grew up at 65 South Third Street. Joseph Papp was born here. *The Amazing Spiderman 2*, the Batman film *The Dark Knight Rises*, and the series *Blacklist* and *Persons of Interest* were shot on location at the old Pfizer headquarters, now known as 630 Flushing Avenue. *OxD, One Extraordinary Day* is a documentary by Craig Lowy about Elizabeth Streb's Williamsburg-based troupe's performance atop the London Eye prior to the 2012 Summer Olympics.

For fiction set here, read the classics *A Tree Grows in Brooklyn*, by Betty Smith, *A Williamsburg Trilogy*, by Daniel Fuchs, and *Tropic of Capricorn*, by Henry Miller. More recently, *The Sunshine Crust Baking Factory*, by Stacy Wakefield, and the indie-published book *Killing Williamsburg*, by Bradley Spinelli, are recommended by local bookstores. *Solos*, by Kitty Burns Florey, depicts life in contemporary Williamsburg.

NOSHES, RESTAURANTS, BARS IN WILLIAMSBURG

Bahia, 690 Grand Street, (718) 218-9592
Bamonte's Restaurant ☎, 32 Withers Street, (718) 384-8831
Bedford Cheese Shop, 229 Bedford Avenue, (718) 599-7588
Best Pizza, 33 Havemeyer Street, (718) 599-2210
Brooklyn Brewery, 79 North 11th Street, (718) 486-7422
Café El Puente Restaurant ☎, 231 South 4th Street, (718) 388-2416
Delaware and Hudson, 135 North 5th Street, (718) 218-8191
Diner, 85 Broadway, (718) 486-3077
Egg, 109 North 3rd Street, (718) 302-5151
Gottlieb's ☎, 352 Roebling Street, (718) 384-6612
Maison Premiere, 298 Bedford Avenue, (347) 335-0446
Marlow & Sons, 81 Broadway, (718) 384-1441
Motorino, 139 Broadway, (718) 599-8899
Peter Luger Steak House ☎, 178 Broadway, (718) 387-7400
Reynard, 80 Wythe Avenue, (718) 460-8004
Sandwich Shop, 495 Lorimer Street, (718) 302-4665
Semilla, 160 Havemeyer Street, (718) 782-3474
Traif, 229 South 4th Street, (347) 844-9578

SELECT DESTINATIONS

Book Thug Nation, 100 North 3rd Street
Brooklyn Bowl, 61 Wythe Avenue, (718) 963-3369
Brooklyn Kitchen, 100 Frost Street, (718) 389-2982
Museum of Food and Drink, 62 Bayard Street, (718) 387-2875

Music Hall of Williamsburg, 66 North 6th Street, (718) 486-5400
Nitehawk Cinema, 136 Metropolitan Avenue, (718) 384-3980
Pete's Candy Store, 709 Lorimer Street, (718) 302-3770
Russian Orthodox Cathedral of the Transfiguration of Our Lord, 228 North
    12th Street, (718) 387-1064
SLAM: Streb Lab for Action Mechanics, 51 North 1st Street, (718) 384-6491
Spoonbill and Sugartown Booksellers, 218 Bedford Avenue, (718) 387-7322
Swords-Smith, 98 South 4th Street, (347) 599-2969
UnionDocs Center for Documentary Art, 322 Union Avenue, (718) 395-7902

☞ Like Williamsburg? Visit Greenpoint and Bushwick (youth culture), Borough
Park and Crown Heights (Hasidic), or Bushwick and Sunset Park (Latino).

Windsor Terrace and Kensington

Windsor Terrace, I know it from way back when it was solidly populated primarily by uniformed services and very parish-driven. In those days, if you wanted a home, you pretty much went through Holy Name RC Church and church publications. A lot of homes passed from grandparents to parents to their kids and so on. Today the ethnic and religious mix has changed significantly and the politics too. Windsor Terrace, . . . today it's very progressive and filled with young families.

—Marty Markowitz, Windsor Terrace resident and former Brooklyn borough president

BASICS

MAPPING: Using GPS, orient to Farrell's Bar and Grill. Use F, G (15th Street, Prospect Park West, Church Avenue) subways. Near Prospect Park and the neighborhoods of Borough Park, Ditmas Park, Park Slope, Prospect Lefferts Gardens, Prospect Park South. Windsor Terrace is bounded roughly by Prospect Park West, Prospect Park Southwest, Green-Wood, 7th Avenue. Kensington is bounded roughly by Caton, Foster, Coney Island, and MacDonald Avenues.

SELFIES AND 'ZA: Selfies on horseback or at Terrace Bagels. For pizza, Enzo's Brick Oven.

GREENMARKETS: Wednesdays year-round, Prospect Park West at 15th Street. Seasonally Sundays at PS 154. Saturdays at Fort Hamilton Parkway and East 5th.

ACCOMMODATIONS: Gowanus hotels, Airbnb.

Visit two side-by-side neighborhoods that have almost nothing in common; welcome to Brooklyn!

Bite-sized, homey Windsor Terrace is sandwiched between Prospect Park and verdant Green-Wood. Come for a drink at historic Farrell's Bar and Grill, a throwback to the neighborhood's Irish past.

Windsor Terrace, population twenty thousand (and majority white), is a fiercely community-oriented place. People on the street stop to talk with acquaintances about their kids and cats, and they lend a hand, whether volunteering at street fairs or shoveling snow for a neighbor. Once a neighborhood of firefighters and cops, Windsor Terrace is less blue collar today. Fewer homes fly American flags, once ubiquitous here. But shopkeepers and customers still know one another; Windsor Terrace is a neighborhood on a first-name basis.

Adjacent Kensington is more than twice as large as Windsor Terrace, and its mix of ethnicities is global—Russian, Polish, Mexican, Ukrainian, Hasidic, Irish, Darfurian, Bangladeshi, and Pakistani (and matched by equally eclectic housing styles).

Unexpected discoveries include Kensington Stables, where Prospect Park's rentable horses are housed, and a slot-car-racing joint, Buzz-A-Rama. Rabbit Hole Ensemble, which has been producing plays in Manhattan and Brooklyn venues since 2005, is based here.

That an immigrant-rich enclave was named after pristine, moneyed Kensington, of London's Kensington Palace fame, is amusing. So is a comment made by the owners of Gold's Horseradish, which was manufactured in Kensington for decades: "When the Dodgers left Brooklyn, they left Gold's to supply the heat."

BEST BETS IN WINDSOR TERRACE AND KENSINGTON

1 Prospect Park: It's nearby and it's fabulous, with facilities for skating, cycling, running, and more (see "Brooklyn's Waterfronts and Parks," section 4).
2 Eat and drink: Have an ice-cold beer out of a Styrofoam cup they call a "container" at Farrell's Bar and Grill (est. 1933). Take out Australian steak and cheese pie at tiny Dub Pies; enjoy a cup of coffee at Elk Coffee. For firefighter-sized portions, eat Mexican at Elora's. Buy fare for an Italian picnic at Piccola or United Meat Market.
3 Ethnic: Explore the ethnic shops on Church and Coney Island Avenues. Have a Russian spa experience at Sadoony USA.
4 How people live: Admire Fuller Place, which often placed high in the Brooklyn Botanic Garden's "Greenest Block in Brooklyn" competition. Enjoy Kensington's riotously varied architecture.
5 Slot-car racing: A rarity! Yes! You can race slot cars at Buzz-A-Rama (check hours).
6 Ride a horse: Rent a horse at Kensington Stables and ride the three-and-a-half-mile bridle path in Prospect Park.
7 Live like a local! Jog in Prospect Park. Bike to Coney Island along Ocean Parkway mall. Meet friends at Terrace Books or Connecticut Muffin.

OLD/NEW BROOKLYN

Oh, about Farrell's . . . Farrell's Bar and Grill, it's said, was Brooklyn's first bar to open after Prohibition was repealed. It's an old-fashioned Irish pub with polished wood, mirrors, and brass—and it's still chairless: everyone drinks standing up. Only in 1972, when Shirley MacLaine, accompanied by journalist Pete Hamill, who attended school down the street, showed up here, did it grudgingly start to serve women. Don't expect a bastion of liberalism here. It's still old school.

CELEBS, FILMS, FICTION

At 174 Windsor Place, author Isaac Asimov's father ran a candy store. The family lived across the street. Al Pacino's 1975 film *Dog Day Afternoon* was shot on

Prospect Park West between Seventeenth and Eighteenth Streets. The movie *Smoke* was shot at a "Brooklyn Cigar Store" set, across from Farrell's Bar and Grill. A rougher, more colorful Windsor Terrace of yesteryear is depicted by authors Joe Flaherty and Patrick Fenton. Read the 2014 graphic novel *Lena Finkle's Magic Barrel*, by Anya Ulinich.

NOSHES, RESTAURANTS, BARS IN WINDSOR TERRACE AND KENSINGTON

Connecticut Muffin, 206 Prospect Park West, (718) 965-2067
Dub Pies, 211 Prospect Park West, (718) 788-2448
Elora's ☎, 272 Prospect Park West, (718) 788-6190
Enzo's Brick Oven, 217 Prospect Park West, (718) 499-3150
Farrell's Bar and Grill ☎, 215 Prospect Park West, (718) 788-8779
Terrace Bagels ☎, 224 Prospect Park West, (718) 768-3943

SELECT DESTINATIONS

Buzz-A-Rama, 69 Church Avenue, (718) 853-1800
Fuller Place, between Prospect Avenue and Windsor Place
Kensington Stables, 51 Caton Place, (718) 972-4588
Sadoony USA, 1158 McDonald Avenue, (718) 951-9000
Terrace Books, 242 Prospect Park West, (718) 788-3475
United Meat Market, 219 Prospect Park West, (718) 768-7227

☞   Like Windsor Terrace / Kensington? Visit Park Slope, Bay Ridge, and Flatbush.

Where to Go, What to Do

BRIC Celebrate Brooklyn! summer festival in Prospect Park. (Photo by E. Freudenheim, 2014)

Brooklyn's Cultural Scene
Fifteen Best Bets

There is no such thing as a typical BAM experience; our programming—
from film to music, theater to dance, literary and family fare—is as varied
as our audiences and the diverse borough of Brooklyn. My advice is to allow
for surprises!   —Katy Clark, president, Brooklyn Academy of Music

"Allow for surprises" is good advice. Brooklyn's cultural life isn't exactly where, or
what, one conventionally might expect it to be. In this multimedia, multitasking
cultural environment, you can hear indie rock concerts in a bowling alley (Williamsburg's Brooklyn Bowl), dance the rueda de casino outside an architectural
icon (Brooklyn Central Library), and go to a concert in a cemetery (Green-Wood)!
To help you traverse this cultural landscape, here's a rundown of the geography
of Brooklyn's six major cultural hubs and thumbnail sketches of the fifteen top
cultural destinations.

OVERVIEW: BROOKLYN'S SIX CULTURAL HUBS

Cultural Hub 1: Brooklyn Cultural District and BAM Area

The Brooklyn Cultural District is Brooklyn's version of Manhattan's Lincoln Center but more diffuse and more diverse. More than fifty cultural organizations,
small museums, and performing arts groups, all driven by their singular passions,
missions, and artistic visions, coalesce into this cultural nerve center. BAM is the
heart of it. Public transportation here is awesome; almost every train in the New
York City system stops nearby at the Barclays / Atlantic Avenue station and many
at Brooklyn Borough Hall, near the New York Transit Museum and the Brooklyn
Historical Society. Visitors at any time of year have a rich set of options: performances, films, exhibitions, discussions, and artist talks.

Performing arts venues include BAM, BRIC House, Theatre for a New Audience, Irondale Ensemble Project, Roulette, and more. Barclays Center draws big-
name talent. The renovated 1928 Paramount Theater at Long Island University's
Brooklyn campus, known for its rare 1920s Wurlitzer organ, opens around 2018
as the Brooklyn Paramount. In terms of visual arts, BAM is opening a new gallery at the BAM Strong. The Museum of Contemporary African Diasporan Arts
(MoCADA) has long been in the area. At UrbanGlass, the Agnes Varis Art Center and Robert Lehman Gallery host exhibitions of art glass.

"The growth of the Brooklyn Cultural District has brought an infusion of different audiences and numbers of colleagues in a similar pursuit of their own artistic missions," said BAM's executive producer, Joseph Melillo. "This energizes and animates the art community here. We aren't alone anymore at BAM! There are new and innovative things that we hadn't thought possible but that we can do with this art community."

A plaza at the intersection of Flatbush Avenue and Lafayette Avenue will be the site for performances, outdoor movies, and public art, opening soon. Behind the scenes, the Brooklyn Cultural District houses dozens of offices, workshops, and studio spaces for arts organizations. They range from internationally celebrated Mark Morris Dance Company, which holds dance classes at its headquarters across from BAM, to 651 Arts, a nonprofit that has created cultural programming rooted in the African Diaspora since 1988.

Entertainment and culture are in this area's DNA. Before World War II, theaters and movie houses thrived along Fulton Street and Flatbush Avenue. Some abandoned theaters, like the Paramount and the Strand, have been revamped for twenty-first-century productions.

Tips: Don't ask directions to the "Brooklyn Cultural District," a name invented by officialdom. Just ask for the name of wherever you are going, like BAM. To see a list of all the organizations in the Brooklyn Cultural District, look online at the Downtown Brooklyn Arts Alliance website.

Cultural Hub 2: North Brooklyn along the L Train

For less formal productions and a younger crowd, head to Williamsburg, Greenpoint, and Bushwick. You'll find dozens of venues for indie bands and film screenings, art shows, spoken word and performance art, dance, and collaborative, multimedia events. Expect a flexible scene where an indie band from Berlin might be playing in a bookstore that doubles as a bar and gallery. Bushwick is the place to go to see art galleries. (See section 3, "The Neighborhoods.")

Cultural Hub 3: The Brooklyn Museum / Eastern Parkway Hub

As in European cities where the cultural heavyweights are located close together, the Brooklyn Museum, Brooklyn Central Library, Prospect Park, and the Brooklyn Botanic Garden are all within walking distance along elegant Eastern Parkway. Not far away are the Brooklyn Children's Museum and the Weeksville Heritage Center.

Cultural Hub 4: Dumbo and Brooklyn Bridge Park

Dumbo's cultural calendar is packed with many attractions: art galleries, Bargemusic concerts, and the St. Ann's Warehouse theater's performances, plus public art installations, literary events, and concerts in Brooklyn Bridge Park. The Brooklyn Historical Society and Brooklyn Children's Museum opened satellites in Dumbo in 2016.

Cultural Hub 5: Literary Life Borough-Wide

Literary events and readings are held all over the borough in bookstores, bars, and other venues. (See details in the following pages.)

Cultural Hub 6: Public Spaces—Parks and Libraries

The parks serve as outdoor museums, movie theaters, and summertime concert halls. Try to catch a memorable event, such as the annual outdoor reading of Walt Whitman's "Song of Myself" in Brooklyn Bridge Park or an outdoor play or mausoleum tour in Green-Wood. The public libraries, notably the Dweck Center in the Central Library in Grand Army Plaza, offer a marvelous schedule of free multicultural films, lectures, readings, and performances.

TOP FIFTEEN BROOKLYN CULTURAL DESTINATIONS

1. BAM—Brooklyn Academy of Music

BAM is a performing and cinema arts complex that showcases innovative dance, theater, music, opera, and film. A world-class venue, it's been likened to London's Barbican Centre.

One of BAM's hottest tickets is for its signature Next Wave Festival, an international showcase for cutting-edge performance. BAMcinématek presents film classics, premieres, festivals, and retrospectives. Year-round, literary events and artist talks are convened. BAM's DanceAfrica is the nation's largest festival dedicated to African and African-diasporic dance, performance, art, and film. It includes a weekend-long outdoor African marketplace. BAM also runs the city's largest Martin Luther King Day program. Executive producer Melillo described the combination of BAM's community and international programming to the author as "authentically who we are as a cultural institution."

BAM's physical empire is growing. By 2018, it will span four buildings on three different streets. On Lafayette Avenue in Fort Greene, you will find the Peter Jay Sharp Building, the Howard Gilman Opera House, BAM Rose Cinemas, and the upstairs Lepercq Space and BAMcafé. Next door, at 321 Ashland Place, is the more affordable BAM Fisher, which shows more experimental works and serves BAM as a training ground or "field team." The new BAM Karen will have four new cinemas plus the never-before-open-to-the-public BAM Hamm Archives, located in a new multiuse building, also on Ashland Place. At 651 Fulton Street, the BAM Harvey Theater will anchor BAM Strong, a new integrated complex with BAM's first permanent gallery for visual art exhibitions, a terrace, a café, and a restaurant.

BRIC House and UrbanGlass, the world's largest publicly accessible glassblowing facility, and its gift shop and showroom sit on the same block as BAM Strong. Former BAM president Karen Brooks Hopkins called this "a complete 'culture block' on the northern border of the Brooklyn Cultural District."

To explore BAM, find your way to the area defined by Flatbush Avenue, Fulton Street, Hanson Place, and St. Felix Street.

For information: http://www.bam.org.

2. Brooklyn Museum

The Brooklyn Museum is one of New York City's most significant museums, with an annual attendance of over half a million. Founded in 1823 in Brooklyn Heights, the museum is now located in Prospect Heights adjacent to the Brooklyn Botanic Garden. A public plaza and modern glass entranceway lead inside to the original spacious Beaux-Arts building designed in 1893 by McKim, Mead & White. As of 2015, the Brooklyn Museum stands poised for an exciting future under the directorship of Anne Pasternak, formerly head of Creative Time.

The Brooklyn Museum's more than one million objects range from ancient Egyptian death masks to Central African totem poles to artifacts from the Pacific Islands, Melanesia, and the Andes. The Asian art collection, started in 1903, includes rare Korean art and pieces from Iran's Qajar dynasty. Its Egyptian collection, much of it in storage, is considered one of the world's finest. Well known for its period rooms, including an elaborate 1864 Moorish-style room from the estate of John D. Rockefeller, the museum also has a highly regarded American gallery of paintings, sculpture, and decorative arts.

Embracing new Brooklyn's zeitgeist, Brooklyn Museum was reinvented as a cutting-edge institution under the leadership of Arnold Lehman, its former Shelby White and Leon Levy director. It's one of the world's few major museums with a

---

BROOKLYN VOICES

ARNOLD LEHMAN
Shelby White and Leon Levy Director of the Brooklyn Museum, 1997–2015

The Brooklyn Museum's audience has never been both this young or this diverse. I think those elements—youth and diversity—are almost synonymous with the change that's taken place in much of Brooklyn over the years. Beyond the glass façade and other major improvements at the Museum, it is the human dimension that has changed most dramatically.

Brooklyn today is a very powerful nexus of what's going on in the arts around the world. I do think it's true that when artists are looking for a place to work, Brooklyn is that place, because there's such vibrancy and so many different kinds of art being done here. It's not as if there are just a few well-known artists working here who are stars, and the rest are chopped liver. There are so many outstanding artists in Brooklyn now, you couldn't even try to name them all—and I won't!

Manhattan is a prelude to the arts in Brooklyn—any visitor to New York must see the Brooklyn Museum, must go to BAM, must see artists' studios from Williamsburg to Bushwick to Red Hook, to get a sense of the real vitality of the arts in New York City.

BROOKLYN VOICES

ELIZABETH A. SACKLER

Founder of the Elizabeth A. Sackler Center for Feminist Art at the Brooklyn Museum

Whether you are an artist or not, people who see [Judy Chicago's] *The Dinner Party* talk about what it means to them. When they come with a child or grandchild, brother or sister, grandparents, it starts a conversation. I believe *The Dinner Party* is a transformative exhibition.

We are a center for feminist art, and with that comes a political lens. The Sackler Center is not just about "feminist art." When we look at any art through a feminist lens, we may see things we have heretofore not seen, which is to say we've *all* been brought up with patriarchal eyes. We need to ask, What do we see in art, and why is it that we see what we are seeing? The Sackler Center has raised the bar of inclusion for women. It has also opened a window onto the inequities and disparity between male and female artists.

During the 2016–2017 season, for our tenth anniversary, the Brooklyn Museum is undertaking an unprecedented project: We are reinstalling our encyclopedic collections and temporary exhibitions with programming through a gender lens. This includes our institutional history—the role women have played in our own institution—and didactics. This promises to be revelatory and a game-changer in the museum world.

robust and tangible commitment to feminism, embodied in the Elizabeth A. Sackler Center for Feminist Art, opened in 2007.

An activist feminist art center (not a gallery), the center is an important hub for educational programs and discussions about feminism and art and for the annual "Sackler Center First Awards" for outstanding women. Elizabeth A. Sackler, founder of the center, calls it her "enduring activist declaration." Don't miss the stunning *The Dinner Party* installation by Judy Chicago, on permanent display at the Elizabeth A. Sackler Center for Feminist Art.

The museum has mounted several blockbusters showcasing "material culture." These shows—*Hip-Hop Nation: Roots, Rhymes, and Rage*; *Fashion World of Jean Paul Gaultier*; and *The Rise of Sneaker Culture*—have raised eyebrows in some circles, but they've generated public buzz and critical acclaim, too. You'll also find erudite shows and globally themed exhibitions reflecting and exploring the experience of Brooklyn's various populations, for instance, *Basquiat: The Unknown Notebooks* and *Impressionism and the Caribbean: Francisco Oller and His Transatlantic World*, alongside standing exhibits such as the Egyptian *Mummy Chamber* and *African Innovations*.

"Target First Saturday" at the Brooklyn Museum is a uniquely Brooklyn experience. It's held from about six p.m. until eleven p.m. on the first Saturday of every month (except September). Some five thousand guests descend on the museum for free concerts, lectures, films, open galleries, and hands-on art activities for kids and adults. You'll never forget the Brooklyn cornucopia of varying ages, races, and backgrounds. Everything (except food and drink) is free. Some events require admission tickets, dispensed free at the Visitor Center.

Grab a sandwich at the Counter Café, or splurge at the Michelin-rated restaurant Saul. The museum has an outdoor piazza, a fun fountain with random geysers, and a small archaeological garden. The gift shop sells handmade clothes, jewelry, posters, and books. The museum is open late on Thursdays.

For information: https://www.brooklynmuseum.org.

3. BRIC Arts | Media House

At BRIC Arts | Media House, near BAM, you'll experience a diverse, arty, expressive Brooklyn vibe.

The BRIC House's indoor "stoop" amphitheater is a fine place to meet friends, whatever the weather. You might see an art exhibit, catch a community discussion about a topical issue (the town hall meeting on gentrification in 2015 was packed), or watch a performance. There's free Wi-Fi and a café. Mondays through Thursdays you can watch through the TV studio's glass window as hip Brooklyn anchors interview locals about trends and news on BRIC TV, a 24/7 television channel by, for, and about Brooklyn. It is New York City's biggest community-access TV channel. You can watch it streamed live online or on cable television.

BRIC has a lot of frying pans in the fire. It's a community art and media center, gallery, theater, café, town hall, media-training center, and meeting spot. It's like the thermometer of the borough; if some issue is going on, you're likely to hear about it at BRIC. It's also the organization behind Prospect Park's blockbuster summer series, BRIC Celebrate Brooklyn! and the new BRIC Jazzfest, initiated in 2015. "BRIC is Brooklyn's largest presenter of free cultural programming and likely one of the biggest in the city," said Leslie Schultz, BRIC's president.

"BRIC Celebrate Brooklyn! is a special place," executive producer Jack Walsh told the author. "On tour, these artists play one similar venue after another. Celebrate stands out. I stood on the stage with British rock singer Robert Plant from Led Zeppelin at one in the morning after he performed, and he's looking out at the empty venue saying in that raspy voice, 'Jack, Jack, you've really got a good vibe here. You've really got a good place here.' They get a sense that they're not just playing a show for money but for the people."

"We've had lots of stars" in Prospect Park, he recalled, ticking off Betty Carter ("a fantastic jazz singer from Fort Greene, . . . a massively awesome presence. . . . She was here in the 1980s"), Manu Chao from Spain ("a cult figure, a counterculture socialist rock party band," from the 1990s), Bob Dylan, and David Byrne ("the quintessential New Yorker; this is his city; when he performs here, it's for the people").

Have something to say? Any Brooklyn resident can take a brief orientation class and become a producer on Brooklyn Public Network's Free Speech TV, making a very Brooklyn-esque statement about the importance of the proverbial little guy.

"Today the challenge is to continue to reach the culturally underserved, as Brooklyn's demographics undergo tectonic changes," said Schultz. BRIC represents "old-Brooklyn values in a new shell, in that we value diversity, community, and neighborliness."

Entrance to BRIC House is free; its programs are free or very low cost. BRIC House is located near BAM and Barclays and not far from the Manhattan Bridge.

For information: http://www.bricartsmedia.org.

4. Festivals

Brooklyn's major multiday and multisite festivals include BAM's Next Wave Festival, the Brooklyn Botanic Garden's Cherry Blossom and Sakura Matsuri Festival, DanceAfrica, the Brooklyn Book Festival, BRIC Celebrate Brooklyn!, and BRIC Jazzfest.

The AfroPunk Festival, the Central Brooklyn Jazz Consortium Festival, and Red Hook Jazz Festival, plus summertime concerts in the parks, are other Brooklyn music festival standouts. To give a sense of the size of these events, the Brooklyn Hip-Hop Festival, established in 2005, attracts as many as twenty thousand fans.

Attend the Bushwick Open Studios Festival for art. Williamsburg's sprawling Northside Festival features over a week of bands, "innovators, creators and filmmakers." Attend the relatively new BEAT Festival. Open House New York is a unique program in which the public can visit otherwise-inaccessible places citywide. The Brooklyn Hoops Festival, Renegade Craft Fair, and Taste Talks are popular.

Ethnic festivals in a place as diverse as Brooklyn should be, and are, awesome. Among the most popular are the International African Arts Festival, Williamsburg's religious Giglio festival, and the Great Irish Fair. The biggest is the West Indian American Day Parade.

Brooklyn's literary and film festivals are huge and are covered elsewhere in this chapter.

For information: see "Festivals in Brooklyn" in "The New Brooklyn," section 2.

5. Movies and Indie Films

BAMcinématek runs incredible film series, organized by theme, director, leading star, and era, and shows indie films, classics, and select first-run movies as well. Williamsburg's Nitehawk Cinema doesn't just take the cake; it serves it—you can dine and watch a flick as drinks and food are served at your seat by waiters who float ethereally through the darkened theater. Light Industry screens interesting, if obscure, old films. Bell House in Gowanus and the Wythe Hotel in Williamsburg both occasionally screen films. UnionDocs Center for Documentary Art thoughtfully presents film, video, sound, photography, and other documentary forms. Spectacle is a volunteer-run community screening space for offbeat works. Generic first-run movie houses can be found in Brooklyn Heights (UA Multiplex), Downtown Brooklyn (Alamo Drafthouse Cinema, opening in 2016), Sheepshead

Cobble Hill Cinemas, built as Lido Theater in 1925. (Photo by E. Freudenheim, 2015)

Bay (UA IMAX), and Williamsburg (Williamsburg Cinemas). Only the Alpine in Bay Ridge and Cobble Hill Cinemas remain of the borough's better old, small, neighborhood theaters.

SUMMER OUTDOOR MOVIES (FREE)

You can see a free movie outdoors just about every evening of the week in July and August somewhere in Brooklyn. Some settings are spectacular.

Here are some venues: Classics and blockbusters are shown at Coney Island's Flicks on the Beach (Mondays); Red Hook Park Summer Film Festival (Tuesdays); SummerScreen in Greenpoint's McCarren Park (Wednesdays); Brooklyn Bridge Park's Syfy Movies with a View (Thursdays); Bay Ridge's Narrows Botanic Garden's Outdoor Movie Series (Fridays); Rooftop Film Series (Thursdays, Fridays, and Saturdays, usually ticketed) in various cool locations; and in Fort Greene's Habana Outpost restaurant (Sundays). Movies are also shown in many public parks. The June Northside Festival in Williamsburg screens some films.

For information: look up "free summer movies" on the New York City Parks Department site.

ANNUAL FILM FESTIVALS

Brooklyn has about a dozen film festivals.

BAMcinemaFest is a world-class film festival and shows cutting-edge films.

The annual BFF, the Brooklyn Film Festival, screens over a hundred narratives, documentaries, and animation films from thirty countries every May. It was born in the carefree spirit of early Williamsburg. "We just thought it would be fun. I called all my friends and the artists I knew and issued an invitation to cross the bridge" to Williamsburg, said the festival's founder, Marco Ursino. Local filmmakers and themes are included: BFF's 2014 Brooklyn-themed documentaries included *Born to Fly*, about Williamsburg-based choreographer Elizabeth Streb (profiled in this book), and *Third Shift*, about former workers in Williamsburg's doomed, derelict Domino Sugar Refinery, just then being torn down to make way for construction of a vast apartment complex.

The Brooklyn Film & Arts Festival, held in Downtown Brooklyn in March, specializes in Brooklyn-themed works. The Brooklyn Short Film Festival is held in June. The Art of Brooklyn Film Festival, founded in 2011, shows Brooklyn-centric films or movies by Brooklyn-born or Brooklyn-based filmmakers from around the world. The Red Hook Film Festival is held in October.

The Bushwick Film Festival, founded in 2007 by Liberian-born Kweighbaye Kotee, runs sessions for filmmakers on financing, distribution, and women filmmakers, in addition to showing new-media projects. Consider, too, the Williamsburg Motorcycle Film Festival and the Williamsburg Independent Film Festival. The latter, its website says, aims to showcase filmmakers "in the mecca of hipster and progressive culture, Williamsburg, Brooklyn."

Kickstarter, the global crowdfunding website based in Brooklyn, holds a one-day festival of films financed through a Kickstarter campaign (as is the Kickstarter Film Festival itself).

Brooklyn has two feminist film festivals. The Reel Sisters Festival, cofounded in 1997 by *African Voices* magazine and Long Island University, is devoted to supporting films produced, directed, and written by women of color. The three-day Brooklyn Girl Film Festival features indie films by women.

People with a serious interest in new media and journalism should check out the screenings and events at Williamsburg's UnionDocs Center for Documentary Art.

For information: check individual websites of the above festivals.

INDIE FILM SCENE AND HOLLYWOOD EAST

Brooklyn has a significant movie-making industry. The Independent Filmmaker Project (IFP), the nation's oldest and largest film-advocacy organization, opened the Made in New York Media Center by IFP in Dumbo. Steiner Studios at the Brooklyn Navy Yard is the East Coast's largest soundstage complex. The Brooklyn College Barry R. Feirstein Graduate School of Cinema is the city's first public graduate school of cinema and the nation's only film school actually situated on a working film lot.

As a visitor, you might stumble on a film shoot in a Brooklyn neighborhood. TV shows, commercials, and other productions frequently film on Brooklyn streets. (Some locals make money renting out their homes and businesses; the Mayor's Office of Film, Theatre & Broadcasting has a tip sheet "How to Make Your Home a Star in New York City.")

For information: read "Celebs, Films, Fiction" in section 3 of this book to discover what movies were filmed in dozens of neighborhoods.

6. Theater, Dance, and Music

Brooklyn's performing arts scene is red hot.

THEATERS

What's next on the cultural cutting edge? When asked, Joseph Melillo, BAM's executive producer, said in a phone conversation, "I'd like to construct a contemporary circus festival. Circus is the newest phenomenon on the cultural landscape. It exists in multiple cultures and in multiple forms. It can be many things to many people. I think putting an aesthetic lens on it, on this evolved twenty-first-century form of circus, would be rendering a service."

St. Ann's Warehouse, a hip performing arts center, may have the best real estate of any theater in New York. In a class with Manhattan's Public Theater and New York Theater Workshop, St. Ann's "is the go-to place for American avant-garde theater, such as the Wooster Group and Mabou Mines," founder and artistic director Susan Feldman told the author. For its 2015 season, it opened with an all-female cast from London's Donmar Warehouse playing Shakespeare's *Henry IV*. St. Ann's Warehouse's new Dumbo space on Water Street is spectacular, serving as a waterfront cultural center at the renovated, historic Tobacco Warehouse. Enjoy access from Brooklyn Bridge Park, a pretty public garden with Manhattan views, and food concession from Vinegar Hill House.

The Theatre for a New Audience (TFANA) at Polonsky Shakespeare Center has produced over five dozen masterworks, including twenty-eight works of Shakespeare, other classics, and contemporary plays. TFANA moved from Manhattan into a three-hundred-seat theater in the Brooklyn Cultural District in 2013.

Bushwick Starr, Jack, Irondale Ensemble Project, New Brooklyn Theatre, and other smaller theaters and theater companies each have their own mission. Obie Award–winning Bushwick Starr produces new work in theater, dance, and puppetry. Rabbit Hole Ensemble produces critically acclaimed minimalist productions. New Brooklyn Theatre's board chairman, Jeff Strabone, explained, "We aim to democratize the theater. That means free plays, site-specific productions, new voices, and conversations between the audience and the artists."

Shows on tour come to Kumble Theater for the Performing Arts at Long Island University Brooklyn Campus, Brooklyn Center for Performing Arts at Brooklyn College, and On Stage at Kingsborough Community College. Check out Brick Theater, Target Margin Theater, Falconworks, and community theater groups. Smith Street Stage's free summer shows adapt Shakespearean classics for a neighborhood crowd in Carroll Park.

For tots, classic puppet shows are performed at the vintage Puppetworks theater in Park Slope, beloved by generations. Shadowbox Theater, a musical puppet theater that addresses social issues, is a resident company in PS 3, the Bedford Village School in Bedford-Stuyvesant. For hipster kids, Williamsburg-based Puppetsburg presents hilarious, inventive puppet shows.

For live comedy, check out Freddy's, Littlefield's, Two Boots, and Union Hall in Park Slope and the Cameo Gallery and Knitting Factory in Williamsburg, among others.

For information: check listings and blogs for current shows; see "Tips," section 5.

MUSIC AND DANCE

Barclays Center hosts blockbuster events with huge stars like Jimmy Buffett and Justin Bieber. Midwood's elegantly renovated three-thousand-seat Kings Theatre has had shows by Erykah Badu, Chaka Khan, and the Beach Boys. The fifteen-hundred-seat revamped Brooklyn Paramount will reopen around 2018. Issue Project Room in Downtown Brooklyn presents avant-garde music and performances. Roulette in Boerum Hill has roots in the 1970s Manhattan experimental music scene of John Cage, Philip Glass, and Meredith Monk. A center for contemporary and experimental music, it presents over a hundred music and dance performances annually, some featuring the Brooklyn Philharmonic and the award-winning Brooklyn Youth Chorus. BRIC House has excellent shows in an intimate setting.

Barbès in Park Slope, a bar with its own record label, has a back room where eclectic groups have been playing for years. Bargemusic, a chamber-music venue, is a repurposed old coffee barge permanently anchored near Brooklyn Bridge Park. It was renovated in 1977 as a concert hall, the madcap-genius idea of the late Olga Bloom, a violinist seeking cheap practice space. The exuberant two-day annual Balkan Zlatne Uste Brass Band Festival is held in a former German opera house. You can just go to church and hear the Grammy Award–winning gospel at Brooklyn Tabernacle services near the Fulton Mall. The Brooklyn Music School near BAM and Park Slope's Brooklyn Conservatory of Music have concerts, too.

North Brooklyn is full of venues. Indie bands and stars in Brooklyn include Chairlift, Dirty Projectors, Grizzly Bear, LCD Soundsystem, the National, TV on the Radio, Twin Shadow, Vivian Girls, and Yeasayer. Top tier, in a conventional sense, is the Music Hall of Williamsburg, booking headliners that sell out quickly.

The venue Baby's All Right has a full kitchen and restaurant (it also does brunch) and tends to get the bands that play smaller rock venues in Manhattan. Rough Trade is a well-known record store that hosts concerts, trending toward the obscure and cult-followed, smaller record labels. Union Pool books smaller acts, often local; it's an intimate space with eclectic programming, so on any given night, you might see a delicate singer-songwriter, a folk-rock band from Maine, or a band on tour with a lot of indie buzz. Silent Barn is a nonhierarchically run DIY venue that books local acts and holds launch parties for indie magazines. It is, said a local, "tapped into both the music and independent literary scenes; it feels very much like a community." Shea Stadium is a DIY venue in an old warehouse space. It books fun bands—many local to the neighborhood. Saint Vitus Bar in Greenpoint is a metal bar through and through, with cheap beer, loud bands, and a dark interior. Pete's Candy Store is an intimate space that hosts small acts, from country music to literary readings. Finally, Cameo Bar is a spacious venue in the back of a restaurant, down the street from Music Hall of Williamsburg. Chicago-based *Pitchfork Media*, the online music magazine, has editorial offices in Brooklyn. But as one local put it, a lot of bands are getting priced out, "which sucks." For listings, see Brooklyn Vegan, Free Williamsburg, and OhMyRockness online.

Hip-hop fans know that made-in-Brooklyn hits include Public Enemy's "Fight the Power" (the theme song in Spike Lee's *Do the Right Thing*), "Mos Def & Talib Kweli Are Black Star," and Big Daddy Kane's "Ain't No Half Steppin'." Wesley Jackson, founder of the Brooklyn Hip-Hop Festival—New York City's largest event that showcases the positive aspects of hip-hop culture—described shifts in the hip-hop world during a phone interview. He sees the movement in a values shift back to its political roots, saying, "Brooklyn's still got a lot of people with fire in their belly," but with second-generational wealth in the hip-hop world, others "are investing in galleries and education; we are creating an artist class."

The world's best-known Brooklyn-based dance company is the Mark Morris Dance Group. (Their *Hard Nut*, a takeoff on *The Nutcracker*, is a holiday favorite.) Brooklyn also serves as a home and an incubator for hundreds of emerging dance companies, bands, and performance groups.

For information: check listings and blogs for current shows.

7. Green-Wood and Other Historic Cemeteries

Cemeteries can be a historical treasure trove. In the pre–Civil War era, when Brooklyn was its own city and Manhattan's growing population created overcrowded conditions in church graveyards, the state legislature passed the Rural Cemetery Act of 1847. That stroke of the legislative pen created the commercial mortuary business; heretofore, the private or church property doubled as cemeteries. Brooklyn farmers knew a deal when they saw it; some sold their lands for use as cemeteries.

GREEN-WOOD

Green-Wood is a must-see, a burial ground reinvented as a major cultural venue and historical resource. There's nothing like it in all of New York City. This bucolic retreat is the final resting place of over half a million souls. It's one of Brooklyn's leading historical institutions, an accredited arboretum, and a historic cemetery. History buffs, Civil and Revolutionary War hobbyists, storytellers, and the generally curious will find this a rewarding expedition. Take a guided trolley tour to hear engrossing tales of the heroes and crooks, winners and losers, who are "permanent residents" in this peaceful 478-acre place of rolling hills, paths, and lakes, founded in 1838.

Green-Wood is fantastic for photographs, from the elaborate Gothic gate to beautiful sculptures and ornate Victorian mausoleums. Venture up Battle Hill, so named for the Battle of Brooklyn. At the August Battle of Brooklyn reenactment, costumed actors, some on horseback, even fire an old musket or two. Enjoy the Memorial Day concert and guided nighttime walks. Start at the Visitors Center in the renovated, all-glass, 1895 Wier Greenhouse, opening in 2016. Walking and trolley tours, performances, book talks, and tributes to "special residents" may have a fee; entrance is free.

Who is buried in Green-Wood? One finds among the interred a breathtaking roll call: the artists Nathaniel Currier and James Merritt Ives of Currier & Ives; Louis Comfort Tiffany, the stained-glass artist; the painters Asher Brown Durand, William Merritt Chase, John Kensett, and William Holbrook Beard. The inventors of the safety pin, carbonated water, the sewing machine, and the steam locomotive ended up here, as did Charles Ebbets, of the Dodgers' ballpark fame. So did the Smithsonian's architect, James Renwick, and the corrupt Tammany Hall politician William Magear Tweed, known as Boss Tweed. Big-pharma founders Edward Squibb and Charles Pfizer are here. Others include Samuel Morse, the inventor of the telegraph, and Peter Cooper, who invented Jell-O and founded the Cooper Union. The *New York Times* founder, Henry Raymond; abolitionist Henry Ward Beecher; and Henry Bergh, the founder of the ASPCA, are all here. Well over five thousand Civil War and Revolutionary War soldiers are buried here, too.

Look for terrific nature studies, lectures, and events at Green-Wood; advance ticket purchase is recommended.

For information: http://www.green-wood.com.

OTHER CEMETERIES OF NOTE

Cypress Hills Cemetery, which dates to 1848 and straddles Queens and Brooklyn, is a nonsectarian cemetery and the final resting place of Jackie Robinson, the Baseball Hall of Fame Dodger; Mae West; and artist Piet Mondrian. Early civil rights activists are buried here, too: Thomas Downing (1791–1866), a member of the Underground Railroad; Elizabeth Jennings Graham (1830–1901), a nineteenth-century New York City "Rosa Parks"; leader, writer, and activist Arturo Schomburg (1874–1938); and James McCune Smith (1813–1865), the nation's first African American to earn a medical degree.

Holy Cross Cemetery in East Flatbush is a well-kept secret. Dodgers player Gil Hodges rests here, as do "Murder Inc." mobster Frankie Yale, race-horse trainer Sunny Jim Fitzsimmons, and actor Lenny Montana, who as Luca Brasi played a scene in *The Godfather* at Brooklyn Heights' Hotel St. George.

At Midwood's Jewish Washington Cemetery, shiny black headstones of recent Russian émigrés depict the faces of the deceased, while older gray stones mark graves of nineteenth- and early twentieth-century immigrants. Yiddish theater greats are buried here, along with "Big" Jack Zelig (1888–1912), a gangster with the Eastman Gang. Washington Cemetery has run out of room, because some empty plots belong to defunct *landsmanshaft* burial societies.

For information: http://cypresshillscemetery.org and http://www.ccbklyn.org/our-cemeteries/holy-cross-cemetery.

8. Art and Heritage Parades

Brooklyn turns out for parades—for Veterans and Memorial Days, for Columbus and Norwegian Constitution Days, and twice for Saint Patrick's Day. Over forty thousand people show up for the LGBTQ PRIDE Week parade. Of late, a new parade has started: of unicyclists. Brooklyn's dozen or so big parades are, variously, earnestly family friendly, patriotic, sexy, silly, and homemade. The biggest are the Mermaid and West Indian American Day Parades, marking the beginning and end of summer, respectively. Both attract up to eight hundred thousand spectators, and feature handcrafted, elaborate costumes. Are parades cultural events? Sure!

MERMAID PARADE

Coney Island's arty Mermaid Parade is hot and hilarious, a ribald cocktail of high and low culture. Promoted as "the world's biggest art parade," this is one happy-go-lucky parade that celebrates excess, pokes fun, and flaunts it.

Imagine fifteen hundred marchers, dressed (barely) as mermaids, mermen, Neptunes, octopuses, whales, and fantasy fish from a Freudian playbook. Mermaid paraders show it all off—fleshiness and skinniness, baby-faced youth and encroaching old age, the hairy and the bald. Add in cheering spectators, a procession of antique cars, broiling sun, a honky-tonk King Neptune and Queen Mermaid, strutting bands, and artistic floats.

The Mermaid Parade revives a raucous Coney Mardi Gras tradition that faded after the mid-1950s. Yale Drama School–educated Dick Zigun, founder of the nonprofit Coney Island USA, created the Mermaid Parade in 1983 more or less out of thin air to celebrate what his organization describes as "ancient mythology and honky-tonk rituals of the seaside" and "the beginning of the summer." Quirky as Coney Island, it's art for art's sake.

For information: http://www.coneyisland.com.

WEST INDIAN AMERICAN DAY PARADE ON LABOR DAY

Signaling summer's end, the nation's biggest Caribbean celebration (and one of New York's largest parades) is a spectacle of music, amazing costumes, and steel-drum-playing cultural pride. Caribbean Carnival Week kicks off days in advance of the parade. Thursday night is a "Caribbean Woodstock" folk-heritage event; Friday night, a Brass Band Festival. Saturday is the Junior Carnival Parade and an evening ticketed show, the Panorama brass bands competition. Sunday is the final "Dimache Gras" concert, complete with costumes.

Rain or shine, on Labor Day Monday, the West Indian American Day Parade prances down Eastern Parkway. It's an hours-long, enthusiastic procession of sexy feather-costumed dancers, steel brass bands and outrageous floats, hand-shaking politicians, and flag-waving, scantily clad marchers of all ages and body shapes. Small-business owners, bus drivers, and city employees, whatever their workaday role, get into the fun for their heritage day. Standing or dancing here, oftentimes under a blistering sun, as vendors hawk flags, Bob Marley T-shirts, roasted corn and meat, you might forget you're in . . . Brooklyn. Tourists are advised to avoid late-night events, in the interest of safety.

For information: http://wiadcacarnival.org.

9. Brooklyn Botanic Garden

The Brooklyn Botanic Garden (known as BBG) is one of the borough's great gifts. For just the price of admission, you're transported to a brilliant, timeless natural garden. It's open and lovely in all seasons and beyond gorgeous in the spring. Inhale the beauty of fifty-plus acres of orchestrated plantings: Daffodil Hill, the blooming lilacs, the classic rose gardens, and the cherry blossoms on Cherry Esplanade. Annual event highlights include the month-long celebration of Japanese culture during the Sakura Matsuri Cherry Blossom Festival, Making Brooklyn Bloom, Chili Pepper Festival, and Ghouls & Gourds.

The Japanese Hill-and-Pond Garden has meandering paths, big hungry koi fish, sleepy turtles, and a red Shinto shrine. It's the first Japanese garden created in an American public garden and one of the oldest Japanese-inspired gardens outside Japan. Saunter along Celebrity Path to see the names of about 160 famous Brooklynites from Barbra Streisand to Mae West. Indoors, the Steinhardt Conservatory fascinates with its tropical, desert, and temperate environments. Wander the Shakespeare and Fragrance Gardens.

Check out BBG's suggested itineraries and seasonal guided tours, spring gardening symposia, and famous plant sale.

You can enter through the refurbished Flatbush Avenue or Washington Avenue entrances. The indoor-outdoor Yellow Magnolia Café and gift shop are excellent. So is the expanded and wonderful Discovery Garden space for children.

For information: http://bbg.org.

10. Public Art and Street Art

Brooklyn Bridge Park, Dumbo, and MetroTech Commons have public art programs, featuring sculpture or photography. Brooklyn's street art changes all the time. You can see extraordinary murals by Bushwick Collective's artists, and dotted around the borough are murals done by teens through the nonprofit Groundswell. In 2015, Jeffrey Deitch's Coney Art Walls was shown in Coney Island. Occasionally Brooklyn political street art goes viral, as did Tatyana Fazlalizadeh's *Stop Telling Women to Smile* project. Some works are fixed; many are temporary installations.

For information: see the "Street Art and Public Art" section in the "Brooklyn Cultural Sites" box in this chapter.

11. Literary Haunts

Is everyone in Brooklyn a reader or a writer? Sometimes it seems so. The borough has a slew of independent bookstores and publishers, small presses, and literary magazines. Brooklyn College has a prominent MFA program for creative writers. Brooklyn has an abundance of writing classes and writers groups. Brooklyn "may have more readers per square inch than anywhere in the country," Noreen Tomassi, the executive director of the Center for Fiction, told the author. She was explaining the decision to relocate the center from Manhattan to a site across from BAM, scheduled for 2018. "The borough is home to so many great writers—both well known and emerging—and so many of our audience members already are Brooklyn residents."

SEVEN WAYS TO TAP INTO THE BROOKLYN LITERARY SCENE

How to tap into this Brooklyn literary scene? First, read Brooklyn authors (see a recommended reading list of contemporary Brooklyn authors in this chapter). Attend the Brooklyn Book Festival in September. Go to readings—in bookstores, bars, cafés, the Central Library's Dweck Center, Restoration Plaza in Bed-Stuy, and Park Slope's Old Stone House. They're happening weekly, in a wide range of venues. Patronize Brooklyn's independent bookstores; see "Shopping in Brooklyn" in this section. Many cohost events, such as Greenlight's "Brooklyn Voices"

VOICES ABOUT BROOKLYN

HAROLD AUGENBRAUM
Executive Director of the National Book Foundation, 2006–2015

There was always a literary culture in Brooklyn. In the 1940s, Arthur Miller and even Gypsy Rose Lee, who was a writer as well as a stripper, were there. Norman Mailer was always there. The godfather of the current literary scene is Paul Auster; he's been living there for thirty years.

Brooklyn's contemporary literary culture was created by changes in real estate. Brooklyn was a place to go for a well-educated population when Manhattan became unaffordable. Good transportation and a stock of middle-class housing existed there; the brownstones needed work but hadn't deteriorated beyond repair. You can't be reductive and underestimate the idea that real estate in Brooklyn was one of the reasons it attracted what has become a middle-class literary scene.

And, the establishment of BAM as a cultural center that gave the borough a cultural identity was important. There was this attitude that Brooklyn is the non-Manhattan place to live, that you could do things in Brooklyn you couldn't do in Manhattan, because, in certain parts, Manhattan is culturally static. BAM was a beacon.

We used to think of writers as bohemian; Europeans think of writers as intellectuals. Brooklyn writers might be liberal and open to new ideas and focused on the quality of art, but the scene is not as bohemian as in the Village in the 1950s and 1960s or even the Upper West Side in the 1970s and 1980s. It's focused on culture and art, not lifestyle.

Brooklyn is already the "next" literary community in the United States. I'm not talking about the quality of the work, just the fact that this is a large community of writers that supports the idea of a literary place. The literature scene that's grown up in the past ten or fifteen years there hasn't yet reached maturity. But Brooklyn has a concentration of writers, the city's most interesting independent bookstores—Greenlight, BookCourt, Community Bookstore, and others— access to almost a dozen MFA programs where writers can teach and make a living, small presses, frequent readings, and a major literary festival. The Brooklyn Book Festival is a literary festival; it's less commercial than its Central Park predecessor, New York Is Book Country. What you find in Brooklyn is a local audience hungry for culture, and one that reads.

---

collaboration with St. Joseph's College in Fort Greene. Explore the niches, like Mellow Pages Library in Bushwick, a lending library specializing in small presses and independent publishers. Read Brooklyn literary magazines such as *N+1* and *One Story*. Attend writers' workshops and conferences, from the Slice Literary Writers Conference to the Black Writers Conference at Medgar Evers College.

BROOKLYN BOOK FESTIVAL

The Brooklyn Book Festival is a bibliophile's dream. It's a festive, multineighborhood event with lectures, readings, and get-togethers, plus a huge outdoor bookstall marketplace. It includes a full week of "Bookend Events"—hundreds of lectures, presentations, discussions, and literary mingles—held in venues citywide as the ramp-up to the intense Sunday main event. (It's usually held the third weekend of September.) Some three hundred Brooklyn and international authors from over a dozen countries participate. About forty thousand people attend. Former Brooklyn borough president Marty Markowitz, along with Carolyn Greer, Liz Koch, and Johnny Temple, launched the Brooklyn Book Festival.

Temple is in the thick of the Brooklyn literary scene. He's the head of the Brooklyn Literary Council and publisher of the Gowanus-based Akashic Books. His small indie press is known for its popular "Brooklyn Noir" series, edgy list, and sassy tagline, "reverse-gentrification of the literary world." Formerly a bassist with the rock group Girls Against Boys, Temple moved to Fort Greene in 1990. His comments illustrate how fertile a place Brooklyn has been for cultural entrepreneurship.

NICHE LITERARY FESTIVALS AND SPACES

Williamsburg's annual Grand Comics Festival is a small, curated event, an alternative to New York City's massive comic conventions. The Parachute Literary Arts Festival brings a gathering of poets to Coney Island. Cave Canem in Downtown Brooklyn describes itself as "a home for the many voices of African American poetry" that "is committed to cultivating the artistic and professional growth of African American poets." If there's a literary niche, you'll likely find it in Brooklyn.

BROOKLYN VOICES

JOHNNY TEMPLE
Publisher of Akashic Books, Cofounder of the Brooklyn Book Festival,
Chair of the Brooklyn Literary Council

I was enamored of Brooklyn's, and specifically Fort Greene's, literary history. Richard Wright wrote some of *Native Son* while sitting in Fort Greene Park. Walt Whitman was integral to the founding of Fort Greene Park. I was fascinated. I couldn't help but notice that there was no literary festival in Brooklyn, despite the fact that Brooklyn has a more colorful literary history than most places in the country.

[Now, a decade later], nowhere else do you see as many independent publishers in one place as at the Brooklyn Book Festival.

Whereas the book-publishing world tends to be a bit elitist, we are trying to foster a post-politically-correct environment, one without polite constraints on what you can and cannot say. The Brooklyn Book Festival is a populist way of presenting literature. We include everything from graphic novels to children's literature. Many international authors travel to Brooklyn just for this event. And unlike some book festivals where programming features special panels on, say, gay or black or Latino writers, the Brooklyn Book Festival integrates people across different religious and ethnic groups. . . .

Back in the day, Brooklyn had a grittier blue-collar aesthetic. It's a more gentrified world today, but not without surprises: Brooklyn's a hotbed for writers of Caribbean descent who are producing wonderful literature.

NATIONAL BLACK WRITERS CONFERENCE (NBWC)
AT THE CENTER FOR BLACK LITERATURE AT
MEDGAR EVERS COLLEGE, CUNY

This is a conference for new and emerging black writers, the brainchild of Pulitzer Prize–nominated John Oliver Killens. Participants with a Brooklyn connection include MacArthur "genius grant" winner Edwidge Danticat, author of *Brother, I'm Dying*; juvenile author Jacqueline Woodson, winner of the National Book Award for *Brown Girl Dreaming*; and TV personality Touré, author of *Who's Afraid of Post-Blackness?*; as well as Colson Whitehead, Bernice McFadden, Elizabeth Nunez, and Bridgett Davis. Past honorees include Toni Morrison, Nikki Giovanni, Amiri Baraka, Octavia Butler, Marsye Condé, Quincy Troupe, Walter Mosley, Ishmael Reed, Marita Golden, and poet Sonia Sanchez.

For information: http://centerforblack literature.org/category/nbwc.

THE CENTER FOR FICTION

The nation's only organization devoted only to fiction, this literary organization will be jumping across the East River in 2018, bringing with it programs for readers, writers, and schoolchildren. It's been located in Manhattan for about two hundred years and awards the prestigious First Novel Prize. Executive director Noreen Tomassi cited "the superb location across from BAM, one of the world's great cultural institutions," and being "at the heart of a great cultural district" as reasons for relocating. She added, "We think the notion of Brooklyn as an 'outer borough' and somehow 'lesser' than Manhattan is ridiculously out of date. It's an intellectual and cultural hub in a great city, and we are thrilled to become part of that energy!"

For information: http://www.centerforfiction.org.

LIBRARIES AND ARCHIVES

The Brooklyn Public Library system is the nation's fifth largest and one of its oldest. Of its sixty branches, about one in seven are historic Carnegie beauties. The Brooklyn Central Library at Grand Army Plaza is housed in a 1940 Art Deco

---

CONTEMPORARY BROOKLYN AUTHORS: RECOMMENDED READS

Recommended and notable fiction by Brooklyn-based authors, compiled by Greenlight Bookstore in spring 2015.

New York Trilogy, by Paul Auster
2 a.m. at The Cat's Pajamas, by Marie-Helene Bertino
Open City, by Teju Cole
Visit from the Goon Squad, by Jennifer Egan
Binary Star, by Sarah Gerard
Magicians, by Lev Grossman
Blazing World, by Siri Hustved
Prelude to Bruise, by Saeed Jones
Gods without Men, by Hari Kunzru
10:04: A Novel, by Ben Lerner
Motherless Brooklyn, by Jonathan Lethem
Station Eleven, by Emily St. John Mandel
BlackGirl Mansion, by Angel Nafis
Dept. of Speculation, by Jenny Offill
Only Words That Are Worth Remembering, by Jeffrey Rotter
Vacationers, by Emma Straub
Brooklyn, by Colm Toibin
We the Animals, by Justin Torres
Love Affairs of Nathaniel P., by Adelle Waldman
Land of Love and Drowning, by Tiphanie Yanique
Literary Brooklyn, by Evan Hughes (nonfiction but about Brooklyn writers)

BROOKLYN VOICES

BRENDA M. GREENE

Executive Director of the Center for Black Literature and
Chair of the English Department at Medgar Evers College, CUNY

There is a need for writers throughout the African diaspora to tell their stories from their unique perspective, stories which speak to issues that address all aspects of the human experience and what it means to be a person of color in America and in this global society. Despite the increasing diversity of people and ethnic groups in our society and the blurred boundaries around race and ethnicity, conversations about race still remain charged. The Center for Black Literature . . . provides a "space" in which to study the craft of writing and to document and celebrate writers throughout the African diaspora.

Held biennially in March, the National Black Writers Conference . . . is one of the most significant gatherings of Black writers, scholars, and literary professionals in the Northeast, a four-day public gathering that brings writers and the public together to discuss emerging themes in the literature of Black writers throughout the African diaspora.

---

building shaped like an open book, its shiny bronze panels depicting literary characters. The Central Library's Dweck Center has excellent free cultural programming—and the snack bar, run by the local Four and Twenty Blackbirds, is a pleaser. The Central Library's Brooklyn Collection is a repository and a showcase, filled with rare historic photos, maps, archival documents, and the *Brooklyn Daily Eagle* newspaper (1841–1955). Call (718) 230-2762 for an appointment with a "Brooklynologist." Anyone can obtain a Brooklyn Public Library card for fifty dollars from anywhere, even Kathmandu, and remotely access its collections. "Brooklyn Public Library's core mission—the preservation and free transmission of society's knowledge, history, and culture, has guided our work for more than a century. As the definition of literacy evolves, the Library will adapt its programs and collections," Linda E. Johnson, president and CEO of the Brooklyn Public Library, told the author.

Brooklyn has other interesting archives and special collections. You can find historical materials at the Brooklyn Historical Society, the Brooklyn Visual Heritage photo archive, and the archives of Brooklyn College, the Brooklyn Museum, the Brooklyn Navy Yard, and Park Slope's Lesbian Herstory Educational Foundation. The Red Hook Archives has photos and images of Red Hook; access is by appointment. The Central Chabad Lubavitch Library and Archive Center, a multilingual 250,000-volume repository, is open to researchers by appointment. Oral history projects abound, from the Coney Island History Project to the Brooklyn Navy Yard to Story Corps, located in Fort Greene.

A mother lode is yet to open: BAM's Hamm Archives holds the history of the nation's oldest performing arts institution. "We have an organic archive that goes back to the late nineteenth century, an extraordinary reservoir of BAM-specific materials: tickets and photographs and posters and books. It is fundamentally American cultural history," said Joseph Melillo, BAM's executive producer. The Hamm Archives will open to the public for the first time in the Brooklyn Cultural District, around 2018.

For information: see the websites of the above organizations.

12. Brooklyn Historical Society and the Brooklyn Navy Yard

BROOKLYN HISTORICAL SOCIETY AND MUSEUM

The Brooklyn Historical Society (BHS) boasts the nation's largest collection of Brooklyn history. Its elegant 1880 landmarked building in Brooklyn Heights has rotating exhibits of artifacts and memorabilia. Upstairs the historic wood-paneled library is gorgeous. BHS presents supersmart discussions, tours, book talks, storytelling panel discussions, film screenings, conversations with luminaries, and

---

VOICES ABOUT BROOKLYN

JAMES PEACOCK

Author of *Brooklyn Fictions: The Contemporary Urban Community in a Global Age* and
Senior Lecturer in English and American Literature, Keele University, UK

In Brooklyn fiction, there's a romantic tradition, starting with Betty Smith's *A Tree Grows in Brooklyn* (1943) and including novels such as Jane Schwartz's *Caught* (1985) and Kitty Burns Florey's *Solos* (2004), and there's what you might call a "gritty tradition," which includes Hubert Selby Jr.'s *Last Exit to Brooklyn* (1964), Michael G. Stephens's *The Brooklyn Book of the Dead* (1994), and Loida Maritza Pérez's *Geographies of Home* (1999). Both traditions are interested in immigrant experience, changing neighborhoods, the formation and breakdown of communities, but in recent postgentrification novels, the immigrants are more likely to be hipsters or yuppies from Manhattan.

The romantic tales have gritty elements, of course—poverty, illness, death—but ultimately they affirm certain values that have come to be associated with the borough in the popular imagination: diversity, community spirit, a cherishing of history, down-home neighborliness, and less interest in chasing the dollar than in Manhattan.

In the gritty tradition, Brooklyn is still diverse, but integration is much more difficult and neighborhoods more likely to be immigrant ghettoes than multicultural havens where a pleasing range of ethnic foods can be found in the local shops. These stories—and one should include Amy Sohn's outrageous comedies of ill manners such as *Prospect Park West* (2009)—show the negative consequences of gentrification: massively inflated real estate prices, social exclusion, status anxiety, and paranoia about the "wrong" sort of people ruining one's neighborhood experience.

And add to that list nostalgia—for the "real" Brooklyn, the "authentic" Brooklyn. The big question in all Brooklyn fictions is, Was there ever a "real" Brooklyn, or was it only ever imagined?

events relating to issues both topical and historic. A Dumbo branch opens in 2016, promising to bring the understudied topic of Brooklyn's waterfront history to life. Whatever they do, they do well here. The genealogy service is popular, as is their ground floor, admission-free gift shop.

For information: http://www.brooklynhistory.org.

BROOKLYN NAVY YARD

One of New York City's most extraordinary, not-to-be-missed destinations, the Brooklyn Navy Yard (est. 1801) is on the National Register of Historic Places. The sprawling campus serves many functions. It's part museum and historical site and part modern industrial park with a commitment to environmental sustainability. For the historical perspective, go to the Visitors Center, Building 92, or take a guided tour around the historic yard. Both are memorable. Special exhibits such as *Brooklyn Navy Yard, Past, Present and Future* lay out this institution's role in American life. The Navy Yard's modern industrial park is one leg of Brooklyn's Tech Triangle. It houses innovative and tech companies, Steiner Studios, the Brooklyn College Feirstein Graduate School of Cinema, and many "makers." Opening a new chapter in the Yard's life, Wegmans supermarket and other stores arrive in 2017.

For information on the museum and historical tours, see http://bldg92.org. To learn about the industrial park, see http://brooklynnavyyard.org/about-bnydc.

13. Specialty Museums

CITY RELIQUARY

Williamsburg's nonprofit City Reliquary delights in showcasing the artifacts of living "commonly" used by New Yorkers. Find old seltzer bottles and dolls that may remind you of a grandparent from Brooklyn. Watch for fun special events at this original and civic-minded organization, conceived in Williamsburg circa 2002.

For information: http://www.cityreliquary.org.

CONEY ISLAND USA AND THE CONEY ISLAND HISTORY PROJECT

Freak shows and vaudeville at "Sideshows by the Sea" are the fare at the nonprofit Coney Island USA. Operating out of a landmark building, this arts organization presents revivals of old populist American entertainment forms. It also houses the modest Coney Island Museum, which has a collection of old funhouse mirrors and memorabilia. It organizes the Coney Island International Film Festival and the massive Mermaid Parade. In their words, their approach is "rooted in mass culture and the traditions of P. T. Barnum, dime museums, burlesque, circus sideshows, vaudeville, and Coney Island itself." This operation is run by Coney advocate Dick Zigun. Visit its funky Freak Bar, find T-shirts at the gift shop, and take a step back in time.

The nonprofit Coney Island History Project, a separate entity founded in 2004 with an exhibit space near Deno's Wonder Wheel, is admission-free on summer weekends. It displays interesting artifacts and offers tours.

Brooklyn Navy Yard flag shop, 1917. The photo shows women sewing American flags. (Courtesy Library of Congress)

For information: for Coney Island USA, see http://www.coneyisland.com; for Coney Island History Project, see http://www.coneyislandhistory.org.

MOCADA

Founded in 1999, Museum of Contemporary African Diasporan Arts (MoCADA) was founded by politician-activist Laurie Cumbo in a Bed-Stuy brownstone. As of 2018, it will be one of four cultural organizations in the BAM Karen site, along with the 651 Arts organization. Check their lectures, education programs, programs, and exhibitions.

For information: http://mocada.org.

MUSEUM OF FOOD AND DRINK (MOFAD)

Williamsburg's Museum of Food and Drink is the first such museum in New York City. It opened in 2015, as this book was going to print. Here's what they promise: "Imagine a place where you can use an Aztec kitchen, see cereal made before your eyes, decode food marketing, taste West African street food, make Chinese hand-pulled noodles, learn about agriculture and composting, and see how the body digests a sandwich—all in one museum." Sounds great!

For information: http://www.mofad.org.

MORBID ANATOMY MUSEUM

Inside this big, black building in Gowanus, you will find a curious and curated view of medicine and death, with emphasis on the obscure, taboo, and macabre. There are displays of Victorian mourning artwork, Day of the Dead memorabilia, preserved skulls, and such exhibits as *Anatomical Theatre: Depictions of the Body, Disease, and Death in Medical Museums of the Western World*. Mike Zohn from the Science Channel's show *Oddities* once presented his collection of ancient and modern penises here. The gift shop sells cult books and necromancy curiosities. The taxidermy class is popular.

For information: http://morbidanatomymuseum.org.

NEW YORK CITY TRANSIT MUSEUM

Small museums have the luxury of being quirky, and this underground museum, hidden away in a decommissioned 1936 IND subway station, won't disappoint. Allow an hour to pretend you're driving an MTA bus and sitting on antique subway cars, then emerge into the sunlight with a greater appreciation of mass transit. Explore *Steel, Stone, and Backbone: Building New York's Subways 1900–1925* and interactive fun such as *On the Streets*, an in-depth look at New York City's trolleys and buses. The museum occasionally organizes vintage subway rides and cool tours through the system's innards, all fun and informative, too.

For information: http://web.mta.info/mta/museum.

SCANDANAVIAN EAST COAST MUSEUM

This virtual museum offers information on Brooklyn's Scandinavian heritage.

For information: http://www.scandinavian-museum.org.

14. Culture for Kids

Family-friendly cultural programs are offered by the Brooklyn Public Library, the Brooklyn Museum, Brooklyn Botanic Garden, and BAM. In Prospect Park, you'll find excellent programs at the Audubon House and Lefferts Historic House, puppet shows for little ones, and teen programs for older kids. Check Prospect Park Alliance, Brooklyn College's Brooklyn Center for the Performing Arts, Wyckoff House Museum, and Barclays Center. (See "Forty Things to Do with Kids," section 5.)

Plus, kids can see how things are made at the Museum of Food and Drink, many chocolate makers, Cousin John's Bakery in Park Slope (come early in the morning), UrbanGlass tours of their glassblowing facilities, and more.

BROOKLYN CHILDREN'S MUSEUM

Geared for infants through age six, both of the Brooklyn Children's Museum's locations—its renovated building in Crown Heights and the exciting Dumbo annex, opening in 2016—make a delightful outing. This was the first of the nation's three hundred or so children's museums (indeed, the first in the world) when it

Nathan's Coney Island, by Ivan Koota, acrylic on canvas, 2002. (Photo courtesy of Ivan Koota, Brooklynplaces.com)

was founded in 1899. Combine a visit to the original Crown Heights museum (complete with toy store and snack bar) with a visit to Berg'n or cafés on Franklin and Nostrand Avenues. "We want to be every child's first New York cultural experience," said a museum spokesperson.

For information: http://www.brooklynkids.org.

JEWISH CHILDREN'S MUSEUM

The first-of-its-kind Jewish Children's Museum in Crown Heights offers a view of Orthodox Jewish life and traditions. The museum building is very modern, and there are interactive exhibits. Visitors of all faiths are welcome. Closed late Fridays and Saturdays.

For information and hours: http://www.jcm.museum.

KIDS' FILM FESTIVALS

BAMkids Film Festival is curated for kids and shows a roster of award-winning movies, shorts, and animation from dozens of countries. It coincides with the public school February holiday. The Brooklyn Film Festival (BFF) sponsors a wonderful kids' film fest in May in Dumbo. Year-round, the Brooklyn Public Library branches screen free films.

For information: http://www.bam.org; http://www.bff.org.

HALLOWEEN PARADES AND EVENTS

In October, Brooklyn surrenders to Halloween-mania for nearly two weeks of shows, costume parades, pet costume shows, haunted walks, harvest festivals, and pumpkin patches, culminating on Halloween night, October 31.

For free fun, check out Prospect Park's Halloween Haunted Walk and Carnival, spooky stories at Lefferts Historic House, and the Haunted Halloween Walk and Fairytale Forest in Bay Ridge. BAM presents a free outdoor Halloween Festival. Buy tickets to the Brooklyn Children's Museum's Halloween Monster Mash, Prospect Park's Haunted Carousel, and the Brooklyn Botanic Garden's Ghouls & Gourds, where costumed characters on stilts accompany a cacophonous parade.

Every neighborhood does Halloween. Park Slope's Halloween Parade, also free, is reputedly the nation's largest children's parade. Thousands of children trick-or-treat at local stores, as costume-wearing shopkeepers turned witches, fairies, and cartoon characters dole out the sugar. Fort Greene Park's Halloween Parade features a pumpkin patch and hayrides. Williamsburg events are calibrated for millennials. In Bushwick, you'll find artists parties and a Latino Calabaza Fest. In Clinton Hill, the owners of 313 Clinton Avenue put on a legendary free Halloween-night show. The Coney Island Children's Halloween Parade (requiring preregistration), the Creep Show at Coney Island USA, "Ascarium at Aquarium," and City Tech's deliciously spooky high-tech show, *Gravesend Inn* in Downtown Brooklyn, are fun.

Pets get into the act too. Dress them up and go to Fort Greene Park's Great PUPkin Dog Costume, the Bay Ridge Dog Costume Contest, or Brooklyn Heights' Howl-O-Ween Costume Parade (register in advance).

For information: Google each neighborhood event.

15. Fireworks

Enjoy fireworks on New Year's Eve in Prospect Park (after the New Year's Eve midnight Fun Run) and Coney Island. If the Macy's annual July Fourth celebration is hosted on the east side of Manhattan, over the East River, you can see fantastic fireworks along Brooklyn's shoreline and Brooklyn Bridge Park. Otherwise, you can see July Fourth fireworks in Coney Island. Every Friday night in summer, fireworks are shot off near Coney's boardwalk, and after some Cyclones home games.

For information: for Macy's fireworks, see http://social.macys.com/fireworks; for Coney Island summer fireworks, see http://www.brooklyncyclones.com; for holiday fireworks, see http://www.nycgovparks.org.

BROOKLYN CULTURAL SITES

Major Cultural Institutions (see separate listings for museums and theaters/venues)

BAM (see under theaters)

Barclays Center, 620 Atlantic Avenue, (917) 618-6100

Bargemusic, 2 Old Fulton Street, (718) 624-4924

BRIC Arts | Media House, 647 Fulton Street, (718) 855-7882

Brooklyn Academy of Music (see BAM under theaters)

Brooklyn Arts Council, http://www.brooklyn artscouncil.org

Brooklyn Book Festival, http://www.brooklyn bookfestival.org

Brooklyn Children's Museum, 145 Brooklyn Avenue (Crown Heights) and 1 John Street (Dumbo), (718) 735-4400

Brooklyn College Center for Performing Arts, 2900 Bedford Avenue, (718) 951-5000

Brooklyn Historical Society, 128 Pierrepont Street, (718) 222-4111

Brooklyn Museum, 200 Eastern Parkway, (718) 638-5000

Brooklyn Public Library, 10 Grand Army Plaza, (718) 230-2100 (Central Library)

Center for Arts & Culture at Bed-Stuy, 1368 Fulton Street, (718) 636-6960

The Center for Fiction (under construction), 286 Ashland Place, (212) 755-6710

Mark Morris Dance Center, 3 Lafayette Avenue, (718) 624-8400

Prospect Park Lefferts Historic House and Audubon Center, www.prospectpark.org

For Brooklyn Cultural District, see http://www.dbartsalliance.org/#members and http://downtownbrooklyn.com

Specialized Museums

BAM Hamm Archives (opens 2018), 286 Ashland Place

City Reliquary, 370 Metropolitan Avenue, (718) 782-4842

Coney Island History Project, West 12th Street near Deno's Wonder Wheel, (347) 702-8553

Coney Island Museum, 1208 Surf Avenue, (718) 372-5159

Jewish Children's Museum, 792 Eastern Parkway, (718) 467-0600

Museum of Contemporary African Diasporan Arts (MoCADA), 80 Hanson Place, (718) 230-0492

Museum of Food and Drink, 62 Bayard Street, (718) 387-2875

New York Transit Museum, Boerum Place, (718) 694-1600

Old Stone House Museum, 336 3rd Street, (718) 768-3195

Select Theaters and Performing Arts Venues

BAM

BAM Fisher, 321 Ashland Place, (718) 636-4100

BAM Harvey Theater, 651 Fulton Street, (718) 636-4100

BAM Opera House, 30 Lafayette Avenue, (718) 230-4352

BAM Rose Cinemas, 30 Lafayette Avenue, (718) 636-4100

BAM Strong Gallery, restaurant, café, 651 Fulton Street, (718) 636-4100

BRIC House arts and media center, 647 Fulton Street, (718) 855-7882

Brick Theater, 579 Metropolitan Avenue, (718) 285-3863

Brooklyn Academy of Music (see BAM)

Brooklyn Paramount Theater (opens 2018), 1 University Plaza, (718) 488-1011

Celebrate Brooklyn! See BRIC

Irondale Ensemble Project, 85 South Oxford Street, (718) 488-9233

(continued)

BROOKLYN CULTURAL SITES (*continued*)

Issue Project Room, 22 Boerum Place,
   (718) 330-0313
Jack Arts Center, 505 1/2 Waverly Avenue
   (contact online)
Kings Theatre, 1027 Flatbush Avenue,
   (800) 745-3000
Knitting Factory, 361 Metropolitan Avenue,
   (347) 529-6696
Music Hall of Williamsburg, 66 North 6th Street,
   (718) 486-5400
New Brooklyn Theatre
Roulette, 509 Atlantic Avenue, (917) 237-0363
Smith Street Stage, Carroll Park, http://
   www.smithstreetstage.org.
St. Ann's Warehouse, 45 Water Street,
   (718) 254-8779
Theatre for a New Audience (Polonsky
   Shakespeare Center), 262 Ashland Place,
   (212) 229-2819

Street Art and Public Art:
Sources for Discovering Locations
Art in the Parks, http://www.nycgovparks.org/
   art-and-antiquities/art-in-the-parks
Brooklyn Bridge Park, http://www.brooklyn
   bridgepark.org/places/public-art
Bushwick Collective, https://www.facebook
   .com/TheBushwickCollective
Coney Island Murals, Jeffrey Deitch, http://
   deitch.com/gallery/index.php
DOT Art for Streets, http://www.nyc.gov/
   html/dot/html/pedestrians/dotart.shtml
Dumbo: Walls and Anchorage, http://dumbo.is/

Groundswell, http://groundswell.nyc/
   public-art
Open studios: in Bushwick, Gowanus,
   Red Hook, Clinton Hill, elsewhere (check
   neighborhood chapters in section 3)
Public Art Fund, http://www.publicartfund.org
Street Art NYC, blog, http://streetartnyc.org
Subway Art, http://www.nycsubway.org/perl/
   artwork

Select Landmarks
Brooklyn Army Terminal, between 58th and
   63rd Streets
Brooklyn Borough Hall, 209 Joralemon Street,
   (718) 802-3700
Brooklyn Bridge
Coney Island: Deno's Wonder Wheel, Cyclone
   Roller Coaster, Parachute Jump, Riegelmann
   Boardwalk
1880s Historic Dutch Reformed Church,
   890 Flatbush Avenue at Church Avenue
Flatlands Dutch Reformed Church, 3931 Kings
   Highway, (718) 252-5540
Floyd Bennett Field, 50 Aviator Road,
   (718) 338-3799
Manhattan Bridge
Montauk Club, 25 8th Avenue, (718) 638-0800
Plymouth Church, 75 Hicks Street,
   (718) 624-4743
Weylin B. Seymour's, 175 Broadway,
   (718) 963-3639
Williamsburg Bridge
Wyckoff House Museum, 5816 Clarendon Road,
   (718) 629-5400

Eating and Drinking in Brooklyn

400 Amazing Restaurants

Believe me, you won't starve. Plot your culinary itinerary in Brooklyn as carefully as Napoleon plotted his wars. Try global ethnic cuisines from Ethiopian to Polish, halal to kosher, old-Brooklyn nostalgia foods to farm-to-table new-Brooklyn cuisine. Many chain restaurants including Shake Shack, Smashburger, and Wahlburgers have Brooklyn locations. But why not try something different?

BROOKLYN'S EATING AND DRINKING LANDSCAPE

What are you in the mood for? There are three rough categories of eats.

First, old Brooklyn's populist menu. It is neither green nor—seltzer aside!—slenderizing. It includes Nathan's hot dogs, Junior's cheesecakes, Totonno's and Di Fara's pizza, Peter Luger's steaks, Bamonte's pasta, Mill Basin Deli's brisket, and bagels. Buying wholesale is a time-honored Brooklyn tradition; trek to Acme Smoked Fish for discounted smoked salmon, Fridays only.

Second, the new-Brooklyn cuisine. It is often organic, and the farms from which the food comes, eco-conscious and sustainability minded. ("Local farms" in New York means within a three-hundred-mile radius, more or less.) It's a cuisine "for people who care about food and what they put in their bodies" and who do what they can in their personal lives to respond to metaconcerns like global warming, Katy Sparks, owner of Katy Sparks Culinary Consulting, told the author. In both food and drink, the words "craft," "small batch," and "locavore" describe the new food aesthetic. Restaurateur Andrew Tarlow has built a small empire on these principles; it includes Diner, Marlow & Sons, Marlow & Daughters, and Reynard (all in Williamsburg), Roman's (in Fort Greene), Achilles Heel bar and café (Greenpoint), and *Diner Journal* online.

Third, ethnic fare. Ethnic authenticity is Brooklyn's middle name. So for Russian borscht, go to Brighton Beach; for Polish kielbasa, to Greenpoint. Turkish kebabs and spinach pies are cooking in Sheepshead Bay. Find "Jewish" fare for noshing in Midwood, and variations on both Middle Eastern and traditional southern Italian in Bay Ridge, Williamsburg, and Carroll Gardens. Pizzerias are ubiquitous; you'd be surprised at the soups and nonpizza dishes some turn out, too. A yen for cheap, authentic Mexican or Chinese food may take you to a Sunset Park taco joint or an Avenue U Szechuan restaurant, to Coney Island's Doña Zita, the Red Hook ball fields, and Bushwick. For soul food, try Mitchell's in Prospect Heights. You'll find

"Festivale des Soupes" at Bar Tabac on Smith Street. (Photo by E. Freudenheim, 2013)

creative, upscale riffs on ethnic food across the borough, especially in the pricier eateries in Williamsburg, Carroll Gardens, and Bushwick.

WHERE TO DRINK AND EAT (NOT RESTAURANTS)

Beer Gardens, Craft Beers, and Indie Distilleries

Beer drinkers can swill their way through Brooklyn's beer gardens, small bars, dive bars, and breweries. Some favorites include Radegast Hall & Biergarten and Berry Park in Williamsburg. In Bushwick, try the Well or Arrogant Swine, where you'll find authentic North Carolina–style whole-pig BBQ—with brews, of course!

In Crown Heights, Franklin Park is excellent and has interesting music and events. Berg'n is a cavernous indoor space with several popular food stands. Der Schwarze Kölner / Die StammKneipe in Fort Greene serves a dozen brews and tasty tidbits. In the Park Slope and Greenwood area, visit Brooklyn Bavarian Biergarten or Greenwood Park beer garden.

Brooklyn Brewery in Williamsburg is rightfully credited with reviving Brooklyn's craft brewing industry. Get in line for a tour and to sample seasonal beers in a low-key setting. Their award-winning brew master, Garrett Oliver, is awesome. Visits to smaller breweries are fun: Six Point Brewery in Red Hook, KelSo Beer Company in Fort Greene, and Other Half Brewing Co. in Carroll Gardens. The DIY emporium Bitter & Esters in Prospect Heights sells brewing equipment.

Small-batch distilleries are making a comeback, following a change in New York State laws, so you can visit Van Brunt Stillhouse in Red Hook; Kings County Distillery in the Brooklyn Navy Yard; Breuckelen Distilling in South Park Slope; and Williamsburg's New York Distilling Co. The Brooklyn Winery is also in Williamsburg.

The Cocktail Scene

Savor a good cocktail? Inventive mixed drinks are part of Brooklyn's food scene. "For a little fun, dress up for cocktails before or after dinner," advises culinary consultant Katy Sparks. "Sit at the bar, and watch the bar chefs." (They're neither "mixologists" nor "bartenders" anymore, she told the author.) "The best and most talented are creating recipes out of whole cloth, using extremely innovative

Kings County Distillery at Brooklyn Navy Yard (est. 2010). (Photo by E. Freudenheim, 2014)

ingredients, riffing on the classics, and experimenting with new tastes. If rhubarbs are in season, rhubarbs will be on the cocktail menu. Or they might mix small-batch artisanal bourbons with interesting bitters, like celery lime."

An ironic retro look is all the rage, from old apothecary bar décor to the "sartorial splendor" of some bartenders, whose get-ups include, in Sparks's words, "arm gaiters, long sideburns, maybe a hat and mismatched tie," evoking the 1890s or speakeasies. But of course, the scene is hot and sophisticated and morphs quickly; today's hip will soon be tomorrow's cliché.

Sample various signature cocktails at Clover Club in Carroll Gardens; Maison Premier, Extra Fancy, Hotel Delmano, and Dram in Williamsburg; Blueprint in Park Slope; June Wine Bar in Cobble Hill; and Miles in Bushwick.

Farmers Markets and Whole Foods

Brooklyn's two-dozen greenmarkets operate every day of the week in different neighborhoods. We've included them in each neighborhood profile; also check GrowNYC Greenmarkets online. Whole Foods supermarket is located in Gowanus and is opening soon in Williamsburg.

Food Trucks

No need to curb your appetite! These curbside trucks—fitted out with kitchens and licensed by the city—are purveyors of gourmet on the go, like lobster rolls and ice cream and waffles. They park at Brooklyn Bridge Park and other outdoor parks. Search NYCTruckFood.com for locations; just plug in a zip code and identify what cuisine you are looking for—awesome!

Made-in-Brooklyn Gourmet

Brooklyn's small artisanal food producers are inventing and manufacturing hundreds of interesting edibles. They're mentioned throughout this book. Here are some more: Wandering Bear Coffee Company, Up Mountain Switchel, sugar-free Cracked Candy, Mike's flavor-infused Hot Honey products, Lukas Veggie Burger mixes, Sohha Savory Yogurt, Middle Eastern condiments by NYShuk, Sfoglini Seasonal Pasta, and paleo chocolate from Haute Chocolate. (See "Shopping in Brooklyn," section 4.)

Twelve Fab Brooklyn Pizzerias

Pizza is an art form in Brooklyn. Let us count the ways. Is it the cheese you love? Or the sauce? Or the crust, thin or thick, triangle or square? Here are some of the best. See the neighborhood listings in the following pages for contact information.

Di Fara's Pizzeria (Midwood section of Flatbush)
Franny's (Park Slope)
Grimaldi's Pizzeria (Dumbo)

Guiseppina's (Greenwood Heights)
Juliana's (Dumbo)
L&B Spumoni Gardens Restaurant (Bensonhurst)
Lucali (Carroll Gardens / Cobble Hill)
Motorino (Williamsburg)
Paulie Gee's (Greenpoint)
Roberta's (Bushwick)
Saraghina (Bed-Stuy)
Totonno's Pizzeria (Coney Island)

Smorgasburg

Smorgasburg is a moveable feast, literally, a fairground of small-batch, independently crafted food. It rotates locations, through indoor venues, parks, and parking lots, transforming them into a heaven of small food stands selling interesting foods. Started in Williamsburg (hence its punny name), Smorgasburg's successfully launched many aspiring food "inventors." Its twin is Brooklyn Flea, a curated flea market, also with wonderful vendors.

Mimi & Coco's Japanese-style savory dough balls at Smorgasburg. (Courtesy Sam Kolich, 2015)

400 BROOKLYN RESTAURANTS AND BARS

The following list of local Brooklyn restaurants serves up almost a year's worth of daily dining-out suggestions! It includes informal but excellent eateries and Brooklyn's most expensive restaurants, as well as bars. You'll find more restaurant ideas in individual neighborhood chapters in section 3. Many small restaurants don't take reservations for fewer than six people.

About this list: All restaurants on this list had received either an "A" rating from the New York City Department of Health or were pending inspection. A handful of vegan restaurants are so noted. "Michelin rated" means a restaurant won at least one Michelin star between 2014 and 2016; "Michelin Bib Gourmand" means a restaurant won the Michelin "value for money" designation for 2016.

Bay Ridge

Areo, 8424 3rd Avenue, (718) 238-0079
Brooklyn Beet Company, 7205 3rd Avenue, (718) 492-0020
Celtic Rose Restaurant and Tea Room, 8905 3rd Avenue, (718) 238-3355
David's Brisket House, 7721 5th Avenue, (718) 333-5662
Embers, 9519 3rd Avenue, (718) 745-3700
Grand Sichuan House, 8701 5th Avenue, (718) 680-8887
Hazar Turkish Kebab, 7224 5th Avenue, (718) 238-4040
Karam, 8519 4th Avenue, (718) 745-5227
Schnitzel Haus, 7319 5th Avenue, (718) 836-5600
Tanoreen, 7523 3rd Avenue, (718) 748-5600

BARS

Kitty Kiernans, 9715 3rd Avenue, (718) 921-0217
O'Sullivan's, 8902 3rd Avenue, (718) 745-9619
Wicked Monk, 9510 3rd Avenue, (347) 497-5152

Bedford-Stuyvesant

Alice's Arbor, 549 Classon Avenue, (718) 399-3003
DOCD Southern Desserts Shop, 214 Bainbridge Street, (347) 413-8348
Le Paris Dakar, 518 Nostrand Avenue, (347) 955-4100
Manny's, 212 Patchen Avenue, (718) 483-9868
Peaches, 393 Lewis Avenue, (718) 942-4162
Reconnect Café, 139 Tompkins Avenue, (347) 406-9780
Saraghina, 435 Halsey Street, (718) 574-0010
Sugar Hill, 609 DeKalb Avenue, (718) 797 1727

BARS

Black Swan, 1048 Bedford Avenue, (718) 783-4744
Therapy Wine Bar, 364 Lewis Avenue, (718) 513-0686

Bensonhurst

Café Kiev, 1739 West 7th Street, (718) 336-8800
L&B Spumoni Gardens Restaurant, 2725 86th Street, (718) 449-1230
Tomasso's Restaurant, 1464 86th Street, (718) 236-9883
Villabate Alba Café, 7001 18th Avenue, (718) 331-8430

BARS

Draft Barn, 317 Avenue X, (718) 768-0515

Boerum Hill

French Louie, 320 Atlantic Avenue, (718) 935-1200
Hanco's, 134 Smith Street, (718) 858-6818
Mile End Delicatessen, 97A Hoyt Street, (718) 852-7510 (Michelin Bib
    Gourmand)
M.O.B., 525 Atlantic Avenue, (718) 797-2555
Rucola, 190 Dean Street, (718) 576-3209
Sottocasa Pizza, 298 Atlantic Avenue, (718) 852-8758 (Michelin Bib Gourmand)

BARS

Brooklyn Inn, 148 Hoyt Street, (718) 522-2525
Congress Bar, 208 Court Street, http://congressbarbrooklyn.com
Hank's Saloon, 46 3rd Avenue, http://www.exitfive.com/hankssaloon ("ain't
    no phone")

Borough Park

Vostok, 5507 13th Avenue, (718) 437-2596

BARS

The Gallery, 933 McDonald Avenue, (718) 438-9215

Brighton Beach

Café Glechik, 3159 Coney Island Avenue, (718) 616-0766 (also in Sheepshead Bay)
Nargis Cafe, 2818 Coney Island Avenue, (718) 872-7888
National Restaurant & Nightclub, 273 Brighton Beach Avenue, (718) 646-1225
Skovorodka, 615 Brighton Beach Avenue, (718) 615-3096
Tatiana Grill and Café, 3145 Brighton 4th Street, (718) 646-7630
Toné Café, 265 Neptune Avenue, (718) 332-8082

BARS

Kebeer Draft Bar and Grill, 1003 Brighton Beach Avenue, (718) 934-9005

Brooklyn Heights

Colonie, 127 Atlantic Avenue, (718) 855-7500
Heights Café, 84 Montague Street, (718) 625-5555
Henry's End, 44 Henry Street, (718) 834-1776
Noodle Pudding, 38 Henry Street, (718) 625-3737
Tazza's, 311 Henry Street, (718) 243-0487
Yemen Café, 176 Atlantic Avenue, (718) 834-9533

BARS

Brooklyn Heights Wine Bar & Kitchen, 50 Henry Street, (718) 855-5595
The Long Island Bar, 110 Atlantic Avenue, (718) 625-8908
Montero Bar & Grill, 73 Atlantic Avenue, (646) 729-4129
Roebling Inn, 97 Atlantic Avenue, (718) 488-0040

Bushwick

Amancay's Diner, 2 Knickerbocker Avenue, (718) 628-8860
Bizarre, 12 Jefferson Street, (347) 915-2717
Blanca, 261 Moore Street, (347) 799-2807 (Michelin rated)
Bossa Nova Civic Club, 1271 Myrtle Avenue, (718) 443-1271
Bunna Café, 1084 Flushing Avenue, (347) 295-2227 (vegetarian/vegan)
Bushwick Country Club, 618 Grand Street, (718) 388-2114
Café Ghia, 24 Irving Avenue, (718) 821-8806 (vegan options)
Central Café, 108 Central Avenue, (718) 497-3028
Circo's Pastry Shop, 312 Knickerbocker Avenue, (718) 381-2292
Dear Bushwick, 41 Wilson Avenue, (929) 234-2344
Falansai, 112 Harrison Place, (347) 599-1190 (Michelin Bib Gourmand)
Lange Noir Café, 247 Varet Street, (718) 821-2459
La Tortilleria Mexicana Los Tres Hermanos, 271 Starr Street, (718) 456-3422
Momo Sushi Shack, 43 Bogart Street, (718) 418-6666
Northeast Kingdom, 18 Wyckoff Avenue, (718) 386-3864
Pearl's Social & Billy Club, 40 Saint Nicholas Avenue, (347) 627-9985
Pine Box Rock Shop, 12 Grattan Street, (718) 366-6311
Roberta's, 261 North Moore Street, (718) 417-1118 (Michelin Bib Gourmand)
Tina's Restaurant, 1002 Flushing Avenue, (718) 821-9595

BARS

Miles, 101 Wilson Avenue, (718) 483-9172
Old Stanley's, 226 Wyckoff Avenue, (917) 658-8941
Tandem, 236 Troutman Street, (718) 386-2369

Carroll Gardens / Cobble Hill

Angry Wades, 222 Smith Street, (718) 488-7253

Bar Tabac Café, 128 Smith Street, (718) 923-0918

Battersby, 255 Smith Street, (718) 852-8321

Bien Cuit, 120 Smith Street, (718) 852-0200

Buttermilk Channel, 524 Court Street, (718) 852-8490 (Michelin Bib Gourmand)

Café Luluc, 214 Smith Street, (718) 625-3815

Claudine's, 311 Smith Street, (718) 237-4992

Enoteca, 347 Court Street, (718) 243-1000

Frankies 457 Spuntino, 457 Court Street, (718) 403-0033 (Michelin Bib Gourmand)

Jolie Cantina, 241 Smith Street, (718) 488-0777

Karloff, 254 Court Street, (347) 689-4279

La Vara, 268 Clinton Street, (718) 422-0065

Lucali's, 575 Henry Street, (718) 858-4086

People's Republic of Brooklyn, 247 Smith Street, (718) 522-6100

Prime Meats, 465 Court Street, (718) 254-0327 (Michelin Bib Gourmand)

Provence en Boite, 263 Smith Street, (718) 797-0707

Take Root, 187 Sackett Street, (347) 227-7116 (Michelin rated)

Zaytoon's, 283 Smith Street, (718) 875-1880

BARS

Black Mountain Wine House, 415 Union Street, (718) 522-4340

Brooklyn Social, 210 Smith Street, (718) 858-7758

Camp, 179 Smith Street, (718) 852-8086

Clover Club, 210 Smith Street, (718) 855-7939

The Jakewalk, 282 Smith Street, (718) 599-0294

June Wine Bar, 231 Court Street, (917) 909-0434

Waty and Meg, 248 Court Street, (718) 643-0007

Clinton Hill

Aita, 132 Greene Avenue, (718) 576-3584 (also at 798A Franklin Avenue)

Alice's Arbor, 549 Classon Avenue, (718) 399-3003

Crown Fried Chicken, 963 Fulton Street, (718) 399-3181 (multiple locations)

The Finch, 212 Greene Avenue, (718) 218-4444 (Michelin rated)

The General Greene, 229 DeKalb Avenue, (718) 222-1510 (Michelin Bib Gourmand)

Locanda Vini e Olii, 129 Gates Avenue, (718) 622-9202

Marietta, 285 Grand Avenue, (718) 638-9500

Outpost, 1014 Fulton Street, (718) 636-1260

SoCo, 509 Myrtle Avenue, (718) 783-1936

Speedy Romeo, 376 Classon Avenue, (718) 230-0061 (Michelin Bib Gourmand)

Tip Top Bar & Grill, 432 Franklin Avenue, (718) 857-9744

Umi Nom, 433 DeKalb Avenue, (718) 789-8806 (Michelin Bib Gourmand)

BARS

Brooklyn Tap House, 590 Myrtle Avenue, (347) 750-7557

Fulton Grand, 1011 Fulton Street, (718) 399-2240

The Mayflower, 132 Greene Avenue, (718) 576-3584

Putnam's Pub and Cooker, 419 Myrtle Avenue, (347) 799-2382

Columbia Waterfront District

Alma Restaurant, 187 Columbia Street, (643) 643-5400

Ferdinando's Focacceria Restaurant, 151 Union Street, (718) 855-1545

Luzzo's Pizza, 145 Atlantic Avenue, (718) 855-6400

Petit Crevette, 144 Union Street, (718) 855-2632

Pok Pok NY, 17 Columbia Street, (718) 923-9322 (Michelin rated)

BARS

Alma Rooftop Bar, 187 Columbia Street, (643) 643-5400

Coney Island

Doña Zita Mexican Food, 1221 Bowery Street, (347) 589-9396

Gargiulo's Restaurant, 2911 West 15th Street, (718) 266-4891

Nathan's Famous, 1310 Surf Avenue, (718) 333-2202

Paul's Daughter, 1001 Riegelmann Boardwalk, (718) 449-4252

Peggy O'Neill's, 1904 Surf Avenue, (718) 449-3200

Tom's Coney Island, 1229 Riegelmann Boardwalk, (718) 942-4200

Totonno's Pizzeria, 1524 Neptune Avenue, (718) 372-8606

Wahlburgers, 3021 Stillwell Avenue, (718) 881-8888

BARS

Coney Island Brewing Company, 1904 Surf Avenue, (718) 996-0019

Freak Bar, 1208 Surf Avenue, (718) 372-5159

Ruby's Bar and Grill, 1213 Riegelmann Boardwalk, (718) 975-7829

Crown Heights

Barboncino, 781 Franklin Avenue, (718) 483-8834

Café Rue Dix, 1451 Bedford Avenue, (929) 234-2543

Catfish, 1433 Bedford Avenue, (347) 305-3233 (vegan options)

Chavela's, 736 Franklin Avenue, (718) 622-3100 (Michelin Bib Gourmand)

Franklin Park, 618 St. Johns Place, (718) 975-0196

Glady's, 88 Franklin Avenue, (718) 622-0249 (Michelin Bib Gourmand)

Mayfield, 688 Franklin Avenue, (347) 318-3643

Pearl Indian Restaurant, 738 Franklin Avenue, (718) 622-9500

Sweet Basil, 709 Franklin Avenue, (718) 399-3388

BARS

Berg'n (also food), 899 Bergen Street, (718) 857-2337

Glorietta Baldy, 502 Franklin Avenue, (347) 529-1944

King Tai Bar, 1095 Bergen Street, (718) 513-1025

Downtown Brooklyn

Archives Restaurant at New York Marriott at Brooklyn Bridge, (718) 222-6543

Junior's Cheesecake, 386 Flatbush Avenue Extension, (718) 852-5257

Katz's Delicatessen (opening 2017 in City Point)

Ganso Ramen, 25 Bond Street, (718) 403-0900 (Michelin Bib Gourmand)

Queen, 84 Court Street, (718) 596-5955

Chains such as Chipotle, Hill Country BBQ, Dallas BBQ, Shake Shack

BARS

Livingston Manor, 42 Hoyt Street, (347) 987-3292

Dumbo, Fulton Ferry Waterfront, Vinegar Hill

Brooklyn Ice Cream Factory, 1 Water Street, (718) 246-3963

Brooklyn Roasting Co., 50 Washington Street, (718) 522-3498

Fornino, Brooklyn Bridge Park, Pier 6, (718) 422-1107

Gran Eléctrica, 5 Front Street, (718) 852-2700 (Michelin Bib Gourmand)

Grimaldi's Pizzeria, 1 Front Street, (718) 858-4300

Juliana's, 19 Old Fulton Street, (718) 596-6700

River Café, 1 Water Street, (718) 522-5200 (Michelin rated)

Superfine, 126 Front Street, (718) 243-9005

Vinegar Hill House, 72 Hudson Avenue, (718) 522-1018 (Michelin Bib
  Gourmand)

BARS

Olympia Wine Bar, 54 Jay Street, (718) 624-7900

68 Jay Street Bar, 68 Jay Street, (718) 260-8207

Flatbush

Am Thai Bistro, 1003 Church Avenue, (718) 287-8888

Bahar Masala, 984 Coney Island Avenue, (718) 434-8088

Café Madeline, 1603 Cortelyou Road, (718) 941-4020

Chikurin Sushi, 1777 Ocean Avenue, (718) 338-1818

Di Fara's Pizzeria, 1424 Avenue J, (718) 258-1367

El Mexicano Restaurante & Cafe, 2102 East 15th Street, (718) 676-2700

Essen New York Deli, 1359 Coney Island Avenue, (718) 859-1002 (kosher)

Farm on Adderley, 1108 Cortelyou Road, (718) 287-3101 (vegan options)

Fisherman's Cove, 4 Newkirk Plaza, (718) 859-1580 (five locations)

Highway Bagels Corp., 1921 Kings Highway, (718) 336-9200

Lea, 1022 Cortelyou Road, (718) 928-7100 (Michelin Bib Gourmand)

Memo Shish Kebob, 1821 Kings Highway, (718) 339-8001

Michael's of Brooklyn, 2929 Avenue R, (718) 998-7851

Milk and Honey, 1119 Newkirk Avenue, (718) 513-0441

Mimi's Hummus, 1209 Cortelyou Road, (718) 284-4444

Mish Mash Gourmet, 1103 Kings Highway, (718) 375-5100 (kosher)

Moldova Restaurant, 1827 Coney Island Avenue, (718) 998-2892

Oxcart Tavern, 1301 Newkirk Avenue, (718) 284-0005

Purple Yam Restaurant, 1314 Cortelyou Road, (718) 940-8188 (Michelin Bib Gourmand)

Shayna's Restaurant, 907 Church Avenue, (718) 282-8190

Tacis Beyti Turkish Restaurant, 1953–1955 Coney Island Avenue, (718) 627-5750

Top Café Tibet, 1510 Cortelyou Road, (718) 941-2725

Wheated Pizza, 905 Church Avenue, (347) 240-2813

BARS

Bar Chord, 1008 Cortelyou Road, (347) 240-6033

Castello Plan, 1213 Cortelyou Road, (718) 856-8888

Fort Greene

Black Iris Middle Eastern Cuisine, 228 DeKalb Avenue, (718) 852-9800

Chez Oskar, 211 DeKalb Avenue, (718) 852-6250

Graziella's, 232 Vanderbilt Avenue, (718) 789-5663

ICI: French Country Kitchen, 246 DeKalb Avenue, (718) 789-2778

Lean Crust, 737 Fulton Street, (718) 852-7567 (vegan options)

LuLu & Po, 154 Carlton Avenue, (917) 435-3745 (Michelin Bib Gourmand)

Roman's Restaurant, 243 DeKalb Avenue, (718) 622-5300

The Smoke Joint, 87 South Elliott Place, (718) 797-1011

Walter's, 166 DeKalb Avenue, (718) 488-7800

BARS

Brooklyn Public House, 247 DeKalb Avenue, (347) 227-8976

Frank's Lounge and Bar, 660 Fulton Street, (718) 625-9339

Gowanus

Ample Hills Creamery, 305 Nevins Street, (347) 725-4061 (multiple locations)

Dinosaur BBQ, 604 Union Street, (347) 429-7030

Du Jour Bakery, 365 5th Avenue, (347) 227-8953

Fletcher's Brooklyn Barbecue, 433 3rd Avenue, (347) 763-2680

Four and Twenty Blackbirds, 439 3rd Avenue, (718) 499-2917

Ghenet Brooklyn Ethiopian Restaurant, 348 Douglass Street, (718) 230-4475

Littleneck, 288 3rd Avenue, (718) 522-1921

Monte's Restaurant, 451 Carroll Street, (718) 852-7800

The Pines, 284 3rd Avenue, (718) 596-6560

Runner & Stone, 285 3rd Avenue, (718) 576-3360 (Michelin Bib Gourmand)

Station Diner, 224 4th Avenue, (718) 522-2083

Two Toms Restaurant, 255 3rd Avenue, (718) 875-8689

BARS

Canal Bar, 270 3rd Avenue, (718) 246-0011

Great Harry, 280 Smith Street, (718) 222-1103

Halyards, 406 3rd Avenue, (718) 532-8787

Lavender Lake, 383 Carroll Street, (347) 799-2154

Lowlands Bar, 543 3rd Avenue, (347) 463-9458

Mission Dolores Bar, 249 4th Avenue, (718) 643-2273

Pickle Shack, 256 4th Avenue, (347) 763-2127

Royal Palms Shuffleboard, 514 Union Street, (347) 223-4410

Sheep Station, 149 4th Avenue, (718) 857-4337

Greenpoint

Achilles Heel, 180 West Street, (347) 987-3666

Anella, 222 Franklin Street, (718) 389-8100

Black Rabbit, 91 Greenpoint Avenue, (718) 349-1595

Calexico, 645 Manhattan Avenue, (347) 763-2129

Enid's, 560 Manhattan Avenue, (718) 349-3859

Five Leaves, 18 Bedford Avenue, (718) 383-5345

Glasserie, 95 Commercial Street, (718) 389-0640

Greenpoint Fish & Lobster Company, 114 Nassau Avenue, (718) 349-0400

Greenpoint Heights, 278 Nassau Avenue, (718) 389-0110

Habitat, 988 Manhattan Avenue, (718) 383-5615

Paulie Gee's, 60 Greenpoint Avenue, (347) 987-3737 (vegan options) (Michelin
   Bib Gourmand)

Peter Pan Donut & Pastry Shop, 727 Manhattan Avenue, (718) 389-3676

BARS

Bar Matchless, 557 Manhattan Avenue, (718) 383-5333

Ramona, 113 Franklin Street, (347) 227-8164

Rosemary's Greenpoint Tavern, 188 Bedford Avenue, (718) 384-9539

Greenwood Heights

Guiseppina's, 691 6th Avenue, (718) 499-5052
Korzo Haus, 667 5th Avenue, (718) 499-1199
Lot 2, 687 6th Avenue, (718) 499-5623
Roots, 639 5th Avenue, (615) 419-7877
Toby's Public House, 686 6th Avenue, (718) 788-1186

BARS

Freddy's Bar, 627 5th Avenue, (718) 768-0131
Greenwood Park, 555 7th Avenue, (718) 499-7999 ("B" rating for food)

Marine Park

Brennan & Carr, 3432 Nostrand Avenue, (718) 646-9559

BARS

3rd & 7th, 3622 Quentin Road, (718) 336-6300

Mill Basin Area

Dolly's Italian Ices, 5800 Avenue U at 58th Street, (347) 582-1075
La Torre Pork Store, 4518 Avenue N, (718) 252-0546
La Villa, 6610 Avenue U, (718) 251-8030
Mill Basin Kosher Deli, 5823 Avenue T, (718) 241-4910
Moretti Bakery, 4524 Avenue N, (718) 377-5364

BARS

Saigon Grill & Bar, 4521 Avenue N, (718) 338-8886

Park Slope

al di la Trattoria, 248 5th Avenue, (718) 783-4565
Bareburger, 170 7th Avenue, (718) 768-2273
Bark, 474 Bergen Street, (718) 789-1939
Battersby, 255 Smith Street, (718) 852-8321
Blueprint, 196 5th Avenue, (718) 622-6644
Bogota Latin Bistro, 141 5th Avenue, (718) 230-3805 (vegan options)
Bonnie's Grill, 278 5th Avenue, (718) 369-9527
The Chocolate Room, 51 5th Avenue, (718) 783-2900
Cousin John's Bakery, 70 7th Avenue, (718) 622-7333
Cubana Café, 80 6th Avenue, (718) 398-9818
Dizzy's, 511 9th Street, (718) 499-1966
Fonda, 434 7th Avenue, (718) 369-3144
Franny's, 348 Flatbush Avenue, (718) 230-0221

Ginger's Bar, 363 5th Avenue, (718) 788-0924

Miriam, 79 5th Avenue, (718) 622-2250

Mr. Falafel, 226 7th Avenue, (718) 768-4961

Nana, 155 5th Avenue, (718) 230-3749

Olive Vine, 54 7th Avenue, (718) 622-2626

Palo Santo, 652 Union Street, (718) 636-6311

Pork Slope, 247 5th Avenue, (718) 768-7675

Rose Water, 787 Union Street, (718) 783-3800

Talde, 369 7th Avenue, (347) 916-0031 (Michelin rated)

Taro Sushi, 244 Flatbush Avenue, (718) 398-5240

V-Spot, 156 5th Avenue, (718) 928-8778 (vegan)

BARS

Brooklyn Bavarian Biergarten at Grand Prospect Hall, 263 Prospect Avenue,
    (718) 788-0400

The Gate, 321 5th Avenue, (718) 768-4329

The Owl Farm, 297 9th Street, (718) 499-4988

Sidecar, 560 5th Avenue, (718) 369-0077

Union Hall, 702 Union Street, (718) 636-4400

Prospect Heights

Bearded Lady, 686 Washington Avenue, (469) 232-7333

Cheryl's Global Soul, 236 Underhill Avenue, (347) 529-2855

Chuko, 552 Vanderbilt Avenue, (718) 576-6701

Flatbush Farm, 76 Saint Mark's Avenue, (718) 622-3276

Kimchi Grill, 766 Washington Avenue, (718) 360-1839 (also on Smith Street)

Le Gamin Café, 556 Vanderbilt Avenue, (718) 789-5171

Morgan's BBQ, 267 Flatbush Avenue, (718) 622-2224

Piquant, 259 Flatbush Avenue, (718) 484-4114

Saul, at the Brooklyn Museum, 200 Eastern Parkway, (718) 935-9842

Shake Shack, 170 Flatbush Avenue, (347) 422-7721

Stocked, 635 Vanderbilt Avenue, (929) 234-6554

Taro Sushi, 244 Flatbush Avenue, (718) 398-5240

Tom's Restaurant, 782 Washington Avenue, (718) 636-9738

The Vanderbilt, 570 Vanderbilt Avenue, (718) 623-0570

BARS

Bar Sepia, 234 Underhill Avenue, (718) 399-6680

Soda Bar, 629 Vanderbilt Avenue, (718) 230-8393

Weather Up, 589 Vanderbilt Avenue, (212) 766-3202

Inside Barclays Center are food stands and bars selling a variety of eats for people
    with tickets

Prospect Lefferts Gardens

Culpepper's, 1082 Nostrand Avenue, (718) 940-4122
Delroy's Cafe, 14 Duryea Place, (347) 770-9300
Elberta, 335 Flatbush Avenue, (718) 638-1936 (Michelin Bib Gourmand)

BARS

Erv's on Beekman, 2122 Beekman Place, (718) 936-2122

Red Hook

Baked, 359 Van Brunt Street, (718) 222-0345
Brooklyn Crab, 24 Reed Street, (718) 643-2722
Court Street Grocers, 116 Sullivan Street, (347) 529-6803
Fairway Café, 500 Van Brunt Street, (718) 254-0923
Fort Defiance, 365 Van Brunt Street, (347) 453-6672
The Good Fork, 391 Van Brunt Street, (718) 643-6636 (Michelin Bib Gourmand)
Home/Made, 293 Van Brunt Street, (347) 223-4135
Hometown Bar-B-Que, 54 Van Brunt Street, (347) 294-4644 (Michelin Bib
    Gourmand)
Hope & Anchor, 347 Van Brunt Street, (718) 237-0276
Kevin's, 227 Van Brunt Street, (718) 596-8335
Red Hook Lobster Pound, 284 Van Brunt Street, (718) 858-7650

BARS

Botanica, 220 Conover Street, (347) 225-0148
Brooklyn Ice House, 318 Van Brunt Street, (718) 222-1865
Fort Defiance, 365 Van Brunt Street, (347) 453-6672
Red Hook Bait and Tackle, 320 Van Brunt Street, (718) 451-4665
Rocky Sullivan's, 34 Van Dyke Street, (718) 246-8050
Sunny's Bar, 253 Conover Street, (718) 237-8888

Sheepshead Bay Area

Donut Shoppe / Shaikh's Place, 1503 Avenue U, (718) 375-2572
Istanbul Restaurant, 1715 Emmons Avenue, (718) 368-3587
Jordan's Lobster Dock, 3165 Harkness Avenue, (718) 934-6300
OPera Cafe & Lounge, 2255 Emmons Avenue, (718) 676-2992
Parkview Diner, 2939 Cropsey Avenue, (718) 333-9400
Randazzo's Clam Bar, 2017 Emmons Avenue, (718) 615-0010
Roll-N-Roaster, 2901 Emmons Avenue, (718) 769-6000

BARS

Falada Houka Lounge, 2011 Emmons Avenue, (718) 332-4040

Sunset Park

Ba Xuyen, 4222 8th Avenue, (718) 663-6601

East Harbor Seafood Palace, 714 65th Street, (718) 765-0098 (Michelin Bib Gourmand)

International Restaurant, 4408 5th Avenue, (718) 438-2009

Lucky Eight, 5204 8th Avenue, (718) 851-8862

Mister Hotpot, 5306 8th Avenue, (718) 633-5197

Nyonya, 5323 8th Avenue, (718) 633-0808 (also in Bensonhurst)

Thanh Da, 6008 7th Avenue, (718) 492-3253

BARS

Irish Haven, 5721 4th Avenue, (718) 439-9893

Soccer Tavern, 6004 8th Avenue, (718) 439-9336

Williamsburg

Allswell, 124 Bedford Avenue, (347) 799-2743

Baby's All Right, 146 Broadway, (718) 599-5800

Baci & Abbracci, 204 Grand Street, (718) 599-6599 (Michelin Bib Gourmand)

Bahia, 690 Grand Street, (718) 218-9592

Bamonte's Restaurant, 32 Withers Street, (718) 384-8831

Barcade, 388 Union Avenue, (718) 302-6464

Black Brick, 300 Bedford Avenue, (718) 384-0075

Bozu, 296 Grand Street, (718) 384-7770

Cafe Mogador, 133 Wythe Avenue, (718) 486-9222

Caracas Arepa Bar, 291 Grand Street, (718) 218-6050

The Counting Room, 44 Berry Street, (917) 519-4181

Delaney BBQ, 359 Bedford Avenue, (718) 701-8909

Delaware and Hudson, 135 North 5th Street, (718) 218-8191 (Michelin rated)

Diner, 85 Broadway, (718) 486-3077 (Michelin Bib Gourmand)

Egg, 109 North 3rd Street, (718) 302-5151 (Michelin Bib Gourmand)

El Almacen, 557 Driggs Avenue, (718) 218-7284

The Elm, 160 North 12th Street, (718) 218-1088

Forrest Point Bar, 970 Flushing Avenue, (718) 366-2742

Mable's Smokehouse and Banquet Hall, 44 Berry Street, (718) 218-6655

Maison Premiere, 298 Bedford Avenue, (347) 335-0446

Marlow & Sons, 81 Broadway, (718) 384-1441 (Michelin Bib Gourmand)

Meadowsweet, 149 Broadway, (718) 384-0673 (Michelin rated)

Motorino, 139 Broadway, (718) 599-8899

Peter Luger Steak House, 178 Broadway, (718) 387-7400 (Michelin rated)

Reynard, 80 Wythe Avenue, (718) 460-8004 (Michelin rated)

Rye, 247 South First Street, (718) 218-8047 (Michelin Bib Gourmand)

Semilla, 160 Havemeyer Street, (718) 782-3474 (Michelin rated)
Shalom Japan, 310 South 4th Street, (718) 388-4012 (Michelin Bib Gourmand)
Smorgasburg, various locations, http://www.smorgasburg.com
Traif, 229 South 4th Street, (347) 844-9578 (Michelin Bib Gourmand)
Zenkichi, 77 North 6th Street, (718) 388-8985
Zizi Limona, 129 Havemeyer Street, (347) 763-1463

BARS

Alligator Lounge, 600 Metropolitan Avenue, (718) 599-4440
Brooklyn Winery, 213 North 8th Street, (347) 763-1506
East River Bar, 97 South 6th Street, (718) 302-0511
Extra Fancy, 302 Metropolitan Avenue, (347) 422-0939
4th Down, 750 Grand Street, (917) 744-6522
The Gutter, 200 North 14th Street, (718) 387-3585
The Ides Bar at Wythe Hotel, 80 Wythe Avenue, (718) 460-8006
Kilo Bravo, 180 North 10th Street, (347) 987-4379
Masha & the Bear, 771 Grand Street, (718) 384-5000
New York Distilling Co., 79 Richardson Street, (718) 412-0874
Noorman's Kil, 609 Grand Street, (347) 384-2526
OTB, 141 Broadway, (347) 763-1481
Radegast Hall & Biergarten, 113 North 3rd Street, (718) 963-3973
Spike Hill, 186 Bedford Avenue, (718) 218-9737
Spritzenhaus, 33 Nassau Avenue, (347) 987-4632
Spuyten Duyvil, 359 Metropolitan Avenue, (718) 963-4140
Teddy's Bar, 96 Berry Street, (718) 384-9787
Turkey's Nest Tavern, 94 Bedford Avenue, (718) 384-9774
Union Pool, 484 Union Avenue, (718) 609-0484

Windsor Terrace and Kensington

Brooklyn Commune, 601 Greenwood Avenue, (718) 686-1044
Double Windsor, 210 Prospect Park West, (347) 725-3479
Elk Coffee, 154 Prospect Park Southwest, (718) 853-5500
Elora's Restaurant, 272 Prospect Park West, (718) 788-6190
Le P'tit Paris Bistro, 256 Prospect Park West, (718) 369-3590
Piccoli, 157A Prospect Park Southwest, (718) 788-0006

BARS

Farrell's Bar and Grill, 215 Prospect Park West, (718) 788-8779

BROOKLYN COOKBOOK SHELF

Well, you can't eat everything in Brooklyn—but you can take some of it home in a cookbook.

For old Brooklyn flavors, check out *Welcome to Junior's! Remembering Brooklyn with Recipes and Memories from Its Favorite Restaurant,* by Marvin and Walter Rosen. New and old are combined in *Brooklyn Chef's Table: Extraordinary Recipes from Coney Island to Brooklyn Heights,* by Sarah Zorn and Eric Isaac. The first of this genre was the 1991 *Brooklyn Cookbook,* in preparation for which author Lyn Stallworth trekked around the borough wresting classic Brooklyn recipes for popular food joints including Mrs. Stahl's knishes and Lundy's Manhattan clam chowder.

For twenty-first-century Brooklyn recipes, check out *Edible Brooklyn: The Cookbook,* compiled by Rachel Wharton, or *The New Brooklyn Cookbook: Recipes and Stories from 31*

Brooklyn Farmacy & Soda Fountain, in a renovated 1920s apothecary on Henry Street (est. 2010), has its own cookbook. (Photo by E. Freudenheim, 2014)

Restaurants That Put Brooklyn on the Culinary Map, by Melissa Vaughan, Brendan Vaughan, and Michael Harlan Turkell.

The hottest new-Brooklyn restaurants all have cookbooks. Roberta's, Bushwick's celebrated pizzeria, has *Roberta's Cookbook*, by Carlo Mirarchi and Brandon Hoy. The eatery Saltie published the eponymous *Saltie: A Cookbook*, by Caroline Fidanza and Anna Dunn. *The Frankies Spuntino Kitchen Companion & Cooking Manual* captures the flavors of the Carroll Gardens favorite Frankies 457. Egg, the breakfast-sensation eatery, shares some of its secrets in *Breakfast: Recipes to Wake Up For*, by George Weld and Evan Hanczor et al. Plan-ahead Type A cooks will enjoy *Battersby: Extraordinary Food from an Ordinary Kitchen*, by Joseph Ogrodnek and Walker Stern, who advance-prep amazing meals at a tiny, highly rated eatery. Jewish tastes are reflected in *The Mile End Cookbook: Redefining Jewish Comfort Food from Hash to Hamantaschen*, by Toronto-born deli owners Noah and Rae Bernamoff, of the Mile End Deli.

Bakeries have popped their own books out of the oven: *Baked, Ovenly*, and *First Prize Pies: Shoo-Fly, Candy Apple, and Other Deliciously Inventive Pies for Every Week of the Year (and More)*, by Allison Kave, and *The Four & Twenty Blackbirds Pie Book: Uncommon Recipes from the Celebrated Brooklyn Pie Shop*, by Emily Elsen and Melissa Elsen. Ice-cream-aholics will melt at the recipes in the cookbook called *Brooklyn Farmacy*. Meanwhile, the owners of Ample Hills Creamery, named after a line in a Walt Whitman poem about Brooklyn, authored *Ample Hills Creamery: Secrets and Stories from Brooklyn's Favorite Ice Cream Shop*.

In the alcohol aisle, there's *Brooklyn Spirits: Craft Distilling and Cocktails from the World's Hippest Borough*, by Peter Thomas Fornatale and Chris Wertz, and *The Kings County Distillery Guide to Urban Moonshining: How to Make and Drink Whiskey*, by entrepreneur David Haskel, who started the Kings County Distillery in the Brooklyn Navy Yard.

Brooklyn's first dedicated cookbook store opened in 2015 in Greenpoint: Archestratus.

Shopping in Brooklyn
Over 260 Places to Shop

BROOKLYN'S SHOPPING LANDSCAPE

Brooklyn does not have one famous shopping street, like Manhattan's Madison or Fifth Avenues or the Champs-Élysées in Paris. Though there are malls in Brooklyn, in general shopping here is not a uniform, mall-like experience. Interesting stores might be tucked on a block among other workaday businesses, perhaps a bagel shop, nail salon, real estate agency, animal hospital, and bodega. This dispersed quality of shopping in Brooklyn makes it an exploratory affair, not efficient but fun.

Strap on your sneakers.

Gifts and Souvenirs

Puhleeeze, skip the plastic Brooklyn Bridge key chains for souvenirs. This is *Brooklyn*. Why not get some artisanal lime-pickle-flavored mayonnaise instead? Or just take a selfie with a Brooklyn pizzeria guy, and frame it for your mom.

Shop at Brooklyn Flea, street fairs, museum stores, and quintessentially Brooklyn boutiques in Bushwick, Williamsburg, Greenpoint, Carroll Gardens, and Park Slope, on Atlantic Avenue, and elsewhere. You can sit right down and write yourself a letter on the hand-designed stationery at Foxy & Winston. For home gifts, Journey in Dumbo specializes in modern, vintage, and one-off artists' pieces, housed in a former cardboard-factory building. Should you find yourself at Marlow & Sons for dinner, you can also buy a leather bag (it might come from the same cow as your beef-neck entree; the restaurant is dedicated to using the *whole* animal).

Wear Brooklyn: Check out the hats, hoodies, backpacks, and shirts sold at Brooklyn Brewery, Coney Island, and BRIC Celebrate Brooklyn! concerts and in museum shops—and even at some pizzerias trying to get in on Brooklyn fever. Wear a T-shirt saying "Randazzo's Clam House"—and for sure you'll get a thumbs-up from expat Brooklynites in LA.

Clothing emblazoned with team logos (Nets, Rangers, Cyclones, Dodgers) is ubiquitous. Anyone who's a cyclist will love a Brooklyn bike jersey. At the New York Transit Museum, you can get T-shirts with the letters or numbers of New York City subways. Brooklyn Industries sells messenger bags with lifetime warrantees and collectible T-shirts designed by Brooklyn artists. The Brooklyn Botanic Garden's gift shop sells Claudia Pearson tea towels adorned not with frumpy roses but with brownstone buildings. Carry it all home in a Brooklyn-themed tote.

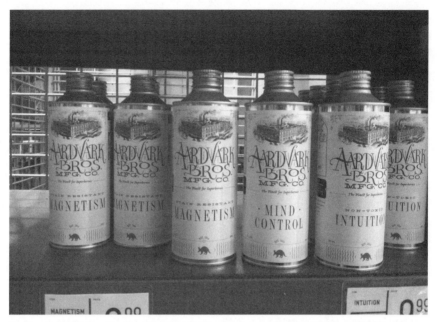

Merchandise in the Brooklyn Superhero Supply Store, a tutoring center founded by novelist Dave Eggers (est. 2004). Its motto is "Ever vigilant, ever true." (Photo by E. Freudenheim, 2015)

For gifts of food, shop at the Brooklyn Kitchen, BKLYN Larder, or other farm-to-table food emporiums. Mast Brothers' chocolate bars never fail to please (also try the Chocolate Room, Nunu's Chocolates, or Jacques Torres), nor do made-in-Brooklyn alcoholic beverages, Brooklyn Beet Company ketchup, Vendome's five-star macaroons, JoJo's small-batch sriracha, Peter Luger's steak sauces, or treats from Brooklyn Sesame. Try "Anarchy in a Jar Spiced with Beer Jelly." Nonedible kitcheny winners include Brooklyn Brewery barware and Brooklyn Slate Company cheeseboards. And see the list of Brooklyn cookbooks included in this book!

For books: Consider graphic novels, zines, comics, kids' books, works by Brooklyn authors, and photo-filled coffee-table books showing the awesomeness of Brooklyn's street art, Green-Wood, the Brooklyn Navy Yard, Prospect Park, and Coney Island. Buy histories galore of the Brooklyn Bridge, the Brooklyn Dodgers, Brooklyn gangsters, and individual neighborhoods. Brooklyn chefs have published enough cookbooks to fill a Costco shopping cart. Not sure what to buy? See "Contemporary Brooklyn Authors" and "Bibliography: Seventy-Five Works of Fiction Set in Brooklyn" in this book.

Splurge on a painting, print, or sculpture at a BWAC art show in Red Hook or from a gallery in Dumbo or Bushwick. Peruse the posters at Brooklyn Frame Works and the Brooklyn Museum. Buy a decked-out skateboard from KCDC or Skate Brooklyn and handcrafted jewelry at Catbird or Erie Basin. Men's hats are big; check out the traditional hats at Bencraft and Goorin Brothers and hip men's fashion at Brooklyn Circus. Make your own bracelet at Brooklyn Charm. Shop online for Brooklyn-made goods at By Brooklyn in Carroll Gardens, the website With Love from Brooklyn, or the Brooklyn Museum gift shop. Cat Studio makes pillows and home gifts with arty drawings.

For gifts reflecting diversity: A mere $9.80 buys you a sheet of twenty U.S. Post Office postage stamps, orderable online, featuring the "Unbought and Unbossed" Brooklyn congresswoman Shirley Chisholm. Clothes with Brooklyn attitude are the specialty of Fort Greene's Moshood Creations. Buy a history of Weeksville or gospel music by Grammy-winning Brooklyn Tabernacle Choir. You can find ethnic goods in their respective neighborhoods: Barbadian sorrel syrup, nutmeg-tamarind sauce, or a CD of

> ### POPULAR BROOKLYN GIFTS
>
> Bagels
> Brooklyn Superhero Supply's tins of Immortality, Inspiration, Chutzpah, and AntiMatter
> Posters or stationery with a Brooklyn logo or the Brooklyn Bridge
> Fresh spices and condiments from Sahadi's
> Brooklyn-logo clothes: T-shirts and baseball caps, bike jerseys
> Coney Island stuff: funny shirts, towels
> Cool jewelry, housewares, and finds from craft fairs
> Brooklyn-made craft brews, whiskey, chocolates, and pickles

Merchandise sold at Brooklyn Brewery in Williamsburg (est. 1988). (Photo by E. Freudenheim, 2014)

soca music for a Caribbean-themed gift; Jewish goods (fancy a yarmulke, klezmer music, perhaps a seventy-three-volume Schottenstein Talmud in English?). A host of potentially wonderful gift items are sold in stores serving Brooklyn's Latino American, Polish American, Russian American, Irish American, Pakistani American, Afro-Caribbean American, and Italian American communities.

Homesick for Brooklyn? Order a Junior's cheesecake, some pickles, or both, online. Surf Dumbo-based Etsy's one hundred thousand Brooklyn-made items, from a rocking chair priced at $9,000 to a shower curtain depicting the Brooklyn Bridge.

One-of-a-Kind Stores

For one-of-a-kind stores, browse boutique-rich neighborhoods: Greenpoint, Williamsburg, Carroll Gardens, Cobble Hill, Red Hook, Dumbo, and Park Slope in particular. Popular women's clothing stores you won't find elsewhere include Bird, Iris Lingerie, Kiwi, Diane T., and Tango for relaxed, sophisticated women's clothes, and Flirt for the young and, well, flirty.

If you play guitar, banjo, or mandolin, visit the extraordinary Retrofret Vintage Guitars (one of several outstanding instrument stores in the borough). Spacecraft, a hobbyist shop, is one of many selling "maker" equipment. Owl and Thistle General Store in Crown Heights, self-described as "urban mercantile specializing in local, green, fair and direct-trade products," represents the new-Brooklyn zeitgeist. The Clay Pot is known for wedding and engagement rings, some designed by Brooklyn artists.

In Carroll Gardens, walk along Smith Street from Union Street to Wyckoff Street, to explore over a dozen small, independent stores. In Williamsburg, you'll find a ton of options, starting with Mociun (picked by *Vogue* as one of Brooklyn's top fashion shops) and Jumelle for sophisticated women's office clothes. Thistle & Clover features up-and-coming designers. Atlantic Avenue between Hoyt and Smith Streets has a fab potpourri of clothing, antique furniture, vintage boutiques, and, unexpectedly, bridal ateliers.

While visiting ethnic neighborhoods, you can find all kinds of stuff, from cherry preserves imported from Poland to red Chinese New Year party favors, for unusual gifts.

What Are Brooklyn Flea and Smorgasburg?

The institution known as Brooklyn Flea is a destination cultural experience, not just a flea market. Imagine about a hundred vendors selling interesting artifacts, vintage clothes, collectables, jewelry, curios, and DIY handmade items. It's super-curated; you won't find undervalued treasures. This year-round weekend event is a fun social scene. Indoor and outdoor locations vary seasonally, usually with summer Saturdays in Fort Greene and Sundays in Williamsburg.

Smorgasburg, begun in 2011, is Brooklyn Flea's twin. It's an indie food festival, showcasing local and regional artisanal food vendors. It moves locations, from churchyard lots to Coney Island to Brooklyn Bridge Park to Industry City. Again, the offerings are broad: as many as a hundred vendors serve up yummy bites, rain or shine. Favorites include Asia Dogs with Asian-inspired toppings, Mighty Quinn's slow-cooked barbequed meats, and Samesa's knockout chicken shawarma. Smorgasburg's so popular that it's even been exported—to Manhattan.

Vintage, Thrift, Stoop Sales, Markets

Explore Brooklyn's epic thrift-and-vintage sector, in all price ranges from dirt cheap to "really?" Selections include clothes, comics, shoes, furniture, housewares, jewelry, art, books, you name it. Some stores are tiny; others are cavernous.

For designer vintage, try Antoinette Vintage and Amarcord. For bargains, head to Buffalo Exchange or Beacon's Closet. North Brooklyn is vintage-jammed; start in Williamsburg (Artists & Fleas, 10 Ft. Single by Stella Dallas, and a dozen others) or Bushwick (Green Village, a stage-set designer's dreamland) or Greenpoint (People of 2morrow and Fox & Fawn, the latter also in Bushwick). Carroll Gardens has interesting vintage stores. Walk a mile and a half from Bergen Street to Eighteenth Street on Park Slope's Fifth Avenue to explore a dozen secondhand and consignment shops. Try L Train Vintage, Life Boutique, and Two Lovers. For limited decorating budgets, cheap gear, and Halloween costumes, check the Salvation Army. Housing Works, a thrift store that raises money for AIDS, has shops in Brooklyn Heights and Park Slope; items in the window displays are sold through an online auction.

At weekend stoop sales (definition: an urban garage sale, with items displayed on a brownstone stoop or the sidewalk), you can find bargains on books to clothes to kids' gear to furniture.

Build It Green in Gowanus is a cavernous reuse center specializing in recycled goods, from old iron gates, wooden doors, and antique bath tiles to the occasional rolltop desk. Across the street is New York Old Iron, a sometimes-open high-end salvage yard, always fascinating to scour even if you don't need an iron fence. Town Square in Greenpoint runs greencycle swaps, toy exchanges, and Halloween-costume exchanges.

As for markets, aside from Brooklyn Flea, there are a few worth visiting. In Williamsburg, Artists & Fleas is a showcase for indie designers, vintage artists, and emerging artists. The smaller Bushwick Flea is located at 52 Wyckoff Avenue. A small weekend flea market takes place in Park Slope at PS 321.

December holiday pop-up markets sell everything from soap to clever clocks to jewelry, pottery, clothing, handmade teddy bears, and artistic bric-a-brac. At Brooklyn Pop Up Market in Fort Greene and Bushwick, shop for arty one-off items, handcrafted housewares and furniture, some made by Brooklyn artists.

Malls, Brands, Discount Stores

Brooklyn has several midpriced malls, plus an Ikea store in Red Hook and Costco in Sunset Park.

- Fulton Mall in Downtown Brooklyn is an outdoor pedestrian mall, created by closing off city streets. Decades old, it has a funny mix of shops: a smattering of family-owned businesses, national chains, and City Point, an indoor mall opening in 2016 and anchored by a Century 21 discount department store. Some of the national stores currently here: Macy's, Nordstrom Rack, Aéropostale, American Eagle, Banana Republic, Gap, and T. J. Maxx. Locals (and Japanese tourists, too!) shop for urban-style sneakers, T-shirts, and wigs. Check out Afrikart and Ragga Muffin for street-style fashion and Dr. Jays for shoes. Accessible by subway; parking impossible.
- Atlantic Terminal and Atlantic Center Malls is a complex at the Atlantic Avenue subway station near BAM and Barclays Center. It has Target, Best Buy, Uniqlo, Men's Warehouse, Victoria's Secret, Old Navy, Party Center, Office Max, Burlington Coat Factory, and DSW shoes, along with Chuckie Cheese and other brands. Accessible by subway; parking lot underground.
- Kings Plaza Mall on Flatbush Avenue, near the Queens border, has as anchor stores Macy's and Sears, along with H&M, American Eagle, Express, Footlocker, Aéropostale, and Bolton's. Best by car, a schlep by mass transit; parking lot.
- Gateway Center mall, off the Belt Parkway in Canarsie, has a Home Depot, Bed Bath & Beyond, Target, Michael's, and Babies R Us. Accessible by car.
- The Junction is a building near Brooklyn College in Flatbush, with Target, David's Bridal, Models, and Men's Warehouse, plus a cluster of smaller stores. Street parking or public transit.

American Apparel, Banana Republic, MAC Cosmetics, Ann Taylor Loft, Free People, Ralph Lauren, Sephora, and others have stores in Williamsburg, Brooklyn Heights, Park Slope, or Carroll Gardens. There's a chic Barney's store in Cobble Hill.

Major discount stores include Century 21 in Bay Ridge and Fulton Mall, and T. J. Maxx, Nordstrom Rack, and Neiman Marcus Last Call, in or near the Fulton Mall. The family-owned Nathan Borlan's sells high-end traditional children's clothing at a deep discount, Frankel's sells work clothes and awesome boots, and Borough Park's S&W sells discounted women's coats. In Williamsburg, find Cucina & Tavola for fine cookware; Fred Perry; Paul Smith; and a Brooklyn Industries factory outlet. Search online for Nine West, Gap, Old Navy, and other outlets.

OVER 260 PLACES TO GO SHOPPING IN BROOKLYN

Brooklyn's a big marketplace. Here are some tips on souvenirs and gifts; shops specializing in Brooklyn-made items, bookstores, clothing boutiques, food stores selling both new artisanal products and traditional Brooklyn fare, breweries, chocolate makers, home and jewelry shops, kitchen and home-brew shops, toy stores, and dozens of vintage shops.

Buy Brooklyn: Thirty Iconic Brooklyn Stores

CULTURAL INSTITUTIONS WITH GIFT SHOPS

BAM (FG), 651 Fulton Street, (718) 636-4100, http://www.bam.org
BRIC Celebrate Brooklyn! (PS), kiosks in Prospect Park (in person only)
Brooklyn Botanic Garden (PH), 990 Washington Avenue, (718) 622-0963,
   http://www.bbg.org
Brooklyn Historical Society (DU), 128 Pierrepont Street, (718) 222-4111,
   http://www.brooklynhistory.org
Brooklyn Museum (PH), 200 Eastern Parkway, (718) 638-5000, http://
   www.brooklynmuseum.org
Brooklyn Navy Yard (BNY), Building 92, http://bldg92.org/store/

KEY TO NEIGHBORHOOD ABBREVIATIONS

BB = Brighton Beach	F = Flatbush
BE = Bensonhurst	FG = Fort Greene
BH = Brooklyn Heights	GH = Greenwood Heights
BNY = Brooklyn Navy Yard	GO = Gowanus
BOH = Boerum Hill	GR = Greenpoint
BP = Borough Park	MB = Mill Basin
BR = Bay Ridge	MP = Marine Park
BS = Bedford-Stuyvesant	MW = Midwood
BU = Bushwick	PH = Prospect Heights, Pacific Park
CA/ENY = Canarsie, East New York	PLG = Prospect Lefferts Gardens
CG/CH = Carroll Gardens, Cobble Hill	PS = Park Slope
CH = Crown Heights	RH = Red Hook
CI = Coney Island	SB = Sheepshead Bay
CLH = Clinton Hill	SP = Sunset Park
CW = Columbia Waterfront District	W = Williamsburg
DB = Downtown Brooklyn	WT = Windsor Terrace
DU = Dumbo, Fulton Ferry Waterfront, Vinegar Hill	

Coney Island USA gift shop (CI), 1208 Surf Avenue, (718) 372-5159

Green-Wood (GH), http://www.green-wood.com, (718) 210-3080

Jewish Children's Museum (CH), 792 Eastern Parkway, (718) 467-0600, http://www.jcm.museum

New York Aquarium (CI), 602 Surf Avenue, (718) 265-3474, http://nyaquarium.com

New York Transit Museum (DB), Boerum Place and Schermerhorn Street, (718) 694-1600, http://web.mta.info/mta/museum

FUN PLACES THAT ALSO SELL BROOKLYN SOUVENIRS

Brooklyn Bowl (W), 61 Wythe Avenue, (718) 963-3369, http://www.brooklynbowl.com

Brooklyn Brewery (W), 79 North 11th Street, (718) 486-7422, http://brooklynbrewery.com

Brooklyn Cyclones Shop (CI), MCU Park, Surf Avenue at West 17th Street, (718) 37-BKLYN

Brooklyn Flea (it moves around; check website for locations), http://brooklynflea.com

Brooklyn Industries (PS), 206 5th Avenue, (718) 789-2764, http://www.brooklynindustries.com

Brooklyn Nets, at Barclays Center (PH), 620 Atlantic Avenue, (917) 618-6100, http://www.barclayscenter.com

Junior's (DB), 386 Flatbush Avenue Extension, (718) 852-5257, http://www.juniorscheesecake.com

Lola Starr (CI), 1205 Boardwalk West, (646) 915-2787

MCU Park (CI), 1904 Surf Avenue, (718) 449-8497, http://www.brooklyncyclones.com/splash/

Nathan's Famous (CI), 1310 Surf Avenue, (718) 333-2202, http://www.nathansfamous.com

Park Slope Food Coop (PS), 782 Union Street, (718) 622-0560, http://www.foodcoop.com (you must be accompanied by a member)

Peter Luger Steak House (W), 178 Broadway, (718) 387-7400, https://peterluger.com

Roberta's (BU), 261 Moore Street, (718) 417-1118, http://robertaspizza.com/shop

Spikes Joint, 40 Acres and a Mule (FG), http://spikesjoint.com

WEBSITES AND SHOPS SPECIALIZING IN BROOKLYN STUFF

BklynDesigns Expo (GR), http://bklyndesigns.com (annual event)

By Brooklyn (CG/CH), 261 Smith Street, (718) 643-0606, http://bybrooklyn.com

Etsy, https://www.etsy.com

With Love from Brooklyn, http://www.withlovefrombrooklyn.com/

Ten Brooklyn Bike Shops

Bay Ridge Bicycle World (BR), 8916 3rd Avenue, (718) 238-1118
Bicycle Habitat (PS), 560 Vanderbilt Avenue, (718) 783-3609
B's Bikes (GR), 345 Myrtle Avenue, (347) 889-5338
Dixon's Bicycle Shop (PS), 792 Union Street, (718) 636-0067
Dog Day Cyclery (RH), 115 Van Brunt Street, (347) 799-2739
R&A Cycles (PS), 105 5th Avenue, (718) 636-5242
Red Lantern Bicycles (FG), 262 Driggs Avenue, (718) 349-1212
Ride Brooklyn (PS), 468 Bergen Street, (347) 599-1340
Roy's Sheepshead Cycle (SB), 2679 Coney Island Avenue, (718) 648-1440
718 Cyclery (PS), 254 3rd Avenue, (347) 457-5760

For high-end specialty fittings and custom bikes, Acme Bicycle Co. (GO),
    597 Degraw Street #2F, (917) 355-3397.

Twenty-Six Bookstores

Barnes & Noble (BH, PS), 106 Court Street, (718) 246-4996; 267 7th Avenue,
    (718) 832-9066
Better Read Than Dead (BU), 867 Broadway
BookCourt (CG/CH), 163 Court Street, (718) 875-3677
Bookmark Shoppe (BR), 8415 3rd Avenue, (718) 853-5115
Book Thug Nation (W), 100 North 3rd Street
Boulevard Books & Cafe (BE), 7518 13th Avenue, (718) 680-5881
Freebird Books (CW), 123 Columbia Street, (718) 643-8484
Greenlight Bookstore (FG), 686 Fulton Street, (718) 246-0200
Here's a Book Store (SB), 1964 Coney Island Avenue, (718) 645-6675
Hullabaloo Books (CH), 711A Franklin Avenue, (917) 499-3244
Human Relations (BU), 1067 Flushing Avenue, http://humanrelationsbooks.com
Molasses Books (BU), 770 Hart Street, (631) 882-5188
Park Slope Community Bookstore (PS), 143 7th Avenue, (718) 783-3075
powerHouse Arena (DU), 38 Main Street, (718) 666-3049
P.S. Bookshop (DU), 76 Front Street, (718) 222-3340
Spoonbill and Sugartown Booksellers (W), 218 Bedford Avenue, (718) 387-7322
Swords-Smith (W), 98 South 4th Street, (347) 599-2969
Terrace Books (WT), 242 Prospect Park West, (718) 788-3475
Unnameable Books (PH), 600 Vanderbilt Avenue, (718) 789-1534
WORD (GR), 126 Franklin Street, (718) 383-0096

SPECIALIZED BOOKSTORES

Archestratus (cookbooks) (GR), 60 Huron Street, (718) 349-7711
Berl's Poetry Shop (poetry) (DU), 126A Front Street, (347) 687-2375
Black Sea Bookstore (Russian) (BB), 3175 Coney Island Avenue, (718) 769-2878

Desert Island (comics) (W), 540 Metropolitan Avenue, (718) 388-5087
Idlewild (travel, foreign language) (CG/CH), 249 Warren Street, (212) 414-8888
Singularity & Co. (sci-fi) (DU), 18 Bridge Street, (347) 460-7724

Forty Clothing Boutiques

FOR HIM OR NEM

Bencraft Hats (W), 236 Broadway, (718) 438-9649 (also BP)
By Robert James (W), 193 Grand Street, (349) 529-6392
Cadet (W), 46 North 6th Street, (718) 715-1695
Epaulet (CG/CH), 231 Smith Street, (718) 522-3800
Fred Perry Surplus Shop (W), 306 Grand Street, (347) 689-2096
Goorin Bros. (W), 181 Bedford Avenue, (718) 599-4287 (also PS)
Kinfolk Store (W), 90 Wythe Avenue, (347) 799-2946
Moshood Creations (FG), 698 Fulton Street, (718) 243-9433
Oat Brooklyn Hat (W), 240 Kent Avenue, (718) 662-0091
Robinson Brooklyn (W), 85 North 3rd Street #117, (718) 218-9800
Steven Alan (BOH), 349 Atlantic Avenue, (718) 852-3257

FOR HER OR VER

Baggu (W), 242 Wythe Avenue #4, (800) 605-0759
Bird (PS), 316 5th Avenue, (718) 768-4940 (also CG/CH and W)
Brooklyn Charm (W), 145 Bedford Avenue, (347) 689-2492
Brooklyn Circus (BOH), 150 Nevins Street, (718) 858-0919
Diana Kane (PS), 229 5th Avenue, (718) 638-6520
Diane T (CG/CH), 174 Court Street, (718) 923-5777
Esti's (MW), 1888 Coney Island Avenue, (718) 645-2600
Flirt Brooklyn (CG/CH), 93 5th Avenue, (718) 783-0364
Hudson + Lawrence (BOH), 355 Atlantic Avenue, (718) 624-2969
Iris Lingerie (BOH), 366 Atlantic Avenue, (718) 422-1149
Joinery (W), 263 South 1st Street, (718) 889-6164
Jumelle (W), 148 Bedford Avenue, (718) 388-9525
Kimera (BOH), 366 Atlantic Avenue, (718) 422-1147
Kiwi (PS), 119 7th Avenue, (718) 622-5551
Little Red Boutique (BS), 374 Lewis Avenue, (718) 443-1170
Malchijah Hats (CH), 942 Atlantic Avenue, (718) 643-3269
Marietta's (RH), 392 Van Brunt Street, (718) 596-2225
Martine's Dream (CH), 681 Nostrand Avenue, (347) 750-7668
Michelle New York Brides (BOH), 396 Atlantic Avenue, (718) 643-1680
Mociun (W), 224 Wythe Avenue, (718) 387-3731
Myths of Creation (W), 21 Graham Avenue, (718) 389-3036
Pema NY (W), 255 Bedford Avenue, (718) 388-8814

Refinery (CG/CH), 248 Smith Street, (718) 643-7861
Steven Alan (BOH), 349 Atlantic Avenue, (718) 852-3257
Tafari Tribe Globe Trade (PLG), 593 Flatbush Avenue, (347) 365-6197
Tango (BH), 145 Montague Street, (718) 625-7518
Thistle & Clover (FG), 221 DeKalb Avenue, (718) 855-5577
Vinnie's Styles (PH), 239 Flatbush Avenue, (718) 636-9787
Wolves Within (GR), 174 Franklin Street, (347) 889-5798

Forty-Five Food Stores, New and Old Brooklyn

NEW BROOKLYN: ARTISANAL, HAND-CRAFTED, SMALL BATCH, ORGANIC, LOCALLY SOURCED

Baked in Brooklyn Store (GH), 755 5th Avenue, (718) 788-3164; also Baked (RH)
Bedford Cheese Shop (W), 229 Bedford Avenue, (718) 599-7588
BKLYN Larder (PS), 228 Flatbush Avenue, (718) 783-1250
Brooklyn Brine (GO), 574 President Street, (347) 223-4345
Brooklyn Kitchen (W), 100 Frost Street, (718) 389-2982
Brooklyn Roasting Company (DU), 25 Jay Street, (718) 855-1000
Brooklyn Victory Gardens (CLH), 920 Fulton Street, (718) 398-9100
Bushwick Coop (BU), 2 Porter Avenue, (347) 450-1087
Clinton Hill Pickles (CLH), 431 DeKalb Avenue, (212) 334-3616
Dough (CLH), 448 Lafayette Avenue, (347) 533-7544
Eastern District (GR), 1053 Manhattan Avenue, (718) 349-1432
Empire Mayonnaise (PH), 564 Vanderbilt Avenue, (718) 636-2069
Foragers Market (DU), 56 Adams Street, (718) 801-8400
Greene Grape Provisions (FG), 753 Fulton Street, (718) 233-2700
Heavenly Crumbs (CLH), 355 Franklin Avenue, (718) 623-6271
Jordan's Lobster Dock (SB), 3165 Harkness Avenue, (718) 934-6300
La Nueva Union Bakery (F), 1114 Cortelyou Road, (718) 284-7218
Marlow & Sons (W), 81 Broadway, (718) 384-1441
Meat Hook and The Kitchen (W), 100 Frost Street, (718) 349-5032
Nablus Sweets (BR), 6812 5th Avenue, (718) 748-1214
One Girl Cookies (CG/CH), 68 Dean Street, (718) 675-4996
The Pickle Guys (MW), 1364 Coney Island Avenue, (718) 677-0639
Red Hook Lobster Pound (RH), 284 Van Brunt Street, (718) 858-7650
Smith & Vine (CG/CH), 268 Smith Street, (718) 243-2864
Smorgasburg (various locations), http://www.smorgasburg.com
Steve's Authentic Key Lime Pies (RH), 185 Van Dyke Street, (718) 522-7425
Vendome's Macaroons (CG/CH), 233 Smith Street, (917) 892-2127

OLD BROOKLYN: ETHNIC

Aiello Brothers Cheese Company (SP), 145 48th Street, (718) 666-4462
Bari Pork Store (BE), 158 Avenue U, (718) 372-6405

Caputo's Fine Foods (CG/CH), 460 Court Street, (718) 855-8852
Court Pastry Shop (CG/CH), 298 Court Street, (718) 875-4820
D'Amico Coffee (CG/CH), 309 Court Street, (718) 875-5403
Elza Fancy Food (BB), 3071 Brighton 4th Street, (718) 942-4088
Family Store (BR), 6905 3rd Avenue, (718) 748-0207
G. Esposito & Sons Pork Store (CG/CH), 357 Court Street, (718) 875-6863
Gold Star Bakery (BE), 7409 13th Avenue, (718) 236-8560
Leske's Bakery (BR), 7612 5th Avenue, (718) 680-2323
Mansoura Pastries (MW), 515 Kings Highway, (718) 645-7977
Monteleone's Bakery (CG/CH), 355 Court Street, (718) 852-5600
Napoli Bakery (W), 616 Metropolitan Avenue, (718) 384-6945
Oriental Pastry and Grocery (CW), 170 Atlantic Avenue #A, (718) 875-7687
Sahadi's (BH), 187 Atlantic Avenue, (718) 624-4550
Schmura Matza Bakery (BP), 1285 36th Street, (718) 438-2006
Terrace Bagels (WT), 224 Prospect Park West, (718) 768-3943
Weiss Homemade Kosher Bakery (BP), 5011 13th Avenue, (718) 438-0407

Fifteen Breweries, Distilleries, Wineries

Brooklyn's craft-brewing and microdistilleries are super visitor friendly. Many give tours and host events on-site.

BREWERIES (TOURS, BARS)

Brooklyn Brewery (W), 79 North 11th Street, (718) 486-7422
Coney Island Brewing Company (CI), 1904 Surf Avenue, (718) 996-0019
KelSo (FG), 529 Waverly Avenue, (718) 398-2731
Other Half Brewing Co. (CG/CH), 195 Centre Street, (347) 987-3527
Sixpoint Brewery (RH), 40 Van Dyke Street, http://sixpoint.com
Threes Brewing (GO), 333 Douglass Street, (718) 522-2110

DISTILLERIES (TOURS, BARS)

Breuckelen Distilling (GH), 77 19th Street, (347) 725-4985
Kings County Distillery (BNY), 63 Flushing Avenue, in Brooklyn Navy Yard
    Building 121, (347) 689-4211
New York Distilling Co. (W), 79 Richardson Street, (718) 412-0874
The Noble Experiment (BU), 23 Meadow Street, (718) 381-3693
Red Hook Winery (RH), 175 Van Dyke Street, (347) 689-2432
Van Brunt Stillhouse (RH), 6 Bay Street, (718) 852-6405
Widow Jane Distillery (RH), 214 Conover Street, (347) 225-0130

WINERIES (TASTINGS)

Brooklyn Winery (W), 213 North 8th Street, (347) 763-1506
Red Hook Winery (RH), 175 Pier 41, at 204 Van Dyke Street, (347) 689-2432

Ten Chocolate and Caramel Makers

Cacao Prieto (RH), 218 Conover Street, (347) 225-0130

The Chocolate Room (PS), 51 5th Avenue; also on Court Street (CG/CH),
   (718) 783-2900

Fine & Raw Chocolate (BU), 288 Seigel Street, (718) 366-3633

Jacques Torres (DU), 66 Water Street, (718) 875-1269

JoMart Chocolates (MP), 2917 Avenue R, (718) 375-1277

Liddabit Sweets (SP), 220 36th Street, Industry City, (718) 788-4000

Li-Lac Chocolate Factory (SP), 68 35th Street, Industry City, (212) 924-2280

Mast Brothers Chocolate Makers (W), 111 North 3rd Street, (718) 388-2625

Nunu Chocolates (BOH), 529 Atlantic Avenue, (718) 834-1818 (also PS)

Raaka Chocolate Factory (RH), 64 Seabring Street, (855) 255-3354

Twenty-Five Gift, Home, and Jewelry Shops

A&G (W), 111 North 6th Street, (718) 388-1779

Abode (W), 179 Grand Street, (718) 388-5383

Babeland (PS), 462 Bergen Street, (718) 638-3820

British Sterling Silver Corporation (BP), 4922 16th Avenue,
   (718) 436-2800

Brooklyn Superhero Supply Store (PS), 372 5th Avenue, (718) 499-9884

Brooklyn Women's Exchange (BH), 55 Pierrepont Street, (718) 624-3435

Catbird (W), 219 Bedford Avenue, (718) 599-3457

Clay Pot (PS), 162 7th Avenue, (718) 788-6564

Eichler's Religious Articles Gifts Books (BP), 5004 13th Avenue,
   (718) 633-1505

Erie Basin (RH), 388 Van Brunt Street, (718) 554-6147

Exit 9 Gift Emporium (CG/CH), 127 Smith Street, (718) 422-7720

Honey Gifts (W), 110 North 6th Street, (718) 302-1760

House of Small Wonder (W), 77 North 6th Street, (718) 388-6160

In God We Trust (W), 129 Bedford Avenue, (718) 384-0700

Journey (DU), 72 Front Street, (718) 797-9277

Life:Curated (W), 186 Grand Street, (347) 689-9143

Milly and Earl (W), 351 Graham Avenue, (718) 389-0901

Mongo Jewelry (CG/CH), 246 Smith Street, (917) 671-7696

Owl and Thistle General Store (CH), 833 Franklin Avenue,
   (347) 722-5836

Pier Glass (RH), 499 Van Brunt Street, (718) 237-2073

Pink Olive (W), 370 Bedford Avenue, (718) 576-3915

Reclaimed Home (CLH), 945–947 Carroll Street, (917) 652-4325

Shag Brooklyn (W), 108 Roebling Street, (347) 721-3302

Shops at the Loom (BU), 1087 Flushing Avenue, (718) 417-1616

Species by the Thousands (W), 171 South 4th Street, (718) 599-0049

Fifteen Hobbyist, Kitchen, and DIY Shops

Artist & Craftsman Supply (GO), 307 2nd Street, (718) 499-8080
Brooklyn Gallery of Coins and Stamps (BR), 8725 4th Avenue, (718) 745-5701
Brooklyn General (CW), 128 Union Street, (718) 237-7753
Michael's (CA/ENY, BH), Gateway Center, 252 Atlantic Avenue, (347) 694-4067
Panda Sport (BR), 9213 5th Avenue, (718) 238-4919
Train World (BP), 751 McDonald Avenue, (718) 436-7072
Utrecht Art Supplies (CLH), 536 Myrtle Avenue, (718) 789-0308
W.C. Art and Drafting Supplies (DB), 351 Jay Street, (718) 855-8078

KITCHEN AND HOME BREW

Bitter & Esters (PH), 700 Washington Avenue, (917) 596-7261
Brooklyn Kitchen (W), 100 Frost Street, (718) 389-2982
Brooklyn Slate Company (RH), 305 Van Brunt Street, (877) 648-8333
A Cook's Companion (CW), 197 Atlantic Avenue, (718) 852-6901
Cucina & Tavola (W), 235 Grand Street, (718) 963-3131
The Peppermill (BP), 5015 16th Avenue, (718) 871-4022
Whisk (W), 231 Bedford Avenue, (718) 218-7230

Twelve Malls and Outlets

MALLS

Atlantic Center Mall and Atlantic Terminal Malls (FG), 625 Atlantic Avenue, (718) 622-7893
Fulton Mall (DB), including City Point, Fulton Street between Flatbush Avenue and Boerum Place
Gateway Center (CA/ENY), 409 Gateway Drive, (718) 235-4756 (for directory: bit.ly/1kbgJ1i)
Kings Plaza Shopping Mall (MB), 5100 Kings Plaza, (718) 253-6842 (for directory: http://www.kingsplazaonline.com/Directory)

DISCOUNT, OUTLETS

Brooklyn Industries Outlet (W), 162 Bedford Avenue, (718) 486-6464; multiple locations
Century 21 (BR, DB), 472 86th Street and in Fulton Mall, (718) 748-3266
Costco (SP), 976 3rd Avenue, (718) 965-7603
Cucina & Tavola (W), 235 Grand Street, (718) 963-3131
Frankel's (SP), 3924 3rd Avenue, (718) 768-9788
Fred Perry Surplus Shop (W), 306 Grand Street, (347) 689-2096
Fulton Mall (DB), various shops, between Boerum Place and Flatbush Avenue
Neiman Marcus Last Call (BH), 210 Joralemon Street, (929) 324-3150
Paul Smith (W), 280 Grand Street, (718) 218-0020

Four Markets

Brooklyn Flea (this market moves around; check the website for locations),
   http://brooklynflea.com
Bushwick Flea (BU), 52 Wyckoff Avenue, http://www.bwflea.com
Park Slope Flea at PS 321 (PS), 180 7th Avenue, weekends, rain or shine
Various pop-up holiday markets in December

Four Skateboard Shops

Aegir Boardworks (DU), 99 Water Street, (347) 987-3825
Homage (CG/CH), 64 Bergen Street, (718) 596-1511
KCDC (W), 85 North 3rd Street, (718) 387-9006
Skate Brooklyn (PS), 78 St. Marks Place, (718) 857-5283

Eight Toy Stores

Acorn (BOH), 323 Atlantic Avenue, (718) 522-3760
Brooklyn Superhero Supply Store (PS), 372 5th Avenue, (718) 499-9884
Flying Squirrel (GR), 87 Oak Street, (718) 218-7775
Heights Kids (BH), 93 Pineapple Walk, (718) 222-4271
Kaleidoscope (BR), 8722 3rd Avenue, (718) 491-2051
Little Things Toy Store (PS), 145 7th Avenue, (718) 783-4733
Mini Jake Toy Store (W), 178 North 9th Street, (718) 782-2005
Norman & Jules Toy Shop (PS), 158 7th Avenue, (718) 987-3323

Thirty Vintage, Preused, Secondhand Stores

Antoinette Vintage (W), 119 Grand Street, (718) 387-8664
Artists & Fleas (W), 70 North 7th Street, (917) 488-4203
Beacon's Closet (PS), 92 5th Avenue, (718) 230-1630; also on Guernsey Street
   (GP)
Brooklyn Flea (check the website for locations), http://brooklynflea.com
Buffalo Exchange (CG/CH), 109 Boerum Place, (718) 403-0490
Build It Green (GO), 69 9th Street, (718) 725-8925
Domsey Express (BU, W), 1379 Myrtle Avenue, (718) 443-4343; 431 Broadway,
   (718) 384-6000
Fox & Fawn (GR), 570 Manhattan Avenue, (718) 349-9510 (also BU)
Green Village Used Furniture and Clothing (BU), 276 Starr Street, (718)
   599-4017
Housing Works (PS, BH), 266 5th Avenue, (718) 636-2271; 122 Montague Street,
   (718) 237-0521
Hush Hush Closet (W), 240 Kent Avenue, (347) 863-6741
Life Boutique Thrift (PS), 515 5th Avenue, (718) 788-5433
L Train Vintage (BU), 1377 DeKalb Avenue, (718) 443-6940; multiple locations

Mary Meyer + Friends Vintage (W), 56 Bogart Street, (718) 386-6279

Miss Master's Closet (BS), 1070 Bedford Avenue, (718) 783-2979

No Relation Vintage (GO), 654 Sackett Street, (718) 858-4906

Olive's Very Vintage (CLH), 434 Court Street, (718) 243-9094

One of a Find (PH), 633 Vanderbilt Avenue, (718) 789-2008

People of 2morrow (GR), 65 Franklin Street, (718) 383-4402

Rough Trade NYC (W), 64 North 9th Street, (718) 388-4111

Salvation Army Thrift Store (BOH, CLH), 436 Atlantic Avenue, (718) 834-1562; 22 Quincy Street, (718) 622-4535

Seven Wonders Vintage (GR), 606 Manhattan Avenue, (954) 609-2403

10 Ft. Single by Stella Dallas (W), 285 North 6th Street, (718) 486-9482

Trailer Park (PS), 77 Sterling Place #A, (718) 623-2170

Two Lovers (PS), 227 Fifth Avenue, (718) 783-5683

Union Max (CW), 110 Union Street, (718) 222-1785

Urban Jungle (BU), 120 Knickerbocker Avenue, (718) 381-8510

Vice Versa (W), 241 Bedford Avenue, (718) 788-1925

Yesterday's News, 328 Court Street, (718) 875-0546

Brooklyn's Waterfront and Parks

Urban jungle? Interspersed within the seventy-one square miles of the borough are more than four hundred parks. Like a box of Valentine's Day chocolates, they come in all shapes and varieties: pocket parks and waterfront expanses, marshland and rolling greens, golf courses and ball fields. And Brooklyn's twenty-six-mile coast touches the Atlantic Ocean, New York Harbor, the East River, Jamaica Bay, Gowanus Canal, and Newtown Creek.

BROOKLYN'S WATERFRONT

Experience the waterfront. There are many ways to do so.

Itching to be *in* or *near* the water? Brooklyn has three Atlantic Ocean beaches: Brighton, Coney, and Manhattan Beaches. The excellent New York Aquarium is just off the Coney Island boardwalk, a fishy, family-friendly world of hands-on edutainment. Go line fishing off a pier in Canarsie, Bay Ridge, Red Hook, or Coney Island. Watch NYC Swim's annual Brooklyn Bridge Swim (don't try it alone). You can run and cycle along the Brooklyn Greenway waterfront. Stroll the Ikea Esplanade or Bush Terminal Park. Brooklyn Bridge Park, with its meandering pathways, funky beach, pop-up pool, environmental education programs, and kayak launch site is a huge amenity. In Greenpoint, have brunch on the East River waterfront. Jog along Shore Parkway in Bay Ridge. Visit funky little Plumb Beach and the Salt Marsh Center.

Or go *on* the water. Kayak from a half dozen sites. In Red Hook, go aboard the Waterfront Museum in the hundred-year-old *Lehigh Valley No. 79* barge, a landmark listed on the National Register of Historic Places. Check out PortSide NewYork, based on a historic oil tanker, the *Mary A. Whalen*, its "living lab for twenty-first-century waterways." Enjoy a concert aboard Dumbo's Bargemusic or take a boat tour on the Gowanus Canal. You can kayak in Sebago Bay or paddle with the hip North Brooklyn Boat Club. Go fishing in a Hobie Outback with New York Kayak Fishing Guide Services. Sail off Brooklyn Bridge Park. Take a party-fishing boat, popular with locals out of Sheepshead Bay. Take the seasonal ferry connecting Greenpoint, Williamsburg, and Dumbo or to Governors Island. An Ikea ferry shuttles between its Red Hook megastore and Wall Street. Go pedal boating in Prospect Park Lake, or boat in Jamaica Bay. Buy a ticket for the *Queen Mary 2*—it sometimes sails out of Red Hook!

BROOKLYN'S PARKS

Brooklyn's parks are wonderful and varied. McGolrick Park feels European, and Marine Park has golfing, cricket, and the Salt Marsh Center. Jamaica Bay, a national park, has many things to do including bird-watching during their annual migratory flyover.

Brooklyn Bridge Park

Brooklyn Bridge Park stretches from Atlantic Avenue past both the Brooklyn and Manhattan Bridges. It flows artfully along the East River coastline, with basketball and soccer courts, a sandy beach, concert and dance spaces, 1 Hotel, and more. Brilliantly designed, with goose-bump-inducing views, this eighty-five-acre park spans about a mile and a half of riverfront, facing Manhattan, the Statue of Liberty, and New York Harbor.

It weaves together promenades, gardens, grassy hills, playgrounds, benches, many sports fields, and picnic spaces. A nearly manic roster of free activities includes dancing, sunrise yoga, kayaking, stargazing, and movies and concerts. There are restaurants, the Brooklyn Bridge Garden Bar, and novelty food trucks. This park was designed for both action and contemplation by the award-winning firm of Michael Van Valkenburgh Associates. Sustainability is inherent in the design; many structures were made of recycled materials from the old piers and other New York City bridges, the Willis Avenue and Roosevelt Island Bridges.

Rising like a phoenix from the ashes, this park resurrected an abandoned, dangerous industrial waterfront, where decaying piers were an eyesore (and a waste of riverfront property) for decades. Brooklyn Bridge Park was born after Sisyphean efforts over decades by community activists. It was realizable only through the formation of a private-public partnership. A bargain was struck that to ensure the park's long-term financial sustainability private enterprise would be allowed in the park. That arrangement explains why Brooklyn Bridge Park is the site of the 1 Hotel and Pierhouse, a large complex of apartments, offices, condos, restaurants, retail spaces, and a fitness center on Pier 1, to open in 2016.

Many visitors arrive first at historic Fulton Ferry Landing. It's a popular photo-op site for brides and grooms. It was also the place from which ferries first plied the water between Brooklyn and Manhattan—in 1642. Enjoy amazing views of Manhattan, Bargemusic (the landmarked barge turned concert hall), and Brooklyn Ice Cream Factory (housed in a landmarked lighthouse building). Luke's Lobster, No. 7 Sub, and Shake Shack are here, too.

From Fulton Ferry Landing to the south: At Pier 1, you will find the East River Ferry dock, food, drink, and bar concessions, a playground, and eye-popping views of Manhattan and the Brooklyn Bridge. Pier 2 has basketball, handball, bocce, shuffleboard courts, a roller rink (with skate rental), and fitness equipment. Pier 3's Greenway Terrace has lawns and greenway, with a jogging path. The weird grassy

Squibb Bridge, leading to Brooklyn Bridge Park. (Photo by E. Freudenheim, 2014)

hill is a sound wall, built to muffle nearby highway noise. There's a "beach" on Pier 4, though you cannot go in the water; the sandy area with tidal pools is fun for tots. The area was constructed using bits of an old sunken railroad float transfer. Pier 5's the place for hockey and soccer fields, picnicking, fishing, and Ample Hills Creamery ice cream. The dock for the free weekend Governors Island ferry is on Pier 6, where there's also a flower meadow, viewing platform, sand volleyball courts, playgrounds with summertime sprays and water elements, a dog run, and Fornino's wood-fired-oven pizza. Plans to build two towers with over three hundred apartments at the Atlantic Avenue entrance to Pier 6 remain controversial as of this writing.

From Fulton Ferry Landing to the north: Enter the park from Dumbo's Washington Street. Jane's Carousel is a jewel box of a merry-go-round, its restored vintage horses revolving in a pretty, retractable glass enclosure. Main Street Park has a bouldering wall for climbers, Pebble Beach, a nautically themed playground, and a dog run. John Street Park, accessible from a Jay Street pedestrian bridge, has little walkways over a tidal salt marsh and a gathering lawn. Look down and note the cobblestones and tracks from the old Jay Street Connecting Railroad.

Squibb Park Bridge—a gently springy $5 million zigzag pedestrian ramp made of black-locust timber, bronze, and steel—leads from Brooklyn Heights down to Pier 1 in Brooklyn Bridge Park. (If you dislike swaying in the air, walk down Columbia Heights; it's the same quarter-mile distance.)

Come on foot, by bike, by cab, or by mass transit; parking is impossible. You can take the East River Ferry, New York Water Taxi, or Governors Island Ferry to get to Brooklyn Bridge Park.

For information, see http://www.brooklynbridgepark.org.

Prospect Park

Prospect Park's 585 acres of beautiful rolling hills, woodlands, waterfalls and a lake, playgrounds, and sports facilities attract some ten million visits annually. (Thank you and *namaste* to the architects Olmsted and Vaux for giving to posterity this and other urban pastoral landscapes in Brooklyn.) It is listed on the National Register of Historic Places. Brooklyn is the city's least-forested borough; of the borough's one hundred acres of forest, most is in Prospect Park.

About the only things you can't do in Prospect Park are camp overnight or swim. Enjoy New Year's Eve fireworks here, cook dinner (if it's a BBQ), bike, jog, or skate the 3.3-mile loop. There are places to play ball, fly a kite, romp with a dog, kayak and pedal boat, ice-skate and roller-skate, and sunbathe. The historic Boathouse, pretty Picnic House off Prospect Park West, and other landmarked structures are used for photo shoots, weddings, and parties. Kensington Stables rents horses to ride in the park. Groove to the Sunday-afternoon Drummers Circle, join nature walks and volunteer cleanups, hear extraordinary acts at the summer outdoor BRIC Celebrate Brooklyn! concerts in the band shell. The area near the Picnic House has free Wi-Fi. You'll find many charity walks and bike and running races.

Destinations include LeFrak Center at Lakeside, which has wintertime ice-skating, seasonal roller-skating, novelty bike rentals, and in summer, the Splash Pad. The Tennis Center operates indoor and outdoor courts. The Audubon Center and Lefferts Historic House offer free educational programming. The "Children's Corner" includes the Prospect Park Zoo, the century-old Carousel, Imagination Playground, and an inventive Natural Exploration Area, built from huge tree trunks and limbs downed during Superstorm Sandy in 2012.

The park's old monuments are terrific photo ops. You can find panthers (at the Third Street entrance), lions (in the zoo, where else), and metal sculptures of a snake eating a frog and an octopus and five garden eels, as well as classical busts depicting Mozart, Beethoven, Grieg, and the like near the Concert Grove, close by LeFrak Center. A famous statue of Lincoln is there, also.

At the main Grand Army Plaza entrance, there's a Saturday greenmarket and events such as the lightings of a thirty-foot high Hanukkah menorah (by a rabbi aloft a cherry picker) and Christmas tree during the December holidays. Grand Army Plaza's Bailey Fountain, tucked in a piazza, is *bellisimo* and reminiscent of Rome.

The park is closed between one a.m. and six a.m. Dogs can go unleashed from nine p.m. to one a.m. and six a.m. to nine a.m.

For information, contact the Prospect Park Alliance, https://www.prospect park.org.

Other Parks by Neighborhood

In Bay Ridge, the twenty-four-acre Owl's Head Park, on a bluff overlooking New York Harbor, has woods and rolling hills and views of the Verrazano-Narrows Bridge and Staten Island. Runners, cyclists, and walkers exercise on Shore Parkway Promenade, which is lovely despite being adjacent to a highway. Narrows Botanical Garden was carved from a sliver of underutilized green in Bay Ridge. In Leif Ericson Park nearby, descendants of Norwegian immigrants built a playground in the shape of a Viking ship.

Elite runners in the forty-fourth New York Marathon, mile 7. (Photo by E. Freudenheim, 2014)

Bedford-Stuyvesant's Herbert Von King Park (originally Tompkins Park) was designed by Olmsted and Vaux. Visit the Eubie Blake Auditorium and a recording studio decorated with murals by African American artists, both in the Culture Center in the park. Fulton Park, called "one of Brooklyn's little-known oases" by civic environmentalist Adrian Benepe, is a place to relax.

Bushwick's Maria Hernandez Park has a running track, playgrounds, special events, summer concerts, and a dramatic backstory, described in the Bushwick chapter in section 3.

Carroll Park in Carroll Gardens, under two acres in size, is a well-used neighborhood park with a long history. Enjoy bocce, summer theater, and special family-friendly events.

Coney, Brighton, and Manhattan Beaches: In addition to broad, sandy Atlantic Ocean beaches, the three-mile Riegelmann Boardwalk between Coney Island Beach and Brighton Beach affords people-watching, refreshing breezes, and expansive views. You can start at one end with cotton candy and end at the other with borscht.

Brooklyn's two eighteen-hole public golf courses, Dyker Beach and Marine Park Golf Courses, are open year-round, weather permitting.

The green malls lining Ocean Parkway and Eastern Parkway, both long, tree-lined pedestrian areas, offer benches and shade trees.

Floyd Bennett Field was named in honor of a Brooklyn pilot who flew over the North Pole in 1926. It opened in 1931 as New York City's first municipal airport. It's now under the jurisdiction of the National Park Service, with old runways (built for a prejet era), vast property, and a handful of historic buildings. Amelia Earhart flew from here. Facilities include bike trails, a model-airplane area, camp sites (unsupervised; requires advance booking). Occasional public programming runs the gamut from an annual Indian powwow to megagardening. Get maps at the visitor center to avoid getting lost. (Learn more about Mill Basin and Floyd Bennett Field in section 3.)

Vast Green-Wood, located in Greenwood Heights between Park Slope and Sunset Park, is part arboretum, part cemetery. It's peaceful and beautiful.

Thirty-acre Fort Greene Park has a powerful monument to the degradations of war and has ties to Walt Whitman. The Fort Greene Park Conservancy produces excellent cultural and family programming; there's a greenmarket, too. Commodore Barry Park hosts the AfroPunk Fest, International African Arts Festival, and concerts and has ball fields and an outdoor pool. (See the Fort Greene chapter in section 3.)

Jamaica Bay Gateway National Park is the nation's largest urban park, with twenty-six thousand acres of coastline and marsh. It includes Floyd Bennett Field, Canarsie Pier, and Plumb Beach, a neglected site where there are horseshoe crabs and some kite boarding. You can kayak, stargaze, rent a horse at nearby Jamaica Bay Riding Academy, or bird-watch.

At 530 acres, Marine Park (in a neighborhood by the same name) offers interesting things to do, too. At the Salt Marsh Nature Center, children can play Neptune by raising and lowering tide levels in tidal tanks. Hike along a one-mile nature trail, or rent a boat to explore Gerritsen Creek. Enjoy a running track at East Thirty-Third Street. Community events include kite-flying, bird-watching, biking, a back-to-school festival, Santa in the Park, bocce and cricket tournaments, summer concerts, and the Clyde Beatty–Cole Brothers Circus. Paerdegat Basin Park is popular for summer kayaking and canoeing.

Ocean Parkway and Eastern Parkway, Brooklyn's main interior traffic arteries, have miles of green pedestrian corridors for strolling, bench sitting, and slow-paced cycling.

Park Slope's three-acre J. J. Byrne Park has ball courts and a playground. The on-site Old Stone House is picturesque and is also a cultural center and museum. Enjoy the Sunday organic greenmarket, summer concerts, movies, plays, and festivals here.

In Red Hook, fifty-eight-acre Red Hook Recreation Area is scruffy but functional, with ball fields, outdoor pools, and on summer weekends, makeshift food stands selling amazing Latino food. The Ikea Esplanade is a nearly mile-long, restored, publicly accessible waterside walkway, including a pier extending into the Erie Basin—Brooklyn's funky Highline. You can picnic and sit in ridiculously giant-sized metal chaises (big enough for three). It's an outdoor museum of sorts. Louis Valentino Jr. Park and Pier's four and a half acres boast nineteenth-century buildings and stunning views of the Statue of Liberty, Governors Island, Manhattan's skyline, Staten Island, and the New York Harbor. Summertime movies shown here have a heck of a backdrop.

Sunset Park is a twenty-four-acre park with views of New York Harbor. Its recreation center houses an Olympic-size outdoor swimming pool. Down by the waterfront, there's the evocative Bush Terminal Park near Industry City, with views of industrial buildings, tidal pools, and the Bay Ridge Channel. Enter at Forty-Third Street.

In North Brooklyn, straddling North Williamsburg and Greenpoint, thirty-five-acre McCarren Park has a large outdoor swimming pool and playing fields. Greenpoint's Transmitter Park, once the working home of the WNYC radio transmission towers, has places for active recreation, a lawn, and a recreational pier where you can fish and just gaze at mid-Manhattan's skyline. McGolrick Park, just nine acres, has a family feel, inviting benches, and the *Monitor Monument*. The as-yet-unbuilt Bushwick Inlet Park is supposed to be a twenty-eight-acre park on the East River.

Williamsburg's seven-acre waterside East River State Park has that sine qua non of real estate: location, location, location. The views of midtown Manhattan and the Empire State Building are great. There's picnicking and BBQs and sometimes free concerts, ticketed events, and the foodie's flea market, Smorgasburg. This park is located on the site of a nineteenth-century dock, which explains the cobblestone streets and railroad tracks embedded in concrete. It's next to Northside Piers Park, a publicly accessible green space near the upscale housing development called Northside.

For more information on additional parks in Brooklyn, see http://www.nycgov parks.org.

WHERE TO PLAY OUTDOORS IN BROOKLYN

Where can you bird-watch during the bird migratory flyover? Or go ice-skating? This section lists some of the best public places in Brooklyn for all kinds of activities.

Beaches for Sunning and Swimming. Brighton Beach, Brooklyn Bridge Park (sunning only), Coney Island Beach, Manhattan Beach Park. Lifeguards are on duty from ten a.m. until six p.m., Memorial to Labor Day. Swimming is prohibited unless a lifeguard is present. It's serious; every year there are off-hours drownings due to riptides.

Biking. Bike paths go everywhere: Brooklyn Greenway, Brooklyn Bridge Park, Coney Island Riegelmann Boardwalk, Floyd Bennett Field, Marine Park, Ocean Parkway bike path, Prospect Park, Shore Parkway Promenade.

Boating and Kayaking. Brooklyn Bridge Park, Gowanus Canal, Marine Park, North Brooklyn Boat Club, Prospect Park, Paerdegat Basin Park, Sebago Canoe Club, Valentino Pier.

Bocce Courts. Brooklyn Bridge Park, Dyker Beach Park, Carroll Park, Marine Park, McCarren Park.

Cross-Country Skiing. Brooklyn Bridge Park, Marine Park, Prospect Park.

Fishing. Brooklyn Bridge Park, Canarsie Pier, Coney Island Pier, Pier 69 in Bay Ridge, Emmons Avenue fishing boats, Prospect Park (annual fishing contest), Transmitter Park, Valentino Pier.

Golf. Dyker Beach Golf Course, Brooklyn Golf Center (driving range), Marine Park Golf Course.

Horseback Riding. Jamaica Bay Riding Academy, Kensington Stables (Prospect Park).

Ice-Skating. LeFrak Center at Lakeside (Prospect Park); indoors at Abe Stark Rink; also privately run Aviator Sports.

Kite-Flying. Brooklyn Bridge Park, Fort Greene, Prospect Park, Marine Park, Shore Parkway Promenade.

Outdoor Running Tracks (quarter-mile tracks unless otherwise noted). Brooklyn Bridge Park (path, no track), Betsy Head Memorial Playground, Fort Greene Park (no track), Fort Hamilton High School Athletic Field, Leon Kaiser Playground, Kaiser Park, Coney Island, McCarren Park, Prospect Park (path and road, no track), Red Hook Recreation Area, Shore Road Park (no track), among others.

Roller-Skating. Brooklyn Bridge Park Pier 2 Roller Rink, LeFrak Center at Lakeside (Prospect Park).

Skateboarding. Shore Parkway Promenade, Owl's Head Park.

Swimming Pools. Brooklyn's outdoor public pools are free. There are over a dozen outdoor pools, some with special kiddie pools, lap-swim times, and classes. All have changing facilities, security and lifeguards, and entrance requirements such as a lock; check the website before you go. Seasonal "pop-up pools" are fun.

Tennis (public courts; permit required). Fort Greene Park, Manhattan Beach Park, Marine Park (between Fillmore Avenue and Avenue U), Prospect Park, and many more.

Trapeze. The privately run NYC Trapeze school operates out of Coney Island.

Wildlife and Zoos. Audubon Center (Prospect Park), New York Aquarium for Wildlife Conservation (Coney Island), Prospect Park Zoo, Salt Marsh Nature Center (Marine Park).

For information on the above, see http://www.nycgovparks.org, unless privately owned.

Rentals

Citi Bikes (http://www.citibikenyc.com) are the blue bikes with stations all around New York; you pay a fee to join and pick them up and drop them off as you like. At Prospect Park's LeFrak Center, (718) 462-0010, you can rent novelty pedal bikes for the whole family in season! Rent bikes and boats in Marine Park from Wheel Fun Rentals, (917) 533-6196, http://wheelfunrentals.com.

Also see parks under "Brooklyn's Cultural Scene," section 4, and read about the Brooklyn Botanic Garden and Green-Wood.

Visitor Information

Opening day for Luna Park's Thunderbolt ride in Coney Island. (Photo by E. Freudenheim, 2014)

DIY Tours

When I do a tour of Brooklyn, I start at Borough Hall . . . and end up in Carroll Gardens. In between, it's a very full day.

—Carlo A. Scissura, president and CEO,
Brooklyn Chamber of Commerce

Why not strike out on your own for a few hours? To go it alone, here are fifteen general itineraries. Please use your mobile device for maps.

TOUR 1: BROOKLYN CULTURAL DISTRICT

(Where: Downtown Brooklyn, Fort Greene. Duration: three hours. Start: Brooklyn Borough Hall at 209 Joralemon Street. Optional: walk across Brooklyn Bridge before tour.)

See a few key destinations in the Brooklyn Cultural District. Best to combine with a performance; get tickets in advance.

Start at Brooklyn Borough Hall (209 Joralemon Street). Choose to visit either the New York Transit Museum (Boerum Place and Schermerhorn Street) or the Brooklyn Historical Society (128 Pierrepont Street). Explore Fulton Mall, walking through to Flatbush Avenue, past Junior's restaurant. Visit the Museum of Contemporary African Diasporan Arts, MoCADA (80 Hanson Place), or see a performance at BAM (30 Lafayette Avenue), Irondale (85 South Oxford Street), Theatre for a New Audience (262 Ashland Place), or BRIC House (647 Fulton Street). Check out the UrbanGlass gallery at the same address. Dine in Fort Greene, perhaps at French ICI (246 DeKalb Avenue).

TOUR 2: BROOKLYN BIKE MANIA

(Where: borough-wide. Duration: one to three hours. Start: rent a Citi Bike, helmet advised.)

You can go almost anywhere in Brooklyn on a bike. Here are three suggestions.

Bedford Avenue is one of Brooklyn's longest streets—and it has a bike lane. Start in Williamsburg and go through to Crown Heights, and you'll see Latino, Hasidic, hipster, and other neighborhoods along the way.

To ride the Brooklyn Greenway, start at Bushwick Inlet, where the ironclad Civil War–era USS *Monitor* was launched. Ride past the Brooklyn Navy Yard, Brooklyn Bridge Park, and Brooklyn Cruise Terminal, where the *Queen Mary 2* sometimes docks. Bike in Red Hook past the Erie Basin, where some working barges are still visible, especially from Beard Street Pier, off Van Brunt Street. Pass Red Hook Recreation Area, nip over to observe the Gowanus Canal, and bike south to Industry Park on Sunset Park's industrial waterfront. Note: The Brooklyn Greenway is still evolving. (See http://www.brooklyngreenway.org.)

Finally, bike down Ocean Parkway from Prospect Park to Coney Island and the beach, along a protected bike path on a greenway.

TOUR 3: WOODY ALLEN'S CHILDHOOD HAUNTS IN MIDWOOD

(Where: Midwood section of Flatbush. Duration: thirty to sixty minutes on foot or by car. Start: Q subway station at Avenue M and East Sixteenth Street.)

American filmmaker Woody Allen was born Allan Stewart Konigsberg and grew up in Midwood. Find out a little about his childhood homes and haunts in this tour, based partly on Eric Lax's authorized *Woody Allen: A Biography* and PBS's *Woody Allen: A Documentary.*

The Q subway station was Allen's stop for trips to Manhattan, Coney Island, and Brighton Beach, as well as to Sheepshead Bay when he performed at Pips on the Bay comedy club.

Allen hated school. He attended PS 99 elementary school (1120 East Tenth Street) and Midwood High School (2839 Bedford Avenue). Lax recounts that Allen liked to play hooky and got in trouble frequently. He was once hauled into the principal's office for writing a story with the line, "She had an hourglass figure, and I'd like to play in the sand." However, his talent was already being recognized; Allen was being paid for writing jokes for well-known comedians even before he graduated high school.

Not surprisingly, going to the movies was an important part of Allen's youth. You can visit the site of the old Elm Theater (now Emigrant Savings Bank, Avenue M and East Sixteenth Street), the Kingsway (now Walgreens, 946 Kings Highway), and the still-operating Kent Theater (1170 Coney Island Avenue). The Kent and Jewel theaters might have been the inspirations for the movie houses in Allen's films *Purple Rose of Cairo* and *Broadway Danny Rose.*

Allen, his parents, and his sister, Lax reports, lived with a changing cast of relatives in a big, raucous family, moving a dozen times to different apartments in Midwood. He lived upstairs at 968 East Fourteenth Street until he was seven, reports Lax. If you stand in front of another of his former homes (1144 East Fifteenth Street), you can hear the rattling subways that make an appearance in some of his movies. Better yet, the real-life Allen dyed his mother's fur coat with his chemistry set when living here; a similar scene appears in the 1987 *Radio Days.* A high school photo of Allen shows his address as 1402 Avenue K. A block away, on Avenue K and East Fifteenth, some aunts and uncles lived in the large, red corner building.

Allen grew up in a kosher home, attended Hebrew school, and was bar mitzvahed at a synagogue on Coney Island Avenue (likely one that is still there). Marion Meade's unauthorized *The Unruly Life of Woody Allen: A Biography* reports among other tidbits that at his bar mitzvah party, Allen entertained the crowd by doing an imitation, in blackface, of Larry Parks as Al Jolson in *The Jazz Singer*.

Visit nearby Brooklyn College (2900 Bedford Avenue). For snacks, try Di Fara's Pizzeria (1424 Avenue J).

TOUR 4: FAMOUS WRITERS IN BROOKLYN HEIGHTS

(Where: Brooklyn Heights. Duration: forty-five minutes. Start: 102 Pierrepont Street, where Norman Mailer [1923–2007] briefly lived with his parents after graduating Harvard.)

This itinerary covers the homes of nine literary greats who lived in Brooklyn Heights.

From Mailer's family home, walk to where Joseph Brodsky (1940–1996), a Nobel Prize winner, U.S. poet laureate, and persecuted Russian exile, lived (22 Pierrepont Street). In 1939, W. H. Auden (1907–1973) lived nearby (1 Montague Terrace) before moving to 7 Middagh Street. (The group house at 7 Middagh was started by the *Harper's Bazaar* editor George Davis and the writer Carson McCullers and was home to a colorful cast of artists, would-be artists, lovers, friends, and lovers' friends over the years.) Thomas Wolfe (1900–1938) lived in the area for a year (5 Montague Terrace), shortly before the *New Yorker* published "Only the Dead Know Brooklyn." Backtracking via Pierrepont, find the home of Arthur Miller (1915–2005), author of *Death of a Salesman* and *A View from the Bridge* (155 Willow Street). He later decamped to 31 Grace Court, where he finished the former work. Interestingly, Miller sold his Willow Street property to an elderly W.E.B. Du Bois.

Truman Capote (1924–1984) wrote *Breakfast at Tiffany's* and other works here (at 70 Willow Street). Nearby, at Plymouth Church (57 Orange Street), a stop on the Underground Railroad, is a statue of the church's leader, abolitionist activist Rev. Henry Ward Beecher. His sister was Harriet Beecher Stowe, the author of *Uncle Tom's Cabin*.

Returning via Orange Street, see where the poet and essayist Hart Crane (1899–1932) and the novelist John Dos Passos (1886–1970) lived (110 Columbia Heights). Crane, the author of the epic poem *The Bridge*, lived in several houses on this block. Unfortunately, the bohemian group home at 7 Middagh Street was torn down. Return by heading south past the home of Norman Mailer (142 Columbia Heights). Enjoy a snack on Montague Street or the views from the Brooklyn Heights Promenade.

TOUR 5: ELEGANT CLINTON AVENUE IN CLINTON HILL

(Where: Clinton Hill. Duration: fifteen minutes by bike. Start: site of the original Drake's Cake bakery, now Benjamin Banneker Academy, 71–77 Clinton Avenue.)

Take this quick bike tour of the homes of wealthy industrialists in landmarked Clinton Hill near Pratt Institute.

Charles Pratt, an early partner of the Standard Oil Company and the Pratt Institute founder, lived here (252 Clinton Avenue). He commissioned homes for three of his four sons nearby, in different styles: a Tuscan villa (229 Clinton Avenue); a Romanesque Revival brick building, now the residence of the Catholic bishop of Brooklyn (241 Clinton Avenue); and a neo-Georgian, owned today by Saint Joseph's College (245 Clinton Avenue). Also see the Gallery House, a progressive nonprofit event space described by the NYC Landmarks Preservation Commission as "typical of the hundreds of neo-Grec row houses built in Brooklyn during the 1870's" (272 Clinton Avenue).

Elegant homes were built in 1894 for one of the first U.S. watch-case manufacturers, Joseph Fahys (287–293 Clinton Avenue).

A home built here for A. G. Jennings of the nearby 1871 Jennings Lacework Factory (on Park Avenue and Hall Street) is a landmark. It has also been a Halloween destination since 1994, when its owners started to stage an elaborate, free, spooky Halloween show as an alternative to potentially dangerous trick-or-treating (313 Clinton Avenue).

The Church of Saint Luke and Saint Matthew, a hundred-year-old Romanesque church with Tiffany windows (520 Clinton Avenue), is a New York City landmark.

Finally, detour a few blocks to Pratt Institute's Sculpture Park (200 Willoughby Avenue). It lays claim to being New York City's biggest sculpture garden. Also, at the corner of DeKalb and Classon Avenues, note the sign stating, "Clinton Hill is representative of an upper-class urban neighborhood and streetscape of its day."

TOUR 6: FULTON MALL

(Where: Downtown Brooklyn. Duration: one hour, on foot only. Start: Brooklyn Borough Hall. Optional: walk across Brooklyn Bridge before tour.)

Take in Fulton Mall and the New York Transit Museum, historic homes belonging to antislavery leaders, Brooklyn Tabernacle gospel church, and Junior's, where you can dig into a calorie-laden slice of cheesecake.

From Borough Hall, go to the New York Transit Museum (130 Livingston Street), below ground in an actual decommissioned subway station. See the Quaker Meeting House, where Quakers have been worshiping for over three hundred years (110 Schermerhorn Street). Nip south on Livingston toward Smith Street and turn left to find the Brooklyn Tabernacle, known for its Grammy Award–winning gospel choir (17 Smith Street). Backtrack to the Fulton Mall to see the landmarked Gage & Tollner's 1897 restaurant building (303 Fulton Street), now defunct but once famous for its Victorian mahogany tables, gas chandeliers, wall mirrors, and flashy clientele like Diamond Jim Brady, Jimmy Durante, and Mae West.

Along Fulton Street, notice the mix of ethnic and upmarket stores; that's old and new Brooklyn staring you in the face. Walk past Macy's in the historic A&S building, and turn left onto Albee Square. Note the stately 1908 Dime Savings Bank (9 DeKalb Avenue) and the new City Point shopping mall (1 DeKalb Avenue).

Head to the 1847 First Free Congregational Church (311 Bridge Street). It is a New York City designated landmark and was home of one of Brooklyn's oldest black congregations, rich in stories. It's said that congregants celebrated the signing of the Emancipation Proclamation for three days. Frederick Douglass encouraged blacks to enlist in the Union Army here in February 1863. Harriet Tubman, a "conductor" on the Underground Railroad, addressed the congregation in 1865; a section of Fulton Street is named for her. The congregation has since decamped to Bed-Stuy, and the building is part of the NYU-Poly campus.

On "Abolitionist Place," see four nineteenth-century homes of pre–Civil War abolitionist activists (182–188 Duffield Street). Nearby, MetroTech Center, a sprawling office complex from the 1990s, was the first sign of revivification in the area. Return through Fulton Mall, or have a snack at Junior's (386 Flatbush Avenue Extension).

(Read about Downtown Brooklyn in section 3, "The Neighborhoods.")

TOUR 7: BOROUGH HALL SKYSCRAPER HISTORIC DISTRICT

(Where: Downtown Brooklyn. Duration: ten minutes, by foot only.)

On this brief walk, see a slice of Borough Hall Skyscraper Historic District. These nineteenth- and early twentieth-century buildings are neither so remarkable nor terribly tall—but given the galloping pace of development in Downtown Brooklyn, it's notable they've been preserved for posterity.

From Brooklyn Borough Hall, go west on Court Street. Turn right to the Franklin Building, an 1877 Romanesque Revival midget that boasted, briefly, of being Brooklyn's tallest building (186 Remsen Street). Backtrack to the 1901 Beaux-Arts–style Temple Bar Building (44 Court Street). Walk south (away from the Brooklyn Bridge) to the 1924 Brooklyn Municipal Building, designed by McKenzie, Voorhees & Gmelin (210 Joralemon Street). On Joralemon, head west to the Romanesque and neo-Gothic Brooklyn Chamber of Commerce Building (75 Livingston Street). End with a visit to the Fulton Mall, Brooklyn Heights Promenade, or Emanuel Celler U.S. Courthouse to see *The Role of the Immigrant in the Industrial Development of America* murals from the 1935 Works Progress Administration era (Cadman Plaza East).

TOUR 8: HISTORIC GOWANUS

(Where: Gowanus. Duration: forty-five minutes on foot, less by bike or car. Start: Fourth Avenue and Union Street R subway stop.)

Community activists are working to place a swath of Gowanus on the National Register of Historic Places to preserve its nineteenth-century character and ward off excessive development. The following are already individual landmarks, except for the ball field.

See Public Bath #7, a 1911 New York landmark and one of many public bathhouses in the city, on the corner of President Street and Fourth Avenue. Walk west on Union Street to the 1910 National Packing Box Factory Building (543 Union Street).

The so-called Green Building was formerly Paulson & Son's brass foundry (450–460 Union Street). It's been repurposed as an event space; a residential tower may one day rise there.

Head toward the 1899 Carroll Street Bridge and Engine House (Carroll Street between Nevins and Bond Streets). Listed on the National Register of Historic Places, it's the oldest of only four retractable bridges in the nation. There are two other historic bridges on this canal.

Walking toward Third Street, take a long look at the Gowanus Canal. Use your imagination; when this Superfund site is fully remediated, it could be Brooklyn's Little Venice. Things are already changing fast.

The 1870 showcase headquarters of the New York and Long Island Coignet Stone Company, an industrial concrete pioneer near Third Street and the Whole Foods, was the city's first all-concrete building (370 Third Avenue).

Washington Park, a baseball field used by the Brooklyn Superbas, the team that became the Dodgers, opened in 1898 (Third Avenue and Third Street intersection, Con Edison site). It's said that Third Avenue is about where third base would have been. The Third Avenue wall of the Con Edison yard at 222 First Street is said to have been part of the clubhouse wall.

See the Old American Can Factory, formerly Somers Brothers Tin Box Factory (232 Third Street, across from Whole Foods). This retrofitted 1885 canning facility produced eighteen hundred tin boxes a day. Today it houses small firms and studios. Sonic Youth recorded its first three albums here.

Backtrack to see a massive, red, graffiti-covered 1902 Romanesque Revival building, built by the Brooklyn Rapid Transit Corporation, which had at that time a monopoly on every steam railroad, elevated line, and streetcar in Brooklyn (322 Third Avenue).

TOUR 9: VICTORIAN FLATBUSH: PROSPECT PARK SOUTH

(Where: Prospect Park South section of Flatbush. Duration: one hour by foot, less by bike or car. Start: Dutch Reformed Church at 890 Flatbush Avenue.)

You won't believe the gracious nineteenth-century homes in Prospect Park South, the gemstone of Victorian Flatbush, built when boomtown Brooklyn was an independent city. Victorian Flatbush's development was spurred by the extension of the Brighton subway line and the 1880s opening of Prospect Park and the Brooklyn Bridge.

The Dutch Flatbush Reformed Church (890 Flatbush Avenue) on the border of the neighborhood sets the stage. In 1892, the church sold a tract of farmland to the developer Dean Alvord, who built this "suburban" neighborhood, which offered more space and privacy than brownstone town houses did. Note the old gravestones in the cemetery. One of Brooklyn's best-kept secrets is the Victorian Knickerbocker Tennis Club, about four blocks away at 114 East Eighteenth Street. Welcome to Victorian Flatbush!

Nearby is the Colonial Revival home built by the neighborhood's chief architect for himself (1510 Albemarle Road). A romantic favorite is the decorative Queen Anne mansion (1501 Albemarle Road). It once belonged to Elmer Sperry, of Sperry-Rand fortune, who moved here from the smaller 100 Marlborough Road, which proved too tight for the inventor's experiments with gyrocompasses.

Around the corner is the "Japanese House" (131 Buckingham Road). It reflects the Victorian infatuation with Asian exotica (a pagoda grows in Brooklyn) and was featured in 1903 ads to lure both people with new fortunes and those with family money to an elite Brooklyn outpost, far from the industrial grit of the docks, warehouses, and grimy factories where many residents' fortunes were made. Don't miss the green median strip, which touts the regal title of Buckingham Road Mall, designed in the preautomotive era, when people traveled by horse-and-buggy.

One block west is the former home of the iconoclast Nellie Bly (184 Marlborough Road). That was the nom de plume of Elizabeth Cochrane Seaman, an intrepid reporter who feigned insanity in order to cover conditions inside Bellevue Hospital and then wrote *Ten Days in a Mad-House* in 1887. She traveled the world and at age thirty-one married the seventy-three-year-old magnate Robert Seaman. A former Bensonhurst kiddie amusement park, Nellie Bly, was named in her honor.

Another block west, look for the "Honeymoon Cottage," built for a Guggenheim (308 Rugby Road); the "Swiss Chalet" (100 Rugby Road); and the "pink house" (now gray) of Meryl Streep's 1982 movie *Sophie's Choice* (101 Rugby Road).

The next block is Argyle Road, where, it's said, there was a private botanic garden on a double lot (145 Argyle Road). A few blocks down were the homes of the president of the American Can Company and the founder of the Fruit of the Loom empire (1519 and 1215 Argyle Road, respectively). The latter, a Spanish-styled home, was designed by the firm Severance and Van Alen, architects of Manhattan's Chrysler Building.

Exit back to rude reality from Albemarle Road onto Coney Island Avenue through brick stanchions marked with the letters "PPS," for Prospect Park South.

TOUR 10: BATTLE OF BROOKLYN AND REVOLUTIONARY WAR SITES BY NEIGHBORHOOD

(Where: multiple neighborhoods; design your own tour. Duration: one hour to one day, by bike or car. Start: your choice of sites.)

Brooklynites celebrate and reenact the Battle of Brooklyn as though "our side" won. We didn't. But in the spirit of "live to fight another day," George Washington escaped and eventually won the war.

The Battle of Brooklyn (also called the Battle of Long Island) took place in August 1776. "It was a decisive and crushing defeat for the Americans. It was by the merest chance that the whole American army was not captured, which might have brought the War of the Revolution to a summary end. By herculean efforts Washington succeeded in ferrying his defeated troops across the East River. Then began a rapid retreat, with the English in hot pursuit, who received a check just north of Central Park" is how the lengthy 1908 booklet *Dedication of the Prison Ship Martyrs' Monument* (accessible on the Internet Archive) described it. It was, in short, a rout.

Here are nine places where the Battle of Brooklyn played out, organized by neighborhood. For a chronological listing, access the Old Stone House's "Battle of Brooklyn Walking Guide to Sites and Monuments" online.

Bay Ridge and Bensonhurst

Get a sense of the early hours of the fateful Battle of Brooklyn here. On August 27, 1776, the British general William Howe and admiral Richard Howe (brothers) landed a larger-than-expected force of about twenty-seven thousand soldiers at Denyse's Ferry, near today's Fort Hamilton, built much later in 1831. It's worth a visit to the fort's Harbor Defense Museum, listed on the National Register of Historic Sites, and to see the plaque dedicated to the 1776 resistance in John Paul Jones Park, sometimes called Cannonball Park, nearby. Revolutionary War–era Barkaloo cemetery, a family plot, at Narrows Avenue and Mackay Place, is Brooklyn's smallest cemetery.

In Bensonhurst, visit New Utrecht Liberty Pole, the New Utrecht Reformed Dutch Church Cemetery, and Milestone Park. "Both Continental Army General George Washington (1732–1799) and British General William Howe (1729–1814) used this area as a military prison during the Revolutionary War," says the New York City Parks Department. The cemetery has an unmarked grave for Revolutionary War soldiers. In nearby Milestone Park, a replica of New York's oldest milestone (the original is at the Brooklyn Historical Society) shows the distance to New York and Denyse's Ferry, where the British landed.

Brooklyn Heights Promenade

At the Clark Street and Columbia Heights entrance to the Promenade, a 1924 plaque marks the location of Fort Stirling. This rural area was known as Clover Hill. A plaque at Montague Street and the Promenade marks the site of the Cornell House: "In this house, used as a headquarters by George Washington during the Battle of Long Island, the Council of War on August 29, 1776, decided 'to withdraw the American Army from Long Island' and escape across the East River to Manhattan."

Cobble Hill / Carroll Gardens / Gowanus

On the corner of Atlantic Avenue and Court Street (now the site of a Trader Joe's grocery store), a plaque marks the site of Cobble Hill Fort, variously known as Corkscrew Fort, Spiral Fort, Ponkiesbergh Fort, and Smith's Barbette. On August 27, 1776, from this spot, a signal shot warned that the British armies had landed, and Washington watched the fighting, including in swampy Gowanus near the site of Old Stone House. Carroll Street Bridge in Gowanus is the former Porte Road at Denton's Mill, the path taken by patriots fleeing the battle. Denton's Mill is memorialized in tiny Denton Place, between First and Carroll Streets. Carroll Park honors Charles Carroll, a 1776 Continental Congress member, the only Roman Catholic to sign the Declaration of Independence.

Dumbo / Fulton Landing

The floating concert hall Bargemusic sits near where Washington's troops retreated, ceding Brooklyn and Long Island to the British, crossing the East River in the dead of night aboard all manner of craft laden with soldiers, horses, cannons, and supplies on August 27, 1776.

Flatbush

A plaque on the Flatlands Reformed Dutch Church, founded in 1654, at Kings Highway and East Fortieth Street north of Flatbush Avenue, reads, "1636: The Kings Highway, formerly the road to Flatlands Neck, passed this site. Over it the Indian braves and Captain John Underhill with his colonial soldiers passed. Lord Cornwallis, on August 26, 1776, at the head of British troops, silently marched in the night to outflank the Continental army at the Battle of Long Island. President George Washington drove over this road April 20, 1790 on his journey around Long Island. [Erected by] Battle Pass Chapter, DAR, 1935."

Fort Greene Park / Brooklyn Navy Yard

An important site, the Prison Ship Martyrs' Monument in Fort Greene Park holds the remains of some 11,500 patriots who died aboard British prison ships moored near the Brooklyn Navy Yard. The conditions of their captivity make today's Geneva Convention standards for prisoners of war seem luxurious. Dedicated in 1908, the monument commemorates what may be the nation's largest Revolutionary War cemetery.

Park Slope

The Old Stone House, a reconstruction of a colonial-era Dutch farmhouse in Washington Park, has exhibits on the Battle of Brooklyn. It was lost by midday on August 27, 1776, when the American general William Alexander, Lord Stirling, surrendered. The original home on this site, mentioned by Stirling in correspondence with George Washington, was possibly Stirling's temporary command post.

Prospect Park

As you're biking or walking up the park's northernmost hill toward Grand Army Plaza, following the one-way direction of the car traffic, see two plaques set in stones on either side of the road. They mark the location of the Valley Grove Inn and the Dongan Oak, the site of a battlefield massacre. They are between the Prospect Park Zoo and Grand Army Plaza.

Red Hook

Fort Defiance, near Beard Street, guarded Buttermilk Channel and Gowanus Bay, its cannons ready to fire at British ships in New York Harbor. It was one leg of a multisite defense that included Manhattan's Battery Park and Governors Island, named Nutten Island.

Tip: If time is limited, concentrate on the Old Stone House, Fort Hamilton, the Washington plaque, and the Prison Ship Martyrs' Monument in Fort Greene.

(Sections of this tour were excerpted with permission from the "Battle of Brooklyn Walking Guide to Sites and Monuments" pamphlet, published by the Old Stone House online.)

TOUR 11: CIVIL WAR SITES BY NEIGHBORHOOD

(Where: multiple neighborhoods; design your own tour. Duration: one hour to one day, by bike or car. Start: your choice of sites.)

You'll find no Civil War battlefields here. Some prominent Brooklyn landowners owned slaves, including the Wyckoff, Lott, and Cortelyou families, several of whose surnames survive today as Brooklyn street names. But slavery was abolished in New York State by 1827, three decades before the Civil War.

Brooklyn's four most impressive Civil War destinations are Weeksville, a preserved free black community that predated the Civil War; Green-Wood Cemetery, where some five thousand Civil War veterans are buried; the homes and churches of abolitionists in Downtown Brooklyn and Brooklyn Heights; and in Greenpoint, the launch site of the ironclad warship the *Monitor*. (See Greenwood Heights and Crown Heights chapters in section 3.)

In Green-Wood, the thirty-five-foot, 1869 Civil War Soldiers' Monument on Battle Hill honors the 148,000 men from New York City who enlisted for service in the Civil War. The grave of abolitionist preacher Henry Ward Beecher (1813–1887) is on Dawn Path, off Hillside Avenue. The Civil War Soldiers' Lot contains the markers of men who died at Shiloh, Antietam, Gettysburg, and other battlefields and many who died of disease. Soldiers Lot includes the grave of "Our Drummer Boy," Brooklyn's first Civil War casualty, twelve-year-old Clarence Mackenzie, a drummer with Brooklyn's Thirteenth Regiment who was killed by friendly fire. Civil War nurse Abigail Hopper Gibbons, a Quaker, abolitionist, and prison reformer, is buried here. Her home was a stop on the Underground Railroad; her father, Isaac Hopper, is credited with the "railroad" concept. (See *Final Camping Ground: Civil War Veterans at Brooklyn's Green-Wood Cemetery, in Their Own Words*, by Jeffrey I. Richman, published by Green-Wood Cemetery.)

Sites near the Brooklyn Bridge include the abolitionist Plymouth Church and, in Downtown Brooklyn, "Abolitionist Place," honoring nineteenth-century abolitionists Thomas and Harriet Truesdell, who lived at 227 Duffield Street, and their neighbor William Harned, an Underground Railroad conductor.

In Greenpoint, the first ironclad warship, the battleship *Monitor*, which helped win a Union victory, was built at the Continental Iron Works. You can see a sign at 56 Quay Street, Bushwick Inlet and East River, dedicated in May 2015. It is one of a series of signs along the National Oceanographic and Atmospheric Administration's Monitor Trail. (Other Monitor Trail signs are located at the Richmond National Battlefield at Drewry's Bluff; the North Carolina Maritime Museum in Beaufort, North Carolina; and along the Noland Trail at the Mariners' Museum in Newport News, Virginia.) A Greenpoint Monitor Museum is under discussion.

In Greenpoint, McGolrick Park's 1938 sculpture *Monitor*, by Antonio de Filippo, depicts a heroic nude pulling a rope attached to a capstan, honoring the memory of the men of the *Monitor*. In Prospect Park, the Grand Army Plaza's Soldiers' and Sailors' Memorial Arch features multiple bas-relief sculptures celebrating the Union army and navy and an immense quadriga. It's the largest of three Civil War monuments at this Prospect Park entrance.

In Flatbush, an excavation unearthed slave accommodations at the Hendrick I. Lott House (1940 East Thirty-Sixth Street), the homestead of a wealthy Brooklyn family. Documents indicate the Lott family owned twelve slaves in 1803. The historic house is expected to reopen in 2016–2017.

The Brooklyn Historical Society has an extensive collection of photos, letters, scrapbooks, memorabilia, and online African American history sources, including sermons for and against abolition. You can access digitized Civil War documents via the Brooklyn Collection at the Brooklyn Central Library.

TOUR 12: WORLD WARS I AND II AND LATER WARS

(Where: multiple neighborhoods; design your own tour. Duration: one hour to one day, by bike or car. Start: your choice of sites.)

Several Brooklyn sites played important roles in the wars of the twentieth and twenty-first centuries: the 1801 Brooklyn Navy Yard, 1902 Bush Terminal, and 1919 Brooklyn Army Terminal.

The Brooklyn Navy Yard, the biggest such facility of its kind in the world, was active during World War I and in World War II. During the war years of 1942–1945, it geared up to a seven-days-a-week, twenty-four-hours-a-day operation with seventy-five thousand employees. The site covered nearly three hundred acres. Its stats suggest the enormity of the operation: seven dry docks, nineteen miles of paved streets, a dedicated power plant and on-site hospital, dozens of mobile cranes, and eight piers. Battleships and aircraft carriers were built and repaired there, as well. The Brooklyn Navy Yard's Building 92 has exhibits. Group tours are conducted by Turnstile Tours.

Sunset Park's Bush Terminal (now called Industry City) and the Brooklyn Army Terminal were key. Starting in 1917, the U.S. Navy commandeered the commercial Bush Terminal piers and manufacturing facilities. The Brooklyn Army Terminal wasn't finished until 1919, after the end of World War I, but this immense area, with two eight-story factories, was active during World War II. Funnily, Elvis Presley shipped out from the Brooklyn Army Terminal during the Korean War, while the paparazzi snapped; you can see his photo in the lobby. The United States Naval Clothing Depot, a manufacturing plant for military uniforms, was nearby at Third Avenue and Twenty-Ninth Street.

Fort Hamilton in Bay Ridge rapidly expanded when the United States entered World War II in 1942 and became a staging area for troops shipping out to the European front from the New York Port of Embarkation. Manhattan Beach, near Sheepshead Bay, was among the nation's largest Coast Guard training centers. In North Brooklyn, the Pfizer Plant (today reconfigured as 630 Flushing Avenue, a site for incubators and labs for small food start-up companies, among other businesses) was where penicillin was first mass-produced, saving the lives of countless soldiers. A red-light district called the Barbary Coast, off Sands Street in what is now Dumbo, was patronized by troops who had a few days in New York before shipping out.

Cadman Plaza War Memorial in Downtown Brooklyn, a granite and limestone structure, is dedicated to the more than 300,000 "heroic men and women of the borough of Brooklyn" who died in World War II; some 11,500 names of Brooklyn service members are inscribed inside. It may reopen as an educational center.

Dozens of memorials commemorate the Korean War, the Vietnam War, and twenty-first-century conflicts in Afghanistan and the Middle East. Brooklyn celebrates Memorial Day with two parades, in Bay Ridge and in Greenpoint. Green-Wood presents an annual Memorial Day concert.

See New York City Parks Department's website for information on war memorials in Brooklyn's public parks.

TOUR 13: SEPTEMBER 11, 2001, MEMORIALS

(Where: multiple neighborhoods; design your own tour. Duration: one to three hours, by bike or car. Start: your choice of sites.)

Brooklyn has more than a dozen homegrown 9/11 memorials, mostly created by citizen volunteers. They honor the 298 victims (about one in ten of the nearly 2,800 same-day victims of the World Trade Center attacks) who were from Brooklyn. It was a deeply traumatic day. Many Brooklyn residents witnessed the attack's aftermath from Brooklyn's shoreline communities. Thousands streamed over Brooklyn's bridges, escaping Manhattan. Many Brooklyn-based first responders who were not Brooklyn residents also died.

Near the Brooklyn Bridge are two Fire Department of New York (FDNY) sites. Visit FDNY Engine 205 / Ladder 118, to see a patriotic mural (74 Middagh Street). Proceed to the FDNY Memorial Wall at FDNY headquarters

9/11 memorial at Engine Company 205 / Ladder Company 118 in Brooklyn Heights. (Photo courtesy Sam Kolich, 2015)

(9 MetroTech Center). It lists the names of over five dozen firefighters who died from diseases caused by exposure to the rubble's toxic stew. Eerily, the wall is big enough for dozens of additional names.

In Park Slope, a dozen elite FDNY Squad 1 firefighters who raced to the scene of the attack died there, among some three hundred firefighters who lost their lives that day. A wooden sculpture in their honor sits outside the firehouse, poignantly titled *Out of the Rubble* (288 Union Street).

Small plaques can be found on the Brooklyn Botanic Garden's Esplanade and in Prospect Park's Long Meadow at Memorial Grove.

In Bay Ridge at Pier 69 (also called the American Veterans Memorial Pier), the towering bronze "Beacon" memorial, cast by the sculptor Robert Ressler at Greenpoint's Bedi-Makky Foundry, marks a spot where bystanders watched the World Trade Center's twin towers burn (Sixty-Ninth Street and Belt Parkway; access from Shore Road via the pedestrian bridge). Ten blocks off Ninety-Second Street and Shore Road were renamed 9/11 Memorial Way, in honor of residents who died at the World Trade Center. Saint Ephrem Church has a memorial Garden of Hope (929 Bay Ridge Parkway).

Coney Island's bronze Brooklyn Wall of Remembrance at the MCU Park (1904 Surf Avenue) is one of the most moving 9/11 memorials. It's dedicated to hundreds of first responders.

The memorial Daffodil Project, initiated by a philanthropic Dutch bulb grower, contributed thousands of daffodil bulbs to New York City in the aftermath of the attack. Some five million daffodil bulbs have since been planted.

TOUR 14: VOLUNTEER TRAVEL: SOCIAL JUSTICE, PRESERVATION, AND ECO TOURS

(Location and duration will vary.)

Brooklyn has many small nonprofit political, environmental, gay rights, and arts groups. A handful offer volunteer opportunities or topical tours. Uprose, Groundswell, the Gowanus Conservancy, Billie Holiday Theatre, and Prospect Park Alliance may welcome volunteers, seasonally. It's a good idea to get in touch well in advance, and consider making a financial contribution to the cause. Find more nonprofits in the Brooklyn Community Foundation directory, and the Historic Districts Council list of "neighborhood partners," both online.

TOUR 15: ANNUAL HISTORIC HOUSE TOURS

(Where: multiple neighborhoods, variously held in spring and autumn. Duration: one hour to one day. Tickets must be ordered in advance. Also, see Open House New York's October series.)

Bedford-Stuyvesant House Tour: Brownstoners of Bedford-Stuyvesant, http:// brownstonersofbedstuy.org

Brooklyn Heights House Tour: Brooklyn Heights Association, http://www
.brooklynheightsassociation.org

Clinton Hill House Tour: Society for Clinton Hill, http://societyforclintonhill
.org

Fort Greene / Clinton Hill House Tour: Society for Clinton Hill, http://society
forclintonhill.org

Green-Wood Cemetery: Mausoleum "House Tour," http://www.green-wood.com

Park Slope House Tour: Park Slope Civic Council, http://www.parkslopecivic
council.org

Prospect Lefferts Gardens House Tour: Lefferts Manor Association, http://
www.leffertsmanor.org

Victorian Flatbush House Tour: Flatbush Development Corporation, http://
www.fdconline.org

GUIDED TOURS

For guided tours, see what's offered by the major cultural organizations: the Brooklyn Historical Society, the Brooklyn Navy Yard, the Brooklyn Public Library, the Coney Island History Project, Green-Wood, the Historic Districts Council, the Municipal Arts Society (MAS), the Gowanus Dredgers, Open House New York (an annual event), and neighborhood preservation groups. All are excellent. So are group or private tours by such touring companies as Big Onion, Foods of New York, Levy's Unique Tours, New York City Walking Tours, New York Like a Native, Turnstile, and Urban Oyster. Visitors enjoy the Made in Brooklyn, Slice of Brooklyn Pizza Tour and Free Tours by Foot. You can also find biking tours, Jewish tours, brewery tours, architectural tours, and guided walks across the Brooklyn Bridge. Of course, double-decker tourist buses also offer tours.

LeFrak Center at Lakeside, in Prospect Park, has ice-skating, roller-skating, and a splash pad in the summer. (Photo by E. Freudenheim, 2014)

Forty Things to Do with Kids

Stuck for ideas of what to do with the kids? Use this alphabetical list of twenty ideas each for indoor and outdoor fun.

TWENTY OUTDOOR ACTIVITIES

1. Baseball: Watch the Brooklyn Cyclones play in Coney Island.
2. Beaches! Coney Island, Brighton Beach, and Manhattan Beach.
3. Brooklyn Botanic Garden Discovery Center and special events.
4. Brooklyn Bridge and Brooklyn Bridge Park: Walk or bike across the Brooklyn Bridge, then head to Brooklyn Bridge Park for boating, art, and many special children's events (free).
5. Coney Island amusement park rides at Luna Park and Deno's Wonder Wheel Amusement Park.
6. Ferry ride to Governors Island (free, summer weekends) or from Dumbo to Williamsburg.
7. Festivals and parades: Asian Lunar New Year, Saint Patrick's Day, PRIDE Parade, International African Festival, Coney Island Sand Sculpting, Make Music New York (free), and annual powwow in Floyd Bennett Field.
8. Floyd Bennett Field: fly kites, bike, camp out (some free).
9. Merry-go-rounds, outdoors: Jane's Carousel in Dumbo, Prospect Park Carousel.
10. Movies under the stars: Some free summer outdoor films are programmed for kids.
11. New York Aquarium Aquatheater, Walrus and Penguin Sea Cliffs.
12. Nosh: Try Brooklyn food-truck fare; visit Smorgasburg.
13. Pools! Swim outdoors; there are small wading pools for tots (free). Check the New York City Parks Department website.
14. Prospect Park: Fishing in the lake (return the catch), Audubon Center, Prospect Park Carousel, playgrounds, rent a pedal boat or family novelty bike at LeFrak Center. Watch the Afro-Caribbean drummers in the Sunday Drummers Circle (some free).
15. Ride a horse: Jamaica Bay Riding Academy or Prospect Park.
16. Skate: Ice-skate, roller-skate at LeFrak Center; skateboard park at Owl's Head Park.

17 Street fairs in summer, Halloween events, Christmas-tree and menorah light-ings (free).
18 Urban Park Ranger Tours: Very popular; you have to enter a lottery the night before, http://www.nycgovparks.org/programs/rangers.
19 Watch and cheer! Unicycle Parade, Ragamuffin Parade (of kids), New York Marathon, Coney Island fireworks (free).
20 Waterfront Museum on the *Lehigh Valley No. 79* barge: see a show aboard a boat in Red Hook.

TWENTY INDOOR ACTIVITIES

1 Aviator Sports: Indoor ice-skating, wall climbing, events.
2 Books: Check out story hours at dozens of libraries and bookstores (free).
3 Bowling and climbing: Bowl at Brooklyn Bowl or the Gutter; climbing walls at Brooklyn Boulders.
4 Brooklyn Children's Museum, in Crown Heights and Dumbo (limited free hours).
5 Brooklyn Museum: Special kids events, Target First Saturday event, galleries.
6 Chocolate factory tours: Tour Cacao Prieto, Raaka Chocolate, Mast Brothers Chocolate Makers, and LiLac Chocolates.
7 Floyd Bennett Field: Watch historic airplane restoration (free).
8 Hair cuts in a toy store: LuLu's and Mini Max.
9 Harbor Defense Museum at Fort Hamilton.
10 Indoor playgrounds (two!) in Williamsburg/Greenpoint: Klub4Kidz and Play.
11 Jewish Children's Museum.
12 Lefferts Historic House Museum or Wyckoff House Museum.
13 Merry-go-rounds, indoors: Jane's Carousel inside the glass-enclosed carousel house in Dumbo; historic B&B Carousel in Coney Island.
14 New York Aquarium Sharks and Rays, Glovers Reef, Conservation Hall, 4-D Theater.
15 New York Transit Museum.
16 Paint a Pot, in Carroll Gardens or Park Slope.
17 Puppet shows at Puppetworks (Park Slope), Shadowbox Theater (Bed-Stuy), or Puppetsburg (Williamsburg).
18 Salt Marsh Center at Marine Park (free, weekends April to October).
19 Slot-car racing at Buzz-A-Rama.
20 Theater and shows for kids at Barclays Center, Brooklyn Center for the Per-forming Arts at Brooklyn College, and On Stage at Kingsborough, as well as Brooklyn Nets and New York Islanders pro sports games.

Monthly Calendar

YEAR-ROUND

The Brooklyn Museum's free Target First Saturday takes place the first Saturday of most months.

JANUARY

Have a bracing New Year's Day brunch, or join the crowd watching hundreds of brave-hearted "Polar Bears" take a January 1 dip in the Atlantic Ocean in Coney Island. BAM hosts the annual Martin Luther King Jr. memorial program, the city's largest MLK Day event, on the third Monday of January. On Super Bowl Sunday, friendly crowds jam local sports bars. Quirky but smart indoor programs at the Brooklyn Botanic Garden are fun. Don't miss the Lunar New Year celebration in Sunset Park and Bensonhurst (sometimes February). There are postholiday shopping sales.

FEBRUARY

Black History Month events kick off at the Brooklyn Museum, Brooklyn Public Library, Medgar Evers College in Crown Heights, and elsewhere. Public schools close for vacation. Find family-friendly programming at the Brooklyn Children's Museum, the BAMkids Film Festival, and in parks. Shop the Presidents' Day sales.

MARCH

Saint Patrick's Day parades in Bay Ridge and Park Slope plus Women's History Month lectures and films make a rich, if sometimes weather-challenged, month. Visit a matzo factory before Passover in the Williamsburg or Borough Park Hasidic neighborhoods. Change clocks for daylight savings on the second Sunday of the month.

APRIL

Sakura Matsuri, the Brooklyn Botanic Garden's month-long Cherry Blossom Festival, is a must. The Brooklyn International Film Festival opens. The Brooklyn

Folk Festival convenes for a weekend. Luna Park's historic wooden Cyclone roller coaster and dozens of Coney Island rides open. Attend Good Friday processions in Italian Bensonhurst and Carroll Gardens, Easter Egg Rolls in the parks, the monthly Brooklyn Quilters Guild show, and Earth Day celebrations, notably in Greenpoint and Gowanus.

MAY

Outdoor dining starts as the weather warms. Memorial Day weekend features Fleet Week, Green-Wood's Annual Memorial Day Concert, and the three-day DanceAfrica festival at BAM. Brooklyn's Memorial Day Parade, dating to 1867, is the oldest such parade in the United States. Do the Brooklyn Half Marathon and 5 Borough Bike Ride (both require advance registration). Enjoy dance parties at Brooklyn Bridge Park, the opening of Governors Island, accessible by ferry from Brooklyn, and neighborhood house tours in Fort Greene, Clinton Hill, Brooklyn Heights, Prospect Lefferts Gardens, Flatbush, and Park Slope (see "DIY Tours," section 5).

Cinco de Mayo is celebrated in Bushwick and Sunset Park. The May 17 Norwegian Constitution Day enlivens Bay Ridge. It's Ramadan for many Brooklyn residents (depending on the lunar calendar), with public events in the parks. There's Park Slope's Fifth Avenue Street Fair, SONYA's Studio Stroll in Fort Greene, Wallabout in Clinton Hill and Bed-Stuy, free "Weekend Walks" organized by the city, and Brooklyn Public Library's Bike the Branches. In May or June, don't miss the Red Hook Fest and BKLYN Designs.

JUNE

Brooklyn erupts into party mode, though school isn't out and the outdoor pools don't open until month's end. The Mermaid Parade in Coney Island is a must-see. Stoop sales and street fairs are in full swing: Carroll Gardens' Smith Street Funday Sunday Fair, Bay Ridge's Fifth Avenue Festival, Midwood's Mardi Gras, and Park Slope's Seventh Heaven on Father's Day. Special celebrations include the Italian Gigolo procession (Bensonhurst and Williamsburg), Juneteenth emancipation commemorations, and the PRIDE Parade and events. At Floyd Bennett Field, you can bird-watch, sleep under the stars, and attend the Redhawk Native American heritage celebration, a powwow.

SUMMER!

Atlantic Ocean beaches (Coney Island, Brighton Beach, Manhattan Beach) open and dozens of public outdoor pools are free. Concerts and films, including

SummerStage performances and BRIC Celebrate Brooklyn! series in Prospect Park are free. (See "Brooklyn's Cultural Scene," section 4.)

Enjoy events, dancing, and concerts in Brooklyn Bridge Park, BAM's midday jazz in Downtown Brooklyn's MetroTech Center, soul and hip-hop at Martin Luther King Jr. concerts in Wingate Field, shows at the new Coney Island amphitheater, and waterfront concerts at Sheepshead Bay's Kingsborough Community College. The Metropolitan Opera performs once, for free, in Prospect Park or Brooklyn Bridge Park.

Coney Island explodes with sun and surf, amusement-park rides, Brooklyn Cyclones baseball games at MCU Park, and shows at the New York Aquarium. Walk along Coney Island's Riegelmann Boardwalk. Fish on a pier. Enjoy fireworks on Friday evenings and after home Cyclones games (when they win).

Foodies graze at Smorgasburg, the weekend food fest. Sunday is famous for home-cooked Latino fare at the Red Hook ball fields. Seasonal farmers markets open, listed in this book by neighborhood.

You can see a free movie every night of the week. (See "Movies and Indie Films" in "Brooklyn's Cultural Scene," section 4.)

JULY

July Fourth events include Macy's fireworks, the Nathan's Famous Hot Dog Eating Contest and fireworks in Coney Island, free outdoor films in the parks, and Bastille Day in Carroll Gardens (July 14). Perennial favorites include the International African Arts Festival, DanceAfrica, BWAC art shows in Red Hook, the Brooklyn Hip-Hop Festival, and events at the Brooklyn Children's Museum. In Williamsburg, see the Feast of Our Lady of Mount Carmel and San Paolino Di Nola. Go aboard the educational Waterfront Museum and *Mary A. Whalen* barges.

AUGUST

Brooklyn's beaches and pools are packed. Street fairs include the Brighton Jubilee (Brighton Beach). Go to the AfroPunk festival in Commodore Barry Park or the ten-day Festa de Santa Rosalia in Bensonhurst. Watch the Battle of Brooklyn reenactment at Green-Wood. Celebrate Pakistani Independence Day in Flatbush. Watch the West Indian American Day Parade on Labor Day Monday (sometimes September). Back-to-school sales start.

SEPTEMBER

The big Atlantic Antic street fair; Coney Island's Great Irish Fair; and Carroll Gardens' Court Street Crawl beckon. The Brooklyn Book Festival culminates on a Sunday following a week of citywide author readings, discussions, and literary events. Car lovers won't want to miss the Antique Automobile Association of Brooklyn event at Floyd Bennett Field. BAM's Next Wave Festival opens, through December. Greenmarkets overflow with agricultural abundance. September 11 marks the anniversary of the 2001 World Trade Center attack, including the Stephen Siller Tunnel to Towers 5K Run & Walk. Public school commences. Children have off in observance of Jewish and Muslim holidays.

OCTOBER

Halloween! Enjoy harvest festivals, a three-day Columbus Day weekend, many Halloween parades, and inventive Green-Wood events such as the annual mausoleum tour. Don't miss the Rock 'n' Roll Half Marathon in Prospect Park. During Open House New York, you can enter cool sites and landmarks. October brings FW|BK (Fashion Week Brooklyn) and Bed-Stuy's annual house tour. (Read more about Halloween in section 4, "Where to Go, What to Do.")

NOVEMBER

The weather turns brisk. It's Thanksgiving! Over fifty thousand runners tackle the New York Marathon, following a course that's mostly through Brooklyn. Enjoy Thanksgiving-morning Turkey Trot running races in Prospect Park and Coney Island. Veterans Day is a three-day weekend. November brings Black Friday, Cyber Monday, Thanksgiving sales, winter coat drives for charity, Election Day, and daylight savings time on Marathon Sunday.

DECEMBER

Christmas, Hanukkah, and Kwanzaa holidays spark multicultural celebrations: concerts, holiday craft and gift markets, public lightings of thirty-foot-tall menorahs and gorgeous, huge Christmas trees, performances of the *Messiah* and the *Nutcracker* ballet, and caroling. The MTA offers vintage holiday rides on historic trains. Enjoy Christmas lights in Dyker Heights, the kids' Reindeer Run and Jingle Jog in Prospect Park, and the Winter Festival at Lefferts Historic House. Ice-skate at Prospect Park's LeFrak Center. On New Year's Eve, walk across the Brooklyn Bridge, see midnight fireworks in Coney Island or Prospect Park, and watch the ball drop at the Parachute in Coney Island. Brooklyn's hopping with parties, festivities, and midnight runs and bike rides on New Year's Eve.

Tips
Accommodations, Transportation, Safety, Blogs

ACCOMMODATIONS

There are about sixty-five hotels in Brooklyn, with more popping up like clover. Between 2012 and 2016, twenty hotels opened in Brooklyn. Many are chains. This book doesn't list them all (find them online) but offers a key piece of advice: choose your location first, and check real proximity to subways, restaurants, and amenities.

There are two clusters of hotels: in Downtown Brooklyn and Gowanus and in North Brooklyn.

In Downtown Brooklyn and along Fourth Avenue in Gowanus, you'll find several Marriotts including a Fairfield Inn, plus a Sheraton, Holiday Inns, and Super 8s. Sleep Inns are in Sunset Park and Coney Island. For independents, try the Nu Hotel, Hotel le Blue, or Gowanus Inn and Yard. Esplendor Bossert and 1 Hotel in Brooklyn Bridge Park (opening soon) offer upmarket alternatives. A Marriott Autograph Collection Hotel is being built near BAM.

To date, North Brooklyn has Pointe Plaza and the Pod and boutique and luxury hotels such as the Wythe Hotel, the Hoxton, William Vale, McCarren Hotel, and in Greenpoint, the popular Box House and Henry Norman hotels. Bushwick's first hotel, under construction as of this writing, is at 232 Siegel Street. Bay Ridge and Borough Park have their own longstanding hotels.

Staying at an Airbnb is a good way to see a neighborhood.

Some bed-and-breakfasts are in lovely Victorian homes. Of the borough's sixty B&Bs, a few popular ones include the following; the abbreviations indicate neighborhoods (see the key in "Shopping in Brooklyn," section 4).

Akwaaba Mansion, 347 MacDonough Street, (718) 455-5958 (BS)
Bibi's Garden B&B, 762 Westminster Road, (718) 434-3119 (MW)
Blue Porch, 15 DeKoven Court, (718) 434-0557 (MW)
Carroll Gardens House, 284 President Street, (917) 992-5052 (CG/CH)
DeKoven Suites, 30 DeKoven Court, (718) 421-1052 (MW)
Downtown Brooklyn B&B, 136 Lawrence Street, (347) 762-2632 (DB)
Eve's B&B, 751 Westminster Road, (347) 256-2577 (MW)
Garden Green B&B, 641 Carlton Avenue, (718) 783-5717 (MW)
Honey's Home B&B, 770 Westminster Road, (917) 873-9493 (MW)
House on 3rd Street, 422 3rd Street, (718) 788-7171 (PS)
Inn on Second, 60 Second Street, (718) 596-3185 (PS)

Lefferts Manor, 80 Rutland Road, (347) 351-9065 (MW)
Lorelei, 667 Argyle Road, (646) 228-4656 (MW)
Midwood Suites, 1078 East 15th Street, (718) 253-9535 (MW)
Park Slope B&B, 604 5th Street, (718) 965-2355 (PS)
Rugby Gardens, 317 Rugby Road, (718) 469-2244 (MW)

WHAT'S FREE?

Public library events, some festivals (most of the Brooklyn Book Festival), outdoor concerts, dances, and events in parks, public beaches, and outdoor public pools are free. Some cultural institutions offer periodic free entry, notably the Brooklyn Children's Museum (Thursday afternoons) and the Brooklyn Museum (Target First Saturdays).

TEN BEST FREE THINGS TO DO IN BROOKLYN

1   Walk the Brooklyn Bridge. Go in the direction of Manhattan. It's gorgeous.
2   Hear amazing concerts at BRIC Celebrate Brooklyn! summer festival and dozens of free concerts and movies in the parks.
3   Stroll the Coney Island boardwalk, any time of year. It's picturesque, the air's fresh! In summer, sunbathe, ride the waves. Visit Coney Island History Project's exhibits.
4   Explore the brownstone neighborhoods on Sunday mornings; the streets are beautiful and peaceful.
5   Luxuriate in the parks. Brooklyn Bridge Park offers so much to do, you could spend an entire weekend. Prospect Park, Fort Greene Park, Marine Park, and Floyd Bennett Field each offer something special.
6   On summer weekends, hop the ferry to Governors Island and look around this old military installation; it's another world.
7   Attend a parade, street fair, or ethnic celebration! Spirits are high, the music is good, it's a party.
8   Try Free Tours by Foot.
9   Go to the beaches, swim in outdoor pools, explore Green-Wood.
10   Visit Plymouth Church for its gospel choir and abolitionist history.

TRANSPORTATION

Subways run 24/7. MetroCards work on subways and buses, with time-limited free transfers. Consider seven- and thirty-day passes (http://web.mta.info/nyct/fare/FaresatAGlance.htm) and the "New York Pass" (https://www.newyorkpass.com).
  Area airports are LaGuardia (LGA), Kennedy (JFK), and Newark (EWR). Rapid-transit "Train to the Plane" is available only for JFK (http://web.mta.info/

TEN BROOKLYN SUBWAY TIPS

1 Subways run twenty-four hours a day, 365 days a year.
2 Consult websites for real-time transit information, like MTA.gov or apps like Embark. Weekend and late-night track repairs can cause crazy-making, elaborate reroutings. Subway broadcast announcements are *never* clear.
3 Not all "downtown trains" go to Brooklyn.
4 Pay attention to express versus local trains. They usually run on different tracks. Express trains skip stations.
5 Keep bags on your lap; you can be fined for using more than one seat.
6 Be prepared for stairs. Only some stations have elevators. Consult the MTA website for "accessibility."
7 Beware similar names: Manhattan's Fulton Street station isn't Brooklyn's Fulton Street station. Borough Hall station isn't in Borough Park.
8 Avoid riding in an empty car.
9 Open containers of coffee or drinks are not allowed.
10 Watch the show! As the Q or B trains cross the Manhattan Bridge, you might see kids break-dancing or doing the "Flex in Brooklyn."

---

mta/airtrain.htm). Allow an hour to cab to JFK or LaGuardia and longer for Newark.

Yellow cabs roam everywhere. Green cabs roam in Brooklyn, with limited operations in Manhattan. Both are city licensed and metered. "Car services" are licensed, unmetered cabs you must call—ask the fare in advance. Black sedans are expensive car services. Uber and other web-based cabs are widely used.

The ferry system can be a little confusing, because different operators are involved. East River Ferry runs on varying seasonal schedules from Greenpoint to Dumbo and in summer to Governors Island (http://www.eastriverferry.com). Free ferries are run by New York Water Taxi daily from Manhattan's Pier 11 to Ikea in Red Hook, Brooklyn. The New York Water Taxi All Day Access Pass also stops in Pier 1, Dumbo, and Red Hook Dock on Van Brunt Street.

Rent bikes from Citi Bikes (http://www.citibikenyc.com). Download bike maps from NYC.gov.

THIRTEEN AVOIDABLE CONFUSIONS

Alas, Brooklyn can be confusing!

1 BRIC is a cultural organization based at BRIC House in Fort Greene; they aren't related to Williamsburg's Brick Theater.
2 Columbia Heights is a street in the neighborhood of Brooklyn Heights, not in the Columbia Waterfront District.

3 Don't confuse Brooklyn's Fulton Street with Manhattan's Fulton Street. Both
   are subway stations! In Brooklyn, Old Fulton Street is in Dumbo; Fulton
   Street is in Downtown Brooklyn.
4 Greenpoint is miles from the neighborhood of Greenwood Heights and from
   Green-Wood, the cemetery and arboretum.
5 The "Heights" might refer to Brooklyn Heights or Crown Heights.
6 Kings Highway differs from Kings Plaza. Kings County is the administrative
   name for Brooklyn. (All honor British royalty.)
7 Morgantown is sometimes called East Williamsburg or Williamsburg.
8 SummerStage is a citywide program of the City Parks Foundation. Summer-
   Starz is a movie series in Williamsburg.
9 The Prospect Park subway station is a mile from Prospect Park's main
   entrance at Grand Army Plaza, near the Grand Army subway station.
10 Prospect Park West and Prospect Park Southwest are streets. Prospect Park
    South is a neighborhood. All border Prospect Park.
11 South and Southside Williamsburg differ. The former is largely Hasidic; the
    latter is largely Latino. Only the Williamsburgh Savings Bank in Fort Greene
    is spelled with an *h*.
12 Wyckoff Street and Wyckoff Avenue, in Boerum Hill and Bushwick, respec-
    tively, are miles apart.
13 The Gowanus Expressway and Brooklyn Queens Expressway (BQE)
    are stretches of Interstate 278. Some locals call the Gowanus Expressway
    the BQE.

SAFETY AND SLANG

New York is one of the nation's safest cities. Still, be street smart. Carry a valid
driver's license or a copy of your passport and a health-insurance card. New York's
emergency number is 911, and the city's all-purpose information line is 311.

And because the King's English is not always spoken in Kings County, we've
included a list of Brooklyn slang.

FORTY-FOUR AMAZING BROOKLYN BLOGS

General

Bklynr: http://bklynr.com
Brooklyn Based: http://brooklynbased.com
Brooklyn Daily Eagle: http://www.brooklyneagle.com
Brooklyn Independent Television's BK Live and other shows: BRICartsmedia
   .org/BKindiemedia
Brooklyn the Borough: http://www.brooklyntheborough.com
Brooklyn Magazine: http://www.bkmag.com

BROOKLYN GLOSSARY: THIRTY WORDS

1. agita: Yiddish for anxiety, upset
2. alternate side: New York City's idiosyncratic parking rules
3. boro: the same as *borough*, of which New York City has five
4. bridge: usually the Brooklyn Bridge
5. bridge and tunnel crowd: people who must use a bridge or tunnel to get to Manhattan; derogatory
6. brown bag laws: New York City laws disallowing public consumption of alcohol
7. brownstone Brooklyn: neighborhoods with nineteenth-century row houses made of a material called brownstone: Bedford-Stuyvesant, Boerum Hill, Brooklyn Heights, Carroll Gardens, Clinton Hill, Cobble Hill, parts of Crown Heights, Fort Greene, Park Slope, Prospect Heights, Sunset Park
8. CUNY: City University of New York, a vast public educational system
9. deep Brooklyn: a vague term suggesting the speaker isn't sure where it is, likely Flatbush or Flatlands
10. food truck: vans fitted out with kitchens that sell food while parked on streets
11. fuhgeddaboudit: Brooklyn phrase meaning "no way"
12. grandma's slice: thin-crust pizza squares
13. 'hood: neighborhood
14. maven: Yiddish for an expert or big shot
15. meh: an expression suggesting something is blah, uninteresting, a Seinfeld-ism
16. not fuh nuttin: Brooklynese suggesting that an action had good reason—"it's not for nothing"
17. outer borough: Brooklyn, Queens, Staten Island, Bronx; not Manhattan
18. regular coffee: coffee with milk and sugar ("black" has neither)
19. schlep: as a noun, a long trip; as a verb, to carry a lot of bags or take an uncomfortable journey
20. schlock: Yiddish for cheap, not good quality
21. schmuck: Yiddish for a low-life person; derived from the word for penis
22. slice: a slice of pizza, not the entire pie
23. slope: usually refers to Park Slope
24. stoop sale: Brooklyn equivalent to a garage sale
25. stop 'n' frisk: New York City police policy of stopping and frisking black males; found unconstitutional by the U.S. Supreme Court in 2013
26. 'sup?: urban slang for "what's up?"; a greeting
27. the city: Manhattan
28. the 1, the 2, the D, the B, etc.: refers to subway lines
29. train: the New York subway
30. upstate: north of the Bronx

Brooklyn Rail: http://www.brooklynrail.org
DNA: http://www.dnainfo.com/new-york/brooklyn
Explore Brooklyn: http://explorebk.com

Current Events and Listings

Brooklyn Paper: http://www.brooklynpaper.com
Brooklyn Vegan: http://www.brooklynvegan.com
Bushwick Daily: http://bushwickdaily.com
Bushwick Galleries: http://bushwickgalleries.com
Downtown Brooklyn Events: http://downtownbrooklyn.com/events
Free Williamsburg: http://freewilliamsburg.com
New York Times: http://www.nytimes.com/events
Pitchfork Media: http://pitchfork.com/news
Time Out New York: http://www.timeout.com/newyork

Family-Focused Blogs

Mommy Poppins: http://mommypoppins.com
Park Slope Parents: http://www.parkslopeparents.com

Food Blogs

Chowhound: http://www.chow.com
Diner Journal: http://dinerjournal.com
Edible Brooklyn: http://www.ediblebrooklyn.com
Grub Street: http://www.grubstreet.com

Local Trends and Real Estate Blogs

Brownstoner: http://www.brownstoner.com
Curbed: http://ny.curbed.com
Home Reporter: http://homereporter.com
Voices of New York ethnic media in English: http://voicesofny.org

Neighborhood and Hyperlocal Blogs

Most neighborhoods have at least one blog. For starters:

Bedford-Stuyvesant: The Bed Stuy Blog, http://thebedstuyblog.com
Brooklyn Heights: Brooklyn Heights Blog, http://brooklynheightsblog.com
Bushwick: Bushwick Daily, http://bushwickdaily.com
Cobble Hill / Carroll Gardens / Gowanus: Pardon Me for Asking, http://pardon
    meforasking.blogspot.com
Coney Island: The Coney Island Blog, http://www.theconeyislandblog.com
Ditmas Park: Ditmas Park Corner, http://www.ditmasparkcorner.com
Dumbo: Dumbo NYC, http://dumbonyc.com

Gowanus: Gowanus Your Face Off, http://www.gowanusyourfaceoff.com
Greenpoint: Greenpointers, http://greenpointers.com; Town Square, http://
www.townsquareinc.com
Park Slope: F'd in Park Slope, http://www.fuckedinparkslope.com
Prospect Lefferts Gardens: Q at Parkside, http://theqatparkside.blogspot.com
Red Hook: Red Hook Waterfront, http://redhookwaterfront.com/blog
Sheepshead Bay: Sheepshead Bites, http://sheepsheadbites.com
Sunset Park: The Sunset Park Blog, http://thesunsetparkblog.blogspot.com
Williamsburg: Free Williamsburg, http://freewilliamsburg.com

SELECT ZIP CODES

Brooklyn's postal codes begin with 112. Here are a few: BAM/Barclays (11217); Bay
Ridge (11209); Bedford-Stuyvesant (11205, 11206, 11216, 11221, 11233); Boerum Hill
(11201, 11217); Borough Park (11219); Brighton Beach (11235); Brooklyn Heights,
Cobble Hill, Downtown Brooklyn, Dumbo, Vinegar Hill (11201); Brooklyn Navy
Yard (11205); Bushwick (11221, 11237); Carroll Gardens, Columbia Waterfront
(11231); Clinton Hill (11205); Coney Island (11224); Crown Heights (11225, 11213);
Cypress Hills (11208); Ditmas Park (11218); East New York (11207); Flatbush
(11226, 11210); Flatlands (11234); Fort Greene (11205); Gowanus (11217); Greenpoint
(11222); Greenwood (11232); Kensington (11218, 11223, 11229); Marine Park (11234);
Midwood (11230); Mill Basin (11234); Park Slope (11215, 11217); Prospect Heights
(11238); Prospect Park South (11226); Red Hook (11231); Stuyvesant Heights
(11233); Sunset Park, Industry City / Bush Terminal (11220, 11232); Weeksville
(11213); Williamsburg (11206, 11211, 11249); Windsor Terrace (11215).

Brooklyn Bridge, walking from Manhattan to Brooklyn. (Photo by E. Freudenheim 2014)

Bibliography
Seventy-Five Works of Literature
Set in Brooklyn

Here's another way to "see" Brooklyn: in literature. This list includes seventy-five works by classic and recent authors, some acclaimed and others obscure. Most live or have lived in Brooklyn. These novels are also listed by neighborhood in section 3 (except Brownsville, which has a literary history too rich to omit here).

1 James Agee, *Brooklyn Is: Southeast of the Island: Travel Notes* (boroughwide) (essay)
2 Yelena Akhtiorskaya, *Panic in a Suitcase* (Brighton Beach)
3 Dallas Athent, Daniel Ryan Adler, and Nathaniel Kressen, eds., *Bushwick Nightz* (Bushwick)
4 Paul Auster, *Winter Journal* (Park Slope)
5 Paul Auster, *The Brooklyn Follies* (Park Slope)
6 Paul Auster, *Sunset Park* (Sunset Park)
7 Kevin Baker, *Dreamland* (Coney Island)
8 Emily Barton, *Brookland* (East River waterfront, imaginatively Dumbo area)
9 Gemma Burgess, *Brooklyn Girls* series (Brownstone Brooklyn)
10 Truman Capote, *A House on the Heights* (Brooklyn Heights)
11 Michael Chabon, *The Amazing Adventures of Kavalier and Clay* (Flatbush)
12 Mark Chiusano, *Marine Park* (Marine Park)
13 Kate Christensen, *The Astral* (Greenpoint)
14 Gabriel Cohen, *Red Hook* (Red Hook)
15 Reed Farrel Coleman, *Onion Street* (Sheepshead Bay / Manhattan Beach)
16 Reed Farrel Coleman, *Soul Patch* (Sheepshead Bay / Manhattan Beach)
17 Andrew Cotto, *Outerborough Blues: A Brooklyn Mystery* (Fort Greene)
18 Julia Dahl, *Invisible City* (Borough Park)
19 L. J. Davis, *A Meaningful Life* (Boerum Hill)
20 Dagmara Dominczyk, *The Lullaby of Polish Girls* (Greenpoint)
21 Amram Ducovny, *Coney* (Coney Island)
22 Boris Fishman, *A Replacement Life* (Brighton Beach)
23 Joe Flaherty, *Tin Wife* (Windsor Terrace)
24 Kitty Burns Florey, *Solos* (Williamsburg)
25 Paula Fox, *Desperate Characters* (Brooklyn Heights)
26 Daniel Fuchs, *Williamsburg Trilogy* (Williamsburg)

27   Emily Gould, *Friendship* (Carroll Gardens and Dumbo)

28   Joshua Halberstam, *A Seat at the Table: A Novel of Forbidden Choices* (Borough Park)

29   Pete Hamill, *The Christmas Kid and Other Brooklyn Stories* (South Slope / Park Slope)

30   Pete Hamill, *Snow in August: A Novel* (various neighborhoods)

31   Peter Hedges, *The Heights* (Brooklyn Heights)

32   William Heuman, *Strictly from Brooklyn* (Flatbush)

33   Alfred Kazin, *A Walker in the City* (Brownsville)

34   Neil Kleid, *Brownsville* (Brownsville)

35   Salvatore La Puma, *The Boys of Bensonhurst* (Bensonhurst)

36   Robert Leary, *May Wine on Brooklyn Heights* (Brooklyn Heights)

37   Jonathan Lethem, *Fortress of Solitude* (Boerum Hill)

38   Jonathan Lethem, *Motherless Brooklyn* (Cobble Hill)

39   H. P. Lovecraft, *The Horror of Red Hook* (Red Hook)

40   Bernard Malamud, *The Assistant* (Flatbush)

41   John B. Manbeck, *Brooklyn Heights Crime Series* (Brooklyn Heights)

42   Paule Marshall, *Brown Girl, Brownstones* (Bedford-Stuyvesant)

43   James Mason, *Positively No Dancing* (Columbia Waterfront District)

44   Tim McLoughlin, ed., *Brooklyn Noir* (various neighborhoods)

45   Tim McLoughlin, ed., *Brooklyn Noir 2: The Classics* (various neighborhoods)

46   Tim McLoughlin and Thomas Adcock, eds., *Brooklyn Noir 3: Nothing but the Truth* (various neighborhoods)

47   Arthur Miller, *Death of a Salesman* (Midwood) (play)

48   Arthur Miller, *The Hook* (Red Hook) (play)

49   Arthur Miller, *A View from the Bridge* (Red Hook) (play)

50   Henry Miller, *Tropic of Capricorn* (Williamsburg and Bushwick)

51   Henry Miller, *Black Spring* (Williamsburg and Bushwick)

52   Reggie Nadelson, *Red Hook: An Artie Cohen Mystery* (Red Hook)

53   Daniel José Older, *Shadowshaper* (Bedford-Stuyvesant)

54   Ivy Pochada, *Visitation Street* (Red Hook)

55   Ernest Poole, *The Harbor* (Red Hook)

56   Chaim Potok, *The Chosen* (Crown Heights and Flatbush)

57   Norman Rosten, *Under the Boardwalk* (Coney Island)

58   Ariel Schrag, *Adam* (Bushwick)

59   Tom Seghini, *The Borough of Churches: A Novel about Brooklyn in the 1970s* (Brooklyn College / Midwood / Flatbush)

60   Hubert Selby Jr., *Last Exit to Brooklyn* (Red Hook, elsewhere)

61   Hubert Selby Jr., *Requiem for a Dream* (Brighton Beach)

62   Amy Shearn, *The Mermaid of Brooklyn* (Park Slope)

63   Neil Simon, *Brighton Beach Memoirs* (Brighton Beach) (play)

64   Betty Smith, *A Tree Grows in Brooklyn* (Williamsburg)

65 Amy Sohn, *Prospect Park West* (Park Slope)

66 Gilbert Sorrentino, *Steelwork* (Bay Ridge)

67 Bradley Spinelli, *Killing Williamsburg* (Williamsburg)

68 Darcey Steinke, *Milk* (Brooklyn Heights)

69 Michael Stephens, *Brooklyn Book of the Dead* (East New York)

70 William Styron, *Sophie's Choice* (Victorian Flatbush)

71 Colm Toibin, *Brooklyn: A Novel* (Cobble Hill)

72 Anya Ulinich, *Lena Finkle's Magic Barrel* (Kensington-ish)

73 Stacy Wakefield, *The Sunshine Crust Baking Factory* (Williamsburg)

74 Adelle Waldman, *The Love Affairs of Nathaniel P.* (Prospect Heights)

75 Thomas Wolfe, *You Can't Go Home Again* (Gowanus—a telling, if brief, quote about the Gowanus Canal)

(This list was complied with input from the Brooklyn Collection of the Brooklyn Public Library; WORD bookstore; Liz Koch and Johnny Temple of the Brooklyn Book Festival; and Ezra Goldstein, coowner of the Park Slope Community Bookstore and Terrace Books; and with acknowledgments to *Brooklyn Magazine*'s 2014 "A Brooklyn Literary Map: The Best Book for Each Brooklyn Neighborhood," Evan Hughes's *Literary Brooklyn*, and James Peacock's *Brooklyn Fictions: The Contemporary Urban Community in a Global Age*.)

Index

Due to space constraints, this index lists only a selection of the hundreds of restaurants, shops, and venues recommended in this book. Photos and figures are indicated by "f" after the number and tables by "t" after the number.

About the Author

Since 1991, Ellen Freudenheim has written four guidebooks to Brooklyn (the third won a travel book award) and over a thousand articles online about Brooklyn. Her other books include a guidebook to Queens, a guidebook to baby boomers' retirement, and a public health dictionary. She has lived in Brooklyn since the 1980s. To keep up with Ellen's Brooklyn articles or to share tips of great Brooklyn places, visit her website, http://brooklynguidebook.com, or Facebook page, "BrooklynAmbassador."